PUSHING THE BOUNDARIES

CRICKET IN THE EIGHTIES

PUSHING THE BOUNDARIES

CRICKET IN THE EIGHTIES

Playing Home and Away

Derek Pringle

HODDER &
STOUGHTON

First published in Great Britain in 2018 by Hodder & Stoughton
An Hachette UK company

1

Copyright © Derek Pringle 2018

A CIP catalogue record for this title is available from the British Library

ISBN 978147367492 9
Ebook ISBN 9781473674943

Typeset in Minion Pro by Hewer Text UK Ltd, Edinburgh
Printed and bound in Great Britain by Clays Ltd, Elcograf S.p.A.

Hodder & Stoughton policy is to use papers that are natural, renewable
and recyclable products and made from wood grown in sustainable
forests. The logging and manufacturing processes are expected to conform
to the environmental regulations of the country of origin.

Hodder & Stoughton Ltd
Carmelite House
50 Victoria Embankment
London EC4Y 0DZ

www.hodder.co.uk

'You're up and coming until you are over the hill'

Keith Fletcher

For Dad, who sadly saw none of this but handed down the cricket genes.

For Mum and Janet, who put in the overs.

And for my team-mates at Essex CCC. Let's face it, we smashed the Eighties.

CONTENTS

ACKNOWLEDGEMENTS

I would like to thank David Luxton, who has been urging me to write a book for a while, and Roddy Bloomfield and Fiona Rose at Hodder and Stoughton for their encouragement and hard work. A big thank you is also due to Tim Waller for his helpful suggestions while editing the manuscript and for correcting my often errant maths regarding various scores. This book is mostly about cricket in the 1980s, a now distant decade. Although recalling detail was often a challenge, the following were unfailingly helpful in racking their memories on my behalf:

David Acfield, Winston Bynorth, Steve Church, Chris Cowdrey, Tim Curtis, Phil DeFreitas, Paul Downton, Ray East, Matthew Engel, Keith Fletcher, Graeme Fowler, Pat Gibson, Graham Gooch, Martin Johnson, John Lever, Ken McEwan, Kevin Palmer, Paul Prichard, Chris Pugh, Mike Selvey, Robin Smith, John Stephenson.

PHOTOGRAPHIC ACKNOWLEDGEMENTS

The author and publisher would like to thank the following for permission to reproduce photographs:

Tony Debenham Collection, Winston Bynorth, Patrick Eagar/ Popperfoto/Getty Images, Patrick Eagar/Patrick Eagar Collection via Getty Images, Bob Thomas/Getty Images.

Other photographs from private collections.

Every reasonable effort has been made to trace the copyright holders, but if there are any errors or omissions, Hodder & Stoughton will be pleased to insert the appropriate acknowledgement in any subsequent printings or editions.

PREFACE

I SPENT MUCH OF the 1980s playing cricket for Cambridge, Essex and England. In itself, representing those three sides was not especially remarkable, except for the decade in which I played. Timing, they say, is everything in sport and playing then was as fortuitous as being first in the queue at the January sales, although in the Eighties just about everything else went too, on and off the field.

Every generation believes their era to be the definitive one but only now, with the clarifying perspective of time, can we see what a bizarre, divisive and defining decade the 1980s really was, especially on the cricket field. It proved a period of flux both fascinating and disorientating as cricketers were suddenly granted access to personal freedoms, only to have them withdrawn as coach culture came in and consolidated itself.

At the start of the Eighties, despite being preceded by decades known as the 'Swinging Sixties' and 'Sleazy Seventies', cricket still wallowed in a bucolic, sepia-tinged age in which tea ladies ruled and a team's tail began at number eight. Yet, all that changed during a decade in which Margaret Thatcher was the country's sole Prime Minister. Under her Conservative government, Britain became locked in a battle royal as the old ways lost out to the new in a bid to join the modern world. The biggest changes were social and economic, bringing prosperity to many but also the decline of some treasured institutions. In cricket, it was the maverick player who suddenly became an endangered species.

As an all-round cricketer good enough to play for county and country, I was at the heart of the transformation. From my formative years on the greensward of Fenner's with Cambridge University until the fruition of my career with Essex and England I experienced the change in the zeitgeist. It wasn't always pretty but it was a hell of a lot of fun.

With a rich cast of characters like Ian 'Beefy' Botham, Mike Gatting, Phil Edmonds, Bob Willis and Derek Randall for England, along with Keith Fletcher, John Lever, Ray East and Graham Gooch for Essex, all rubbing shoulders with celebrities like Eric Clapton, Elton John and Peter Cook, the decade was rarely dull.

There were thrills, spills and more than the odd catastrophe along the way as cricket went through a transition both painful and comical. As my own experiences in this book will lay bare, few cricketers left the 1980s wealthy, but we did depart rich in experience, with some sparky tales to tell.

It was also a time when the media experienced seismic change. The press's relationship with cricketers altered drastically over the period, as newspapers began to use sport to fight their circulation wars. At the start of the Eighties players could be found carousing with journalists in bars, with an omertà observed. But by the end of the decade subpoenas were being served more readily than pints as every peccadillo became fair game for the Fourth Estate.

As in cricket, the more maverick operators among the press corps became hunted men, accountants steadily culling those who racked up expenses to keep their sources sweet and their mistresses even sweeter. Today, media organisations will never again see the likes of a Chris Lander or Martin Johnson, the cricket correspondents of the *Independent* and the *Mirror*, with readers the poorer for it.

Those men lived more than a little – in the real world rather than on Wikipedia or the Twittersphere – and it informed their copy. You only have to read Frank Keating's *Guardian* reports from

England's tour of India in 1981–82, where he regularly got drunk with Botham, to see the false economy of today's unenterprising approach.

At the beginning of my career, players mostly liked and trusted the press. That relationship was all but eroded by the time I retired from professional cricket in 1993.

The 1980s began for me with a conviction for criminal damage following some high-spirited jinks while at Cambridge (the judge preferred to call it 'oikish behaviour'). It should, on the face of it, have given me enough street cred to be one of the mavericks I so admired. But, having started out as an aggressive middle-order batsman and swing bowler, in possession of both an ear stud and a sponsored Porsche, I quickly discovered that my place in the professional game was best served if I reined in the excess, at least in the middle. It disappointed many, myself included, but with the controversial ear stud quickly consigned to a sock drawer and the Porsche withdrawn by the sponsors, line-and-length and play-the-ball-on-its-merits was essentially how the buccaneer in me ended up.

University, and the cricket played there, was crucial to my development. My generation were fortunate to have both grants and tuition fees funded by the taxpayer. No debt for us unless you were one of those undergraduates who kept a bear in their rooms. I was still at Cambridge when I was first selected to play for England. It surprised everyone, me included, and the novelty kept the media buzzing for weeks.

My unexpected selection also meant that I had to cope with the tag of being the 'new Botham', despite the old one being very much alive and in the same England team. The maverick's maverick, Beefy Botham did things his way and he did them with bravado and style, most of the time. Compared to him, I was just a young pretender on the cricket field, though one with a better haircut.

Despite the press trying to rev up some rivalry between us, we got on well, both being cricketers who embraced the whole experience playing for England gave you back then. There was no going to bed early and sticking to isotonic drinks when you could party the night away. In any case, by the time I played for England Botham had been permanently ingrained in the folklore, his deeds of derring-do, especially against Australia, the kind to be recounted for centuries, even millennia. His fame also meant he was feted by all manner of celebrities, with rock stars like Mick Jagger, Eric Clapton and Elton John particularly fascinated by him.

Although we were essentially competing for the all-rounder's spot, the selectors picked Beefy and me in the same England team on several occasions, yet at times it was difficult to see why. I did manage to get an extended run in 1986 (four successive Tests) while Beefy sat out a three-month ban for possession of cannabis, but I was dropped for his return against New Zealand, which he announced by taking a wicket with his first ball. Only true forces of nature can claim the situation with such timing and elan.

At Essex, a bunch of disparate characters combined their zany talents to produce entertaining cricket and win trophies. Ray East, John Lever, Graham Gooch and David Acfield all looked at life and cricket obliquely without ever jeopardising the team project. They were wild, they were woolly, or at least some of them were, but they knew when to put their game face on.

They were also fortunate to have a sage captain, in Keith Fletcher, who allowed them room for self-expression. To this day I give thanks to having played county cricket for Essex, with its zest for fun and winning ways. It was professionalism without prescription and, refreshingly, a coach-free zone.

During my 15 years with the club we won six County Championship titles, three Sunday Leagues, one NatWest Trophy and one Benson & Hedges Cup, not to mention the Refuge Assurance Cup in 1989, something I dubbed the 'Afterthought Cup' when it was suddenly foisted upon us midway through the decade.

Not every school leaver would have relished guidance from East and Lever, but I lapped it up. Their nurture, which involved everything from sound advice to leading me astray, was as privileged an education as anything I'd received to that point. It was, for all concerned at the club, a golden era, which sadly came to an end in the Nineties.

The Ashes might be the biggest show in town these days but the best Test team in the Eighties was the West Indies. From 1980 until 1995, when Australia eventually defeated them in the Caribbean, they remained unbeaten for 29 Test series. They were the one team Botham never really collared during his career, England managing just one win from 20 Tests against them when he was in the team.

During that period of West Indian dominance, England suffered back-to-back 'Blackwashes' against them, in 1984 and 1985–86, as well as a 4–0 thrashing in 1988. That last defeat was overseen by no fewer than four England captains, five if you count the two sessions I did at The Oval during the final Test when Gooch was forced to leave the field with a badly split finger.

Having been involved in four of the five Tests in that 1988 series, including the drawn first match at Trent Bridge, I was privy to one of the most shambolic episodes in England cricket – and the bar is set high. That shambles was precipitated by Mike Gatting's sacking after the first Test, when a barmaid sold her story of their alleged dalliance during the match to a tabloid newspaper. John Emburey was appointed for Tests two and three, though when both were lost he made way for Chris Cowdrey, godson to Peter May, the chairman of selectors. Cowdrey took over for the Headingley Test and has since based a hilarious after-dinner speech routine on his five days in charge. Unsurprisingly, England lost that one too, though when a broken toe ruled him out of leading us in the final match at The Oval, Gooch was handed what was rapidly becoming the most short-lived job in sporting history.

Many will point to the freedom the players had then as reason for our calamities, but there was no doubt that the game was badly run, as seen by the controversial rebel tours to South Africa which roughly bookended the decade. Neither of those tours would have occurred, nor would there have been any need for four captains, had players been content with how the game was being managed by the Test and County Cricket Board.

Although England had already appointed a coach, Mickey Stewart, by the time of that 1988 farce, full-strength, puritanical professionalism only really took hold at the end of the decade when Graham Gooch, after some toing and froing between other candidates, was awarded the captaincy for more than just the odd match. Gooch had transformed his own game through a more disciplined approach to fitness and practice, to become England's finest batsman. As the country's new captain, he sought to spread his work ethic to the team to see if it would rub off on others. For all those it benefited, it rubbed an equal amount up the wrong way, including Gower, England's other world-class batsman of the time.

Although amateurism technically ended in the early 1960s, a classic professional-versus-amateur row ensued, with Roundhead Gooch pitted against Cavalier Gower. Earlier in the decade the pro-Gower lobby might have succeeded in their agitations, but the mood had changed. Coaches were about to be given licence to domesticate the maverick and their feral instincts.

I recall the exact moment it started, too, during the Nehru Cup in India that predated England's West Indies tour of 1990. Instead of nets, one day we spent our time doing shuttle runs in 90 °F heat.

Afterwards, Gooch told everyone that from now on as much effort would be spent on improving fitness as skills.

The book concludes with the 1992 World Cup, a personal swansong despite it not ending in glory. With England losing their third final in four tournaments, it proved a natural conclusion for several high-profile careers, with Ian Botham, David Gower and Derek Randall all retiring the following season, along with Chris Tavaré, Neil Foster and me. For most of those players cricket was about fun, joy and self-expression, not the endless and often futile quest for constant self-improvement.

People will look back and consider the Eighties in cricket a decade of extroverts and excess, and maybe it was. To those in its midst, though, it just seemed the top end of normal. With nobody to tell you what to do, creativity abounded. For us, nothing seemed impossible, and that was our lasting reward.

1

BLUE MOODS

I saw in the 1980s before most people on the planet. Not because I had exceptional eyesight or was standing on the shoulders of giants, because I don't and I wasn't. No. I did so because I was further east than the majority of the world's population that New Year's Eve, as my gilded youth ended and unknown but exciting adulthood began.

I was in Tasmania, longitude 147° E, on a university cricket tour, getting steadily sozzled with my team-mates, surrounded by the finishing crews of the Sydney to Hobart yacht race. If the location was exotic, the scene was not: lots of drunken people seeing in the new decade by trying to cop off with one another before sobriety returned and they realised their New Year hadn't got off to such a good start after all.

And yet, looking out over the Derwent river that night at the fireworks dancing on the dark water, and taking in that fresh, briny smell, it was impossible not to feel optimistic about the future. True, Soviet tanks had just rolled into Kabul, and the grim dystopia of George Orwell's *1984* seemed to be closing fast, but that and the Red Army seemed far away as the *pffsstcks* of ring-pulls rang out beneath the Southern Cross.

Things were certainly going well for me. I was the youngest member of a combined Oxford and Cambridge cricket team and enjoying my first taste of Australia, the great cricketing foe. As you'd expect, the Aussie jaunt had been a lot of fun and the cricket had been pretty good, too. The team, under Ian Greig and Greg Marie (Cambridge and Oxford respectively), had settled quickly and played well, remaining unbeaten throughout our five-week visit.

For many, it was the highlight of their university careers. As a result, several team photos were taken to commemorate the trip, the most outlandish on Maslin Beach near Adelaide. A nudist hangout, we were snapped au naturel. Fortunately, the air temperature at Maslin was much warmer than the sea, which enhanced morale.

My cricketing education, if not my scholastic one, was certainly advanced on that trip. Not so much by the opposition or the differing conditions, but from watching Peter Roebuck and Paul Parker, two Cambridge graduates enjoying successful careers in county cricket. Both men had graduated in the late 1970s, so were not current members of the university. Their presence on tour owed as much to geography (both were playing club cricket in Australia that winter) as to our insecurity – specifically, the need to strengthen our ranks with proven talent.

Bespectacled and intense, Roebuck had an insatiable curiosity and a need to analyse those around him. He was happy to share his findings, too, even if they made for uncomfortable hearing. He was that curious mix of stick and carrot, and while capable of praise, he felt nothing at humiliating people, often in the same sentence.

He'd taken a first in Law, so had brains to burn – as did John Claughton, who later took a first with applause in Classics at Oxford, an even greater accolade. Listening to the verbal jousts between those two on tour was to earwig the squabbles between Wittgenstein and Russell in Trinity quad 60 years earlier.

A decent batsman, Claughton was probably the brightest player on tour. I mean, how many people sleepwalk reciting Latin, something he did when the team was billeted together in a dorm in Adelaide? It spooked the hell out of the Cambridge lads. Thankfully, one of the Oxford lot had seen it before and gently led him, *sine strepitu*, back to his bed.

Roebuck, too, was prone to eccentricity. On that trip he seemed less interested in cricket than in espousing his vision of things, mostly with regard to life and education. During one match, at Monash University, he stood at second slip and completed crossword after crossword, a man entirely unengaged save by his own brilliance.

Parker was less cerebral than Roebuck but no less intense. At times, both gave the impression that hounds were gnawing at their core. Parker went on to play for England the following year, but one Test was all the selectors saw in him, a poor return for such a gifted batsman and athlete.

He looked our best player on that trip and I noted the fearless way he used his feet to spinners. But noting and emulating are far apart, and I was never able to summon the bottle to shimmy down the pitch as he did. Being out stumped was, for me, the most humiliating dismissal possible and one that denoted a subnormal IQ.

Without knowing their history, it was obvious from that trip that Parker and Roebuck didn't really get on. In one of his more reductive theories, Roebuck divided the world into frauds and non-frauds, placing Parker in the first camp without ever giving his reasons. When I asked him, more in cheek than cross-examination, in which camp he saw himself, he threw a wobbler, telling me to grow up and to go and achieve something before having the impertinence to challenge him. Chastised but not chastened, I watched myself around him after that.

On the tour I gravitated towards those I knew from the Cambridge team the previous summer, as well as the Oxford one we'd trounced in the Varsity match at Lord's. Chief among the latter camp was Simon Clements, a talented left-hand batsman most knew as 'Lamps', on account of the unwieldy spectacles he wore whenever he'd misplaced his contact lenses – which was often.

Aside from winning two blues at Oxford, Lamps was a stalwart for Suffolk in the Minor County Championship, a cricketing prowess that sat askew – like the broken nose on his face – with his unconventional look and manner. Sporting long, lank hair and with a penchant for smoking roll-ups, as well as using hippy expressions like 'bread' and 'man', he was Neil in *The Young Ones* several years before the character was invented.

Talented, bright, unconventional, rebellious and defiantly anti-establishment, Lamps was everything I admired in someone who had, like me, come through the public-school system. I relished his company and he was generous in granting me admission to it, something that would not have happened had we still been at school, where even a year's difference is insurmountable, socially.

The tour was meant to begin with a warm-up game in Singapore, though somebody had messed up as we didn't play. When we turned up at Singapore Cricket Club we were told the season had ended – quite some time ago judging from the knee-high grass on the outfield. Instead, we did some light training and took in the sights.

Singapore was still a racy place back then, having not been completely sanitised by Lee Kuan Yew, a reformed communist and a former student of Fitzwilliam, my Cambridge college. We had been warned about the transsexuals and men who'd transitioned to become 'women' who frequented an area known as Bugis Street, and told not to be lured by their siren calls. Known locally as 'shims', a conflation of 'she' and 'him', they dressed like Hollywood starlets, had husky voices, thick wrists, Adam's apples and sucked Strepsils.

I have photographs of several shims, and unless that is your thing, it is possible to see how some unsuspecting bloke, with a few beers inside him, might mistake them for the fairer sex. Not that any of us did. Still, there must have been plenty willing to engage them in trade, though exactly who was not clear until one of their pimps told us, 'Shims very popular with British Army.'

To a naive undergraduate like me, this was serious exotica. On our last night there, two ladies of the night latched on to me and Lamps in a bar. Their insistence that they would show us a 'very good time' came with a very high price tag. One of them even tried to charm me, saying, 'You so handsome, Dereeek, you look just like Preence Chaaarles.'

Imagine my relief, then, when we didn't even have enough money to buy them a drink (these being the days before students had credit cards). The next day, as flight QF2 rose above Changi and turned south-east for Brisbane, I felt more wordly as a result of my short stay in Singapore, even without any money changing hands.

A lot of people believe I got into Cambridge because I was a talented schoolboy cricketer, but there have always been plenty of those. I reckon it was down to the final question of my interview at Fitzwilliam College to read Geography, the question where the Director of Studies, having gently sparred with you, tries to trip you up.

'One final question, Mr Pringle: why Fitzwilliam?' he asked, with the hint of a checkmate smile.

The question might appear harmless, but for those who know little about Cambridge, especially in the late 1970s, Fitzwilliam was an unlovely, modern building set up the Huntingdon Road about a mile north of the city's historic centre. In short, it was ugly, inconvenient and lacked the tradition of the much-vaunted colleges down the hill, so I couldn't exactly effuse about what a great place it was.

There were rumours, too, which naturally I had acted upon, that the Admissions Tutor at Fitz, a Professor Brian Johnson, might be sympathetic to letting in the odd academically underpowered sportsman. But that reason was unlikely to wash well with the Director of Studies.

Nor could I come out with the usual blather about what a privilege it would be to follow such famous alumni as Isaac Newton, Francis Bacon and Alfred Lord Tennyson, something always open to those applying to Trinity. Fitz had nurtured two Normans, Lamont and St John-Stevas, as well as David Starkey, all famous-ish, but hardly supernovas of achievement.

Miraculously, and before anything that could be construed as an awkward silence passed between us, the answer came to me in an epiphany: 'Because I don't like city centres,' I blurted, pleased as much with the improvised nature of my riposte as with its speed and geographical angle.

How did I know it had hit the spot? Well, because the Director of Studies, who'd probably suspected the real reasons I'd applied to Fitz all along (less competition for places than Trinity, as well as Prof Johnson's love of sport), snapped shut my CV and wet himself laughing.

A year later, in 1978, I moved into Room 23 on L Staircase, just above the kitchens, to spend the next three terms in a small, nondescript space filled with the cloying odour of well-boiled sprouts. The summer term, with its promise of first-class cricket and the heady smell of new-mown grass at famous Fenner's, could not come soon enough.

University, and the cricket it offered, was crucial to my development as both a person and a player. When he was Prime Minister, John Major, who famously never went to university, said to me at a dinner we both attended, 'I hope you didn't go to Cambridge to get an education.'

'No,' I said. 'I went to have a good time.'

My generation were fortunate, and not only because National Service had ended when we were in short trousers. We also had our university tuition fees funded by the taxpayer, as well as means-tested maintenance grants, though there would be a riot now if working folk knew what we spent the latter on (it wasn't textbooks).

Once, on receipt of his grant cheque, my mate Muttley, who read History at St Catharine's, ran up to the side of his college quad and waved the cheque about in a ritual of mock urination. His intention, that he was going to piss it up the wall, being only too clear.

That first year was interesting, especially the cricket, which I suspect was not your typical student fare. Cambridge's captain was Ian Greig, younger brother of Tony who, before he became Kerry Packer's recruiter-in-chief for World Series Cricket, had captained England.

Like his big brother, Greig minor had been schooled in South Africa and had that contradictory mix of bluntness and charm typical of the white males of that country. Until he stumbled in his finals at Cambridge, you sensed he'd never had a moment's self-doubt in his life or, if he had, he'd kept it well hidden.

Before coming up to Cambridge, I'd spent a season on the staff at Essex County Cricket Club, where I'd begun to absorb the ways of the professional cricketer. This was a student set-up, though, not a pro club, so imagine my surprise when Greigy, as he was unimaginatively known, began to lay down the law as if we were Sussex Firsts.

'And finally,' he said, after issuing a long litany of dos and don'ts before our first game of the season, 'if any of you buggers come off the field with less grass stains on your trousers than me, there'll be hell to pay.' Naturally, many of us wanted to tell Greigy that the correct usage was 'fewer' grass stains not 'less', but nobody had the nerve.

This was just one of many diatribes from him, most met with silent nods by the team. When someone did eventually answer back, Greig was rendered speechless, the metaphorical mirror held up reflecting an image of himself he'd clearly never seen. That brave man was Aziz Mubarak, a postgraduate chemist with what seemed, at best, a sketchy command of English, though I suspect that was more the scientist in him than the Sri Lankan.

As a dashing opening bat, Az, as he was known, held no fear of reputation. He'd just as happily cut and carve Test bowlers as college trundlers. He did not discriminate. His demolition of Colin Croft, when Combined Universities played West Indies at Fenner's in 1980, was thrilling to watch, though it wound up the fast, nasty Croft no end. When Deryck Murray, West Indies captain in that match, asked Croft to take a blow after lunch, the fast bowler insisted on continuing.

'If I don't get him out, cappie, I put him in hospital,' said Croft, loudly enough for us all to hear. He did get his man, eventually, but not before Az had humiliated him with a run-a-ball 86.

Az didn't say much, but when he did it was usually worth hearing, unless it was his calling between the wickets, which was hazardous. His 'Yes, Fosh. No, Fosh. Sorry, Fosh' had gone down in Cambridge folklore – and probably hastened the talented Matthew Fosh's decision to quit top-level cricket.

This time Az's call was unerring but equally devastating, coming as it did over a meal at a Berni Inn near Buckingham, as the Cambridge contingent picked for a Combined Universities side to play a Benson & Hedges group match in Oxford broke their journey. I don't recall the exact details of Greigy's monologue, but it was about politics, with his, predictably, being well to the right. Anyway, his point made, there was a short pause before Az, normally a silent presence at such meals, began to speak, very slowly.

'Greigy,' he said, carefully weighing his words, 'you are a ------- National Front ------.'

After a stunned silence, a look of such surprise appeared on Greigy's face as to challenge the gurning champion of Britain.

The cricket season at Cambridge ends with the Varsity match against Oxford at Lord's, the only occasion on which a player can win a blue. I played in three Varsity matches, the most notable of which was the first, when I took seven wickets and scored an unbeaten 103 to help Cambridge win. I contributed very little to the next two, both of them weather-affected draws.

In that first match against Oxford, in 1979, I went from 93 to 99 with a six. Their pace bowler, Aamer Hameed, who'd played two one-day internationals for Pakistan, banged one in from the Nursery End and I pulled it high and hard over midwicket. I was seeing the ball well and absolutely nailed the stroke. For a brief moment during the ball's soaring arc I thought I might have hit it over the Grand Stand and out of Lord's (we were playing over on that side of the square). Instead, it struck the topmost ridge of tiles, breaking one, to leave a visible kink in the roof line.

Over the years I've dined out on how I'd left a permanent mark on Lord's, though that all went when the Grand Stand was rebuilt in 1998 to a design that did not recycle those old tiles. Progress swallows us all in the end, though I still curse the MCC and their dratted modernising programme for reducing, by one, my tales of self-aggrandisement.

Before the Varsity match there were eight weeks of playing various county sides at Fenner's in what was then considered first-class cricket. While we relished the opportunity to play against the leading players of the day, most of our opponents saw the games as little more than a chore.

In those matches, defeat came often for us, with draws considered something of a triumph. In my time, we did prevail once, against Lancashire in 1982, but actual victories by Cambridge over county sides in the 55 years between 1963 and 2018, the professional era, can be counted on one hand.

Fenner's, though, was a fabulous place to play cricket, especially if you didn't mind having salad for lunch every day. There were no cooking facilities other than to boil water so, for four years, I had ham or chicken salad with boiled potatoes, every day of every match. Puddings varied, mind. As the Essex players used to joke – at least there was a choice of custard or sump oil to go with it, depending on whether or not Tony Pocock, the head groundsman, had put his thumb in the bowl while serving them. We didn't mind, and most county teams accepted the lack of variety with good humour. One team that did refuse to eat our lunches was the West Indies. During their match against the Combined Universities in 1981, the salads lay untouched as they sent out for buckets of Kentucky Fried Chicken from nearby Mill Road.

The pitch at Fenner's, being both docile and slow, ensured county sides rarely ran through us unless we batted like numpties or unless the opposition's crackerjack fast bowler was particularly motivated, something that didn't happen often. Of course, a flat pitch also made bowling tough against professional batsmen, but it focused the mind on being accurate, so was great for discipline. Like Plato, line and length were required reading at Cambridge.

I certainly benefited from playing against county players, a pact from which they also gained, with us students usually providing them with easy runs and wickets early in the season. After all, come contract-renewal time in August, when some old buffer on the county committee was perusing the averages, a player might have had cause to be thankful for that unbeaten 100 against

Cambridge. It was, after all, first-class and counted as such in the records.

There were more challenges to playing cricket at Cambridge than just those on the field, considerable though they were. It being the summer term, the game, time-consuming in the extreme when measured in revision hours, had to compete with exams – finals being seen, rightly or wrongly, as the Big Bang moment of one's adult life.

As undergraduates, we all reported to a college tutor who assessed our progress, or not, twice a term. As providers of so-called pastoral care (they never taught us), tutors didn't have much to go on regarding our academic work, so their default tended towards criticism and condemnation, with full-blown shellackings reserved for the truly idle. Occasionally, they were known to praise, though I never had any experience of that myself.

As individuals handed responsibility for our own destiny, we didn't have to attend lectures if we didn't fancy it. The only compulsory element to student life at Cambridge was to spend 56 nights a term in college, to satisfy taxpayers' largesse, and to complete a weekly essay assigned by your supervisor. With the year above's work available to crib from for the price of a beer, there was little to indicate whether you were destined for a first or a fail until exams were completed.

My tutor at Fitz was Dr Tony Edwards, or 'Doc E' as the college wags called him. A medic who specialised in vivisection, Doc E was not sentimental. Generally, our tutorials were sociable and pleasant, but not during exam term. On those occasions, he would pour two sherries, hand one over, fix his eviscerating stare upon me – and start effing and blinding like a man with acute Tourette's syndrome.

The gist, from the few words not blue, was that more work was needed or I'd be doomed to let both myself and the college down. It was always a bravura performance, complete with reddening face and bulging veins, and one which no doubt struck fear into the unassuming. But I knew Doc E well, and I knew he liked cricket, so once he'd finished his rant, he'd always want to know which county was next up at Fenner's and which decent players they might bring along for his delectation.

The examinations for bachelor's degrees at Cambridge follow a 'Tripos' system which, despite being suggestive of something split into three, actually comprises a Part I, completed after one or two years depending on your subject, and a Part II, also known as Finals.

It was possible to change course after Part I, which is what I did. If I'd stuck to Geography, I would have had to write a 15,000-word dissertation and the fieldwork for that would have interfered with my season at Essex, for which I was paid, so I did my Part II in Land Economy. I'd wanted to swap to Law but the Law don in Fitz told me that he would only accept my request if I gave up cricket. 'I'm not having you bring standards down,' he said. I told him cricket standards would be even lower if I gave the game up.

Both sets of exams tend to send the student population into a five-week funk every year during April and May, at least until they are over. One of the unexpected bonuses of playing cricket was the copper-bottomed excuse it provided to avoid lectures and miss the pre-exam angst, which I found liberating, if not especially conducive to a good degree.

Once exams were completed, the euphoria of release unleashed a mass two-week binge, the climax of which was something called 'Suicide Sunday', when just about every college sporting society had its summer cocktail party, cunningly staggered for maximum inebriation. Unsurprisingly, the Accident and Emergency Unit at Addenbrooke's Hospital was placed on red alert that weekend, stomach pumps at the ready.

It was during this post-exam period in 1980, while nervously awaiting the outcome of our Part Is, that me and my housemates, Muttley, Magoo and Red Wils, went for a beer or six one evening in the Fort St George pub by the river on Midsummer Common. We'd already swung by the Senate House to see if our results had been posted on the noticeboards there, but there was nothing, so our anxiety levels remained high.

Beer mixed with unease rarely results in pleasurable intoxication, so when we left the pub after closing time, we were probably still open to a bit of mischief. It wasn't long before we found some either, our curiosity as well as our inner yob pricked by a group of 'Townies' throwing wooden stakes at a cluster of lights in the middle of the common. A big fair was due in Cambridge and the chunky stakes had been hammered into the ground to mark where the various attractions would be sited. Indeed, we'd tripped over a few on our way to the pub, almost turning an ankle or two in the process. There was, then, a degree of vengeance in our decision to join the others as they tried to hit the lights shining 20 feet above us.

I'd thrown my arm out in Australia the previous winter, so could only underarm the stakes. But Magoo scored a direct hit, which broke one of the plastic covers surrounding the light. Despite the blow, it continued to shine brightly. This spurred us into collecting more ammunition, though no sooner had we plonked down our store than out of the shadows came the police, mob-handed, to apprehend us by any means necessary.

Whether it was because the booze had slowed our 'flight' response or our brains were just too sluggish to assess the danger, but most of us were nabbed before we could even think about fleeing the scene, halted by some impressive rugby tackles. Muttley was one who did manage to escape, despite a copper giving chase. Red Wils, who'd been with us in the pub, was also at liberty, having earlier gone off to a party which we'd pooh-poohed on account of the bird-to-bloke ratio being 1 to 10, though that was fairly standard at Cambridge before most of the colleges became mixed.

Bundled into two Black Marias, we were taken the short distance to Parkside police station, an unlovely, Stasi-looking building by Parker's Piece. There Magoo and I were processed and split up, presumably to prevent collusion.

Until that moment, I'd only ever had one dealing with the police: when the bloke across from our digs on Mill Road smashed our front window with his wife's head. It was a vicious assault which left her barely conscious and needing multiple stitches and us facing the expense of replacing a big piece of broken glass, our digs being an old shop in a rough part of town. The broken pane was part of Muttley's bedroom, and while he tried Sellotaping cardboard and newspaper over the hole, his running repairs were never entirely successful at keeping either the elements or the tramps at bay.

Although the victim had been grateful for our intervention and for calling the ambulance, she refused to implicate her husband. Perhaps realising that a future without him was bleaker than a shoe-ing every now and then, she would not press charges, so the police brought them instead. Eventually, our window was paid for, though not before mushrooms had begun to grow in Muttley's carpet.

If the police had been helpful enough then, my view of them was about to change. Deciding that honesty was probably the best policy, I started out telling it exactly how it had been, save for dobbing in Magoo as the man who'd delivered the decisive throw.

'Well, that's very interesting,' said the sergeant. 'Shall I read you my report based on what I saw?' So he did and it was not dissimilar to my account, except that he claimed it was me who'd broken the lights, striking them not once but twice. 'I saw it with my very own eyes,' he said, as if he might occasionally use other people's.

I could get that the sergeant was determined not to let a smart-arse student get away with something like this, but his statement had been coloured by the say-so of one of his special constables, who also happened to work as an assistant groundsman at Fenner's. After all, I'd heard him tell the sergeant that I was a university cricketer good enough to have had my name in the papers.

It was sufficient information, when collated in the sergeant's mind, to make my throw hard and unerring despite my claims that I'd injured my arm, specifically my rotator-cuff muscle, and couldn't manage anything so dynamic. I might have been able to strike the lights, I told him, but my efforts would have lacked the force to break the hard plastic case surrounding them.

My protestations of innocence ignored, I was asked to hand over my wallet, watch and coins, as well as my belt and shoes, the last two items in case I should get the urge to kill myself. I was then slung into a cell with a bloke who could not stop being sick or voiding his bowels. It was probably 2 a.m. by now and I was tired and just a little emotional. But sleep, in that freezing, stinking cell with its thin, plastic mattress, and with matey-boy steadily purging himself of his bodily contents, proved elusive.

The police also seemed keen to stop us getting some shut-eye. In what appeared a deliberate ploy to wind us up, every hour or so some copper or other would pop in to ask (a) where we were from and (b) what we were in for. Silence, my cellmate's general response, would be followed by a shove or two in what seemed to me to be a deliberate attempt to bait him.

Both Magoo and I were charged with criminal damage and released at around 7 a.m. the next morning, a process which included our mugshots and fingerprints being taken. When I asked the desk sergeant whether we might get a cup of tea before we headed off, I was told in no uncertain terms to '---- off, you ------- student scum.'

Our day in court saw us both plead guilty, though I made an arse of myself when the judge asked how I might plead to the charge of 'causing criminal damage or behaving in a manner likely to cause criminal damage'. Confused, I said, 'Not guilty to the first, but guilty to the second.'

'It's all one charge, Mr Pringle.'

'Er, in that case, guilty, Your Honour.'

We were fined £90 and told, at least by my solicitor, that our records would be expunged after three years, providing there were no further offences.

The incident, which we kept from Doc E and Fitzwilliam (Magoo shared not only the same college but also the same subject and tutor), did present one minor repercussion, and not from the bare-faced lie I placed on my visa application to Australia a few years later in the section that asked 'Any criminal convictions?'

In my final year, I'd been at Grange Road watching Magoo and a few other mates play rugby against the Steele-Bodger's XV, arguably the university's biggest game outside the Varsity match at Twickenham. Somehow, during the action, wallets had gone missing from the home dressing room. One of the University subs that day, Simon Cooke, was asked by police investigating the incident to look at a few mugshots of nefarious characters, to see if he recognised anyone.

'Well, I know these two,' he said, picking out me and Magoo, our photos still on file.

Before the police could stamp the case closed, Cooke went on to explain that we were friends of his and that Magoo had been on the pitch the entire game, while I'd been in the stand over on the other side of the ground.

There was another loose strand to the story. Three years after I left university, I bought a house in Cambridge, from where I commuted to Essex to play cricket. It was a few years after that, so around 1988, that I found myself on Midsummer Common not far from the scene of our crime. Curious, I went to have a look. It had been eight years since our puerile rush of blood had given us a night in police cells. The light cover broken that night had still not been fixed.

A university like Cambridge is meant to broaden the mind as well as furnish undergraduates with a degree and therefore a passport to a better life. For those so motivated you can cram in all manner of worthy things when you are 'up' at college, like joining the Union Society for grown-up debate or, if you preferred something more infantile, societies dedicated to debauchery, such as the Wylies, now sadly defunct.

The trouble is, it is all over in a flash. Three or four years, comprising three terms of eight, eight and seven weeks, fairly whizz by. You arrive, get dropped off by your parents, and no sooner have you settled on a favourite pub, admittedly after a bit of trial and error, than it is time to go home for the 'vac'.

One bit of extracurricular activity I did manage to fit in, which involved neither work, drinking nor sport, was to appear in the film *Chariots of Fire*, some of which was made in Cambridge in 1980. The film portrays the journey of two athletes to the 1924 Paris Olympics. One of them is a devout Christian: Eric Liddell, who runs for God's glory. The other is Harold Abrahams, a Jew, who went to Cambridge, and who runs, in the film at least, to overcome prejudice.

A mature student at Fitzwilliam, Iain Reid, was recruiting extras, so a few mates and I thought it a wheeze to get involved. Already owning a blues blazer helped, and I was given the role of vice-captain of athletics for the Societies Fair scene, which was shot at the Senate House on King's Parade. Male extras were paid £10 and given a severe, short-back-and-sides haircut. The added bonus, for me at least, was to miss a couple of days of pre-season nets, which were the epitome of dull, especially if the weather was bad.

The role was not a speaking one, though I was expected to ad-lib something with my mate Dick Tyler, who had blagged his way into the scene. 'Not too audible,' was the instruction from Hugh Hudson, the director, after we'd overdone the enthusiasm on an early take. The intricate shot, almost two minutes uncut, took all day, and it was fascinating to see movie-making in the raw. I'm on screen for about 30 seconds, which is longer than Stephen Fry, a Cambridge contemporary. Fry, a Footlights regular by then, did, however, manage to wangle a front-row seat for the cast photo, where he cuts a svelte figure wearing a boater.

I was invited back for further scenes later in the summer, specifically those depicting the 1924 Paris Olympics. They were shot in Liverpool, one of the few places that still had an authentic cinders track. I turned them down. I was back playing at Essex by then, my 'summer job' better paid than most of my contemporaries'. Anyway, nobody I knew felt the film would amount to much due to the relatively unknown leads, Ben Cross and Ian Charleson. We were all gobsmacked when the following year it won four Oscars.

Unlike Abrahams's experience of running for Cambridge, playing for its cricket team meant getting used to defeat. After all, we were students playing against professional sportsmen. And yet that period provided me with some of the most enjoyable moments of my career – a carefree time when bold experimentation had little downside, at least on the pitch.

A lack of expectation may have had something to do with it. Let's face it, who isn't unburdened when the pressure of winning, and to a large degree the shame of losing, is more or less removed from the equation? I certainly was, and while the county pros were always

likely to prevail over the duration of a three-day match, I was determined to take the game to them when I could.

That attitude, in harness with the fascinating and generally good-
humoured people I played with, plus the hilarious ministry of Brian
Taylor, our coach, played a huge part in making those years ones of
sheer, unadulterated joy. It felt unique – that heady feeling of being
young at Cambridge, with all options still on the table.

Taylor, whose nickname 'Tonker' had been acquired during his
long career at Essex, a team he'd captained between 1967 and
1972, was the perfect fit as coach to a university side like ours. His
ability to deliver the right amount of gravitas, in hearty sergeant-
major tones, while simultaneously being able to laugh at himself
made him extremely popular. His imperfections, in a city where
people were taught to hide them well, made him both authentic
and real.

If Tonker's knowledge of the game was extensive and multi-
faceted, his psychology was strictly binary. Opponents were either
'prats' or 'plonkers', while his own team were 'diamonds' or 'champions'. I knew him well from my time playing with the Essex Second
XI immediately after school. Tonker was our captain and mentor,
and while his county brief required him to knock us into some sort
of shape, so that we might one day become fully functioning professional cricketers, he was able to adjust the tone when it came to
dealing with university players of that era, most of them talented
amateurs at best.

Still, that did not stop him reading the riot act to us occasionally,
such as in 1981 when Sussex made 348 for nine declared, their
dominant batting display having followed a swingeing defeat for us
in the previous game.

'Right, numbers one, two and three, you are all going to make a
hundred and stick it to these fucking show ponies from the south
coast,' he bellowed, pointing at our top order.

'Excuse me, Brian,' said Ian Peck, one of the openers, 'but this is only my second game of the season, and a hundred does seem to be asking a lot.'

'All right, son,' said Tonker, 'you go and get fifty.'

So much for the power of positive thinking – an hour later we were 28 for four, going on to lose the game by an innings and 40 runs.

It was not always so one-sided. In my final year, 1982, when I captained the team, we actually competed pretty well on a few occasions, even managing to beat Lancashire fair and square: i.e., without the inducement of a declaration. That was the season when both my batting and bowling impressed enough people to get me picked for England, the first time an undergraduate had been selected for such an accolade since Ted Dexter, 24 years earlier.

Two counties also approached me that season to be their captain, Worcestershire and Glamorgan. Both were good offers, with substantially more money than I was getting at Essex, but both teams looked weak at the time. Graeme Hick would not join Worcestershire for another two years – so I stayed put with Essex, a team who sought glory and good times over monetary gain.

Anyway, Cambridge should also have beaten Glamorgan that season at Fenner's. But for my faulty maths, we might have had two notches on our middle stump that season. The improbability of actually beating a county had confused me. I'd turned my left ankle playing football during pre-season training, so when Glamorgan arrived to start our season I played as a batsman only. On a pitch that offered some bounce and movement, both unusual for Fenner's, Ian Hodgson, normally my first-change bowler, took eight for 68 in a superb display of controlled seam bowling. Even so, we did not bowl Glamorgan out and they declared their first innings on 281 for nine.

Our reply was to make 222 all out, with me making 127 of them in a surprisingly commanding innings, considering the state of my ankle. Rodney Ontong, Glamorgan's overseas player, then pummelled us for his own hundred, enabling them to set us 326 on the final day in just under five hours.

We had reached 256 for five, 70 runs short, with eight overs to go, when I decided to accept their offer of the draw. I was still at the crease on 73 and Hodgson, no mug with the bat, had just walked in. We had a chat and while he seemed keen to give it a crack my errant maths conspired to place the equation at over 10 runs an over, which it wasn't. It was our first game of the season and we didn't have much to come after Hodge and me, so not losing definitely had its attractions.

Afterwards, Matthew Engel, covering the game for the *Guardian*, asked me why I had taken the draw when the glory of a rare victory might have been in the offing. I fudged some half-arsed excuse before admitting my errant arithmetic. Even so, I should have been bolder and gone for it. What really did we have to lose except another game, something we did all the time? It was, perhaps, the first time that the swashbuckling cricketer I so wanted to be had been subjugated by dull pragmatism.

I didn't bowl in the next game against Nottinghamshire either, though I batted even better in terms of pure ball-striking, smashing 81 in next to no time. The pitch was true, and when Notts replied, their openers, Paul Todd and Bruce French, pasted our opening bowlers Richard Dutton and Bob Palmer all over Fenner's. It didn't help that it was bitterly cold, with a biting northerly wind coming off the Fens. Sensing we might be in for a long day, I waved for our 12th man to bring me another sweater. But before he could respond, Derek Randall, next man in for Notts, appeared on the balcony shouting, 'What do you want, a bloody white flag?'

It was a good, if cruel, line but one that led to a reckoning soon when we took a wicket. Randall arrived at the crease, all jaunty banter and good cheer, eager to continue the carnage. Instead, he was rapped on the pad first ball from Bobby Palmer, which swung in sharply, and given out lbw – a decision he did not take gracefully.

'That were bloody never out,' he said, to the keeper and slips. His protestation was met by dumb shrugs. 'Bloody umpire only gave me 'cos I shouted from pavilion.'

Desperate to get some time in the middle, he opened the batting in Notts' second innings, blocking the hell out of it for 29 while Todd made an unbeaten 104 at the other end. It was enough, though, to see them through for a 10-wicket victory after our second innings had folded for 154.

The weather had warmed by the time we met Lancashire on 12 May. They had a strong team out, missing just four first-team regulars, including Clive Lloyd, the captain. They made 304 all out in their first innings and we responded with 274, which gave them a modest lead.

I'm not sure where Lancashire were staying but our good fortune was that, through their dashing but slightly unhinged batsman Frank Hayes, they had just discovered Grolsch beer, sold in bottles with flip-top stoppers. Laboratory-chic we called it, and luckily it was beyond our pocket. Hayes, an enthusiastic imbiber of most things alcoholic, seemed particularly smitten and had spread his obsession throughout the team. Their mission that game seemed to be to drink Cambridge dry of the stuff and, as resourceful opponents, we were only too happy to show them where that might be accomplished.

Lancashire were perhaps a bit slow to get going on the second morning while we laboured over our first innings, but not enough to account for what happened in the afternoon when, with sun shining, they were despatched for 128 in their second innings.

I took six for 33, my best first-class figures at that juncture. I bowled well, the new Imran Khan leap I had incorporated into my action allowing for a good rhythm from the Pavilion End. I'd like to think it was all down to skill and pace, but there were definitely elements of good fortune involved, aside from any lingering Lancashire hangover.

The first of these was that a plate-sized patch, on which the topmost crust of the pitch had dusted up, had appeared right on an awkward line and length for left-handers – of which they had five in their top eight. The second was that I'd just been picked for MCC to play against the touring Indian side at Lord's, a great accolade for a student and a timely confidence-booster.

Obviously, any bowler had to keep hitting the awkward spot with an upright seam, which I did, and the batsmen had to keep nicking it, which they did. Even so, we still needed 159 on a wearing pitch to win, happily something we managed after Stephen Henderson and I had stilled some early wobbles with an unbroken partnership of 103.

It was a great moment for the players – the university's first victory over a county for 11 years. Word had got round, too, and by the time the winning runs came, in blazing sunshine after tea, over 1,500 students were at Fenner's to witness it.

University teams rarely beat counties in the professional era, but Frank Hayes had known that it was in the offing by the second evening. Grolsched-up in the Anchor pub, he grabbed me in a headlock and hissed, 'If you don't beat us tomorrow you'll have me to answer to.' It was only when I got back to Essex, and rejoined players like Ray East who'd toured with Hayes, that I realised the headlock was a sign of affection.

Lancashire's humiliation was not yet complete. The club's committee demanded an explanation, summoning David 'Bumble' Lloyd, Lancashire's acting captain during the match, to explain himself.

'We didn't lose any points and nobody died,' was Lloyd's brusque assessment as he faced his inquisitors. Except that matters did not improve for Lancashire much after that in the Championship. They finished 12th out of 17.

In contrast, things had started to look up for me. I was awarded a 2:2 and got picked for England, though there was some suggestion that the second achievement was less miraculous than the first.

2

ENGLAND CALLING

I T WAS DURING my last few weeks as a Cambridge undergrad that I was selected to play for England, while some of my inner Corinthian remained.

One wag in the press felt my surprise promotion was due to me being the son that Peter May, the chairman of selectors and a man with four daughters, had never had. There were even rumours circulating at the time that I was sleeping with two of the four May girls. A complete fabrication, as I hadn't met any of them by that stage.

I was certainly perplexed by my sudden promotion, though perhaps not as much as May when he rang my digs to break the news. I'd just finished Finals, but what he didn't know, and I never sought to explain, is that a few months earlier a mate from Fitzwilliam, Dick Tyler, had perpetrated a hoax on Magoo, another good friend. Magoo and Tyler were both rugby blues and the latter had recently duped the other by posing as an England Under-23 rugby selector over the phone.

Determined not to be tricked as well, I hissed, 'Piss off, Tyler,' before slamming down the receiver.

Fortunately, a puzzled May rang back a few minutes later, his persistence and formality persuading me the call was in fact genuine. Basically, he had invited me to play for England in the first Test against India. If I accepted, I should be at Lord's the following Wednesday, ready for nets at 3 p.m. sharp. Despite my disbelief, I think I said, 'Yes.'

A formal, handwritten invitation duly dropped through my letterbox a few days later to confirm I'd not been drinking too much

Camp Coffee and imagined the entire thing. Still, it was hard not to wonder if I was one of those frauds Roebuck was hell-bent on exposing and, therefore, completely undeserving of selection. I'd played just 55 first-class matches, most of them for Cambridge, so my abilities as a cricketer had not exactly been forged in the white heat of meaningful struggle.

Then again, I hadn't applied for the post, so it was hardly my fault if someone – actually, more than one person, as it happened – in either wisdom or stupidity, had gone and picked me for England. Anyway, it hadn't been lucky dip, or maybe it had? I just couldn't decide. I'd been batting and bowling well, so my form backed the pro-selection argument. But then Fenner's was a featherbed and full of runs for anyone reasonably competent. That, surely, was one for the cons, so back to square one on whether or not my selection was warranted.

Thesis followed by an equally valid antithesis played out a constant tug of war in my mind over the following days, the victor changing by the hour. What compounded matters, once news had got out, were the murmurings that privilege had once again eased the direction of travel for someone considered part of the Establishment – Cambridge having also been Peter May's alma mater. Doubt, the performer's great curse and something I'd never previously been overly consumed by, at least on a sportsfield, suddenly crowded out any rational thought. Eventually, the endless analysis proved exhausting and it left me cursing the effects of a decent education.

What I failed to realise, despite my qualms, was how much being at university had sheltered me from the shock my selection had wreaked upon the public – until, that is, I went to play a Sunday League match for Essex against Somerset at Chelmsford, the university having yet to resume its fixture list following exams. When I arrived at the ground, the England squad for the first Test against India was just being read out over the club's tannoy.

The disbelief among the Essex faithful when my name was announced was tangible. Tellingly, there was no applause. It had caught them off guard as much as it had me, a few days earlier. These, after all, were proper cricket supporters and not Cambridge cheerleaders, so their reaction cut deep. Even Essex's sage scorer, Clem Driver, sounded surprised and he'd seen it all, having fought with the Desert Rats in North Africa, played bridge against Omar Sharif, run his own business and followed Essex around for decades.

It made me feel slightly sick, especially when, on the dressing-room balcony, I heard the incredulity in Botham's voice when he said, 'Has he?' after someone told him of my inclusion.

The feeling did not improve when rain prevented the match from starting on time. The press were especially eager to take the opportunity to interview me, but somehow I managed to avoid them. To justify my selection without sounding trite, or suggesting the selectors had been dropping LSD, would have been difficult.

Eventually, the rain relented and we played a 10-over slog, which Essex won by a single run. I bowled my two overs and took a wicket, but batted at nine, hardly a strong endorsement from Keith Fletcher, my Essex captain, that I was England material.

To be fair, Fletch was still smarting from being sacked as England captain the previous week, so was not concerned with massaging egos. Under him, England's Test series in India six months earlier, which was lost 1–0, had been a PR as well as a cricketing disaster. With reports of petulant behaviour, as well as cynically slow over-rates (by both sides), that frustrating tour was seen, rightly or wrongly, as the breeding ground for the 1982 rebel tour of South Africa. It hadn't helped, either, that in one match Fletch had deliberately knocked the bails off his stumps in order to show displeasure at the poor umpiring decisions which had blighted the series.

Back in September 1981, Peter May's appointment as chairman of selectors was seen as a new broom, and his first act had been to appoint Fletch, arguably the greatest county captain of his generation, as Brearley's successor. In an interview with Christopher Martin-Jenkins, he was asked whether he intended Fletcher, then 37, to be a long-term appointment. 'I hope so,' said May. 'There's no point in chopping and changing.' Yet chop Fletch is exactly what May did nine months later, bringing in Bob Willis, or Robert as May called him, to take over the helm.

I had the utmost respect for Fletch, but the irony was inescapable that, had he still been England captain, I would not have been picked for Test cricket at that moment. He was an old pro and they don't deal in potential or the romantic notion of gentleman cricketers, just hard evidence of excellence. That, and whether you could be relied upon to get the job done.

May and Bob Willis were clearly more idealistic. I'd met Willis a few times when Cambridge had played Warwickshire, and I got on well with him and his county team-mates, one of whom, John Claughton, I'd toured Australia with in 1979–80 for Oxford and Cambridge. Between them, and David Brown, the Warwickshire coach, they'd even tried to persuade me to leave Essex and join them, something I said I'd consider if Claughton was ever made captain. Regrettably, he never was, a nasty knee injury bringing his first-class career to a hasty end a few years later.

I found Willis a curious mix of ascetic and bohemian. The fast bowler in him knew that hard, physical work was essential to his craft, and he was a stickler for sacrificing things that would inversely affect his fitness. Yet, at the same time, he liked a drink and gravitated towards people who pushed boundaries, whether in sport, music or life. After all, he'd added a third forename, Dylan, by deed poll, to follow Robert and George, as a tribute to Bob Dylan, whose songs he revered to the point of obsession.

He must have known May was going to appoint him in place of Fletch as England captain by the time Warwickshire began their three-day match against Cambridge on 1 May. Willis didn't play in the game but came along to watch and to spend the evenings with Newmarket's horse-racing crowd. He and David Brown, as well as Andy Lloyd and David Smith, Warwickshire's two opening batsmen, all liked the gee-gees and were close to those who owned, rode and trained them.

The locus of their carousing was the Red Lion pub in Cheveley, a village three miles south-east of Newmarket. They repaired there every evening of the match. On their final night they invited me to join them. What a session it proved. Although a Monday night, the lock-in that ensued was unplanned, which made it all the more thrilling. With everyone far too drunk to drive back to Cambridge, most of us bedded down in the saloon bar with the odd dusty rug for warmth, there being no spare rooms at the inn.

When dawn arrived, in what seemed a blink, we headed back to Cambridge and the Blue Boar hotel on Trinity Street, where Warwickshire were staying. With my bike at home – I usually walked to Fenner's, the ground being about 400 yards away from the flat I shared with my old mucker Muttley – Willis offered me the spare bed in his room. It was a fine gesture, for which I promptly thanked him by throwing up in his bath.

The extra 40 minutes' kip I got as a result of not having to walk home didn't do me much good. Faced with making an interesting declaration to keep spectator interest high on the final day of the match, I kept dropping down the order, unable to face even taking guard for fear that I might be sick on the pitch.

At least I made it to the ground on time. Andy Lloyd didn't arrive until lunch, a late showing that cost him a substantial fine. He'd recovered enough by the afternoon to lead Warwickshire's attempt to chase the 296 needed to win. Happily, the rain gods smiled on us both and brought an early conclusion.

I had not sparkled that match. Willis had also seen that I was no 'Horlicks and slippers' sportsman, carefully looking after myself and tucked up early every night in pursuit of a good eight hours. I didn't know then that he was about to be made England captain, so when his elevation came and was followed, subsequently, by my own selection, it gave me comfort to know that he'd seen me at my worst and still wanted me in the team – peccadillos and all.

University life can be sheltered, and while I considered myself reasonably worldly and well-travelled, having been brought up in Africa, nothing prepared me for the media onslaught which followed my selection.

There were interviews, photoshoots, editorials, all about little me – enough to swell even the most cynical head. Reporters were despatched from Fleet Street just to get a word. It baffled me. After all, I was 23 and therefore no freakish, teenage wunderkind.

Nicholas Coleridge, who'd been at Cambridge a few years before me, turned up at my flat, immaculately attired, to pen a piece for the *Evening Standard*, for whom he was a columnist. Coleridge is now chairman of Condé Nast, but this was his first pukka job in journalism. British *Vogue*, now a part of the Condé Nast stable, even rang to ask if they could do a fashion shoot with me and the Cambridge team dressed in our whites and, this a specific request, 'wearing those sexy cable-knit sweaters cricketers wear'. They seemed charming enough, until I asked how much we might get paid. The dialogue then went dead.

My background was dredged up and my credentials analysed, but most interest, at least in the tabloids, lay with the ear stud I had taken to wearing just a few months earlier. 'It was done for a bet with a university mate,' I told them, which was true. They seemed to want to have fun with it, though, so when someone asked why I wore just a single ear stud, I told them it was because I'd look pretty stupid with two. It provided good copy, which is what they wanted, yet there was a whole other hinterland to the story I did not reveal,

not least the passionate romance which resulted in the piercing and
the choice of stud, both supplied for free.

The piercer was Claire, a medical student at the University of Cape
Town, and a few years older than me. I had been in South Africa on
another Oxbridge tour, though this one had not been a great success.
At one stage, the entire team had been placed on a sporting blacklist
by SAN-ROC, South Africa's Non-Racial Olympic Committee. It
earned us 15 minutes of notoriety until I pointed out that having a
bunch of students on the blacklist would surely dilute its impact. At
which point they took us off.

The political sensitivity of having the slightest tie with apartheid
South Africa meant we had been advised not to go. But we were
student cricketers and not in the habit of looking gift horses in the
mouth. So when the offer of an all-expenses-paid tour to the Rand
Republic was made, few of us looked to our principles and declined.
The University Cricket Club didn't block us either. Their sole stipu-
lation was that instead of touring as Oxford and Cambridge, we
should have a different name. So we did, calling ourselves 'The
Jazzhats', a term hardened pros used for public-school cricketers,
the etymology harking back to the gaudy cricket caps – usually
from their old school – such players traditionally wore irrespective
of the team they were representing. For instance, Douglas Jardine,
England's captain during Bodyline, would wear his stripy Harlequins
cap from Oxford days, even when playing Test matches.

I met Claire once the tour was over. An old Cambridge team-
mate from my second year, André Odendaal, had taken up a post
teaching history at the University of Western Cape, and had invited
me and another Cambridge cricketer, Neil Russom, to stay with
him in Cape Town. First, though, and due to the tour finishing in
Port Elizabeth, he suggested we hire a car and drive the Garden
Route, which winds round the southern tip of that vast continent.

We took his advice, but a combination of rain squalls and squabbles meant we made haste to Cape Town instead. Foot down and with loo breaks kept to a minimum (we'd wee into empty water bottles to save time), we arrived just as André was heading off to join friends for New Year's Eve on a deserted beach on South Africa's Atlantic coast.

The setting, near Elands Bay, was remote and impossibly romantic, even more so when I hit it off with Claire, one of his friends. It was an improbable coupling – her a gorgeous, feisty 4 ft 11 in ball of energy, me a laconic 6 ft 5 in dope. Mother Nature, though, still found a way. Against André's countenance (she was going out with his housemate), we shared a sleeping bag under clear, desert skies. Naturally, I told André that nothing had gone on, but heavy condensation on the bag the following morning suggested otherwise.

That initial dalliance was as delicious as it was unexpected, the melodrama magnified by the unspoilt vistas of nature in the raw. The sea, though, was freezing, and rough, especially when compared to the warm bath of Mombasa where I'd spent many a happy childhood holiday. Big though I was, I braved only a dipped toe. Claire and her friend Sue were fearless, donning their wetsuits and gloves, and diving among the great tangles of kelp to grab crayfish for our table. Incredibly, both were allergic to crustaceans, which meant the rest feasted like kings.

Back in Cape Town, there was an awkward scene with André's housemate, even though Claire told me they had parted prior to our assignation. What followed, once the recriminations had subsided, was a blissful week of sex, drinking and personal instruction – one of the things taught being the best way to make Bobotie, a classic Cape curry. To my shame, I have forgotten the recipe, though not those seven heavenly days, which stirred emotions hitherto dormant.

I mentioned to Claire a bet I had made with Magoo back in Cambridge, his wager being that I wouldn't have the bottle to get my ear pierced. 'We can do that right now if you like,' she said, as we lay about one evening. Intrigued, I agreed, and off she went, returning before long with two ice cubes, a sewing needle, a candle, matches and a bottle of rough Tassenberg red wine.

As a pre-med, I was told to take a few swigs of the Tassie, something Claire did as well, pointing out that it was she who would need the steady hand should I start squealing. Needle sterilised in the flame, left earlobe deadened by ice cubes – and then, bang, she skewered me through with a stroke both swift and sure. She even had a spare stud for me to wear, having lost one previously, with orders to keep twirling it round, to stop the hole sealing up.

The ear bled, went slightly green and wept a bit. The bet, all of a fiver, was won, and I collected when I returned to Cambridge. Best of all, Claire had left a mark on me, evidence that the whole delicious episode had actually happened.

Our parting wasn't easy. Goodbyes had been part of life in Kenya, a place of temporary postings as well as friendships, but this felt a wrench. We agreed to write and did, her letters mature and focused, mine saccharine and trite, as I tried to capture the profundity of it all by channelling my inner Byron. We also decided that she would fly over and visit me in Cambridge, after my Finals, which she did, walking straight into the maelstrom of me being picked for England.

The timing was dreadful. My vistas had changed, utterly. Suddenly, and it was something I couldn't immediately get my head around, women wanted to sleep with me. As a perennial wearer of eyeglasses and loather of contact lenses, which I only wore when playing sport, I'd always assumed that alpha-male desirability, at least in the eyes of the fairer sex, was not something I particularly exuded. Yet, incredibly, even though I hadn't done much more than get picked for the England cricket team, I was big news. And that turned heads, mine included.

Claire arrived but I was, perhaps understandably, distracted. I didn't ignore her completely but I might as well have done. Muttley and Magoo looked after her nobly while I played the 'big I am', but I could tell she was confused. I was winging it and I'm sure it showed, but that was no consolation for her as she vainly searched for any remnants of what we'd had six months earlier.

It was selfish, small-minded and weak-willed of me, but I was a bloke responding to type and reverting to all the old atavisms. By the end of the third Test against India I'd slept with more women in two months than I had done in four years at Cambridge. Back then, only a saint or a confirmed celibate would have spurned an opportunity like that.

Unsurprisingly, things ended messily with Claire. With me preoccupied, she decided to travel round England to see old friends while I got on with playing cricket, a game she could scarcely conceal her scorn for. Come August, she'd decided to return to Cape Town, though not before one last evening together in London.

We met for dinner in Covent Garden, along with Magoo and his girlfriend, Suzy, with whom Claire had been staying. I was in the middle of the second Test against Pakistan, at Lord's, which wasn't going well, adding to the strain of the evening.

We'd settled for an outdoor table at one of the restaurants beside the piazza. Our waitress warned Claire and Suzy not to hang their handbags on the back of their chairs in case of pickpockets and bag-snatchers. At some point in the evening Claire forgot. When it came time to divvy up the bill, her bag had gone.

There was panic, tears and finally frustration, as we reported it at the local police station. Her memory of that evening (amazingly, we have remained friends) is that the police seemed more interested in getting my autograph than in taking her statement, though I do not recall that. All I know is that by the time the police had sent some-one round to Paddington Station, where she had stowed her luggage in a locker, her suitcase had gone – the locker key having been in her stolen handbag along with purse, credit cards, money and camera. The only slice of good fortune was that she'd left her passport and air ticket at Suzy's flat, so was able to travel as planned the next day, albeit in the same clothes and with her worldly possessions wrapped in a plastic bag. I loaned her £20 so she could get to Heathrow, money she assures me she paid back, though there would have been no expectation of that.

It was a symbolic end to our relationship, yet in truth that had concluded, for me at least, as soon as the temptation of other women had begun to swirl around. Unlike some, I find deceit, at least to those close to me, impossible to pull off without the tell-tale churn of unease being written all over me. As a result, I can only get away with telling porkies, and then only slight ones, to complete strangers, which is not a particularly useful skill, given they are unlikely to be questioning one's veracity in the first place.

It wasn't my finest moment. Without seeking to make excuses, it perhaps reveals the recessive but ruthless streak possessed by all sportsmen with a whit of ambition. Here was a girl I thought I had cared for deeply just a few months earlier, now seemingly sacrificed on the bonfire of my vanity. That is not to say I did not feel guilt or have regret. It is just that I found those sentiments distracting when most of my emotional heft was being required to deal with the pressures of international cricket – pressures that had simply not existed for me a few months earlier.

Maybe that is what defines experience in top-level sport – the ability to compartmentalise one's feelings so they don't bleed into one other. I was a novice, though, and lacked the skill to contain any mess. As a result, there'd already been an innocent victim cast aside – though, to my shame, it wasn't something I dwelt on for long.

Test cricket was very different from any I'd experienced before. For starters, there was that written invitation to play for England. It was very formal and required an RSVP to the Secretary of the Test and County Cricket Board, then Donald Carr, one of the more likeable patricians behind English cricket. In addition to nets the day before the match, there was a team dinner to negotiate, a gut-busting four-course affair with wine and port to be consumed just 14 hours before you were expected to take up cudgels against the opposition – India, in the case of my debut.

The dinner doubled as a team meeting at which tactics were also discussed, though rarely in great detail. 'Sunil Gavaskar, what do we think about him?' would be a typical opening gambit after the cheese. 'Well, he's good at pulling and cutting and is strong off his legs, so keep it outside off stump on a good length,' might come the reply from one of the seasoned campaigners. At which point Ian Botham, never one for lengthy analysis, would interject, 'Maybe, but he's only 5 ft 2 in tall, as are the rest of the top order, so let's bounce the shit out of them. Now, come on, let's get to the bar before last orders.'

I was not the only potential debutant for that Lord's Test against India. Allan Lamb, another who'd grown up in Africa, had also been picked in the squad. He exuded calm, though, having already met most of the team during the two one-day internationals which had preceded the Test series, something for which I'd not been picked.

England had won both matches comfortably, with Lamb making a decisive 99 in the second one, at The Oval. A strong contribution like that can cut through the uncertainty most new players feel when they take the step up to international cricket. Believing you belong, a frustratingly elusive feeling for many, remains one of the great confidence-boosters in team sport.

To engender that confidence, almost everyone – captain, selectors, senior players, though not, tellingly, those who feel their place is under threat from your arrival – tries to relax the new boy with an encouraging word. It can be a fine line, though, between receiving the odd helpful tip and being hen-pecked to distraction by well-meaning advice. This is done in various ways, from telling you to play just as you do for your county (not particularly helpful bearing in mind the greater nature of the challenge), to giving you chapter and verse on the dos and don'ts of one's opponents.

For example, bowling to Gavaskar, you would be told not to stray anywhere near his middle stump or he'll clip you through the leg side all day long. Don't drop short or he'll cut and pull you, and don't give him too much width or he'll belt you through the covers. It is all meant to help, except that, with all the perils of getting it wrong, newcomers might wonder if it is worth letting the ball go at all. In May's case, the advice proffered was that in order to get good batsmen out, seam and swing bowlers like me needed to bring them forward rather than push them back – sound guidance, especially if you are getting extra bounce or making the ball move laterally.

Ian Botham's way of getting me to relax before my first Test, at Lord's on 10 June 1982, was rather different and involved dragging me to the bar in the Westmoreland hotel after the team dinner.

'You need to come with me,' he said. 'A few more beers will help you sleep better, otherwise you'll be wide awake worrying about tomorrow.'

He was wrong. I spent a fitful night fretting and peeing, but it meant a lot that he had made the effort to make me feel part of the side.

Except I was not yet part of it, not officially. True, I'd been handed two England sweaters sporting the three lions and a crown, a royal blue cap bearing the same, and six shirts embossed with another lion. The bounty was still part illusion, though, coming as it did with the instruction that I must return it if I wasn't in the final XI. This only added to the suspense, as the team, I was told, would only be decided after Willis had looked at the pitch again on the morning of the match.

It was standard practice, though that did not prevent me from running through the pros and cons of me playing as against those I saw as my immediate rivals – in this instance, Paul Allott, Geoff Miller and Phil Edmonds, depending on the balance between seam and spin preferred by Willis. In this sort of situation, the others up for debate probably mull it over as well, though it isn't long before rational thought is replaced by all manner of fancy theories, usually why you should be the one to miss out. Everyone tells you to relax, though their well-meaning reassurance means you end up worrying even more.

The next morning I was told that I was in. Willis informed me himself, then shook my hand and wished me luck, as did most of the other players. The joy was not overwhelming, as I still needed to prepare for the match. I had made the team but now I needed to get grounded, quick. The warm-ups helped, as did fielding practice, though the banter on the previous days had all but disappeared as the rising tension began to silence even the most confident voices.

One man's joy is another's sorrow, though in a 12-man squad I could not help but become aware of the player whose place I had taken. In this case, Geoff Miller.

Players take disappointment in different ways and Dusty, as everyone called him, swore and cursed and threw a bit of a wobbler. This surprised me. Growing up, I'd always been taught, at every school I'd ever been to from Nairobi to Essex, that setbacks were best met with a stiff upper lip. Indeed, it was compulsory. Yet here was Dusty openly showing his disappointment in a way that went beyond a token strop.

His response was a salutary lesson in the sense of betrayal that exists at the heart of every team sport, and why only Test captains possessing the thickest of skins have ever wanted to be involved in team selection. Dusty had been on most England tours since 1977, bonding strongly with all the leading protagonists, including Willis.

Then along comes an upstart who displaces him for no obvious reason. Suddenly, those friendships feel very false indeed.

Some players hold it against the rival who has displaced them and career-long enmities are formed. But Dusty, once he'd cooled down, was grown up about it. He might have cursed the selectors but he never let it infect our relationship, which has never been less than good – he even joined Essex in the late 1980s, bringing some of his less salubrious habits with him.

England won the toss and batted first in that opening Test. Mum and my sister, Janet, were there to watch from Q Stand, a small section of Lord's where two of a player's four guests – usually a melange of wives, partners or close friends – could watch the day's play in comfort and relative privacy.

In Q Stand it was Gin O'Clock from noon onwards and the G&Ts kept coming all day if you wanted them. A slap-up lunch, including decent wine, would take place at the customary hour, with tea served around 4 p.m. The flow of alcohol was ceaseless, all gratis. People of drinking age would enter as part of genteel society and leave looking, and behaving, like drunken bums.

At lunch on that opening day, Mum and Janet sat next to Mick Jagger and his brother, Chris, so were given an extra thrill. According to Mum, Mick scarcely touched the food or the wine. As I tried to explain to her later, rock stars, unless they are named after food, like Meat Loaf, don't tend to do the lumpy stuff.

My nerves, which had been building steadily for days, reached a crescendo when the fifth wicket fell and I had to make my way down the cork-tiled steps through the Lord's Long Room. There, amid all the portraits of great players, MCC members, all sporting tie and jacket, give you a polite clap to send you on your way. Then down the Pavilion steps you go, through the white swing gate and out onto the beautiful ground, surrounded by more people than you have ever seen in one place, save for Howrah railway station in Kolkata, which I had been to.

Human responses to big moments differ, but as I walked to the crease my mind felt stuffed with cotton wool and my legs felt heavy. I hadn't experienced anything like it since waiting to swim my leg of the 50 metres house relay at St Mary's School in Nairobi, an event that used to fill me with dread, a feeling mostly down to the chlorine sting in the eyes (no goggles back then) and the fact that I'd never cracked the breathing for front crawl. Yes, it was that intimidating.

A quick word with Derek Randall, the other batsman in the middle, who wished me luck, and I was asking for middle and leg and trying my best to look calm. As I glanced round the field, I couldn't help thinking that I had to pull myself together, fast. I mean, there was some bloke walking down St John's Wood Road, not 100 yards away, completely oblivious to my predicament. He's not crapping himself, I thought, and his reality is just as relevant as mine. So what's the big deal?

Feeling bat on ball reduced the flutters a bit, though the situation, with such a big crowd, still seemed unreal and I struggled to find any of the fluency that I'd managed all season batting for Cambridge. Essentially, I spent 26 balls making seven scrappy runs before being adjudged caught at silly point by Gavaskar off Dilip Doshi.

I didn't feel it was out, believing that my bat had struck pad, rather than ball, which made the second noise and convinced umpire David Evans that I'd given a catch off bat and pad. With the Decision Review System still 30 years away, we'll never know, but as I walked off I couldn't help feeling that, out or not, it was a wimpish way to go.

Still, England, having been 96 for four, made 433, following a fine hundred from Randall and some hearty wagging by the tail. We – and I felt that acquainted with my new team – were in good shape.

*   *   *

On the third day, Claire and Muttley were my Q Stand guests. Enthusiastic drinkers both, they were also mickey-takers and brutally honest. Yes, both had seen the 'momentous' event of my first Test wicket the previous day, Yashpal Sharma lbw for four, taken during my first over in Test cricket, but they were people-watchers and didn't rate it as much as the entertainment provided by Frances Edmonds, wife of Phil Edmonds, England's left-arm spinner.

I didn't know Phil that well then, at least not as well as Claire and Muttley now did, thanks to his wife's tipsy tirade against him. 'I know he cavorts around the country, but I don't give a damn,' she declaimed at one point, and not sotto voce. According to Frances, all cricketers were conniving, low-life scum and not to be trusted. She warned Claire about the groupies and not getting involved with me, though I suspect Claire had already realised the perils by then.

I took a second wicket in India's first innings, Ashok Malhotra, who was also one of four I'd bagged in the MCC match against India at Lord's three weeks earlier. (It was that performance, I believe, rather than my good form for Cambridge, which had sealed my selection for England.) With India making a paltry 128 in their first innings, Willis enforced the follow-on, as you did in those days. Second time around he led the line, his six for 101 central to dismissing them for 369. Requiring 67 to go one up in the series, we won by seven wickets.

I took two wickets in India's second innings, which meant I could be pleased with my first foray into Test cricket. Although more solid than spectacular, at least I hadn't disgraced myself. I was concerned, though, at how timid I'd been with the bat. Quality spinners were rarely encountered at Fenner's, and while Dilip Doshi and Ravi Shastri were not the finest tweakers India have ever produced, they were among the best I'd faced to that point.

Leaving Lord's to head back to Cambridge, I promised myself I would not to be so circumspect when facing them again.

ENGLAND V INDIA
(1st Test)

Played at Lord's Cricket Ground, London, 10–15 June 1982

Umpires: DGL Evans & BJ Meyer
Toss: England

ENGLAND

G Cook	lbw b Kapil Dev	4		lbw b Kapil Dev	10
CJ Tavaré	c Viswanath b Kapil Dev	4		b Kapil Dev	3
AJ Lamb	lbw b Kapil Dev	9	(4)	not out	37
DI Gower	c Viswanath b Kapil Dev	37	(5)	not out	14
IT Botham	c Malhotra b Madan Lal	67			
DW Randall	c Parkar b Kapil Dev	126			
DR Pringle	c Gavaskar b Doshi	7			
PH Edmonds	c Kirmani b Madan Lal	64			
RW Taylor†	c Viswanath b Doshi	31	(3)	c Malhotra b Kapil Dev	1
PJW Allott	not out	41			
RGD Willis*	b Madan Lal	28			
Extras	(1 b, 5 lb, 9 nb)	15		(2 lb)	2
Total	(148.1 overs)	**433**		(19 overs)	**67**

INDIA

SM Gavaskar*	b Botham	48		c Cook b Willis	24
GA Parkar	lbw b Botham	6		b Willis	1
DB Vengsarkar	lbw b Willis	2		c Allott b Willis	157
GR Viswanath	b Botham	1	(5)	c Taylor b Pringle	3
Yashpal Sharma	lbw b Pringle	4	(6)	b Willis	37
AO Malhotra	lbw b Pringle	5	(7)	c Taylor b Willis	0
Kapil Dev	c Cook b Willis	41	(8)	c Cook b Botham	89
RJ Shastri	c Cook b Willis	4	(4)	b Allott	23
SMH Kirmani†	not out	6		c Gower b Willis	3
Madan Lal	c Tavaré b Botham	6		lbw b Pringle	15
DR Doshi	c Taylor b Botham	0		not out	4
Extras	(1 lb, 4 nb)	5		(2 lb, 11 nb)	13
Total	(50.4 overs)	**128**		(following on, 111.5 overs)	**369**

INDIA	O	M	R	W		O	M	R	W
Kapil Dev	43	8	125	5		10	1	43	3
Madan Lal	28.1	6	99	5		2	1	2	0
Shastri	34	10	73	0	(4)	2	0	9	0
Doshi	40	7	120	2	(3)	5	3	11	0
Yashpal Sharma	3	2	1	0					

ENGLAND	O	M	R	W		O	M	R	W
Botham	19.4	3	46	5		31.5	7	103	1
Willis	16	5	41	3		28	3	101	6
Pringle	9	4	16	2		19	4	58	2
Edmonds	2	1	5	0	(5)	15	6	39	0
Allott	4	1	15	0	(4)	17	3	51	1
Cook						1	0	4	0

Fall of wickets:

	Eng	Ind	Ind	Eng
1st	5	17	6	11
2nd	18	21	47	13
3rd	37	22	107	18
4th	96	31	110	–
5th	149	45	252	–
6th	166	112	252	–
7th	291	116	254	–
8th	363	116	275	–
9th	363	128	341	–
10th	433	128	369	–

Close of play: Day 1:   England (1) 278–6 (Randall 84*, Edmonds 59*)
                 Day 2:   India (1) 92–5 (Gavaskar 41*, Kapil Dev 28*)
                 Day 3:   India (2) 61–2 (Vengsarkar 30*, Shastri 6*)
                 Day 4:   England (2) 23–3 (Lamb 6*, Gower 2*)

Man of the match: Kapil Dev
Result: **England won by 7 wickets**

*   *   *

The second Test against India was at Old Trafford. Unfortunately, it clashed with the Varsity match against Oxford, forcing me to choose between country and university. Seen very much as the coming young thing, within cricket circles at least, I opted for England over Cambridge – and received an avalanche of stick. Puzzlingly, to me at least, Fleet Street's finest saw it as wholly unacceptable that I should put my own ambitions before duty to one's university.

To me, there was no choice to be made. I'd already played in three matches against Oxford, two of them dull draws. Yes, I was captain, but my responsibilities surely didn't extend to missing a Test match in order to satisfy an old tradition – the first Varsity match having predated the first Test by 50 years.

Peter May was never captain of Cambridge but he did play in the 1952 Varsity match, despite having already been picked several times for England, his Test debut having come the previous year in July 1951. There were differences, however. His match against Oxford did not clash with a Test, so there was no choice for him to make. Also, the university match was still a big deal then, with 10–15,000 paying spectators attending the event at Lord's. Although its status had now changed, with the numbers watching having dwindled to family members and friends, May clearly felt the match still carried cachet.

Drawing me aside after the first Test, he said he would abide by my decision, whatever it was, and that if I should choose to play for Cambridge, it would not affect my chances of playing in the third Test. I told him there was, to my mind, no dilemma to consider, but he told me to go away and think about it anyway.

This confused me. Happily, the sensible counsel of Jack Davies, the University Cricket Club treasurer and a man who'd bowled Bradman for a duck at Fenner's in 1934, was on hand to point me towards Old Trafford. It would, he told me, 'be unthinkable to turn down the opportunity to play for England,' a team he'd represented once, in 1945, in a non-Test match against the Dominions. With Jack on my side, I phoned May to let him know that I'd be travelling to Manchester for the Test and not Lord's for the Varsity match.

My decision was big news, at least in the broadsheets. It wasn't cast as good news, though, with columnists and leader writers fulminating at how I could abandon my university for the sake of a mere Test match. Tony Lewis, a former England captain as well as a Cambridge graduate, was particularly critical in the *Sunday Telegraph*. Back in Lewis's day, the Varsity match was often the sporting highlight for those involved and a plum fixture in the social calendar. Even so, I was genuinely puzzled by the ferment caused. But then I'd only just finished being a naive student and was largely ignorant of the press and the pet itches they liked to scratch. So I handed the captaincy to my old mate Peter Mills and headed north from Cambridge to play India, instead of south to play Oxford.

Cricket requires travel and, to help me get around, that summer Mum had bought a Citroën 2CV for me to share with my sister, Janet. I could just about decant myself in and out of it, but if it had any kind of load on board, such as other passengers or cricket bags, you had to change up into third gear at the slightest incline, even on a motorway.

Mum had moved back to England from Kenya six years earlier after Dad had been killed in a car crash, following a cricket match at a place outside Nairobi called Limuru. A fine cricketer himself, he'd just taken six wickets for 17 before making his fatal journey home. I was at boarding school in Essex at the time and, with the cost of air travel being what it was then, did not fly back to Kenya for his funeral. It is one of the few regrets I still have.

Mum settled in Marks Tey, near Colchester in Essex, the place being roughly equidistant from Felsted, my school, and Culford, the one my sister attended in Suffolk. I was living there with Mum and Janet when my cricket career took off. But I needed subsidised transport, having yet to build up sufficient profile in cricket for a sponsored car like those driven by my team-mates. The Citroën was the third car Mum had provided for us and the first that was not an old banger.

Its shiny newness and colour (it was a bright canary yellow) did not prevent Beefy Botham from christening it 'The Flying Dustbin' as I arrived in it for nets at Old Trafford before my second Test. After practice, Beefy nobly offered to show me the way to our hotel, Mottram Hall, which I'd never been to before. It was about 20 miles away, yet he could not resist trying to lose me as he bombed through Cheshire's leafy lanes in his Saab Turbo. He succeeded too, and I only found the place after several stops to ask the locals.

Peter May had a penchant for booking the England team into secluded hotels miles from the ground. While it meant that distractions such as pubs, restaurants and nightclubs were not on our doorstep, it made the commute to the match, through rush-hour traffic, a right faff. 'Allow at least 45 minutes to get there in the morning,' I was told at breakfast in Mottram Hall. I did, but it was still not enough.

That Test failed to develop into any kind of contest, the Manchester rain preventing either side from even starting their second innings. There were, though, a few incidents of note. Beefy belted a superb hundred, while the returning Geoff Miller, preferred to Paul Allott on his home ground, made 98.

I batted with more gusto for 23 before being stumped giving Doshi the charge, a dismissal, you will recall, I considered to be the province of tail-enders and eejits. But then, this was me being less cautious, if still less savvy, against spin.

Taking the new ball with Big Bob Willis (Beefy's hundred had tired him out), I bowled tidily to dismiss Dilip Vengsarkar, India's best batsman behind Gavaskar. Big Bob had taken India's first two wickets cheaply, but later had his figures ruined when he took the second new ball and Sandeep Patil struck six fours off his first over with it.

It was a curious onslaught, coming, as it did, only after Patil had been struck on the head with the first ball of the over, which also contained a no-ball. He was wearing a helmet, so the blow did not force him from the field. It did spark the beast in him, though, his subsequent blitz not only setting a world record for runs scored off a single over in a Test match (since surpassed), but also speeding him to a memorable hundred.

The 1982 Football World Cup in Spain was drawing to a close by the time we assembled at The Oval for the third Test. England, under Ron Greenwood, had gone out after the second round but had remained unbeaten, so had departed with some sort of honour.

Even with football's hegemony over cricket, fan mail still awaited most England cricketers when they arrived at a Test ground, and there was plenty for us that match at The Oval. Beefy, though, used to get twenty times more than anybody else, including death threats, which he handed to the police.

The letters varied from the abusive and lewd to mundane requests for an autograph. On this occasion, one in particular had caught Beefy's eye, and not just for its footballing bent. Indeed, he was so taken with it that he read it out to us before he had reached the end. A mistake, as it turned out.

'"Dear Ian Botham,"' began the letter. '"I love watching you run in to bowl, especially the way you move so forcefully. My fantasy is to lie naked between you and Karl-Heinz Rummenigge – it would be utter bliss."'

Now, Beefy was reading all this out with amused relish when his face suddenly clouded over with anger.

'What's up, Beef?' we asked, eager to see how it concluded.

'It's from a bloke,' he said, his indignation so obvious that it caused the rest of us to wet ourselves with glee.

'Does he want your autograph as well?' asked Dusty Miller, his dry, Derbyshire wit a constant antidote to Botham's extravagances.

Whatever affront Beefy felt from the letter, he took it out on India with one of the great innings seen at The Oval, his 208 scored at a fair old lick. Rarely have I witnessed a cricket ball struck so cleanly or so powerfully as on that day, especially off the spinners.

He even broke a bone in Sunil Gavaskar's shin, after he cut a long hop from Ravi Shastri into Gavaskar's leg while he was fielding at silly point. It made a horrible sound. At Cambridge I'd won a reputation for being a hard-hitting stroke-maker, but this knock had a curious effect on me, making me marvel in admiration but sick with envy at the same time.

When bowling to Botham in that innings, Dilip Doshi, India's senior spinner, would release the ball, then almost instinctively, like a man shielding his head from a demonic force, raise his hands to protect himself as Beefy lurched down the pitch to hit him over the top for yet another boundary. He struck four sixes and 19 fours in his innings (it seemed like more), two of the sixes so enormous that they landed on the pavilion roof.

England were 512 for five when I walked to the crease, so I thought there was no point in hanging about. I hit my first ball for four, a glorious on-drive off Doshi, and struck another boundary soon after that. Another sashay down the pitch to Doshi, though, and I was stumped, again. Suddenly, I was gaining a reputation for messing up against spin, a ridiculous notion since I was blessed with such a long reach.

Despite Beefy's show-stopper, Derek Randall bided his time at the crease, knocking the ball around and forgoing unnecessary risk despite our commanding position in the match. It was a lesson in playing professional cricket, a point he made in no uncertain terms once he'd returned to the dressing room, last man out for 95.

'Listen, big 'un,' he said. 'This is Test cricket and there's an Ashes tour to play for this winter. You don't just give it away like you did.'

It was a hard-nosed and not entirely unselfish view and one at odds with how I'd been raised to play the game, first by Dad, then by Gordon Barker and John Cockett at Felsted School, and finally by Keith Fletcher at Essex. But this was big boys' cricket and a whole new experience, for which these were undoubtedly sage words. After all, you can rely on promise and potential only so long, and while some of the selectors of that era were undoubtedly prone to hastiness when dropping certain players, you still had to give them reasons to keep picking you.

What Randall was essentially saying was this: 'The team might have put 500 on the scoreboard, but you should have picked yourself up a nice little fifty.' According to him, my mistake was not to look further ahead than the match at hand. If I had, I'd have seen the three Tests against Pakistan and the tour of Australia which lay ahead – big deals both, and certainly worth playing for if cricket was your life. Constructing an innings was important, but so too was constructing a career.

I hadn't been very guarded off the field either, but then I hadn't been doing anything most other cricketers wouldn't have done. It was probably naive, but in the middle of that Test I met two Australian girls in the bar of the Westmoreland hotel opposite Lord's (we were staying there and commuting to The Oval). They were a good laugh and while they made it clear they were not up for sleeping over, they were keen to play a few drinking games – one being to stand on your head against a wall and drink a pint of lager upside down. This we did, in full view of everyone in the hotel bar, me and another team-mate managing, almost, to match them pint for pint. We called time at midnight, slightly dizzier than usual from the night's consumption, though I put that down to the callisthenics rather than the booze.

The Test petered out to a draw, the Oval pitch remaining benign to the end. Still, it meant the series had been won. Except I did not feel giddy with joy. I felt as if my own contributions to the victory had barely scratched the surface. On reflection, this was a tad harsh. True, I had never managed to get going with the bat, but my seven wickets at 31.2 meant that I'd finished second in England's bowling averages for the series to Willis. Not so bad for someone the pundits had been saying was not yet ready for Test cricket.

I'd probably done enough to get picked for the Tests against Pakistan, but first there was the one-day series against them, a form of the game I felt suited me better than five-day cricket.

One-day internationals in England then were played over 55 overs, a curious number, with lunch and tea interrupting either innings. There was a further quirk. In summers like 1982, when two teams toured, only four ODIs would be played, two against each opponent. That meant there was no decider, should the series end at one game all, the winner determined instead by run-rate taken over the two matches. The two games against Pakistan were played at Trent Bridge and Old Trafford. Happily, we won both and, even better, I made what I would call a proper contribution, taking two wickets in each and making an unbeaten 34 at number eight in the second match.

Our fee for each one-day international was £350, which was modest even then. For some reason, one-day cricket was seen as no more than a necessary evil by the Test and County Cricket Board (TCCB). As such, it was considered a very poor cousin to Test cricket. For the administrators, it was simply a means of giving the public something they thought they wanted. As with our remuneration, it was not overdone.

Out-of-pocket expenses, being the same as those for Test matches, were more generous, however. While most of us drove to each venue, each player would nevertheless receive a return first-class rail fare from the mainline station closest to their home to that in the city where the match was being played. For those who lived in London, Birmingham, Manchester or Leeds, the direct connections could leave them feeling a bit short-changed. For the rest of us, it was God bless Lord Beeching, British Rail or whoever for those rambling routes and the substantial fares they incurred.

There was also a daily subsistence allowance of £27.50, more than double what Essex dispensed for away games. Everything had to be signed for, which turned the day before matches into a ritual of net practice, bat-signing (mostly for good causes) and the pocketing of expenses – the majority of it overseen by Bernard Thomas, England's physiotherapist.

Thomas, a talented gymnast in his youth, had been a fixture in the England set-up since the late 1960s and, as such, held great power. He owned a successful physiotherapy practice in Birmingham and drove a Rolls-Royce Silver Shadow, a curious ostentation given the privations he clearly observed to keep lean and fit.

Nicknamed Bernie the Bolt, after the catchphrase and crossbowman used on ITV's *Golden Shot* game show, it was certainly wise to keep on the right side of him, though that was never easy considering his sinister role as chief sneak to the selectors and, as I was later to discover, the press.

During this series, journalists continued to have fun with me. An interview with Dudley Doust, an eminent writer with the *Sunday Times*, made merry mention of my attire, which at that stage comprised some thick, felt slacks, all held up by a broad rubber belt. Team-mates at Essex christened them fireman's trousers, though they were probably cool-proof as well. Attention was also drawn to the steel-toecapped Dr Martens boots I wore, as well as the thin leather tie, standard fare for a student, though not perhaps an England cricketer. That, though, was largely the point of Doust's piece – that I was my own man and not someone in thrall to convention.

It was self-indulgent and probably made me seem an attention-seeking poseur, but I was trying to be faithful to what I saw as the slightly bohemian interests I'd nurtured at university – a cultural baggage that included obscure bands, modern art and difficult novels. Not Jackie Collins, Marks & Sparks and Neil Diamond.

Doust's piece was digested by one or two of the tabloids, who proceeded to keep a watching brief on me, ready to pounce on the slightest hint of hypocrisy when the time was right. That moment wasn't long in coming either, and after I turned up at Lord's for the second Test against Pakistan in a staid suit and tie (compulsory dress on match days), they gave me both barrels for being as 'boring as a tailor's dummy'.

Before that came the first Test against Pakistan at Edgbaston, in which I didn't play. There'd been a few changes from the squad against India. Geoff Cook, Paul Allott and Phil Edmonds had been dropped and in their place had come Mike Gatting, Eddie Hemmings and Ian Greig, my old skipper from Cambridge.

Greig's selection was curious, to me at least, as he offered the team exactly the same as I did, but with a few more years of county experience behind him. At Cambridge, I'd considered myself a superior cricketer to him, even though I was a fresher in his final year. He'd been playing well for Sussex, though, and the Greig name, while anathema to traditionalists who never forgave elder brother Tony for his role in Kerry Packer's World Series, was still a byword for audacity in English cricket – even if, in Ian's case, it wasn't quite deserved.

In the days before that first Test, I'd been playing for Essex against Leicestershire at Grace Road, so had accepted David Gower's kind offer to stay with him at his flat not far from the ground there. The next day, we drove, separately, the 42 miles to Birmingham for our 3 p.m. net session with England. Back then, three-day county cricket, one-day Sunday League, two limited-over competitions, as well as five-day Test cricket, with travel in between, were all crammed into a very tight schedule. I'm not sure if it was the work-load, which I had yet to become accustomed to, or whether it was the continued burden of having to justify my presence in the England side, but I began to feel twinges in my back during practice.

The next morning I woke early with my upper back in spasm, something that had happened to me once before. I told Bob Willis at breakfast and he suggested that I get to the ground pronto to see Bernard Thomas, so that he might try to alleviate it. The trouble was I'd only been to Edgbaston twice before, and never from that direction, so did not really know the way (there were no satnavs then). I'd followed Gower to the ground the previous day, then someone else back to the team hotel. So I waited in reception for someone who might know where they were going.

When three team-mates did eventually come along, they asked if I could hang on to give Derek Randall a lift as he'd left his car somewhere. Being the new boy and not wanting to seem ungallant, I agreed to wait. What nobody had told me, and I had yet to work out despite playing with him in the series against India, was that Randall was the most disorganised person in Christendom. When he finally sauntered down to reception, shirt untucked and tie partially knotted, the others had been gone for 20 minutes. Reporting time at the ground on match days was 9 a.m., which gave us about 10 minutes to get there and get changed.

'Plenty of time, youth,' said Randall. 'It's just round t' corner.'

Well, it wasn't round any of the dozen or so corners we took as it became plain that Randall, like me, had no idea where he was going. Round and round the leafy streets of Edgbaston we went in the Flying Dustbin. Eventually, having stopped to ask at least five pedestrians, we found the ground, arriving 15 minutes late.

Willis was not amused. While I was sent to be assessed by Thomas, Randall manfully tried to take the blame. It didn't work, though neither did the muscle-relaxing injection I'd been given by Bernie the Bolt. After a bit of stretching, Thomas pronounced me unfit, then slapped a £75 fine on me and Randall for our tardiness – a fiver for every minute over deadline.

My withdrawal meant a Test debut for Ian Greig which, as he was a direct rival, did not fill me with joy. My fret levels rose, too, when he took four wickets and England went on to win the match. Even without considering Paul Allott and Graham Dilley, there was now additional competition for that third seamer's role.

Players not involved directly in the Test are usually sent back to their counties, but because I was injured I remained for a few days to have treatment with Thomas. It meant staying on at the Plough and Harrow, then considered Birmingham's plushest hotel, though that was not saying much. While there I bumped into a girl I'd known at Cambridge, who'd been posted to the city with her new job. Although part of my wider circle of friends at university, she had never really given me a second look. Now, though, albeit after a few drinks in the hotel bar, she seemed eager to stay the night, something I did not discourage despite my injury.

Scientists are forever changing their minds about the laws of attraction between people. One minute it's our primitive 'lizard brain' driving our urges; the next we're seeking those who most resemble us or our parents. One theory that makes a modicum of sense is that women sniff out mates with a different immune system to theirs, something that would benefit any offspring they then might have together. While some or all of this might hold true, I have a theory of my own to add, and it is that fame, even the merest whiff of it, must either mask all those odours, switch off any olfactory capabilities or scramble our reptile brains into fancying anyone who has ever been on the telly, however briefly. Whatever the trigger, I was not complaining.

With a fortnight between Tests I was fit again for the next one against Pakistan, at Lord's. Willis, though, was indisposed with a severely stiff neck. At Edgbaston, Imran Khan, who'd won the man-of-the-match award despite his side's defeat, had peppered Willis with bouncers. Big Bob had hung around in the second innings to make 28 in a last-wicket partnership worth 79 – a crucial knock, as it turned out. Most tail-enders expect a bit of roughing up, but Willis had been forced to duck and dive for longer than most. He'd been wearing protective headgear, but that is where most of the problem lay.

Back then, batting helmets were still in their infancy and weighed a lot more than they do today, especially if they possessed a thick metal grille, which both Willis's and mine did. The added weight, and the increased frequency with which he had to get that and his head out of the way, sent his neck into a spasm which had not abated by the second Test. His absence meant the job went to David Gower, the first time he'd captained England.

Robin Jackman was called up and Geoff Miller dropped, which left us with a bowling retinue of Botham, Greig, Jackman, Hemmings and me. The off-spinner Hemmings apart, it was a distinctly mono-paced attack. On a good Lord's pitch we got caned, with Mohsin Khan making 200 as Pakistan racked up 428 in their first innings. In response, our batting faltered and we failed, by two runs, to avoid the follow-on. So we had another go, to see if we could improve second time around.

That first innings had revealed a couple of things. First, what a brilliant bowler Abdul Qadir was, and second, how much Beefy disliked Javed Miandad, the brilliant but mischievous Pakistan batsman who played county cricket for Glamorgan. Beefy made 31 in that first innings and Javed, who stood at silly point whenever Beefy faced Qadir, just wound him up ball after ball, his snide barbs working away much as a bullfighter's banderillas wear down the bull.

The tipping point came when Javed fielded the ball and then, for no real reason, threw it hard into Beefy's arm after he'd knelt down to sweep. Javed's excuse was that Beefy's foot had left the crease and he was shying at the stumps, but it hadn't. Beefy snapped and all kinds of threats were issued as insults gave way to finger-poking and some argy-bargy.

It was an unseemly moment but it got worse, because Beefy was dismissed next ball, caught off bat and pad close to the wicket, by Mohsin Khan not Javed. The wicket had been worked by Javed, though, his antics getting Beefy to lose focus, something that further incensed him after he'd been mug enough to fall for it.

There was fury, then, when Beefy returned to the dressing room, with threats of what he was going to do to Javed after play ringing round the walls.

'I'll ------- shoot the ------,' he said, having decided that anything else would not come close to delivering suitable justice.

'Wot wi', a gun?' chuckled Randall, who'd decided he was going to play his usual role of court jester, this time to Beefy's wounded Henry VIII. Except Beefy was not ready to be placated.

He'd been antsy generally that match, the result of him and his family having received death threats through the post all summer. And not just from one source either. I'd been getting some nasty mail since being picked for England, mainly to the tune that I was a useless, toffee-nosed tosser, but nothing like that. According to

Beefy, the police knew about it but were essentially powerless unless they could trace the source – difficult, as the authors had, understandably, not included their address.

Such impromptu theatre wasn't the only entertainment during that Test match. Lord's being the home of cricket, the dressing room there was a cut above the others, having both a TV and one of those newfangled video recorders, procured ostensibly for players to watch their batting and bowling techniques as filmed by the coach. England had yet to use the facility as intended but, egged on by some of the others, I had brought along a bad blue movie entitled *Billy's Big Banana*, loaned to me by some friends in Cambridge. It was puerile and most definitely in bad taste, but most of us will do anything to be one of the boys.

With a lot happening over the first few days we hadn't had time to play it, so when Chris Tavaré dropped anchor in the second innings, we popped it into the machine and watched. The film had little artistic merit, though the dubbed dialogue was so naff as to be hilarious.

Now, being fairly new technology at the time, nobody had worked out how to mute the video, or even switch it off except at the mains. So when Peter May, the chairman of selectors, walked in just as things were getting interesting, in the film as opposed to the match, we improvised by pausing the video on freeze-frame.

Despite standing in front of the telly, which was on a shelf just above head height, May was oblivious. It didn't have a big screen like today's monsters, and because the image was no longer moving, his eye had not been drawn to it, but we held our collective breath anyway, not a sensible thing to do when the head honcho is trying to make small talk. The tension of 'will he or won't he notice' went on for at least 20 minutes, during which time general tittering turned into the nervous laughter of those convinced that this old-school gentleman would not be amused to discover what the England team were watching during a Test match at Lord's, especially one we were losing.

The mood was finally broken by Tavaré's dismissal for 82, which brought to an end his six-and-a-half-hour vigil. To our relief, May chose to leave the dressing room to give Tav some space. We, too, understood the need for reflection, so we thoughtfully left the video on freeze-frame so that Tav, who was changing right beneath the TV, could sort himself out. Never one for histrionics, Tav took off his pads, gloves and box without ceremony and packed them neatly into his bag. Having towelled himself down and patted his damp fringe, he suddenly noticed us all looking at him. It was only then that he glanced up at the screen, to be confronted by in flagrante delicto on pause.

Tav was a man of iron constitution and his face did not shift an iota. Dry as old parchment, he said, 'Nice to see you lads have been watching me bat. I know I'm boring, but it hasn't been that bad, has it?'

It hadn't, actually. At least Tav had hung around in the middle, which is more than I'd managed, out for the second time to Qadir, prodding cluelessly. I can remember thinking that I'd played against some damned good players, even international ones, but I'd never come up against anything like him. It was sobering, bewildering and more than a little frustrating being confronted by somebody to whom you had no answer.

It was not as if advice on how to play Qadir and his fizzing wrist-spin had not been forthcoming; it had, from all quarters: 'You must pick him in the flight; you must pick him off the pitch; you must use your feet; you must play him off the back foot; play him off the front . . .' And so it went. If it is your first time against Qadir, which for me it was, advice like that just confuses. Indeed, so intent do you become on trying to work out which way the ball will turn that you miss out on the loose stuff, though there wasn't much of that.

Graham Gooch was an excellent player of spin. Although not playing in this series due to his ban for being part of the South Africa rebel tour, he went on to play against Qadir later in the Eighties and reckoned him one of the best spinners he'd ever faced.

'He'd show you a googly you could read,' Gooch would later explain. 'Then he'd bowl one you suspected of being a googly but weren't sure about. Then he'd send down one that you'd be completely bamboozled by but it would usually turn out to be another googly.

'Basically, he had three googlies, all bowled with a different action, to complement his leg-break, top-spinner and flipper,' recalled Gooch. 'He had decent control and bowled briskly enough for you not to be able to use your feet with confidence.'

In short, he was a real handful and nigh-on unstoppable in Pakistan in the days before neutral umpires. Certain that he would present problems for me, I'd even stayed behind after England's practice at Lord's to watch how Pakistan's batsmen – especially the brilliant Javed Miandad – dealt with him in the nets. Batsmen tend to be more relaxed in practice than in matches, but even so I'd never seen anything like what unfolded. Javed took Qadir apart. He cut him, he clipped him, he swept him and, just for laughs, he shimmied down the pitch and hit him back over his head. He did not kick him away once or play a single defensive shot, a situation in direct contrast to how most of us went on to play him during the Test.

Suddenly, from cricket seeming a pretty easy game, following my seamless progress up the sunlit slopes into the England team, it began to look impossibly difficult on the craggy peaks, at least the batting part. If the selectors hadn't already placed an asterisk next to my name denoting 'dodgy against spin', they should have done.

*　　*　　*

During that Lord's Test, which ended in heavy defeat for us by 10 wickets, I met two men who wanted to represent me as my agent. Ray Williams and Harry Maloney were partners and had managed pop groups and solo artists in the 1960s and 1970s. One of their acts was Manfred Mann, initially a vehicle for chart hits, before the South African-born Mann turned them into one of the finest Prog bands of the early 1970s. Now, though, they wanted to branch out into sport.

With the help of Mike Selvey (a neighbour of Harry's and a cricketing colleague of mine), they had identified a few promising young cricketers to kickstart their new project. Norman Cowans, a 21-year-old fast bowler with Middlesex, and I were top of their list. Norman had yet to play for England but he'd been bowling fast in county cricket, so it was unlikely to be long before the selectors picked him. Of course, I had already been selected for the national team, though it was the torrent of publicity which attended that, guaranteed catnip to agents of all stripes, which had most likely caught their eye.

Harry and Ray seemed very amiable and like all agents talked an exceedingly good game. Elton John had once described Ray as the best-looking man in the room at some Sixties shindig or other – a compliment Ray dined out on for decades. They had big plans (don't they all) for me and Norman, should we decide to sign for them. Being a natural sceptic, I tried to quash their ardour by saying that they were unlikely to make me much money outside my cricket earnings, but they would not be put off. Back then, Beefy was about the only England cricketer, and maybe David Gower, who might have enjoyed additional revenue streams from endorsements. For most cricketers, even international ones, it was salary plus a modest bat or boot contract, and that was it.

I was lunched in Soho and taken to the Milton Keynes Bowl for a concert, where I met several of their famous musician clients, including Paul Jones, as Harry and Ray chased my signature. Although easily seduced, I thought it prudent to be cautious and told them I wouldn't sign until I'd had a decent lawyer take a look at their proposal – and promptly got in touch with a schoolfriend whose dad was a partner at Linklaters. I just wanted some general advice on whether the contract on offer was good, bad, fair or indifferent. Once you get lawyers involved, though, every comma is analysed lest it represent a booby-trap, and he told me to go and see a mate of his at Boodle Hatfield: 'They have clients in the entertainment business. You'll be better off with them.'

What he didn't tell me was that I'd be charged the thick end of £2,000. By contrast, Norman gave Harry and Ray's offer about 30 seconds' thought and turned it down.

The final Test of that 1982 summer, also against Pakistan, was at Headingley, a ground at which I had not yet played in my short career. A forecast of high winds meant I took the train rather than risk driving The Flying Dustbin up the A1. That involved a circuitous route from Marks Tey station in Essex, which meant going south to London first, then up north to Leeds. With a cricket case, as well as the usual complement of smart and casual gear to carry, it was all a bit of a fag.

Although the series was intriguingly poised at one Test apiece, I played no part in the decider after suffering another back spasm on the eve of the match – something that was becoming a bit of a habit, and one that had begun to raise concerned eyebrows in high places. This was the famous 'hurt his back writing a letter' incident, which has made just about every 'curious injuries' list since. The truth, as it nearly always is, was far more mundane, but the press, especially when fed information by the devious Bernard Thomas, were happy to overlook the prosaic facts to ramp up the humiliation.

As usual, we'd had nets the day before the match, followed by the team dinner. Afterwards, I went to my room and before turning in sat down to sort out my allocation of guest tickets for the following day. After I'd sealed the last envelope, I leaned back in the chair. Being of motel quality, it promptly gave way and I fell backwards, the muscles around my mid-spine going into spasm as a result.

It was late, about 11.30 p.m., so I self-treated, reasoning that it might be better to sleep with the mattress on a hard floor than on a bed which was soft and lumpy. Unfortunately, the act of heaving the mattress off the bed, then moving the bed frame to make room for it, just made the spasm worse.

As I had done when similarly indisposed at Edgbaston earlier in the series, I rose early the next morning (I hadn't really slept) and consulted Bernie the Bolt. He gave me a muscle-relaxing injection, which again did not work, and then gave the press the nudge they needed to ensure that any sympathy would not be coming my way. It was probably calculated psychology on his part, to stop me amplifying every ache and niggle into a catastrophe, but it made me vow never to trust him again with any sensitive information.

My absence meant that Robin Jackman remained in the side despite Bob Willis returning as captain. In addition, Graeme Fowler and Vic Marks came in to replace Ian Greig and Eddie Hemmings. England won by three wickets, though not before a controversial umpiring decision or two had attracted acerbic comments from Imran.

With England touring teams having perennially slagged off Pakistan umpires for being biased, Imran decided to return fire, picking on umpire David Constant and his decision to give Sikander Bakht out caught off bat and pad to Vic Marks. I wasn't there to see it, but I'd say England's players have always been split on it, including Marks, whose diplomatic answer has always been that 'It was probably out.'

Often, complaints against umpires are made in the heat of the moment, but Imran, who'd been batting at the other end when Bakht was given out, was adamant that Constant had been far from impartial all match. As a result, he and Pakistan objected to Constant standing on every subsequent tour they made to England, until the International Cricket Council took home umpires out of the equation by introducing neutral ones in 2002.

My own humiliation, however, was not yet complete. As part of my 'treatment', Bernard sent me down to Birmingham to see an orthopaedic surgeon friend of his – a trip which necessitated a large detour, with heavy bags and bad back, from my return rail journey home. The surgeon's assessment, which Bernard then sent on to Essex, was that he'd never seen such a lack of muscle on an international sportsman, to which my reply was that he cannot have seen many cricketers. I may not have been ripped like Daley Thompson, but I had more definition than some team-mates I could mention – Gatting, Jackman, Hemmings, Marks, or even Beefy by that stage.

This latest appraisal meant the minus marks were stacking up against me: can't play spin, can't stay fit, not very professional in his overall approach – the last point proven by my lateness at Edgbaston (not really my fault) and the fact I'd compounded my back spasm in Leeds by hauling the mattress from my hotel bed (foolish but well-intentioned).

Another potential tick in the unprofessional box was that I'd also allowed mates from school and university, who'd come to watch the various Tests during the summer, to kip on my hotel floor during the match, with three of them bedding down during the Lord's Test against Pakistan. But I don't think the powers that be knew about that. If they did, they had not let on.

The chances of getting selected for the winter's Ashes tour were looking decidedly slim, particularly as I'd failed to shine in the two remaining county games for Essex. Still, somebody must have looked upon me munificently, as there my name was in the 16-man squad for Australia, announced soon after my twenty-fourth birthday.

My selection did come with a proviso: that I spend two weeks training with Ipswich Town FC, 25 miles up the A12 from Mum's house in Marks Tey. The message being sent was that I needed to toughen up physically, and sending me to train with Paul Mariner, Terry Butcher, Arnold Mühren, Russell Osman, Frans Thijssen, Alan Brazil and Mick Mills, great footballers all, was their way of ensuring that.

But this is where theory and practice can diverge. I turned up at their training ground, ready for hard work, but Ipswich, just settling in under new manager Bobby Ferguson, were more concerned with practising their drills from corners and free kicks.

'We did most of our fitness training in July and August,' explained Paul Mariner. 'If you've brought your football boots, you're welcome to join in. But otherwise, the gym's over there.'

I'd actually met Mariner, as well as Mühren and Thijssen, before. They had come to Cambridge to have some treatment with the legendary physiotherapist Harry Willis, whom I was also seeing at the time with a bad ankle. That was when Bobby Robson was still manager, and while Ipswich would have had their own physio, he was obviously a bucket-and-sponge man not to be trusted with the team's thoroughbreds.

With cricket spikes and trainers the only sporting footwear to my name, I headed to the gym, which was about as cutting edge as Bernie the Bolt's plimsolls. A few warm-up jogs and 40 minutes doing a few light weights and off I'd go, back down the A12.

Not once did I do anything meaningful with the footballers. They did not use the gym during the times I went, and I did not join them on the training ground. Indeed, our paths rarely crossed. By midday, which is roughly when I tended to finish up, they'd done their drills, packed up and gone to the pub. British sportsmen at their finest.

Naturally, the selectors, and Essex, checked up on me. But as I was always polite and on time, Bobby Ferguson told them I'd been working hard. Which is exactly what they wanted to hear.

The naughty-boy training (everyone else in the squad had been taking a holiday before the tour began in early October) did do me some good, though not the sort envisaged by the killjoys who had prescribed it. It gave me some thinking time to work out how to approach the game – not just the one on the field but the bigger one surrounding it.

It gave me the chance to take stock. It had been a tumultuous eight months, in which I'd experienced fame, or at least excessive publicity, and had avenues of opportunity open up that I'd only ever fantasised about previously. I'd also discovered what love was, or I thought I had, and then lost it.

As my old mum would say, 'Easy come, easy go.' And she was right. The speed and ease of it all had made me careless.

3
AUSSIE, AUSSIE, AUSSIE
– THE PREAMBLE

THE TOUR TO Australia in 1982–83 was an eye-opener, and not just for the long, hard look at what Test cricket was really like. At university the fact that we lived in pre-Aids days made little difference to the frequency with which most students experienced sex – not very often, unless you committed to a long-term relationship. In Australia, the mood was very different, with women keen to indulge, especially with something as vaguely exotic as a Pommie cricketer.

It may be exaggerating a bit to say that all you had to do to get lucky was to be vaguely pleasant and buy a girl a drink, but not by much. Never the slickest chatter-upper in the world, I nonetheless advanced my sexual experience on that trip, exponentially. My cricket, though, went backwards.

We flew over to Australia Business Class on Qantas. I'd made the same trip with Oxford and Cambridge a few years earlier, though we'd had that short stopover in Singapore and not done the 24-hour flight in one go. I don't know who said that flying was 99 per cent boredom and one per cent sheer terror, but they were onto something. Naturally, there was talk of Rod Marsh's Sydney to London record of draining 44 cans of Foster's, but with none of us weaned on such fizzy muck, nobody made an attempt, not even Beefy.

Sensing that the longueurs might bore the players into drinking too much anyway, Bernard Thomas, once again the team's physiotherapist and Mr Fixit, decided it would be a good time to get the

1,000 autograph sheets we'd brought with us signed. Knowing that he probably wouldn't get everyone by the time we reached Australia, he targeted those who might not be so compliant when not stuck 36,000 feet in the air.

With Botham just starting on a bottle of Shiraz, Thomas began with David Gower. I was sitting nearby, so watched as Gower began in good humour, right-handed, signing his name. A hundred sheets in, though, and his face had begun to cloud over and his name to shorten. What began, like his batting, as a free-flowing and elegant *'David Gower'* on the page had turned into a hasty and jerky *'DI Gower'*. It did not end there either, his mood and signature eventually disintegrating into a barely legible *'D G—r'*. Even then, he'd only done about a third of them.

Feeling he did not want to push Gower too much, Thomas took the sheets over to Botham, by now contemplating a second bottle of Shiraz. Instead of telling him to shove it, Beefy, whose relationship with Thomas was ambivalent at the best of times, was all sweetness and light. Surprised, Bernard dumped a huge wad next to him and disappeared off to get some shut-eye.

Botham had been here before, though, and his feigned obeisance was a cunning ruse. When everyone had settled, Beefy quietly grabbed a large portion and disposed of them in the loo.

'That's a few hundred we won't be signing, lads,' he said when he returned, ever the team man.

When we touched down in Brisbane I was still sporting the ear stud I'd worn when first picked for England. It had brought me an avalanche of unplanned publicity already, which the Australian media were happy to keep milking, at least until they'd worked out that my role on tour would be a peripheral one at best.

One interview, conducted in the room I shared with Geoff Cook in Brisbane's Crest hotel, was with Australian journalist Rod

Nicholson, and it ended up as one long mickey-take. Cooky, who lay on his bed while Nicholson asked his questions, wet himself laughing. It is never wise to take on journalists like that, but Nicholson was old-school and appreciated my refusal to give anodyne responses to his questions. He also liked the beers we shared with him from our minibar, Aussie hacks being thirstier than most.

His piece on me, when it appeared, was considered and relatively generous, a rarity during Ashes hostilities unless you happen to be winning. Then, it all changes, and the Aussies, who have always had a keen respect for top dogs, positively gush goodwill. Still, they obviously weren't expecting much from us, as most had us billed as the weakest England side ever to have toured Australia, and that included the Under-15s.

It was a standard sledging line from the Aussie press, though Willis did, more or less, give the claims credence a few years later when he said, 'We were almost a second eleven. We had five decent players and the others were just making up the numbers.'

Weakened we might have been – from defections to the rebel tour in South Africa – but we did feel like a team. The only odd selection, to my mind, was the choice of three off-spinners but no Phil Edmonds, though that pandered to the theory that Aussie batsmen, especially the left-handers, were less adept at playing the offie than the left-armer. With Australia having, potentially, as many as five lefties in their top eight, there was a scintilla of logic at play. Even so, three seemed overkill, despite the subtle differences between them, and Edmonds's absence was more likely down to a character clash between him, Willis and May than any cunning strategy.

Factions and enmities will exist in any group comprising 16 men, but apart from Beefy finding one or two of his team-mates annoying, the majority of us got on well together and enjoyed one another's success, at least the little there was. Back then, England players were given single rooms at home, but unless you held a position of high office, such as captain or vice-captain, you had to share with another player on tour.

This wasn't as drastic as it might sound, as everyone would have shared, and absorbed the protocols of sharing, while playing county cricket. The downside was that it involved almost no private space. But the upside meant there was little time for players to brood about their form or missing family and home. I don't wish to seem trite, and my evidence is only anecdotal, but the depression that now seems to afflict so many modern cricketers appeared less prevalent when players shared rooms.

Cooky, with whom I shared for the first few weeks of the tour, was a good room-mate, especially on something as big as an Ashes tour. A seasoned pro, he'd toured India with England the previous winter, a trip led by Keith Fletcher, my captain at Essex. He didn't seem to snore either, something of a deal-breaker for Beefy, who refused to room with either Eddie Hemmings or Derek Randall on account of the racket made by their vibrating uvulas.

Foxy Fowler's initial room-mate was Chris Tavaré, but only because Tav, who'd just got married and had brought along his wife, Vanessa, for the entire four-and-a-half month trip, was not allowed to have her with him for the first few weeks, while the team 'bonded'. When asked what rooming with Tav was like, Foxy said he didn't know. 'When I get in he's asleep and when I wake up he's dressed and gone,' said Fowler. 'All I see is this pair of pyjamas neatly folded on the pillow.'

When Vanessa was eventually allowed to join Tav in their own room, it posed challenges most of us never consider. Vanessa, although knowledgeable about cricket, suffered a near pathological fear of both flying and heights. This meant that she had to be sedated before every flight, of which, on that tour, there were 28. It was not like her having a gin and tonic. She was made properly floppy with Valium. Otherwise every bump or air pocket en route would see her emit a blood-curdling scream, which in an enclosed space like a plane fuselage puts everyone on edge. Still, it wasn't foolproof and every now and then you'd find yourself drifting off at 28,000 feet, only for a shrieking Vanessa to wrench you back into the fragility of your situation.

To allay her fear of heights and by extension lifts, which she refused to use, her and Tav's room had to be on either the first or second floor of the hotel and reachable by stairs. Sometimes this would not be possible and you could always tell when their room was on floor three or above by the paleness of Vanessa's complexion. If you knew your Dulux chart you could pretty much match her pallidness with the floor her and Tav's room was on.

Cooky and I both knew we were probably fortunate to be on that Ashes trip as neither of us had performed that strongly for England during the domestic season. But if potential had got me the nod, Willis also liked solid personalities around him, especially on something as trying as an Ashes tour of Australia, and there were few sounder than Cooky.

We spent about 10 days in Brisbane acclimatising before our first tour match. Days were spent training and practising at the Church of England Boys School, or 'Churchie' as it is known locally, the Aussies' penchant for abbreviation so extreme that even the abridged eventually gets compressed. So, for them, the MCG, as in the Melbourne Cricket Ground, becomes 'The G', though never just 'G', which you would think the logical conclusion.

Brizzie, just a letter shorter than the more formal Brisbane, was hot and humid. None of us except for Foxy were what you'd call 'athlete fit'. But in a bid to get us into better shape, we'd start our daily sessions with a run round the athletics track at Churchie. Our task: to run a mile in six minutes and then get quicker over the week, something not everyone managed.

One who didn't even make the initial cut-off time was Ian 'Gunner' Gould, our second wicketkeeper, a man who both smoked and drank with gusto. On his second night in Australia, Gunner had discovered the General Jackson bar beneath our hotel, a place both popular with the locals and convenient for us, being within staggering distance of the hotel lifts.

It also had a Happy Hour in which you could get a very generous three drinks for the price of one. The only catch – their Happy Hour was between 11 p.m. and midnight, though that did not deter Gunner from taking full advantage, usually after a two-hour warm-up. His dedication to GJ's meant his training runs were carnage, with most of the previous night's consumption ending up by the side of the track.

Hints were dropped from the management, but some habits can be hard to break. So when Gunner was again found down in GJ's, following yet another regurgitation in training, he was warned as to his future conduct and told that he risked being sent home unless his drinking diminished and his fitness improved.

On receiving such a sobering ultimatum, most players would have forgone all temptation, but Gunner, a chirpy character who'd briefly been on Arsenal's books as a goalkeeper (hence the nick-name), merely went to General Jackson's earlier in the evening. Once there, the barman, with whom he'd become very friendly, gave him the same three-for-one deal.

As far as the team's management were concerned, he was not up late-night drinking any more, so had made some effort to come to heel. Gunner didn't stop throwing up in training. It's just that the powers that be put it down to his smoking instead, which they let slide. After all, forcing a player to give up his fags as well was a prescription too far.

One day, while training at Churchie, we were paid a visit by Madness, or at least the band's frontmen, Suggs and Chas Smash. Their manager had heard we were in town and were keen to get some publicity shots with us for their forthcoming tour of Australia.

Deathly pale and dressed in baggy shorts held up by braces and wearing some outlandish hats and sunglasses, Suggs and Chas certainly stood out, a quality that made Doug Insole, our tour manager, extremely nervous. Always one to err on the side of caution, Insole refused to allow any photos with us lest it reflect badly on the team. Most of us were disappointed. Cricket is always in need of a bit of street cred, so when Insole was out of earshot Beefy told Suggs to hang around until the top brass had gone. 'You'll get your photos,' he promised.

Both Suggs and Chas Smash seemed decent blokes, being enthusiastic about most things, especially meeting Beefy and Derek Randall. After they'd got what they wanted they handed over a dozen complimentary tickets for their gig at Brisbane's Festival Hall the following night, on 19 October.

Considering we were still three days away from our first tour match against Queensland, I'm surprised only four of us went along: Randall, Foxy Fowler, Geoff 'Dusty' Miller and me. It was a fantastic night, the gig being rambunctious, sweaty and filled with a carefree energy and kick-arse tunes.

Randall, who was a curious case when it came to knowing where his interests lay, was well up for it, ripping off his shirt and generally leaping around like a lunatic. Even so, when we went backstage to thank Suggs and the band, and they invited us back to their hotel for a drink, Randall declined the offer.

My enthusiasm for Jamaican music, generally, made me a big Madness fan. Their stuff was highly derivative, for sure, but done with a genuine love and respect for the source material – which was primarily the ska of the Blue Beat label. There, Prince Buster, whom the Madness boys adored, out-punched his 'royal' designation and was actually King.

As a result of my affinity, Beefy decided to call me Suggs from then on, the stage name of Graham McPherson, the band's lead singer. And what Beefy decided nearly always came to pass, which is why he and most players from that tour still use it to greet me.

At the time, I wasn't that enamoured of the name, but only because it had already been given to Charlie Ellison, one of the bowlers in my last year at Cambridge, whose haircut and general style actually made him look like a bespectacled Suggs. Familiarity, or even worse, unoriginality, was anathema to graduates of Cambridge. Despite that, the nickname has stuck fast, and not just over my playing career.

Beefy's own musical tastes on that tour revolved around two cassettes he carried with him – Dire Straits' *Making Movies* and *Too-Rye-Ay* by Dexy's Midnight Runners. He played them to death, mostly in the courtesy cars that Holden, the Australian car manufacturer, provided for us in the main cities. Beefy also had a boom box, though there were never many opportunities for him to crank it up, at least in public. Occasionally, it would get a workout in the dressing room after a day's play, but mostly it was an accoutrement, like a handbag.

I cannot recall what make it was, but it wasn't JVC, our sponsor that trip, as Beefy liked to be different. These days, companies sponsor all facets of the England team, so that home Tests, away Tests, home shirts, away shirts, the team, the team's official drink, the series etc. are all supported by different companies. Back then, JVC was the sole sponsor of our Ashes tour, though it sometimes seemed to be us who paid for the exclusivity rather than them.

One of the many things they had us do was record a jingle in a studio somewhere in Brisbane. An entire afternoon was given over to getting us to sing something written by an ad-man to a cheesy tune. You could sense Big Bob's impatience by the time take six came round, though several more were required until the 'suits' at Bickering, Barf and Bagle, or whatever the agency was called, professed themselves satisfied with the results.

JVC also arranged visits to several shopping centres in every city we visited throughout the tour, along with various cocktail parties and dinners. These could have been excruciatingly dull had it not been for the fact they also sent along a bevy of female 'models' clad in hot pants and tight-fitting JVC T-shirts. The girls were there, primarily, to rev up the guests and punters, though one or two were keen to party as well. Many of the players were suspicious of them, fearing honey traps, but one or two of us were single, so didn't care. It was through one of the JVC girls that I discovered what an all-over tan looked like.

As far as I am aware, the players saw no monetary benefits from JVC's sponsorship (there was nothing extra on my payslip). There was, though, one moment of largesse. At the end of the tour they took us to their warehouse in Sydney, handed us a few catalogues and told us to choose anything we liked, within reason.

An avid lover of vinyl records, I chose their top-of-the-range record player, an amplifier and a pair of speakers, which they shipped to the UK free of charge or duty. It did great service for the next 20 years, until I got serious and upgraded to some proper kit.

Derek Randall chose a video camera, a relatively new gizmo back then. When challenged that he wouldn't have a clue how to use it, he said, 'It's not for me, it's for the missus, so she can film the kids growing up. That's the bit I miss when I'm on tour.'

*   *   *

The warm-up games threw up a mixed bag of results – a loss to Queensland was followed by a win against Northern New South Wales. Then there was a draw against South Australia and a nail-biting one-wicket win against Western Australia.

I played in every game and was steady rather than standout. On pitches that offered precious little lateral movement, and using a Kookaburra ball that you ideally needed to get your hands on before it was 15 overs old, I realised that taking wickets was not going to be easy. I was not proved wrong.

Being 6 ft 5 in tall, the expectation of me at Essex, and then subsequently England, was that I should run in with purpose, seam upright, and hit the deck as hard as possible. Aggression, pace and extra bounce were the things I should be seeking – or so went the general consensus. Swing, an elusive skill even for those who'd harnessed it, like Beefy, was never really mentioned as something I might explore.

It was a bit like when I first went to play rugby at my boarding school, Felsted. Due to my size, it was assumed I would be a lock or number eight. In fact, I was best at fly-half, a position I eventually filled for the 4th XV, albeit after several stints of getting my ears squashed in scrums. The same height-to-role presumptions were made about my bowling. Eager to please, I bought into it, at least until I learnt to swing the ball consistently a few years later.

The truth is that like many England seamers over the decades, I was just not quick enough to trouble good batsmen on Australian pitches, especially once the Kookaburra ball had gone soft, which it did pretty quickly. I tried to add a yard or two of pace, but I strained to do so, which compromised accuracy and, eventually, my lower back.

My job, I reasoned, and a role which Willis confirmed when he dropped me after the first Test, was to probe away outside off stump, keep the runs down and pick up the odd wicket when batsmen got bored or frustrated. The limits of my ambition with the ball, therefore, were two-fers not five-fers, and to go for fewer than three runs an over. Both were doable but by no means straightforward.

Nowhere was this more graphically illustrated than in the tour match against Western Australia at the WACA in Perth, the world's fastest and bounciest pitch. With a square constructed of clay from a place called Bulli Creek, which gave it trampoline-like qualities whenever a ball was banged into its surface, the WACA had instilled fear into visiting batsmen for generations.

My own introduction to it had been on TV when my housemaster at boarding school had invited me to watch the highlights on BBC news of England's batsmen taking a pummelling from Dennis Lillee and Jeff Thomson during the 1974–75 Ashes series. No helmets, heads snapped back in avoidance of bouncers, batsmen reeling in pain after getting hit in the chest – this was not the genteel summer game I played on the 'School Front' not 100 yards from where I now sat. No, this one looked dynamic and dangerous, and I was captivated.

Except that I did not exactly feel that way when I came to bowl on the WACA against Western Australia's batsmen, players weaned on its unique qualities. Bowling to opener Bruce Laird was particularly frustrating. In with a chance of playing in the series, Laird, who was about 5 ft 7 in tall, would simply leave straight balls on a good length, something batsmen would never do in England. At the WACA, though, the springy bounce meant they sailed harmlessly over the stumps.

It is difficult to overstate just how much that messes with a bowler's radar. Without the extreme pace to hurry and harry batsmen into mistakes, I was forced to pitch it up further, at which point Laird, a player good enough to have played 21 Tests for Australia, would punch it back past me for two or three.

Like most Aussie batsmen, he also loved to cut and pull, so pitching short was not a sensible option. Which meant my margins of

effectiveness were suddenly reduced to a rectangle on the pitch measuring about 40 inches by 12. Try hitting that ball after ball when the temperature is 100 °F and there are flies fizzing about your mouth and eyes. It ain't easy, and even if you do manage it, it's predictable, and good batsmen like nothing more than a predictable bowler.

As it happened, there was a bit in the pitch for bowlers that day, and I eventually got Laird after he miscued a drive off the leading edge. It was my sole wicket as we dismissed them for 167, which rammed home just how difficult it was going to be, unless batsmen took insane risks, for me to make much impact with the ball.

Batting at the WACA was much more fun, at least once you had got used to the bounce, something I'd miscalculated in the first innings when Terry Alderman had me caught at square leg hooking, for not many. In the second innings, with England needing 209 to win, I helped to add 105 with Derek Randall for the sixth wicket, the crucial partnership in our narrow victory.

Many will scoff at the claim, but that match against Western Australia was more intense than any of the four Tests I'd played in up to that point, though I'd yet to play Australia or the West Indies. WA had six players in the squad for the first Test, which made it a quasi-Aussie team anyway. But give any sniff of beating the Poms to alpha males like Lillee and Alderman and they home in for the kill like the sharks off Cottesloe Beach, just seven miles to the west.

It was after watching Lillee and Alderman in that match that I began to cut holes in the end of my cricket boots, to ease pressure on my big toes, which took a pounding when bowling. For years I was accredited with being the first player to take a scalpel to my bowling boots, but it was Lillee and Alderman who'd done it before me, though their holes, cut into the bespoke boots made for them by a sweet old man in Melbourne called Hope Sweeney, were much neater than the great gouges I made in mine.

Holes or not, those two were a handful, especially bowling at the WACA, a ground they knew intimately. Getting on top of them was difficult, even in a State match, though Randall managed it with a brilliant 92, an innings of dash, verve and courage. It also required a rhino's hide, following the verbal barbs he copped, especially from Lillee and Rod Marsh, the wicketkeeper. Almost every ball would bring some taunt or other, none noted for their sparkling wit. But Randall, or 'Arkle' as he was known, after the famous racehorse, gave as good as he got, their 'attentions' and the chance to chat, if anything, spurring him on.

To me, other than the odd scowl, they directed nothing. Unless you posed a real threat, they would not waste good breath to get you out. Which meant that abuse from them, however vicious and underhand, revealed that they rated you. I endured a silent tour.

The preamble complete, we had a team meeting just before the first Test, which started in Perth on 12 November. The chief item on the agenda was that we must not walk under any circumstance, a diktat presented by Beefy. His argument was that none of the Aussies walked, so why should we. In any case, he claimed the Aussie umpires were so bad that we would get sawn off anyway, so why make their job easier by walking?

Most agreed, some begrudgingly, though Chris Tavaré said that he'd always walked and would continue to do so. 'Over my dead body,' countered Beefy, though when Tav refused to back down, Willis said it would be left to individuals, but that we shouldn't be too willing to ease the umpire's lot.

There was also discussion as to which shots it might not be prudent to play, with the hook and sweep both coming close to being banned; the first because you could not control it and Aussie grounds were large with big boundaries; the second because

Aussie umpires were keener than most to give you out lbw should you miss the ball while playing one.

It all felt overly prescriptive. I was happy not to walk, and I didn't really hook as I was too tall to get into position quickly enough. But I did sweep. Indeed, it was probably my best scoring shot against the spinners, whom I'd not exactly mastered in my early Tests against India and Pakistan.

The meeting, instead of filling us with confidence and excitement, sought instead to limit our ambitions. It emphasised the downside of not doing as you were told rather than the upside of doing your own thing, though I suppose that is the English way.

Suitably briefed, we readied ourselves for the old foe in the most isolated city on earth.

4

AUSSIE, AUSSIE, AUSSIE – THE ASHES

PERTH, A PLACE closer to Jakarta, 1,800 miles away, than Australia's own capital, Canberra, was something of a backwater in Australia then. Curling around the Swan river, it was picturesque but not much more than a one-horse or -road town – the four-mile long Hay Street running the entire length of its urban core. The suburbs, though, spread for miles, mostly along the coast on a north–south axis. But we never really explored them, having been told they were full of psychos and bikers.

We stayed in the Sheraton hotel, then on St George's Terrace, about half a mile from the WACA. In a throwback to times when temperance was seen as more than interfering do-goodery, it was the only place you could get a restaurant meal or an alcoholic drink on a Sunday. Even then, the bar closed at 8 p.m. As a result, it was about the only time the team room, a private sanctuary provided for us at each hotel we stayed in, became well utilised.

Perth was also a city that had seen the most recent spate of immigration from Britain, as well as 'white flight' from former African colonies. Indeed, several 'European' families I'd known in Kenya had moved there, and just before the Test I caught up with an old school friend, Paul, from Nairobi. It had been 10 years since I'd last seen him and he'd picked up an Aussie twang in the interim. Despite that, he still supported England, though I suspect he only said that so as not to appear ungallant. Sadly, what had bonded us as timid teenagers in Nairobi had gone, and we parted realising we now had little in common.

The women in Perth, though, were fearless. No qualms for them that I might have a room-mate. At the start of the tour in Brisbane, I'd bumped into Joel Garner, then playing for South Australia, who'd told me that Australia's women were the country's secret 13th man, tiring opponents out with extracurricular activities.

Garner's theory didn't really stack up, at least not in Perth. Three of the four women I met during our stay there had migrated from the UK in the past five years and had yet to transfer their allegiances to the extent of nobbling the opposition. The fourth was an air hostess with a foreign airline, 'the Hostie', who also had no agenda when it came to distracting Pommie cricketers. She did, though, have the accolade of being the best-looking woman I encountered on the trip. Juggling four women over the 12 days we were in Perth did not come naturally to a dilettante like me, however, and unsurprisingly it ended in tears.

In those days, Test matches still featured rest days, which occurred after three days' play. Some welcomed the break, while others felt that it interfered with the flow of the match. In home Tests back in the UK, it was a chance to catch up with family or friends, but away, it mostly translated into more time spent around the hotel, and that tended to be dull, not restful. The rest day during the Perth Test, though, promised to be different.

Courtesy of an Aussie businessman called Ron Marks, who owned a big boat, there was an open invitation for a trip to Rottnest Island, a lump of rock 14 miles to the west of Fremantle. Rotto, as it was known locally, was inhabited by strange, furry marsupials called quokkas, but otherwise not much happened there. Most of those playing in the Test declined, but a few of us, as well as some of the Aussie team, including Allan Border and David Hookes, were up for the trip, which we were warned would take most of the day.

'Bring anyone you like,' instructed Marks, so I did, asking along the best-looking one of the three recently immigrated women I'd met in Perth – the invite being issued a few days before the Test began and before I'd met the gorgeous Hostie.

When the day came, having invited a guest, I felt obliged to be attentive, so we found a quiet corner in which to canoodle. Yet, just as we were getting comfortable, the Hostie, with whom I'd spent the previous night, hopped onto the boat. Talk about wanting to be vaporised and all those other clichés about being somewhere else fast.

The daggers looks she gave me could have cut chain mail, which meant they didn't go unnoticed by the other girl.

'Do you know her?' she asked accusingly.

'Er, yes,' I mumbled.

'Did you invite her today as well?' she snapped.

'Of course not,' I said, realising that whatever I came out with was unlikely to appease.

Not convinced, she stormed off to another part of the boat, leaving me mortified and at a complete loss as to how I might 'manage the damage', as my new agents, Harry and Ray, would say.

Now, I knew that Ron Marks had met the Hostie and her best friend (another air hostess) and wined and dined them. But not that he'd invited them along for the trip – though I should have suspected. As it was, I couldn't see any comeback from this unexpected confrontation. I'd been exposed as a two-timing charlatan in the most shaming way. As a divorce lawyer friend of mine would say, 'There might not have been a bang, but I was to rights.'

The trouble with boats is that once you set off you cannot get off until the skipper decides to moor up. Not unless you fancy swimming, something not recommended around Perth, which boasts several species of man-eating shark. The Hostie's surprise appearance had killed everything – the day, the possibility of further relations with two attractive women, and my pride. With two wronged females angrily prowling the vessel, I just wanted to hide under a rock, and there weren't any of those until Rotto.

Thank heavens, then, for alcohol. Several cans of Swan lager later and at least the self-loathing had abated a bit. A spot of snorkelling round Rotto and some fishing also allowed me to take my mind off matters. Allan Border even managed to harpoon a fish. But then like most Aussies he was used to dealing, decisively, with nature. After a pleasant lunch and walk to see the quokkas on Rotto, and a few more drinks, my mood had mellowed further. Even the glares from the Hostie seemed to be more Ray-Ban than ray gun, though that may have just been the view from behind my beer can.

Some would argue that fretting serves no evolutionary purpose, as it wastes valuable time and energy. As such, it is an indulgence of human beings with time on their hands. They may well have a point. On the return journey, the Fremantle Doctor blew with such gusto that most of my self-pity was deposited in the Indian Ocean. I wasn't the only one sick either. Suddenly, the shame I felt for being exposed as a two-timing sleazebag seemed very small beer indeed.

That is the one thing they never tell you about visiting Rotto. You travel over in the morning, when the sea is like a millpond, but you return stuffed full of food and drink in the afternoon, just as 'The Doctor' begins to huff and puff. It isn't just the size of the swell which makes people wish they'd never left dry land, but the way it makes the boat roll and pitch in a way guaranteed to crush your constitution and loosen the contents of your stomach. 'Heave away' sheds all nautical meaning when you return from Rotto.

It wasn't the first time I'd been on this stretch of water. Just before the game against Western Australia, we'd been invited to watch

Australia II, Alan Bond's yacht, as it underwent sea trials in its bid to win the America's Cup – which it did to incredible fanfare the following year.

Bondy, as he was known locally, had made a fortune from nothing after his family had emigrated to Fremantle from London in the late 1940s. A man with a brilliant eye for a deal, he was nevertheless unscrupulous when it came to ethics and was not above pulling a sharp one. He made fortunes, lost them and then made them again, a flip-flop-flip that eventually saw him jailed for fraud.

In 1982, though, he was our generous host and on his way to becoming the toast of Australia. Although few felt he would succeed in taking the America's Cup off the New York Yacht Club, whose unbroken possession of the trophy had lasted 132 years, it suited Bondy to gain some publicity for his bid – and we were only too happy to oblige.

At sea, we spent most of our time on the tender launch, sinking beers and eating barbecued chicken, watching on as Team Bond put prospective 'grinders', the strong men who hoist the sails up and down, through their paces.

After they'd gone through six or so racing starts, we were invited on board to observe the process up close. It was afternoon and both the chop and 'The Doctor' were just getting up. Yet *Australia II*, with its secret, winged keel, cut through the swell with scarcely a wobble. The poise and stability were astonishing. After a while, the helmsman asked if I'd like to have a go at steering this multi-million-dollar bit of kit.

'I've never done anything like this before,' I warned as I took the helm, with more than a hint of trepidation.

'Oh, it's pretty simple,' he said. 'See that long, flat, line over there? It's called the horizon. Just head for it.'

So we did, shooting along at speeds I didn't think possible in a boat under sail. Crucially, though, because of the way it displaced the water, there was no seasickness, which was definitely not the case on our return from Rotto in Ron Marks's stink boat.

Having exercised my stomach muscles beyond measure with all the wet and dry heaving, I was in no fit state for the powwow the Hostie demanded once back in dock. With the other girl having befriended one of the crew, I had only one person to appease, though it was still not clear how I might defend the indefensible.

So I didn't try. Instead, I told her that my actions were beyond those of any decent, right-thinking human being and that I could not blame her for not wanting to have anything more to do with me. With nothing more to lose, I laid it on thick, admitting that I was a self-regarding rotter and that she was well rid of me.

And then we went our separate ways, or so I thought. Two hours later, she phoned my room to say she was flying back the following day and that we could not part on such bad terms. So I went round to her hotel and we didn't . . . part on such bad terms. In fact, she appeared to have forgiven me to the extent that I continued to see her over the next 18 months, whenever her flying roster took her to London.

Unsurprisingly, the Perth Test match did not live up to the same drama, after ending in a draw, though it still had its moments – not least when Terry Alderman dislocated his shoulder after grappling with a pitch invader who'd attempted to pinch his sunhat.

The incident happened during a drinks break towards the end of our first innings, soon after tea on the second day. England had just reached 400, thanks to a gutsy ninth-wicket partnership between Bob Taylor and Bob Willis. As most people in the ground rose to have a stretch, including the photographers, about 15 drunken oiks ran on. In the fracas that ensued, one of them cuffed Alderman about the head as he tried to make off with his sunhat.

With his temper already worn thin by the two-Bobs stand, Alderman was in no mood to indulge idiots and charged after the thief, bringing him down on the outfield with a thumping rugby tackle. At that point the oik, subsequently named in the papers as Gary Donnison, started to throw punches but was quickly subdued by Dennis Lillee and Allan Border, who pinned him down until the police arrived to take him away.

The umpires suspended play for 20 minutes and Greg Chappell led his team from the field while the police sought to calm the situation. According to eyewitnesses, trouble had been brewing for a while – the taking of strong beer under a hot sun a combustive combination in something as emotive as an Ashes series.

In tackling him, Alderman had landed awkwardly on an outstretched right arm, his bowling arm, and dislocated his shoulder. He was stretchered off and was out of international cricket for 18 months. It was a terrible price to pay for getting involved and one that cost him at least a dozen Test matches. Some say he was never the same bowler again, though his figures over the 25 Tests he played following the injury don't support that.

As a keen photographer, I just happened to have my camera, with 500 mm mirror lens attached, sitting on my lap. I had not long finished batting – if you could call it that after being bowled by Lillee for a 19-ball duck – so was keen to occupy my mind with something other than my negligible contribution to the match. There was no autofocus on cameras back then – so the fast-moving action as the yobs ran on has not been caught pin sharp – but I did capture a sequence, albeit a bit blurred, which includes the moment Alderman took out his tormentor.

As a photograph it may be unique, as I've never seen any images of the actual incident save for TV grabs. Because it was the drinks break, and because it all happened so fast, the official snappers all had their big lenses on tripods pointing down the pitch. By the time they'd realised something was afoot and had swung their cameras round, it was all over and the WACA resembled a battlefield. Along with Alderman, several policemen were injured and 20 arrests were made, the incident having sparked further unrest in the crowd.

Willis, who'd been batting when it happened, later said the incident was as 'sickening' as anything he'd seen on a Test ground. Like many onlookers, he blamed the booze and something he called the 'boot-boy culture of football' coming to cricket. 'That prospect revolted me,' he later stated in one of the newspapers. To counter any repeat, the sale of alcohol was banned during the middle session of play for the remainder of the match.

It was foolhardy of Alderman to react as he did, though his actions were not without official endorsement. The Australian Cricket Board's Code of Conduct, which was given to all players, stated that 'Players must not assault or attempt to assault an umpire, another player or a spectator. The Code does not apply to any spectator trespassing on the ground.'

Now, I doubt Alderman or any of the players had ever bothered to read the Code thoroughly enough to know that, but it meant that anyone who ran onto the field during play was fair game. Not that it looked like a 'here we go, lads, let's duff over these yobs' situation. No, it was more like the aggressive instinct of a sportsman kicking in after a drunken bum had taken liberties.

Although a very serious and ugly business, it did tickle me that the Aussie papers chose to describe Donnison, Alderman's attacker, as a 'teenage expat from the UK', and not an Australian citizen, which is what he'd recently become.

The other notable occasions during the match, at least from England's point of view, were Chris Tavaré's obduracy in our first innings and another brilliant knock from Randall in our second, one of two hundreds in the match, the other made by Greg Chappell, Australia's captain.

Tav opened with Geoff Cook and had been told by Willis to drop anchor, an instruction he obeyed literally by taking occupation of the crease to new levels of self-denial. From the start of play on the opening day, he'd reached 49 by tea and 66 by the close. In fact, he spent an incredible 90 minutes stuck on 66. When Yardley finally prised him from the crease just before lunch on day two, he'd made 89, an innings that had lasted just shy of eight hours and taken 337 balls.

As had occurred in the match against Western Australia, Randall produced another brilliant innings. Also as per that match, messrs Marsh and Lillee continued to sledge him, almost by the ball. You'd have thought they might have learnt. At Essex, Keith Fletcher forbade anyone to even say hello to Randall once the match had begun. Chatting to the opposition on the field, you see, was Randall's way of steadying his nerves. Trading quips with Marsh and Lillee took his mind off the forbidding task in hand, which was to ensure the draw – something by no means guaranteed with our second innings listing at 151 for five after Australia had made 424 in their first innings.

I also came to the party in our second innings, scoring an unbeaten 47, a knock that brought me some pride in that it at least helped to make the game safe. Part of that included a last-wicket stand of 66 with Norman Cowans, who batted ably until he missed a slow full toss from Greg Chappell and was lbw, an error that probably cost me a first Test fifty, and an Ashes one at that.

Still, I had the consolation of Dennis Lillee saying 'well batted' to me when some of us repaired to Australia's dressing room for refreshment after the match. Having a beer while semi-clad in the host's dressing room is something of a tradition in Australia. In Perth, this was raised to the spectacular by Marsh's contacts in the restaurant trade and the delivery of several seafood platters heaving with crayfish, oysters, prawns and other tasty morsels from the Indian Ocean.

Marsh was also expert in showing us how to get fizzy, icy-cold beers down the hatch very quickly, something he called 'The Refresher'. This only works with ring-pulls that you can rip off in one, but back then all Aussie beer cans seemed to have them. Basically, you take a can opener which has one of those triangular points at one end and make a hole in the base of a full, unopened can of beer. You then plug that hole with your thumb and shake the can hard. Your mouth is then placed over the hole and you suck until a seal is created. At that point you rip off the ring-pull and, hey presto, the contents of the can are jet-propelled down your throat. A few of those in quick succession and you can feel lift-off.

Sharing a cold beer with Lillee, Marsh, Chappell and Kim Hughes, while slurping down oysters, suddenly put a very human face on what, for someone fresh out of university, had been a very alien and hostile experience. I'd played cricket at all levels, but this Test had been a peak in terms of aggression and the sheer intensity of the pressure. Of course, I'd yet to play against the West Indies and their intimidating battery of fast bowlers, but this had probed, pushed and provoked like nothing else. To have survived and then even thrived enough to secure the draw (a good result at fortress WACA) was gratifying.

That warm, fuzzy feeling of accomplishment did not last. The next day we had a team meeting before our six-hour flight to Sydney for a State game, in which one of the things Willis made plain was the unacceptability for a bowler like me to go for more than three runs an over (I'd gone for 3.7).

No real surprise then, after the game against New South Wales which we won by 26 runs but where I averaged 3.18 runs an over, that I was dropped for the second Test, which was in Brisbane.

Eddie Hemmings was brought in for me while Graeme Fowler replaced Geoff Cook. Considering we'd drawn and not lost the opening Test, it seemed a lot of change. It also meant playing two off-spinners, though the inclusion of Hemmings, who'd taken five wickets in the second innings on a turner at Sydney, could have been seen as a tactical change, albeit one that lacked variety. Yet Cook had been jettisoned despite making 99 and 77 in the Sydney game, to Foxy Fowler's 12 and 14. For those making the selections, impressions were clearly what counted, not hard numbers.

Mind you, Foxy had been distracted against NSW at Sydney, at least when England were in the field. He'd been patrolling the boundary to the left of the old pavilion when something had caught his eye which even he, with his fevered imagination, couldn't quite believe. At the end of one over he came up to me and said, 'Swap positions with me next over and see if you see what I'm seeing down there at third man. I'm worried that I'm hallucinating.'

Intrigued, I switched and wondered what lay in store. As ever for non-internationals, the stand was sparsely populated, though I could see a good-looking woman sitting on the front row in a short skirt with her legs up on the fence. Checking her out, I realised it was Vivien, or Zelda as some knew her, the Australian wife of one of the cricket reporters on tour.

As I moved to the boundary's edge, which in those days ran right up to the fence, she parted her legs to show me that, yes, she wasn't wearing any knickers, and that I was indeed looking at the promised land. There'd been talk of her feeling players up in the hotel lift, though I had not been one of them. Once a model, Zelda was a troubled soul whose descent into drug addiction made her unpredictable, though I didn't sense any ambiguity here. It was clear she would keep up the display as long as I was prepared to keep looking. At the end of the over I ran over to Foxy to assure him that he was not having visions and to resume my previous fielding position, away from such distractions, which were not covered in the MCC coaching manual.

Sydney was also my first taste of the famous Sebel Townhouse hotel, set at the 'respectable' end of Kings Cross, Sydney's red-light area, as it merges into Rushcutters Bay. Built in the early 1960s, the Sebel had gained a reputation for being intimate and discreet. As such, it became a favoured haunt of celebrities and rock stars, both local and foreign.

The England team were staying there, and had done so on many previous tours. Cricketers aside, the small lobby bar always had a famous face or two in it. While there, we encountered Daryl Hall and John Oates, the former very friendly and charming. Less club-bable were Siouxsie and the Banshees, whom we came across one night in the hotel lounge sipping crème de menthe from balloon glasses.

Sitting there like the Sphinx of Giza, Siouxsie Sioux rebuffed all attempts at conversation with a wall of silence, her disdain for something as unhip as a cricket team written all over her face. While some found her behaviour disrespectful, I thought it condescend-ingly cool – a silent two fingers to a symbol of the Establishment that Punk had, initially, stood against.

While at the Sebel, Foxy and I also met Steve Smith, an American record producer. Smith had production credits on Bob Marley's *Live at the Lyceum* album, released in 1975, which gave him massive street cred in my book, the record being a huge hit generally, as well as with me and my mates at school. In Sydney with his girlfriend, Debbie Raymond, the now deceased daughter of porn king and property magnate Paul Raymond, Smith had been hired to produce some tracks for Aussie rock legends Cold Chisel. When we professed our love of music, Smith invited us along to the studio, where we met Jimmy Barnes and the band. As sons of so-called '£10 Poms' who'd emigrated to Australia in the 1960s, in an initiative by the

Australian government to attract immigrants from Britain, Barnes, whose real name was John Swan, and his band mates still spoke with strong Scots accents.

Through Smith, I also met Michael Gudinski, the founder of Australia's Mushroom Records, a groundbreaking label with all manner of great bands on it, such as Mental As Anything and my personal favourites, the Go-Betweens. It was at Gudinski's pad in North Bondi with Smith and Raymond that I met Mental's keyboard player Greedy Smith. Greedy lived up to his name too, hogging the many delights on offer that afternoon as we chilled overlooking Australia's most famous beach.

For a recent student like me, hotel bars such as the Sebel's were last resorts, being expensive and therefore generally full of wealthy older people. Fortunately, a few of my colleagues shared my values and we sought cheaper but sleazier places to drink, like the bar at the Bourbon and Beefsteak, five minutes' walk away.

You got a good cross-section of people in the B&B, including up-country folk down in the big smoke for a good time. One couple, who eventually turned out to be brother and sister from somewhere beyond the Blue Mountains, came over to Foxy, Geoff Cook and me while we were sinking a beer, and just stood in front of us beaming. We looked at each other, thinking, Do we know these two? But nothing clicked.

Suddenly, by way of introduction, the bloke pointed at Geoff and said, 'You're Cook, the Pommie opener.'

'Indeed I am, sir,' said Cooky, 'pleased to meet you,' and proffered his hand in greeting.

'Yeah, thought so,' said the bloke. 'You're only ------- ordinary with the willow.'

'Well, thank you very much, sir,' said Cooky. 'Now, what are you having to drink?'

It was a brilliant way to defuse a situation that could have turned awkward, but Cooky had the worldly wisdom to know gaucheness from deliberate provocation and he rode the slight with charm. A few hours later, the two of them were the best of mates.

It is amazing how quickly you become disengaged when not directly involved, as I can recall few details of the second Test at the Gabba other than that we lost. Like us, Australia had made some changes, two of them enforced after injuries to Alderman and, as it transpired, Lillee as well, who was now out of the series following knee surgery. Which meant that only one third of their first-choice pace attack remained. A bonus, surely – except that in came Jeff Thomson and a local bruiser called Carl Rackemann, as blond and German-looking as his name would suggest.

The other change Australia made was to bring in South African-born Kepler Wessels for the mercurial Graeme Wood. Wessels, who'd recently played four seasons for Sussex, had emigrated to Australia and qualified to play for them in the same way Allan Lamb had qualified to play for England. He made quite an impact on his Test debut, too, scoring 162 out of 341 as Australia took a first-innings lead of 122.

Willis took five wickets in the innings, but the effort in Brisbane's enervating humidity took it out of him. I ministered to his lunch needs mid-spell, but all he wanted was ice cream. Even so, it seemed an afterthought as he sat there in jockstrap and vest spooning it down, his famous 1,000-yard stare looking out beyond the Gabba's dog track.

We batted better second time around, Foxy making 83, but not well enough to make Australia struggle. Thommo took five in the second innings on his return and Geoff Lawson took the other five, to become the first bowler to take 11 wickets in an Ashes Test at the Gabba. Australia made the 188 needed without undue alarm, to win by seven wickets.

When you go one down in an Ashes series in Australia, there is a sea change in the way the locals react to you. What was once good-ish-natured banter in the build-up, or when the score was still 0–0 (like the man who upbraided Cooky in Sydney's Bourbon and Beefsteak), now gets ramped up to barefaced insults. It is no exaggeration to say that we got reminded of our defeat at every turn. From the checkout girls at the hotel, to the bellhop and the coach driver who took us to the airport. You then fly off to a new city, where a whole new legion of patriots is waiting to bag you, as the Aussies say, their barbs imparted with feeling. A degree of paranoia from the beleaguered is required for it to work, but it was still wearing. Spookily, though, and without orchestration, Aussies of all generations seem to know that and see it as their duty to keep up the needle.

With the public getting on our case, we headed to Adelaide for the third Test. Our billet there was the Sebel hotel on Hindley Street, a seedy part of town which also contained the city's red-light area, so not very different from Sydney in that regard.

I was rooming once more with Geoff Cook, but it was the pairing of Ian 'Gunner' Gould and 21-year-old Norman 'Flash' Cowans which created the best entertainment. A fine figure of a young man, Norman had caught the eyes of Aussie women the moment he had landed. Here in Adelaide, he'd met a female DJ who'd become so smitten with him that she'd packed a suitcase and moved into his room, a room he also shared with Gunner. A team man not beyond making the odd sacrifice for his colleagues, Gunner nevertheless drew the line at the DJ being a constant presence in what, along with the team room, was the sole retreat for us from an increasingly insufferable Australian public.

'It's a nightmare, this bird Flash has met,' he told a group of us in the hotel bar one night. 'She's there the whole time, even when he is out. I can't lie on my bed and fart any more, I can't sit on the bog with the door open any more and I certainly can't lie around without my undies on. It's bang out of order.'

It was selfish of Flash, but as neither he nor Gunner had been picked for the Test, he reasoned that the DJ's constant presence wasn't impinging on anything important. Anyway, he wasn't going to give someone so willing and gorgeous the elbow just to accommodate Gunner's questionable toilet habits.

The manager of the hotel, a decent bloke with a keen sense of humour, tried to alleviate the matter by offering Flash the key to a suite which he kept for special purposes on account of its massive water bed. But neither Flash nor Miss DJ liked its quivering, tidal surges, and Gunner was once more disturbed in the ministration of his daily rituals.

Driven to distraction, Gunner hatched a plot to give Flash his comeuppance, a wind up that anyone with an ounce of scepticism might have detected. With collusion from the manager, Gunner prepared a fake bill for Flash with items on it like:

Use of lift for extra person	$15.00 per day
Extra person in room	$40.00 per day
Towels used by extra person	$20.00 per day

Over our 10-day stay, it mounted up.

Flash should have smelt a rat when he checked out, but he didn't. Perhaps he was distracted by having to bid the DJ farewell – a teary process, from her at least – which then led to him holding up the team coach, usually a fineable offence. Whatever the reason, he did not spot the deception.

Without enough money to settle the bill, he had to ask Mr Fixit, Bernard Thomas, for a sub of several hundred dollars. Playing along with the ruse with deadpan excellence, Thomas refused to pay up without extensive explanation – which, of course, Flash did not want to provide in front of a coach full of players and, by now, quite a few of the wives and girlfriends as well.

Yet, just as Flash's panic threatened to break into hyperventilation, the manager stepped in, waving the real bill, to reveal that it had all just been a joke hatched by him and Gunner, and that Flash should worry himself no longer. It was a great ruse, enjoyed by everyone except Flash, who, perhaps feeling insecure after being dropped for the Adelaide Test, did not see the funny side. Instead, he wore that pursed-lip look of someone hell-bent on revenge.

And revenge is what he attempted to mete out for the remainder of the tour, at least every time Gunner had a bat in the nets. Whenever that happened, Flash would volunteer to bowl, then try to pin his tormentor to the back of the net with a barrage of bouncers. It was petty, it was nasty, but that is just how it was, and Gunner, a natural ducker and diver, took it without complaint – though, thankfully, not on the chin.

Adelaide had seemed very civilised when we played the State game there earlier on tour. During that match, both teams even left the field for 30 minutes in order to watch the Melbourne Cup,. won on that occasion by Gurner's Lane. Yet all that changed for our second foray. Suddenly, with the Aussies having taken a lead in the Ashes, both team and country went for the jugular – something they are programmed to do when they smell the blood of Englishmen.

To hit us hard, again, Australia included Rodney Hogg in their squad, another fast bowler who liked splitting stiff upper lips. To practise for the expected barrage of bouncers, our assistant manager, Norman 'Giff' Gifford, organised for a bowling machine to be installed in our nets. A combination of that and Norman Cowans, prior to his humiliation with the hotel bill, would bombard us with short balls so as to get us used to what was coming.

Bowling machines were in their infancy then and not very relia-ble. This one comprised two rubber rollers spinning round at great speed. Velocity, direction and length were all adjusted manually by the operator, who was Giff. Batsmen came and went, their time spent ducking, swaying and hooking, as well as picking up the odd bruise.

I was back in the frame to play, following Flash's modest showing at the Gabba, which meant I was summoned for a stint against the bowling machine. It was a nightmare. There were no cues as to when the ball might appear, while Giff kept messing with the length. When one didn't bounce as high as expected and thudded into my left forearm at 90 mph, I thought I'd broken it, so screamingly intense was the pain.

It is at moments like that when you suddenly get to see the true order of things. As I returned to the dressing room in the hope of prompt treatment and even some TLC, I was ignored, despite my obvious distress. Instead, the physio, Bernard Thomas, busied himself stretching Willis's hamstring.

When I kicked up a fuss, Thomas told me, 'There's some ice in the bathroom. Go and make yourself a cold compress.'

I was not impressed. Here I was close to puking from pain, with my left arm hanging limply by my side. Dark thoughts formed. I might have a broken arm here, and this bloke wants me to see to it myself. Eventually, it needed Doug Insole, the manager, to order Thomas to minister to me, but the episode revealed just how expendable some of us were in Bernie the Bolt's eyes.

Happily, the bone wasn't broken and, as it wasn't my bowling arm, I was not ruled out of the Test, not that the match went well for me or the team. Persuaded by some of the batsmen, who didn't seem all that keen to face Lawson, Thomson and Hogg on a fresh Adelaide pitch, Willis won the toss and put Australia in to bat – a risky option in a place where the heat tends to make pitches crack as the clay content in the soil dries. Few things make batting in Australia trickier than widening cracks, which tend to have an increasingly erratic effect on the bounce of the ball. And nowhere is that more pronounced or hazardous than in the last innings of a game, especially if the team batting first has posted a good score, which Australia had done by scoring 438, Greg Chappell having made another fine hundred.

I'd managed to get my first Test wickets of the tour, Allan Border caught behind and Rod Marsh taken by Eddie Hemmings in the gully. Before Border nicked off, I remember saying to Dusty Miller that I just couldn't see when I might snaffle a first wicket or how I might take it. Happily, perseverance won through – a bit of extra bounce and a heavy-handed nibble from Border and I had something in the right column at last.

Although I was pleased with my booty, any pride was soon displaced by what were becoming increasingly persistent feelings of inadequacy as Lawson, Thommo and Hogg gave us all a lesson on how to bowl on a not-very-responsive deck. It was not subtle, apart from the occasional cutter from Lawson and Hogg, but it was fast and it was aggressive.

They brutally targeted the lower middle order and tail and simply blew it away. We lost our last seven wickets for 35 runs, pretty much unacceptable when the ball is not moving about much. Thommo worked up some pace and we simply failed to withstand the onslaught. Indeed, for reasons not immediately apparent at the time, we seemed to lack the necessary stomach for the fight.

It was the kind of collapse for which county cricket routinely got the blame in those days. The argument used to run like this. Because of the sheer number of county matches in a season, many teams would simply not bother to scrap hard to get out of a hole. Instead, they would save their energies, which they would not want to waste chasing a lost cause, for the next match in a few days' time. It was a logic I'd heard put forward many times, yet surely players were not that conditioned by their environment? For starters, this was Test cricket and the Ashes. In our little world, that was as important as it got, though you might not have thought so after the careless way we batted in Adelaide.

There was also something to fight for, the follow-on target, though that did not seem to focus minds as much as it should. Instead, we seemed to imagine a fate far worse than the one posed by Thommo, Hogg and Lawson whanging the ball down at a fair lick.

We missed the follow-on by 23 runs and although we batted better in our next innings, it was not well enough to prevent the inevitable slide to defeat – a defeat we'd been staring at ever since our opponents ended the first day on 265 for three. Now we were 2–0 down in the Ashes with two to play, a bleak outlook and one that had become increasingly galling in triumphalist Australia.

Our next port of call was Hobart, where I'd welcomed in the 1980s a few years earlier while on tour with the combined Oxford and Cambridge side.

Scheduled to play a three-day match against Tasmania there and a one-day match against them at Launceston, we stayed in Hobart's Wrest Point hotel, Australia's first casino when it had opened nine years earlier. Although I was not much of a gambler myself, the Aussies loved to punt on just about anything. Which made the place a magnet for high rollers to low loaders and all designations between.

The night before our tour game, I met a tall, blonde girl in the Wrest Point who asked what I would most like to do while I was in Hobart. The slick answer would have been to say, 'Spend a romantic evening with you, my dear,' but I was feeling perverse, so I said, 'I'd like to see the view from up there,' indicating Mount Wellington, a 4,000-foot high peak that overlooks the city.

'Let's go,' she said. 'I've got Mum's car and we can be at the top in 40 minutes.'

I should have demurred. Although I had by now got used to the directness of Aussie women, she was 19 and had put away several glasses of champagne. Drink-driving is a huge no-no in Australia now, but back then, especially somewhere as frontier-like as Hobart, well, it was a risk most took in order to have a hearty Friday night on the town.

So, off we went around midnight, snaking our way up a lonely, unlit road, until she took one bend too quickly, skidded and hit some rocks. Although we were unhurt the damage to the car was considerable and it would not start. She, of course, was beside herself with embarrassment and worry about the awkward conversation she would need to have with Mum.

A romantic assignation atop a mountain, a definite possibility 30 minutes earlier, was now out of the question, so I spent the next few hours, as the wind howled and the temperature plummeted, consoling her and drying her tears as we waited for it to get light.

Except that visibility was not especially comforting when it came. It was only when the inky black gave way to the first grey detail that I saw how lucky we'd been to skid and hit rocks on the inside of the bend and not the outside – over which there was a vertical drop of at least 1,000 feet.

If fortune had smiled upon us there, it gave us another lopsided grin when a car containing a couple who'd no doubt succeeded in their amorous intentions wound its way down from the summit. They picked us up, applied the balm of sympathy and took us back to the Wrest Point, where I sorted out a taxi for my still-shaken chauffeuse.

I then repaired to my room, where Vic Marks, my room-mate, was up and preparing for the first day of the match. 'Had a good night?' he chuckled, before sitting wide-eyed as I recounted my adventure. 'Well, you'd better hope we bat first so you can get your head down,' he said, but of course we didn't – our stand-in captain, David Gower, losing the toss.

Nothing stays secret for long within a team and once the hierarchy had discovered I'd not had a wink of sleep, I was destined to bowl into the wind, which was now approaching hurricane force (I kid you not, as even the heavy bails would not stay put). Incredibly, I bowled 29.3 overs in Tasmania's innings and took three for 58, a performance of which I was most proud given the strength of the wind and the fact I'd spent a traumatic night halfway up a mountain without a wink of sleep. In my fledgling career to date, my body had let me down a few times but not on this occasion. I was also chuffed with the extra resolve I found to get the job done, something those bowling down-gale did not have to summon. It remains the strongest wind I have ever bowled into.

Even better, my companion from our hairy experience up Mount Wellington phoned to say her mum had been more understanding than expected over the mishap. Obviously, she would have to save up to pay for the damage, but could she make it up to me by taking me to dinner? She could, I said, but as it was my crackers idea to go up the mountain in the first place, dinner would be my treat.

Our Tasmanian sojourn had one further gremlin in store, which arose during the one-day game at Launceston, on what proved a spiteful pitch. It was so unpredictable that Michael Holding, Tasmania's overseas player, went off a short run and pitched the ball up, but only after one of his thunderbolts had struck Derek Randall flush in the mouth.

It was a sickening blow that Arkle, or Rags as he tended to call himself, could do little about, the ball having taken off as well as nipped back sharply off a good length. When he could speak again, which took a few days, he regaled us with his version of the incident.

'Ah kept sayin to mi'self, it's a shit pitch and it's Michael bloody Holding, so get back and across, Rags, get back and across. So, I got back and across and t' ball hit me straight in t' bloody gob.'

He didn't lose any teeth, but his mouth and lips were severely cut and swollen, while the impact had clearly shaken him. Sympathy is rarely the default emotion among sportsmen who have been together for several months and within the hour Beefy had christened him 'The Elephant Man', his bloody, swollen and protruding lip so unsightly as to draw a crowd.

I was to see a lot of that battered mouth as we arrived in Melbourne for the fourth Test after I drew Randall, not for the first time, in the room-mate stakes. He was still in pain, though, and pretty despondent. Staying in the Hilton, a stone's throw from the MCG, we had a daily ritual in which I would order him soup with a straw on room service for breakfast, lunch and supper. It was about the only thing he could get down, the straw being crucial.

Since the beginning of the series in Perth, Arkle had endured something of a lean trot in the Tests, so might have been vulnerable anyway to being dropped. But with a mouthful of stitches impeding his speech and, potentially, his courage, in the face of the bouncer barrage that would materialise if he did play, he was omitted from the Boxing Day Test. Naturally, it was a decision that did not please him much, which may have accounted for his militant stance when the manager called a special team meeting, following critical reports in the tabloid press about a drinking culture on the tour.

Most journalists on that trip had been amiable companions in the bar and therefore mute witnesses to any excess, but that changed after we'd gone 2–0 down. Once that happened, Steve Whiting in the *Sun* began to point to a pernicious drinking culture within the team as the principal reason for our defeats. Under pressure from their editors, others began to draw similar conclusions. The main target was, of course, Botham. But while Beefy was undeniably the team's carouser-in-chief, Whiting's attack seemed to be based more on him being a columnist for the *Mirror*, the *Sun*'s arch rival, than on any real concern over the effects of a few jugs of whisky and ice cream that he'd chugged down after midnight.

The type of tipple may have changed but Beefy's habits hadn't really altered since he'd made his England debut five years earlier. Nor had those of most players, which made for a febrile atmosphere when Doug Insole tried to call us to heel. At that stage of a tour, team gatherings beyond those to discuss tactics prior to a Test were viewed as a bit of a chore. Which meant Insole's edict, that we should not be seen drinking in public after midnight, was not given a sympathetic hearing. While most felt it over-authoritarian, the most vocal dissent came from Arkle, neither a big drinker nor a night owl.

'Nobody's going to tell me when I can have a drink or when I should go to bed,' he fumed. 'I'm not bloody six years old.'

'Oh, yes you are,' shouted Botham, in an attempt to inject some levity into proceedings. But Insole was not for moving despite Randall and the objections of other players. The midnight curfew was introduced, with a £1,000 fine for anyone breaking it.

'Well, you may as well take my tour fee off me now,' shouted Foxy Fowler, another adamant that the days of being told what to do had ended when he'd swapped shorts for long trousers.

Foxy's outburst was not over-stated. The tour fee was £10,000 before tax for the entire five-month trip, so a fine or two of that size would have represented a sizeable chunk. How it was to be policed was not made clear either, though the sight of Bernie the Bolt skulking around hotel lobbies in the wee hours probably gave the game away. Except I don't recall many observing the curfew. Equally, though, I don't remember anyone getting fined for breaking it. And it was broken, most nights.

This all came just a day or so before the Christmas party, a lunch-time event that was fancy dress and to which the press were invited for pre-prandial drinks, despite the increasingly strained atmosphere between us. Wives, girlfriends and families were also invited to the drinks bit, though not the lunch, that being about that much-touted phenomenon – team bonding. As we'd been on tour together for more than 60 days by then, it was probably more a case of resticking those bonds which had worked loose than the creation of any new ones.

For first-time tourists like me, Lamby, Flash, Eddie Hemmings and Foxy, tradition demanded that we perform a sketch for the delectation of the others. Fortunately, in Robin Jackman, we had a 'luvvie' disguised as a cricketer to take control. Jackers, who knew a few actors such as Bernard Cribbins, was a natural performer. You only had to watch his antics on a cricket field to know that histrionics were in his blood.

Our sketch was to sing a song about the team management to the tune of The Firm's 'Arthur Daley ('E's Alright)', which had proved popular on the back of the TV series *Minder*. Jackers had already sorted a backing track courtesy of our sponsors JVC, and with the help of Vic Marks had written a witty ditty which had the chorus 'Dougy Insole, shorts and plimsolls, but underrrr . . . neeeeath, ee's alright.'

It went down well, ending with a flourish as Foxy and I mooned the assembled gathering, a move we'd planned just minutes beforehand. I was dressed as a Hell's Angel, while he was decked out as a schoolgirl, our bare bottoms uncannily in character.

The next day, hangovers pulsing, we walked over in dribs and drabs to the MCG to take on Australia and 80,000 screaming Aussies, all looking to continue their Christmas revelry while indulging in one of their favourite pastimes – Pom-baiting.

Unless you have played in front of such a large, hostile crowd, it is impossible to know how your fight-or-flight reflex will respond, and which will be the stronger. The noise just overwhelms you, it being as much a percussive feeling in the gut as an onslaught on the ears.

I'd survived the selection process, while Flash had returned in place of Eddie Hemmings, as we opted for pace over spin. Geoff Cook had also been restored, as one of the openers, while the batting shifted about to accommodate Arkle's absence with a mangled mouth.

Advance intelligence on the pitch at the MCG was that the bounce would become less predictable as the game went on. In recent matches there, grubbers and daisy-cutters were not uncommon on the fourth and fifth days. It was with some surprise, then, that Chappell put us in to bat after winning the toss, though with his team 2–0 up and his bowlers on song, the heavy cloud that hung over Melbourne may have seduced him to go for the kill.

So far, the Ashes had been one big assault, physically from Australia's bowlers as well as verbally from the public. But while we expected more of the same from Lawson, Hogg and Thommo, nothing prepared us for the extra everything dumped on us by the MCG crowd. It was raucous and insulting, and by the end I was the most battered, sonically, I have ever felt on a cricket pitch, apart from a one-day international at the same venue a few weeks later, when an even bigger crowd turned up to give us what for.

There was nothing subtle about the incessant abuse that sought to provoke in the crudest and most personal ways. Except for one taunt that particularly seemed to tickle them: 'Where do you keep your savings, you Pommie ------? Under the soap?' That was more of a puzzle, until one of our opponents explained it was a reference to the Australian conviction that the English rarely wash – a claim whose source has never been explained.

Fielding on the boundary could be a lonely and dangerous experience, especially if you were in front of the infamous Bay 13, now defunct thanks to modern Australia's drive to become a paragon of political correctness. Not only did the vast 90-yard boundaries keep you far from the comfort of colleagues, but the denizens of Bay 13, mostly unsavoury biker sorts, would think nothing of lobbing a full can of beer at your head. If that kind of thing persisted today, the 'Health and Safety' brigade would make helmet-wearing compulsory for all boundary riders.

One who felt the full force of Bay 13's attentions was Gunner Gould, who had come on as a substitute fielder after Jeff Thomson had broken Foxy Fowler's big toe with a yorker. Gunner, who had brilliantly caught Greg Chappell off Norman Cowans during Australia's second innings, was sporting blond streaks in his hair, after a few of us had been persuaded by a local hairdresser to visit her salon. Whether it was because of those highlights or just the fact that he was the nearest Pom to hand, Gunner had a meat pie dumped on his head by a hairy Hell's Angel as he went to pick up the ball from the boundary gutter, just inches from the crowd (no 15-yard buffer zones then).

It could have got ugly if he'd reacted badly. But as he stood up, the gloop slowly dripping from his head, he looked at his tormentor and said, quick as a flash, 'Steady on, sunshine, I've just had me barnet done,' which disarmed the biker and won over the rest of the bay, or at least the few conversant with a bit of Cockney rhyming slang.

Despite the crowd's hostility, the Test was nip and tuck, with neither side's batsmen able to cut loose and dominate. Mindful that we'd been too timid towards Bruce Yardley, Australia's off-spinner, which had allowed him to bowl the long spells their fast bowlers needed to recover, we decided to change tack and attack him more that match. The outcome, in the first innings at least, was that he took four for 89 as we made 284. But in the second it bore dividends. We hit him for four and a half runs an over, a rate that had the knock-on effect of placing bigger workloads on the other bowlers, which in turn proved a factor in us making 294 on a pitch beginning to play tricks.

I made 42, adding a crucial 61 runs with Bob Taylor for the eighth wicket. In Perth, my batting in the second innings of the Test had helped to make the game safe, but here it had given us a real chance of victory. It felt good to contribute, as I was still finding wickets devilishly hard to come by when I bowled.

With Australia having made 287 in their first innings, it left them needing 292 over two days to win the match and secure the Ashes. With what had transpired over the previous three days, it looked pretty much an even contest, except that Willis had picked up a virus and was not well. Manfully, he took the new ball and bowled his quota of overs, but he was not at full bore. Fortunately, Flash Cowans was, and after he had conjured the dreaded grubber a few times, Australia slumped to 218 for nine, Flash having taken six of them with some hostile fast bowling.

It looked all over. Allan Border was still there, unbeaten on 15, but he had not been having a good series. With him was Australia's No 11, Jeff Thomson, a man whose Test average of 12 was just one digit higher than his batting position. What happened next, as Willis played a cagey game of cat and mouse, giving Border, the established batsman, the easy single to get Thommo on strike, had the makings of a controversy, at least for somebody.

Unbeknown to most of us, Beefy had loaned Border, a good friend of his, one of his Duncan Fearnley bats, to see if it would improve his luck. It did. Shaky at first, Border played with growing assurance, as did Thommo. By the close on the fourth day, they'd put on 37 together, so that Australia's score read 255 for nine. That left them needing 37 runs on the final day for a victory few had given them any hope of achieving when the pair had first come together.

Entry was free for that final day, which could have lasted all of one ball. Yet the drama gripped the country, which gave it an epic scope. One Australian journalist, who'd got married on the rest day of the Test, later told me that the denouement had almost brought him immediate divorce. At the start of that final day he'd been driving his wife out of Melbourne for their honeymoon, with the Test on the radio. But once play started and the tension began to gnaw, he told his new bride that he just had to pull over to listen. And there on the verge they remained, her bored and tetchy, him transfixed, for the next 90 minutes.

Despite the potential brevity of the situation, a crowd of 25,000 showed up to see if Border and Thommo could pull off the improbable. They almost did, the deficit having been narrowed to three runs when Willis, resigned to a last throw of the dice, brought on Beefy to work a late miracle. I was fielding at third man and the tension was almost unbearable. Beefy had performed several incredible feats for England during his career, but he'd taken just one wicket in Australia's second innings here, so another marvel looked unlikely.

Just as thoughts of the stick we would get from the press and the Aussie fans began to swirl about my head, for what would be an Ashes-conceding defeat, in bounded Beefy from the Southern End to bowl to Thommo. At this point, Thommo had kept out 61 balls, made 21 runs and begun to believe the improbable. And maybe that was his mistake. They always say that pressure bites hardest when the winning line heaves into view, in which case Thommo felt its teeth on his arse.

The ball was short and wide outside off stump. Emboldened, he shaped to cut. What happened next seemed both quick and slow, as Thommo, undone by some extra bounce or nerves or even some added zip in Beefy's delivery, edged the ball to Chris Tavaré at second slip. Tav must have felt the game had gone, too, as he seemed surprised that the ball should even have come to him. His instincts, though, carried the day, and while his hands were too late into position to effect a clean catch, they did allow him to parry it gently over his head, where Geoff Miller, happily alert at first slip, stooped to conquer by pouching the rebound.

Thommo was utterly distraught and sank to his knees. There was no touchy-feely hand-on-the-shoulder consolation stuff from Beefy, though, only from Border, his batting partner, who remained unbeaten on 62. Instead, Beefy roared off towards the dressing room (my direction), whooping like a dervish. I intercepted him just before the boundary boards and it was like being hit by a charging rhino.

The emotion, principally relief that we had at last won a Test, stirred a gloating triumphalism in me I'd not experienced before. Somewhat ungraciously, I flicked a prolonged double V-sign to the now silent Aussie crowd, which got me into trouble with England's management after it was caught on camera and used in some of the newspapers. I was not regretful. We'd been abused verbally, been used as target practice for beer cans and generally been pilloried by the media. Who wouldn't enjoy avenging that, even with something that childish? It certainly made me feel good.

The relief in the dressing room was even more obvious, though Willis, still suffering from whatever virus he'd picked up, simply looked dazed. We stayed there, in the bowels of the MCG, for most of the day until even the cold, fizzy filth that passes for beer in Australia began to taste good.

Although worn down by all the sledging and adverse comments in the media, here we were, still in with a shout of retaining the Ashes, provided we could win the last Test in Sydney. Redemption, and it really did feel as biblical as that, was still within our grasp.

ENGLAND V AUSTRALIA
(4th Test)

Played at Melbourne Cricket Ground, 26–30 December 1982

Umpires: AR Crafter & RV Whitehead
Toss: Australia

ENGLAND

G Cook	c Chappell b Thomson	10	c Yardley b Thomson	26
G Fowler	c Chappell b Hogg	4	b Hogg	65
CJ Tavaré	c Yardley b Thomson	89	b Hogg	0
DI Gower	c Marsh b Hogg	18	c Marsh b Lawson	3
AJ Lamb	c Dyson b Yardley	83	c Marsh b Hogg	26
IT Botham	c Wessels b Yardley	27	c Chappell b Thomson	46
G Miller	c Border b Yardley	10	lbw b Lawson	14
DR Pringle	c Wessels b Hogg	9	c Marsh b Lawson	42
RW Taylor†	c Marsh b Yardley	1	lbw b Thomson	37
RGD Willis*	not out	6	not out	8
NG Cowans	c Lawson b Hogg	3	b Lawson	10
Extras	(3 b, 6 lb, 12 nb, 3 w)	24	(2 b, 9 lb, 6 nb)	17
Total	(81.3 overs)	**284**	(80.4 overs)	**294**

AUSTRALIA

KC Wessels	b Willis	47	(2)	b Cowans	14
J Dyson	lbw b Cowans	21	(1)	c Tavaré b Botham	31
GS Chappell*	c Lamb b Cowans	0		c sub (IJ Gould) b Cowans	2
KJ Hughes	b Willis	66		c Taylor b Miller	48
AR Border	b Botham	2	(6)	not out	62
DW Hookes	c Taylor b Pringle	53	(5)	c Willis b Cowans	68
RW Marsh†	b Willis	53		lbw b Cowans	13
B Yardley	b Miller	9		b Cowans	0
GF Lawson	c Fowler b Miller	0		c Cowans b Pringle	7
RM Hogg	not out	8		lbw b Cowans	4
JR Thomson	b Miller	1		c Miller b Botham	21
Extras	(8 lb, 19 nb)	27		(5 b, 9 lb, 3 nb, 1 w)	18
Total	(79 overs)	**287**		(96.1 overs)	**288**

AUSTRALIA	O	M	R	W		O	M	R	W		Fall of wickets:				
												Eng	Aus	Eng	Aus
Lawson	17	6	48	0		21.4	6	66	4						
Hogg	23.3	6	69	4		22	5	64	3		1st	11	55	40	37
Yardley	27	9	89	4	(4)	15	2	67	0		2nd	25	55	41	39
Thomson	13	2	49	2	(3)	21	3	74	3		3rd	56	83	45	71
Chappell	1	0	5	0		1	0	6	0		4th	217	89	128	171
											5th	227	180	129	173
ENGLAND	O	M	R	W		O	M	R	W		6th	259	261	160	190
Willis	15	2	38	3		17	0	57	0		7th	262	276	201	190
Botham	18	3	69	1	(3)	25.1	6	80	2		8th	268	276	262	202
Cowans	16	0	69	2	(2)	26	6	77	6		9th	278	278	280	218
Pringle	15	2	40	1		12	4	26	1		10th	284	287	294	288
Miller	15	5	44	3		16	6	30	1						

Close of play: Day 1:   England (1) 284 all out
                 Day 2:   Australia (1) 287 all out
                 Day 3:   England (2) 294 all out
                 Day 4:   Australia (2) 255–9 (Border 44*, Thomson 8*)

Man of the match: NG Cowans
Result: **England won by 3 runs**

*   *   *

New Year's Eve in Sydney is meant to be one of the great global parties, though you don't want to venture too far from home if you are relying on taxis or buses to get you back. After midnight they are rarer than sober Aussies, though they are not that common whatever day of the year it is.

With most of the team having wives and girlfriends in tow, I went to party with some English people I knew down at the Rocks near the base of the Harbour Bridge. It was chaos. Even before I'd managed to have a drink I'd trodden in someone's esky (cool box), my size thirteens breaking several bottles of wine in the process. It was an accident not entirely of my making, having been shoved by some drunks, but thirsty Aussies don't see it that way. I had to give them 50 dollars or take a thumping, so I opted to lighten my wallet.

The fireworks were decent but the whole night just seemed a bit forced, as if you had to have a good time or else. I toasted in 1983 with my friends and some terrible local Seaview champagne, but parted soon after to make the 45-minute walk back to Kings Cross. Once there, I popped into the Bourbon and Beefsteak for a couple more drinks. At about 2 a.m., I bumped into Ray Illingworth, England's Ashes-winning captain from a decade earlier, who was leading a tour group of England supporters.

'Why aren't you in bed?' he asked. 'You've got a Test match in just over a day's time.'

'Because it's New Year's Eve and I'm going to be 12th man anyway, as all talk has been of us playing two spinners,' I replied. 'They keep telling me Sydney will turn.'

'That's as may be, but there might be injuries in practice, in which case you'll be expected to play. You need to get off to bed, now,' he countered.

Whether the drink had taken effect, or the arrogance of youth was holding sway, I thanked him for his advice and ordered another beer. For one thing, I was hacked off that having played a considerable role in our win at Melbourne, I was so readily considered surplus to requirements, even if the change was a tactical one. Getting bladdered was, after all, as much a means of marking disappointment as celebration. And secondly, I was piqued that Illingworth, a hard-bitten northerner with an acute distaste for players he regarded as public-school prats, should be so ready to give me a piece of his mind. Plenty of us had been out later than this for most of the tour, though I didn't tell him that.

When the first day of the final Test arrived, two spinners it was, with me 12th man, though the tactic was pretty much neutralised the moment Australia made 314 after winning the toss and batting first. Things might have been different had opening batsman John Dyson, who'd scored 79, been given run out in the opening over, after a brilliant bit of fielding by Willis off his own bowling. Not for the first time did a howler of an umpiring decision go against us.

The only time Australians walk is when they have run out of petrol, runs the old saw. Even so, Dyson, who was at least two yards short of the crease when the wicket was broken by Willis's direct hit, must have had some brass neck to stay there. More mystifying was how Mel Johnson, the umpire, failed to give it out. There was no Decision Review System then, but when they did show the TV replay, and froze the action, it was embarrassing. Dyson was not even in the frame.

A similar run-out had occurred in the second Test at the Gabba, where the same umpire's poor judgement had reprieved Greg Chappell. On that occasion, Chris Tavaré had been the one to throw down the stumps and, once Johnson had ruled Chappell not out, his sunhat too. It was the most exercised I ever saw Tav on a cricket field, but then the decision was, like the one in Sydney, an absolute shocker.

If we could have posted a big score, we would still have been in the mix, but Jeff Thomson curtailed any ambition of that by taking five for 50 as we were dismissed for 237. Australia batted again and while our two spinners shared six wickets between them, they did not strike quickly enough to hurt our hosts, who made 382. That score left us needing 460 to win in just over a day.

While a draw looked most likely, a further defeat was also possible and it took a remarkable innings of 95 from Eddie Hemmings, who came in as nightwatchman on the fourth evening, to stave it off. Higher than the best scores in the series from any of our top six, bar Randall and Gower, it was an incredible achievement. Eddie chanced his arm and kept going, before another poor decision did for him. Adjudged to have been caught behind off fellow off-spinner Bruce Yardley, to this day Hemmings maintains he never touched it.

Eddie's knock, and the fact that Australia only had one frontline spinner, meant Greg Chappell's team could not force the win. It also meant we'd lost the Ashes 2–1, a result I felt wasn't too shabby. After all, they were at home and had always looked stronger on paper.

The Ashes was over but not the tour. With 10 one-day internationals scheduled in a triangular tournament with Australia and New Zealand, excluding the best-of-three final, there was no time for contemplation or a debrief. Just a team measure-up for the sky-blue one-day kit and unto the breach once more.

Before I'd got on the plane to Australia, I felt the one-day series would be where Willis would see most value in me. How wrong I was. Instead of playing a big part, I played one match, against Australia at the MCG. Willis preferred Trevor Jesty, who'd been flown over as cover for Arkle following his injury at the hands of Michael Holding.

The one-dayers proved tough. One match against New Zealand in Adelaide, over the Australia Day weekend, saw the on-field temperature climb to 48 °C, that is 118 °F. The best that could be said about it was that it was a dry heat, though that did not prevent Big Bob from sending those not playing on a training run. Fortunately, a couple of hundred yards got the sweat running in rivulets, so we hid away for 15 minutes and then jogged the last 200 yards back.

Both teams wilted but we lost by four wickets. The win, though, must have heat-proofed New Zealand. Two days later, they played Australia in even hotter conditions and beat them as well.

Needless to say, we didn't qualify for the finals, which were contested by the antipodeans. Not that it was quite time to head home. We still had three more one-dayers in New Zealand to negotiate.

While embarrassing, not reaching the finals created a hiatus in the schedule of about a week. With no appetite for naughty-boy nets, Willis told us we could have five days off to go where we wanted, though not home. But, he warned, we must return fit and ready for a practice match at the SCG before we flew off across the Tasman for the final leg of our winter travels.

While most opted to stay put in Sydney at the Sebel, the debonair Gower flew to Hayman Island, a destination on the Great Barrier Reef that cost at least A$300 a night. Knowing Gower, he probably cut a deal with someone, as he was never as careless with money as he was when wafting a bat outside off stump.

Foxy, Geoff Cook and I were also keen to get away, though we opted for the far cheaper option of hiring a log cabin close to Katoomba in the Blue Mountains. That cost us A$30 all in, excluding food and beer, which we purchased from the local supermarket.

It was great fun. Three team-mates, not yet tired of each other's company, out in hick Australia, the part modern touring teams rarely see. The scenery was spectacular, too, the unspoilt vistas gratifyingly empty and made heady by the tangy smell of eucalyptus. As an antidote to the pampered but pressurised bubble of touring it was perfect and we returned with our batteries and belief renewed by the simple life.

Unhappily, it did not improve our lot. The three one-dayers in New Zealand were all lost heavily. Although humiliating, defeat did not put a dampener on any high jinks, such as when Beefy organised a side trip with me, Foxy and Allan Lamb as his running mates. The beano was to Whakatane, ostensibly to play in a charity golf day for Lance Cairns, New Zealand's all-rounder, though the main attraction was a day's deep-sea fishing with him in the Bay of Plenty.

After we'd checked into our hotel Beefy, with irony to the fore, called a team meeting. In it, he told us that he was the manager of this particular trip and that there was only one rule – nobody could go to bed before the manager.

Well, you'd think that after four months' carousing the man would be sated, but no. There we were, the morning before we went fishing, still up at 6 a.m. playing a drinking game that involved skill and snooker cues. At 6.15, with a 7 a.m. pick-up, Beefy announced that we could finally grab a quick half-hour's kip.

My sea legs have never been strong, especially when hung-over, so I spent most of the day dozing below deck, while Beefy and Lamby trolled for fish. A hammerhead shark kept the snorkellers vigilant, but after seven hours of them catching a few middling-size kingfish, everyone was ready for port and a hot shower. At this point I decided to toss in a line and was rewarded with the biggest fish of the day, something that hacked Beefy off no end.

Our winter fun was still not done, though, and while not everyone on the tour chose to take Beefy up on his kind offer to earn US$1,000 on the way back home by playing a match in Sharjah, a fair few did, me included.

The match, a benefit game for Zaheer Abbas, was against Pakistan. Aside from watching a camel race, the only incident of note was a spat in the hotel between Beefy and Javed Miandad and a run-in some of us had with the expats. The first didn't quite come to blows, though it did leave Beefy threatening all kinds of retribution, at least until some of the Pakistan players calmed him down. 'Don't worry, Ian, we hate Javed just as much as you,' said one, though that did not placate Beefy one iota.

On 6 March, we eventually landed back at Heathrow, which meant that we had been away for 147 days. In that time we'd taken 28 flights, attended at least 30 functions, and drunk our own bodyweight in alcohol several times over. If it had been a Club Med holiday it would have been a corker, but it wasn't. It was work and we didn't have much to show for it, having lost the Ashes and both one-day series.

To cap matters off, players were given an end-of-tour report which was sent to their respective counties. Generally, unless there had been a disciplinary issue, it just got filed away with all the other guff generated by the Test and County Cricket Board. Except this time, Doug Insole, acting mostly on information supplied by Bernard Thomas, had got stuck into a few of us.

Foxy, who'd had a fitful tour due to his broken toe, was summoned before Lancashire's chairman to be told that he'd received the worst ever tour report by a Lancashire player representing England. As I'd mostly knocked around on tour with him and Beefy, neither exemplars of sensible behaviour, I was expecting the worst.

Except, nothing happened. No summons, no criticism, not even the odd pointed aside. Only the advice that I should try to add a yard or so to my bowling speed. I suppose Insole, our tour manager, was also chairman of Essex, so had not bothered to write himself a report about me. Instead, it was several years before I got any real indication of the impression I'd created on that tour. When the sobering truth was eventually revealed, it was done so by Willis, a few years after he'd retired.

There the two of us were sharing a drink in Sydney's Bayswater Inn, barely a stone's throw from the Sebel Townhouse of yore. England had been conquering all on their 1986–87 Ashes tour and I was playing Grade cricket in Sydney for Campbelltown. Willis was on holiday seeing friends. The grog was flowing, which is maybe why he decided to offload.

'You and Foxy let me down badly on that tour,' he said, suddenly, apropos of nothing in particular. 'I stuck my neck out for you to be in the squad when others had wanted Trevor Jesty. But you just treated the whole thing as if you were playing for Essex at Ilford.'

He went on, the gist being that playing for England required minimum standards of professionalism which Foxy and I had fallen well short of, especially in our close association with Beefy. The tirade, coming as it did four years after the event, took me by surprise. It was hard to disagree with most of what he was saying, at least on face value. But the next day, after I'd had time to digest his grievances, I began to ponder the extent of where any culpability might lie.

Apart from his captaincy on the field of play, which along with his bowling took a lot out of him, Willis had not really led with a sure touch. As ever, there were mitigating circumstances. With England's management comprising four men, three of them over 57, Willis probably felt overwhelmed. None of the others really offered much in terms of the day-to-day running of the side.

This is not criticism, just explanation. Essentially, though, as callow first-time tourists, Foxy and I, as well as Norman Cowans, were left to our own devices. Although not necessarily a bad thing, being let loose in Australia did mean we were like a pack of Billy Bunters suddenly put in charge of the tuck shop.

Once the press had got on England's case that tour, Big Bob's response was to hole up in his room away from the public gaze. When he did present himself, he made a show of drinking mineral water, though most of us knew he enjoyed a bevvy or two as well.

In his diary of the tour he revealed the realities of captaining England, which he found easier at home, where you spend limited time with the team, than when abroad. There you are with them 24/7, for months on end, with nothing but your room for escape.

'It is impossible to be one of the lads as captain,' he wrote. 'I used to spend a lot of time with the managers of the tours rather than with the players, and it was a bit of a lonely job abroad.'

With Gower doing his own thing most of the time, the senior player that Foxy and I gravitated to for guidance, being always full of energy and up for some adventure, was Beefy, whom we both admired and loved in equal measure.

As a team-mate, Beefy was loyal, generous and great fun. His approach to both cricket and life was always positive. It was just that his methods were idiosyncratic, to say the least. He was, on reflection, probably not the best example to follow unless you were supremely talented, had the utmost faith in those talents and nurtured a strong rebellious streak. But he was never less than compelling in everything he did and he turned impressionable heads as a result, mine among them.

With aspirations to be a match-turning all-rounder myself, I was a willing and sentient follower. I don't regret it either, even if the fallout did cost me a place in England's 1983 World Cup squad, also captained by Willis.

When I look back at that Ashes tour, it was exciting and wild, at least by cricket standards. I am reliably informed that it was not as outrageous as the one to New Zealand which took place the following winter. But I wasn't picked for that – Willis's sacrifice of sticking his neck out on my behalf being a one-tour deal only.

5

ESSEX ALMIGHTY –
THE FLETCHER YEARS

AT THE RISK of sounding over-dramatic, and yet this is a feeling that has grown even stronger with age, I thank my good fortune that I played my county cricket for Essex, a team which possessed players both talented and twisted in equal measure.

The club's philosophy, to play attractive, winning cricket, was the joint enterprise of Doug Insole, Essex's chairman, and the club's captain, Keith Fletcher. So often the bridesmaid in the early- to mid-1970s, especially in the John Player Special League, there was now an added determination about the club to seek glory – which is what most of us played professional cricket for in those days, the living from it being less than modest.

Fletch took over the captaincy from Brian Taylor in 1973 and ran the show until the 1986 season, when he handed over, for the first time, to Graham Gooch. As the move did not coincide with Fletch retiring from playing, it was never a straightforward succession, which meant his influence carried on well into the next decade, first as returning captain and then as an unofficial manager/coach.

The Essex Way, as this philosophy became known, was an approach which, unlike the salary, paid off handsomely. While I was on the Essex staff, between 1978 and 1993, the club won six Championships, three Sunday League titles, one NatWest Trophy and one Refuge Assurance Cup. We also contested five Benson & Hedges finals at Lord's, though only one was victorious.

Without even considering the gross injustice which saw us robbed of the 1989 Championship, after being deducted 25 points for a substandard pitch, that is achievement on a grand scale and one only Middlesex, in terms of Championships (they won five over the same period), can come close to matching during those 15 years.

My happy fate was to be in the right place at the right time, with the right people. Like tributaries feeding into one great river, the Essex dressing room of the late 1970s had the just-ripened super-talents of Graham Gooch and Ken McEwan, plus seasoned performers like John Lever, Ray East, David Acfield, Brian Hardie and Stuart Turner, all being melded and directed by the folksy wisdom of the captain, Keith Fletcher.

I am biased, but to my mind Fletch was the shrewdest leader of his time, and that included the venerable Mike Brearley, the sage of St John's Wood, Middlesex and England. Fletch might never have been able to remember anyone's name, including most in his own team. But he knew how they played, especially Essex's opponents, and set traps accordingly.

His talents were like those of the backwoodsman, sifting clues and spotting telltale signs imperceptible to the rest of us. So when an unfamiliar batsman came in, Fletch would know after just a few balls, having watched his feet, grip and demeanour, where his strengths and weaknesses lay. It wasn't always foolproof, but his assessments were more often right than not.

He also had the respect and love of most he captained. As he pre-dated nearly all of the other players at the club, having been on the staff since 1962, he was seen as a father figure, with all the unquestioning loyalty such a role conferred. The only player who would argue with him or give him much lip was Ray East, though David Acfield, the dressing room's intellectual and deepest thinker, would occasionally challenge his wisdom. Otherwise it was a benevolant dictatorship.

Added to that strong core were the undoubted skills and experience of players like Mike Denness and Norbert Phillip, an all-rounder from Dominica and our second overseas player alongside McEwan. Then there was a group of younger players which included Neil Foster, Alan Lilley, Mike McEvoy, David East and me. By the 1980s, the team's substantial parts had begun to coalesce so effectively as to make it a winning force in all four formats of the game – no mean feat considering the variation between three-day cricket, 55-over Benson & Hedges, 60-over NatWest and the 40-over Sunday League.

With all that talent I failed to make an immediate impact. Essex did not have a particularly enlightened youth policy when I first joined the club in 1978, my gap year before university, which meant a first-team place required proof of excellence rather than potential. Indeed, most of the young uncapped players found the first team pretty much a closed shop unless mass injury struck, which was not often.

For that reason, I had no hesitation in taking a place at Cambridge, where I could enhance not only my cricketing education but also my scholastic one, just in case I decided to make a career out of the former and it ended in tears. When I did win a regular first-team place with Essex, in 1981, they stuck with me until I retired in 1993.

Within the good fortune of playing for Essex lay the even greater serendipity of being taken into the tutelage of John 'JK' Lever and Ray East, the county's most reliable pace bowler and its mercurial left-arm spinner. Although both were left-armers who batted right, the pair were very different characters – JK being calm and considered, Easty volatile and highly strung. If the stereotypes had been accurate, JK should have been the canny spinner, Easty the nasty quick.

Not every callow school-leaver would have relished guidance from such a colourful duo, but I lapped it up. Once, on an early-season away trip to play Leicestershire, the pair took me to a nightclub. The only hindrance was that Essex were playing the next day, so I wasn't sure this was the best way to make a good impression. Imagine my relief, then, when the bouncers told us that we needed jackets to get in. The trouble was, JK had three in the boot of his car, including his latest MCC touring blazer, which I'm sure he made me wear as some kind of social experiment. As he gleefully put it at the time, 'No self-respecting bird is going to fancy someone wearing a jacket with piping on it, especially when it's two sizes too small.' He was not wrong.

Then there was the lost weekend in Yorkshire, when day after day of torrential rain made every major ground in the county unplayable. Scheduled to play a Benson & Hedges qualifier at Harrogate (for which two spare days were set aside back then), followed by a Sunday League match at Bradford, the persistent bad weather turned it into one massive drinking binge, punctuated by some token fitness training in the hotel car park. I'm not sure what the other guests of the Post House at Bramhope thought of our shuttle runs between parked cars, but it was done, mostly, to delay our repair to the Fox and Hounds pub up the hill.

Billeted with Easty, I was saved from some of the worst excesses when he warned me off carousing with him and four Yorkshire players, who set about drinking each other to a standstill once the Sunday League game in Bradford was called off because of a submerged pitch. It was good advice. When Easty reappeared on the Monday, he'd lost his jacket and his wallet had been emptied. He even needed to borrow money for the taxi that had returned him with a stinking hangover and tales of pub lock-ins, 18-hour binges and drinking games so wild that he'd woken on a sofa in Bradford, where someone he'd never met offered him a bacon sandwich.

All this came after a Saturday night in a Leeds nightclub where he, JK and Keith Pont had tried to discover the extent of my capacity for drink. In the dimly lit club, of which my only clear memory was rubbish music and a thick shagpile carpet, they plied me with pint after pint. Now, if the beer had been something decent like

Tetley's or Timothy Taylor's, I'd probably have kept drinking. But whatever it was, my constitution rebelled. So, when they weren't looking, I tipped most of it into the carpet, which did a good job of absorbing it – at least to begin with.

Thinking I was drinking this vile stuff down with impressive enthusiasm, they kept the pints coming. By now, though, the carpet had started to smell like a swamp and feel squishy underfoot. So I moved before they discovered my subterfuge. In the end they gave up on their little game, regaling the rest with tales of my impressive constitution.

When we finally did get to play the B&H qualifier, on the Tuesday, it was a 10-over slog in Middlesbrough, the only place within 70 miles where the rain had stopped long enough to set up stumps. Despite passing all the initiation rites, I didn't make the team. But if that disappointed, so too did losing – Yorkshire's 90 for three off 10 overs proving well beyond our batsmen, who responded rather tamely with 64 for five. It then started to rain again in time for the long journey home.

My first foray to Yorkshire had been quite an adventure, though there was one little twist left as we prepared to head back to Essex.

I'd never met Geoffrey Boycott, at least not properly, but suddenly there he was in our dressing room, being all hail-fellow-well-met.

'Bad luck, Essex,' he said through that lopsided mouth of his. 'It's a shite game when t' world's best opening batsman is pushed down the order t' number seven.'

Of course, to me it had seemed obvious that a 10-over slog would see the ball-strikers promoted over finicky technicians like Boycott. For instance, Mike Denness, our usual opener, had also been demoted.

Mike had never got on with Boycott during their England days, but being a Scotsman with a dry sense of humour, he spotted an opportunity to have a bit of fun with his old adversary.

'Why, Geoffrey, that's the nicest compliment you've ever paid me,' declared Denness. 'The world's best opener. You are kind, thank you.'

'Not you, ----, me,' said Boycott, bluntly, jabbing a finger into his own chest just in case there should be any confusion.

He was not finished, either, and turning to our captain, he asked, 'I'm just off for a net now, Fletch, would young Pringle like to come and bowl at me? He's done bugger all today.'

Well, the cheek of the man, addressing Fletch and not me as if I was a chattel that could be deployed at the whim of two overlords. He even made it sound as if he was doing me a favour. Fortunately, Fletch, not best pleased that we had nothing to show for four wet and booze-sodden days in the West Riding, was in no mood for Boycott's petty agendas.

'---- off, Fiewy,' he retorted (Boycs's nickname among England colleagues was 'Fiery' and Fletch said his R's as W's). 'We're off down the woad. We've spent long enough pwatting awound up here. Go and get your own sodding net bowler.'

The Middlesbrough–Boycott nexus also arose a few years later, this time in 1984. That year, Boycs had been awarded a Testimonial by Yorkshire. One of the highlights, in terms of monies raised, was a match at Acklam Park, the cricket ground where we'd lost that 10-over slog. The game pitted Geoff Boycott's XI against an Invitation XI comprised mostly of Test players. Big sponsors were involved, and because Essex did not have any official cricket sched-uled, five of us – Goochie, JK, Ken McEwan, Norbert 'Nobby' Phillip and me – were invited to play.

Boycott is one of those players who has always divided opinion, though not seemingly among his team-mates. On this occasion the rumour was that he'd upset so many of them over the years that he had to go beyond the county borders to get cricketers to play in his Testimonial games. Whatever the reason, this match required outside help, for which Boycs, or at least the sponsors, were willing to pay £250 a man plus travelling expenses, which suited us despite the long trek north.

The game, 40-overs-a-side in front of a big crowd, went without hitch save in one respect, which left me lucky to collect my fee. It involved Boycott, who having opened, got his team so far behind the run-rate that he was suddenly forced to play a few shots. At his first attempt, against me, he thumped the ball back, whereupon I took a smart one-handed catch of which I was justifiably proud.

'Drop it,' hissed Boycott. 'They've come to watch me not you.'

'Sorry, Mr Boycott,' I said, and held on.

'He must really learn to say please,' I told team-mates as they gathered round to enjoy the irony of Boycs being dismissed while trying to hit out.

On the return journey I travelled with Goochie, while JK took Nobby and Kenny Mac, who had the unlikely experience of being stopped by a police roadblock on the A1 just north of Worksop.

Domestic politics, especially in the raw, rarely impinged on the cocooned lives of cricketers apart from the obvious things like taxes, voting and the price of petrol. But this was a time of clashing ideologies and moral imperatives, and the police had stopped JK to check if he and his passengers were flying pickets sent down from Yorkshire by Arthur Scargill, then President of the National Union of Mineworkers.

Scargill was from the same part of Yorkshire as Boycott, whose father had been a miner. Despite that, Boycott was politically distant from the man locked in a battle royal with Margaret Thatcher, the Prime Minister, for the survival of Britain's coal industry. The miners were not united. Nottinghamshire's pitmen had refused to join the strike, so Scargill had sent those who'd already downed tools in Yorkshire to persuade them otherwise. To counter that, Thatcher had ordered the police to set up roadblocks to prevent them arriving and JK, because his car contained more than two adult men in it, had been stopped. Goochie, with just me on board, had been waved through.

By the end of that summer, 165,000 people had been stopped entering Nottinghamshire as Thatcher and the police played hard-ball. Even so, it took another seven months before Scargill and his NUM eventually voted to go back to work. Meanwhile Boycott topped the Yorkshire batting averages and raised over £130,000 in his Testimonial.

Although the best of mates, nowhere was the difference between my two 'role models', JK and Easty, better exemplified than in how they spent their evening-meal money at away games – a per diem then of about £12, with the captain getting a supplement so he could buy the occasional round of drinks. Breakfast was included in the room tariff.

East, who smoked and drank, would use the allowance to buy beer in the bar of the team hotel (usually a Trust House Forte). His 'meal' would consist of several pints of said drink and half a packet of cigarettes, which he smoked rather than ate. The only solids he consumed were the complimentary peanuts and stuffed olives Trust House hotels provided as bar snacks back then.

Being a good pro, JK was more scientific. As the hardest-working fast bowler in the country (the enormous length of his run-up saw to that), he first needed to rehydrate after a day's play and would head to the nearest decent pub to slake his thirst with at least five pints of ale. When he was satisfied that liquid levels had been replenished, the hunt for the best curry house would commence, whereupon poppadoms, starter and main course, washed down by a few more pints (this time lager), would be downed, before he hooked up with Easty for a nightcap back at the team hotel. The next day JK, his eyes clear and hands steady but sweating a noxious mix of beer fumes and garlic, would be ready for the fray – a man of iron constitution.

Not everyone could do that, which is why the decree issued to players by Fletch – 'I don't care what you get up to of an evening, providing it is legal and you are weady to play cwicket the next morning' – required a measure of self-discipline, or certainly knowing one's limits and constitution.

My own path into and within the team was far from seamless. Selection for England, before I'd really earned it, threw the dynamics of the dressing room, with its system of seniority and earned entitlement, into constitutional chaos.

Essex knew there were other teams after my services, so they had to award me my county cap to keep me at the club, even though I scarcely deserved it. I suppose it looked a bit silly, and possibly humiliating to me, that I'd been capped by country and not county. So, one day, during a match at Chelmsford, Fletch just tossed me an Essex 1st XI cap and two first-team sweaters and, with a minimum of fuss and ceremony (presumably in the hope that the fewer who noticed the better), pronounced me an Essex capped player.

One who did take umbrage was Stuart 'Ted' Turner, a stalwart of the team and someone who'd had two goes at establishing a cricket career. It had taken him six years and at least 50 games for Essex to win his cap, and here was I being handed one after just 20 matches. It proved too much for Ted, who stormed out of the dressing room, slamming the door as he went – Mr Disgusted of Loughton.

I understood where his emotion came from, though not perhaps the need to express it that way. Certainly, his petulance did little to quash the impression that he felt I was a spoilt public-school brat whose route through life had presented few hurdles – a view shared not just by him but by quite a few of the club's supporters. I never could work out where this prejudice came from, as it was not based on fact. Back then, public schools were pretty tough regimes, with punishment and privation as much on the menu as advantage and apple crumble.

Yet, despite my schooling, I'd like to think I won over the Essex faithful, eventually, though I never did become close to Ted, who retired in 1986.

My first nickname at Essex was 'Ignell, a dropped-aitch version of 'Hignell', as in Alastair Hignell, a fine cricketer and rugby player good enough to play full-back for England, who'd been at Cambridge a few years before me. The reason for the moniker was a pre-season dinner at Essex where the playing staff were introduced to the committee by Fletch, something of a challenge for a man with such a poor memory for names.

When he got to me I had to stand and he would then introduce me by name and include a short description of what I did as a cricketer, i.e. seam-bowling all-rounder, a process that should have lasted no more than six seconds. That was the theory at least. Instead, there was an echoing silence that lasted at least as long again as Fletch, grasping for inspiration, stammered, 'This is, er, er . . . this is, er . . . oh yeah, this is 'Ignell, and he's at Cambwidge', the name blurted out only after the sotto voce prompts of those sitting nearby hissing, 'Pringle, Pringle, he's going to Cambridge.' Even then, Fletch had converted 'Pringle' into ''Ignell', the Cambridge association somehow conjuring in his mind a stocky, bearded fellow who batted but did not bowl and who would never be mistaken for me in a police line-up. Inevitably, it brought the house down, which meant that ''Ignell' stuck fast for a while.

Still, at least the name was a rough approximation, which is more than Jack Richards, Surrey's wicketkeeper, got when he was the spare gloveman on England's 1981–82 tour of India, of which Fletch was captain. Upon introducing his squad to Indira Gandhi, then India's Prime Minister, Fletch reached Richards and said, 'This is, um . . . this is . . . er . . . oh yeah, this is Tiddler, he keeps wicket.'

His vagueness over names stood in direct contrast to his acute knowledge of players and how to win cricket matches. I remember

Mike Selvey, a room-mate of Fletch's on England's 1976–77 tour of India under Tony Greig but otherwise an opponent, mostly for Middlesex, giving his take on Fletch's unique qualities as a captain.

'Just when you thought the game might be drifting Fletch would move a man, make a bowling change, and gradually harry and hustle the batsmen into making mistakes,' said Selvey. 'It was almost imperceptible, yet at the same time you were left in no doubt that something was going on and that there was not much you could do about it. Fletch was a master at creating a bit of pressure from nowhere and even better at maintaining it until something gave way, usually the other team.'

For Essex players, those talents were tangible on a daily basis. One example, in 1986, came when we were playing Yorkshire on a typically sluggish pitch at Chelmsford. As was often the case in English conditions, line and length had been paying dividends, thanks to occasional movement off the seam.

Having nipped one back through the gate to bowl Neil Hartley, I was ready to try to replicate the ball to David Bairstow, next man in at six. Instead of a banal 'Come on, 'Ignell, let's have another,' up marches Fletch to deliver a more bespoke message.

Although he'd handed the captaincy over to Goochie that year, Fletch still had heft. 'Flooch' is what journalist Matthew Engel dubbed it, the conflation and collaboration of Gooch and Fletcher which essentially ran Essex cricket between 1986 and 1988.

'Don't bowl a single ball in his half for the west of this over, do you hear?' said Fletch. 'Not one ruddy ball.'

So I didn't, banging it in hard and short. Two balls later, hey presto, Bairstow was back in the pavilion for a duck, having fended a bouncer straight to Brian Hardie at short leg.

There are countless other examples, not all of them highlighted in the MCC coaching manual. For instance, whenever Alvin Kallicharran came to the crease for Warwickshire, Fletch would position himself close to the bat so he could sledge him – loud enough for the batsman to hear but not the umpire. A brilliant strokeplayer, who could destroy attacks with his ability to pull bowlers off a good length, Kalli was nonetheless susceptible to a bit of chirp, at least that was Fletch's theory. It must have worked. In 22 first-class innings against Essex he averaged 29.61 and made just one hundred and two fifties. It was his second-worst average against counties after Middlesex, against whom he averaged 28.45.

Even that hundred, made at Ilford's Valentine's Park in early June 1984, didn't hurt us, though perhaps it should have done. Having put Warwickshire in to bat, we ought to have been annihilated, having followed on 220 runs behind after being dismissed for 114 in our first innings. But, typical of our bravado, we batted much better second time around and, led by a fine 97 from Ken McEwan, our South African overseas player, we managed to make 374. That left Warwickshire needing 155 to win on a pitch not offering much except some slow turn.

I had never really seen the contagion of doubt that can infect teams when wickets start falling, but when John Lever whipped out both Andy Lloyd and Kallicharran in his second over, the latter for a duck, you could sense blind panic beginning to spread through Warwickshire's batsmen. They managed a brief rally through Dennis Amiss and Geoff Humpage, who made 26 and 32 respectively, but the others just seemed fearful and resigned to their fate.

JK and I finished with four wickets apiece, while David Acfield snaffled the other two, including the formidable Amiss. It was an incredible win and one which enhanced our reputation as a side who could pull off the improbable, with style. It also bolstered our belief, as reigning county champions, that we could defend our title. After that win, with the empowering feelings of indomitability that it brought, we lost just a single Championship match over the remaining four months of the season.

ESSEX V WARWICKSHIRE
(County Championship)

Played at Valentine's Park, Ilford, 9–12 June 1984

Umpires: WE Alley & B Dudleston
Toss: Essex

WARWICKSHIRE

PA Smith	c Gladwin b Lever	22	(2)	c Fletcher b Acfield	26
TA Lloyd	run out	72	(1)	c East b Lever	4
AI Kallicharran	c East b Lever	100		b Lever	0
DL Amiss	lbw b Lever	7		b Acfield	24
GW Humpage†	lbw b Pringle	21		c Lever b Pringle	32
Asif Din	lbw b Foster	0		c McEwan b Lever	1
AM Ferreira	c East b Foster	36	(8)	lbw b Pringle	11
CM Old	b Lever	43	(7)	lbw b Lever	4
GC Small	lbw b Lever	12		c East b Pringle	0
N Gifford	b Gooch	1		c Gooch b Pringle	0
RGD Willis*	not out	4		not out	4
Extras	(4 b, 9 lb, 2 nb, 1 w)	16		(2 b, 9 lb, 2 nb)	13
Total	(109.1 overs)	**334**		(46.1 overs)	**119**

ESSEX

GA Gooch	c Asif Din b Old	21	b Gifford	54
C Gladwin	lbw b Willis	4	lbw b Gifford	92
KWR Fletcher*	c Amiss b Ferreira	28	lbw b Ferreira	12
KS McEwan	c Humpage b Old	4	lbw b Ferreira	97
BR Hardie	lbw b Gifford	30	lbw b Small	0
DR Pringle	b Ferreira	8	lbw b Willis	25
PJ Prichard	lbw b Ferreira	5	b Small	31
DE East†	c Humpage b Ferreira	5	b Smith	6
NA Foster	c Smith b Gifford	0	c Smith b Gifford	25
JK Lever	c Lloyd b Gifford	0	not out	1
DL Acfield	not out	0	c Humpage b Gifford	0
Extras	(8 lb, 1 nb)	9	(2 b, 4 lb, 25 nb)	31
Total	(48.2 overs)	**114**	(following on, 120 overs)	**374**

ESSEX	O	M	R	W	O	M	R	W
Lever	30	6	89	5	17	3	46	4
Foster	23	5	66	2	6	1	17	0
Pringle	21	6	72	1	6.1	1	13	4
Acfield	26	7	68	0	17	4	30	2
Gooch	9.1	3	23	1				

WARKS	O	M	R	W	O	M	R	W
Willis	11	4	29	1	14	4	28	1
Old	17	10	26	2	4	1	20	0
Ferreira	13.2	2	44	4	24	7	71	2
Gifford	7	3	6	3	47	9	144	4
Small					22	5	49	2
Smith					9	3	31	1

Fall of wickets:

	War	Ess	Ess	War
1st	33	12	99	6
2nd	57	34	120	6
3rd	94	44	183	58
4th	140	70	190	59
5th	149	100	268	64
6th	208	108	317	68
7th	307	110	332	100
8th	329	110	366	102
9th	330	110	374	102
10th	334	114	374	119

Close of play: Day 1: Essex (1) 3–0 (Gooch 0*, Gladwin 2*)
                Day 2: Essex (2) 249–4 (McEwan 54*, Pringle 20*)

Result: **Essex won by 35 runs**

Just as well. We only pipped Nottinghamshire to the pennant by 14 points, the uncertainty going right down to the last over of the season, when Clive Rice's team fell four runs short of chasing the 297 set them by Ian Botham. A win over Somerset at Taunton would have seen Notts crowned champions by two points.

Our final match, against Lancashire, had been concluded in our favour in two days. So the team repaired to the County Ground at Chelmsford in anticipation of a second successive Championship win. There, in the relative comfort of the members' lounge, we listened to the denouement of Nottinghamshire's match against Somerset on a transistor radio.

It made for agonising listening as Notts' last-wicket pair of Mike 'Noddy' Bore and Andy Pick inched their team closer until, with two balls remaining, they needed just four runs off left-arm spinner Stephen Booth.

For some, like Fletch and Stuart Turner, the tension was too much and they left the room to walk their anxieties around. They weren't gone for long. With glory in sight, Bore went for the big hit and perished, caught on the boundary by 12th man Richard Ollis, leaving Somerset as winners of the match and Essex as winners of the Championship.

Cheers and champagne corks rang out, but we couldn't get too drunk. None of us lived in Chelmsford and the county's largesse didn't extend to getting us hotel rooms for the night.

Although we came to rely on our brilliant captain to give us an edge, not all Fletch ploys hit the jackpot. Against Somerset in 1985, he played a cat-and-mouse game with Ian Botham, then in the batting form of his life. Striking sixes almost at will (he set a Somerset record that season with 80 of them, despite playing only half the games because of England commitments), Beefy was dared, goaded almost, with an in/out field (a few close fielders but with most on the boundary), to keep up his six-hitting against Essex's bowlers.

'Tell Fletch I'm not going to fall for it,' said Beefy to Graham Gooch, the vice-captain and one of about three fielders within earshot as Fletch sought to cut off his boundary options.

He was true to his word, too, using clever deflections behind the wicket to score fours and beat Fletch's trap, as he made 152 from 121 balls. Despite that, Beefy only struck four sixes in that innings, a lowly 15.7 per cent of his runs, so Fletch could rightfully claim a sliver of success for his tactic, especially as Essex went on to win the match.

Every season Fletcher would look at the fixture list and surmise that Essex would probably need 12 or 13 victories to clinch the County Championship title. He'd then begin to identify, bad weather notwithstanding, where and against whom they might eventuate.

He would also predict, broadly, how we might clinch those matches: 'JK will win us four with the ball; Goochie four with the bat; the other bowlers and batsmen a couple each,' he used to say. It was a reductive approach, and ridiculously facile for such a complex game, but it was uncanny how often his gnomic prophecies were proved correct.

He'd also keep a blacklist, in his mind, of those opposition captains who would rather settle for a dull draw, should rain reduce playing time, than risk much through creative declarations. I can remember once, after a good win at Chelmsford, Fletch asking who we had next. 'Warwickshire away,' someone piped up. 'Oh lawd,' said Fletch, 'bloody Giff [Norman Gifford] is their captain now, isn't he? Mr Bloody Negative. He never wants to play a game unless evewything's in his favour. Mind you, nor does that other bloke down the road at Worcester, Phil "Not bloody intewested" Neale. They're a wight pair, those two. We'd better hope for no wain intew-wuptions when we play them.'

You see, with no points for the draw, Fletch was prepared to risk everything for the win – well, almost everything. Obviously, he'd be cagier against teams he expected to be pushing for honours with us at the end of the season, and he never set opponents a target if he didn't think there were enough overs left for us to bowl them out. But he was savvy at reading pitches and bolder than most, working on much slimmer margins when setting or chasing a target. Essentially, Fletch backed his players to rise to the challenges of three-day cricket, which often involved personal sacrifice, especially when weather reduced the game's span. Mostly, though, he'd take risks to win. As a result, Essex gained a reputation for audacious cricket, exciting cricket supporters wherever they went.

Those early Championship title wins were essentially built on a template of destructive batting from Gooch and Ken McEwan, and fine, penetrative bowling from Lever, with East and Acfield cleaning up whenever pitches turned. Others would chip in as necessary. There was no coach, no gym, no indoor nets, no standalone outdoor nets, no psychologists; just a scorer, a physio and a captain who dared his team to win, no matter the circumstance.

Bowlers who took wickets quickly, which meant they were either express or moved the ball laterally, were key, and in Lever we had arguably the greatest in county cricket. It was a status hard won by JK, through stamina, swing – and not being an England regular, at least not for home Tests. They say one man does not make a team, but Essex were certainly blessed to have him. And while the wickets he took for the county with his medium-fast swingers can be measured – 2,396 across all first-team formats – what is not so easily calculated is the psychological wellbeing felt by the team whenever JK was in it. Aside from the potency he provided with the ball, his cheery attitude and gentle wisdom were like a comfort blanket, and Essex were more prone to the jitters without him. Thankfully, in the

1980s that was not often, his fitness record being as reliably robust as his bowling.

It is easier to play the game with a smile when you are supremely good at it, and JK rarely failed to see the fun, however taut the situation. While others would eff and blind with anger or frustration, the worst he was driven to by poor fielding or ropey umpiring was a quick shake of the head and, occasionally, an audible exhalation of breath.

Otherwise, it was back to his mark in the deep blue yonder and then, with that pitter-patter of steps which gradually lengthened into an athlete's stride and the easy rhythm swing bowlers need to get the ball moving sideways, he'd chalk up another of the 112,000-odd deliveries he sent down for Essex.

That swing, mostly in to right-handers but also, with a subtle repositioning of the shine and wrist angle, away from them as well, was the main source of his potency. That, and the ability to bowl at least three telling spells a day with scarcely a reduction in pace.

Bowling is really a function of geometry. For those of left-arm persuasion like JK, swinging the ball back into right-handers achieves the perfect alignment for lbws under the Laws. When left-armers start hooping it, any batsman not confident of adjusting his feet late and playing the ball even later becomes a nervous nellie. When he got it right, which was most of the time, JK's booming swingers possessed a Pythagorean purity, and umpires' fingers loosened as a result.

JK always joked that he got far more lbws than he probably deserved, and maybe he did, but he was such a popular figure in the game that few begrudged him them, not even the departing batsman. He worked the umpires too, not in the aggressive, cynical way Shane Warne used to do during his career, but through politeness. Most in the county game thought JK a gent, and umpires, former players almost to a man back then, were no exception.

While the rest of us would have our run-ins with white-coated authority, JK would be all charm and smiles, and the lbws racked up accordingly. You'd have thought that we might have learnt from his example, but he competed with a calmness that seemed to elude the rest of us.

Players considered to be a 'captain's dream' are mostly mythical beasts existing in the minds of fantasists, yet JK managed to embody it for Essex. Whatever the situation on the field, Fletch or Goochie, the former's successor as Essex captain, could rely on him to provide high-quality bowling. Need a wicket, whistle up JK. Need to keep it tight for 40 minutes, bring on JK. Need some yorkers at the death, give the ball to JK. He was a bowling everyman with the endurance to match. On the rare occasions Easty or John Childs were injured or not selected, he'd even turn his hand to left-arm spin, though not, it has to be said, with much success.

He rarely failed to deliver, especially when the pressure was on. I say rarely. There was the occasion at Lord's in the 1989 Benson & Hedges Cup final when his failure to supply the 'perfect' yorker cost Essex the match, after Nottinghamshire required four runs to win off the last ball and got them. Few realise how intense the pressure is in those situations, and that even someone with JK's experience and talent is not immune. The slightest tension in any part of the body can send the ball where it is not intended, and JK's final delivery, only a matter of inches from being blockhole on leg stump, was awry enough for Eddie Hemmings, a man who had made 95 in that Ashes Test in 1983, to have room to slice it past point for four.

Ever the team man, JK was contrite beyond measure, which was entirely in keeping, but unnecessary for someone who had given himself so often and so selflessly to the cause. I don't know whether he had already made his mind up to retire that season, but that moment seemed to seal matters. Two months later he finally called it a day.

Before that, it is not too far-fetched to say that he carried Essex's bowling for the decade between 1977 and 1987. The county certainly based much of their strategy around him. So valuable was JK, especially when it was swinging, that Fletch once sent the entire team after play (bar JK) to go and look for a ball that Imran Khan had hit over the east wall at Hove in 1983. Before it had been lost, JK had been swinging it round corners, while its replacement had not moved off the straight. We found it too, in someone's back garden, and next morning normal service was resumed, with JK running through Sussex, to finish with seven for 55 as Essex prevailed by an innings and 53 runs.

Essex won the County Championship four times during JK's career. On three of those occasions – 1979, 1983 and 1984 – he took over 100 first-class wickets during the season. Only in 1986 did Essex win the title without him being the club's leading wicket-taker, his 58 victims eclipsed on that occasion by both Neil Foster and John Childs. Essex's fortunes, especially in the longer game, were closely linked to JK's fitness and form. In 1987, for example, with knee problems limiting his appearances, he took just 26 wickets at 34, his worst haul since becoming established in the side two decades earlier. As a result Essex finished 12th in the table, their lowest position for 13 years.

The public, especially Essex supporters, loved and appreciated him, yet his on-field heroics were only part of the allure. Fun-loving, stoic, selfless and a coper by nature, he was the ideal companion in a small hunter-gatherer group like a cricket team. Today's coaches talk about having leaders throughout the team, and while JK never sought any office higher than senior pro, his deeds and words oozed authority and commitment.

Serious when it mattered, he also possessed a levity when the moment allowed, like the time he bowled a gentle full toss first ball after tea, with an orange. Not being forewarned, John Hopkins, the

Glamorgan batsman, struck it with relish for what he thought was an easy boundary, his disappointment palpable when instead of four runs, four pips slid from his bat.

Another time, when a final batting point looked beyond Essex in a Championship match against Kent, JK shouldered arms to a straight one from Graham Dilley and lost his middle stump. It was simple, he said, when I asked him whether he had lost sight of the ball. Although he didn't like Kent, he liked Dill and felt, as part of the fast bowlers' union, that he deserved another wicket.

While a respecter of authority, JK was no yes-man, but he was not a rebel either, save for when he decamped to South Africa in 1982 to join other England players for an illicit series against South Africa. A three-year ban from playing for England ensued, with huge benefits for Essex after international duty proved no longer a distraction.

If he disagreed with his captain's tactics he'd debate the subject, sometimes urgently, but always with respect. His advice, too, especially to lesser mortals, was always considered and never less than helpful. He'd factor in skill levels too, so whereas Ian Botham might say to an incoming batsman, 'If Lillee drops short, just hook him for six,' expecting others to do as he would, JK's advice would be more tailored.

In 1986, JK and I played for England together, at Headingley, after the selectors picked him for the second Test against India, at the grand old age of 37. He took six wickets in the match while I took seven, albeit in a losing cause.

Before the match he was his usual calm self, except for his insistence that I wake him early on the first morning and allow him to travel with me to the ground. When I asked why, he said he'd once missed the start of a Test at Trent Bridge after he'd overslept, a massive faux pas, compounded by him getting lost around Nottingham's one-way system. Although he knew he was to be 12th man on that occasion, the public did not, and he recounted his acute embarrassment when other motorists caught in the traffic began tut-tutting at him and pointing to their watches. In those days most players drove sponsored cars with their names displayed on the bodywork, so arriving incognito was impossible.

Ordinarily, such tardiness would have attracted a big fine from the team enforcer, Bernard Thomas. But JK escaped censure, his standing as the paragon of team-mates placing him almost on the same rung as sainthood. In any case, saints get martyred, not fined by the physio.

Most people find it impossible to believe that we had no coaches at Essex during the Fletcher years. It meant that players, albeit with recourse to the wisdom of experienced cricketers like JK and even Fletch himself, largely had to work out any problems for themselves.

We'd also discuss opponents and watch closely how they did things, especially opposition bowlers. I remember JK and I experimenting in the nets, and occasionally in the middle, with what we had come to believe were the techniques required for reverse-swing – a recent phenomenon which had almost acquired the power of voodoo.

It was in 1984, so this was an early incarnation of reverse-swing, as practised to great effect at the time by the so-called 'doctor of swing', Pakistan's Sarfraz Nawaz, who also played for Northamptonshire. Sarfraz guarded his methods closely, and while there has always been a question for some over whether the 'doctor' referred to was verb or noun, he was able to get balls in unpromising states of wear and tear to swing – which to bowlers like JK and me was genius.

Sarfraz only ever allowed his team-mates the bare minimum of information on how to achieve this reverse-swing, swearing them to secrecy. But these things leak out in unguarded moments, usually over drink, and it wasn't long before JK and I were trying the various techniques we'd gleaned from various bar-room conversations, not all of them strictly within the game's Laws.

It was only a minor eureka moment, as we didn't have all the information or know-how necessary to guarantee success every time. For instance, one of the methods we'd heard about was to wet the ball thoroughly on one side with spittle, while allowing the other to roughen but stay dry (both legal). That was the method we used against Middlesex during a three-day county match at Lord's in early August 1984.

Frustration drove us to try it. Middlesex had reached 186 for two before it suddenly started to work, though ironically not for JK. Indeed, it didn't really work for any of our bowlers except for me and Goochie. But swing it did, and from cruising along in control, Middlesex lost their last seven wickets for 143 runs, me finishing with a devilish six for 66, Goochie with two for 16. We went on to win the game, though that was more to do with Goochie hammering an incredible unbeaten 105 as we chased down 214 in 31.4 overs late on the third afternoon. Wetting the ball like that, with the other side kept rough and dry, was legal but it wasn't foolproof, and that match at Lord's was about the only occasion when some of us had notable success with it.

Another method was to lift up the quarter seam on one side of the ball, so that it acted like a rudder, something which had to be hidden from the umpires due to its illegality. That way was also capricious, working better on some occasions than others. One instance where it did hoop about was in Essex's match against Australia at Chelmsford in 1985. On a slow, benign pitch, I decided to lift the seam to see what might happen – with immediate reward. The ball started to swing, a lot, albeit one way only (in to the right-hander). Mostly, though, I was bowling to the left-handed Greg

Matthews, and he could not lay a bat on it. Once again, Gooch and I were the main beneficiaries among the bowlers, finishing with four wickets apiece.

Reverse-swing didn't claim all the wickets we took. For instance, the last few had to be taken with another ball after John Hampshire, the umpire, changed it after suspected ball-tampering. A former England player, Hampshire's suspicions had been raised when the ball, having done not very much for 50 overs, suddenly began to swing. He discovered how we had achieved it after a dozy team-mate forgot to flatten down the quarter seam once the ball had gone through to the keeper. Hampshire asked to see it, saw the flap standing up like a stegosaurus's backpack and promptly changed it.

For some reason which I have never been able to fathom, ball-tampering is seen as the devil's doing, a sin without redemption. After the day's play, Gooch, who was acting captain in Fletch's absence, was summoned to the umpire's room for a 'chat'. The umpires then came with him to our dressing room to explain why the ball had been changed. Gooch asked the miscreant to reveal himself. We all looked at our feet in silence.

Swing bowling is a fickle, will-o'-the-wisp phenomenon, present one minute and gone the next. There are two types, traditional and reverse, though each is achieved by very different means. Traditional swing, which needs a good seam and shine on at least one side of the ball, demands that most of the technique goes into the action, specifically the wrist. In the case of reverse-swing, most of the technique goes into preparing the ball, which can flirt with the Laws of cricket depending on how patient, or not, the bowler is to gain it.

JK was primarily a traditional swinger. As such he'd emphasise the importance of keeping a strong, upright wrist, behind the ball, so that it stayed with its seam upright during flight. At the micro-level, traditional swing relies on the ball having a gyroscopic

Re
Bc
ne
of
th

M·
Ca

Coming right up. Pulling a pint of Suggs' Ale at Colchester's Hospital Arms pub. With most Essex players partial to proper beer, this one had been specially brewed by Mauldons for my Benefit year.

My maiden wicket in my first over of Test cricket, 1982. The ball nipped down the Lord's slope and umpire David Evans sent India's Yashpal Sharma on his way.

These boots are made for bowling. I'd customise footwear with a scalpel to ease the pressure on my big toes, which took a battering.

Unique sequence of Terry Alderman chasing, tackling and then fighting a pitch invader at the WACA during the 1st Test of the 1982–83 Ashes. Alderman dislocated a shoulder and was out for 18 months.

The sailor's life. Me at the helm of *Australia II* during sea trials off Fremantle, 1982, with Derek Randall and Bob Taylor astern. A year on, the Alan Bond-sponsored yacht ended the USA's 132-year monopoly of the America's Cup.

Punks and Hell's Angels. Ian 'Gunner' Gould and me at the players' Christmas party in Melbourne on the 1982–83 Ashes tour. Back then, fancy dress and players performing sketches were a tradition.

Phil Edmonds could be awkward and brilliant, often in the same breath, but I found him engaging company during our few games together with England.

Malcolm Marshall was simply the best bowler I played against. Whether for Hampshire or West Indies, Macco bowled with unflagging pace and precision. A supreme athlete, his premature death, at 41, came as a shock to all.

Derek Randall on the England B tour of Sri Lanka in 1985–86. Hyperactive and slightly barmy, Randall was a superb batsman and fielder, a free spirit on and off the pitch.

Glad I remembered the deodorant. Bowling at Lord's against Pakistan in 1982, a Test we lost by 10 wickets.

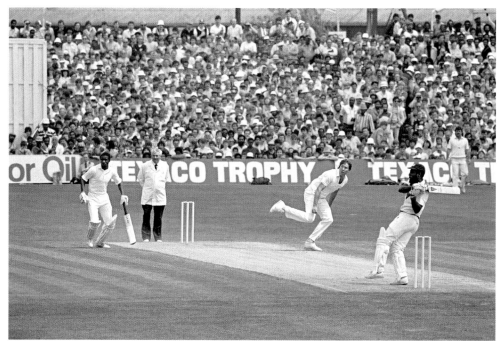

'Toast and jam' – what Viv Richards said to bowlers who dropped short to him, as I did here at Old Trafford in 1984. Viv feasted well that day, making an unbeaten 189, then a world record for ODIs. Eldine Baptiste is the non-striker.

Full house. England v Australia in the 1987 World Cup final at Kolkata's Eden Gardens, which we lost by seven runs. Though also finalists in 1979 and 1992, England have yet to win the trophy.

stability. This is achieved by it backwards-rotating as it travels towards the batsman.

That may sound counter-intuitive, but the backspin helps to keep the seam upright, which in turn dictates the aerodynamics that drives traditional swing – a complicated combination of scientific laws, which include such phenomena as turbulent and laminar airflow, as well as tripped boundary layers. Most swing bowlers don't understand it or think deeply about it – it just comes naturally, or not. Positioning the ball and getting it to behave in a way so as to command those forces requires a lot of skill. It also gives the bowlers so blessed a great feeling of power when it works, though that can be as short-lived as the swing achieved.

For a right-arm bowler like me to bowl an outswinger to a right-hander, the shiny side of the ball would face to the right while the seam would be canted towards second slip. To produce an inswinger, the shiny side would be on the left with the seam angled towards long leg. A higher arm action can also be used to exaggerate the inswinger, though the more eagle-eyed batsmen would spot that. While swing is a great weapon for any bowler to have, the element of surprise, or unpredictability, is even greater.

Even when you possess the means, the precision required for conventional swing is almost surgical, which is why those bowling at high pace (above 87 mph) rarely achieve it. Instead of keeping their wrists cocked and upright to maintain an upright seam, they tend to flick them forward to help generate the extra velocity.

Such need for exactness also explains why swing bowlers don't always get the ball to move sideways through the air. Their arm action or wrist only has to be a fraction out of kilter for the ball to wobble off its axis and go gun-barrel straight.

Balls are also fickle, swinging one moment, then not the next. In the 1980s teams began to be allowed to pick their own balls, not only for each match, but which brand they wanted to use that season. During my first-class career, I encountered Dukes, Readers, Tworts and Surridges. Some, like the Reader, were felt to swing more than others, though that did not mean all teams opted for them.

Before a county match, home or away, the umpires would give you two boxes with six balls of the same brand in each, from which to make your choice – the team fielding first getting first dibs. There would be a set of callipers provided so you could judge the relative sizes of the balls. All were meant to pass through one calliper but not the other. English balls, though, are handmade, so natural variation exists.

JK and I used to be tasked with picking Essex's ball and we'd always go for the smallest, darkest one available. We believed, and this was not based on anything scientific, that the smallest ones swung more. They certainly felt better in the hand, which was probably the point. Although most who picked balls for their teams felt this to be the case, Kapil Dev, India's star swing bowler, did not. He'd pick the biggest ball, his theory being that it was less likely to beat the bat if it moved than a smaller ball. While his reasoning had a certain logic, it was not one that appealed to most bowlers of the era.

Some reckon atmospheric conditions play a part in swing, though if they do it is not yet clearly understood. Certainly bowlers feel that still, humid conditions will aid swing, while gusty days negate it. If the air felt close you'd get a chorus of: 'Ooh, feels like a swinging day.' Yet scientists who've conducted wind-tunnel experiments reckon there is no link between raised humidity and increased swing, which shows there are still unexplained mysteries out there.

Most bowlers who swung the ball conventionally back then had their own pet theory as to why it worked some days and not others. Imran Khan felt that grounds surrounded by trees enabled swing. So not Hove, Imran's home ground when he played for Sussex, or

The Oval, or Old Trafford. But certainly places like Worcester's New Road and Chesterfield. Nowadays, the theory is that big structures make it swing, the addition of new stands and a sponsor's block at Trent Bridge turning it into a ground where swingers now find it almost impossible to bowl a straight ball.

Reverse-swing does not require such technical rigour with hand or bowling action, but it does require some sophistication and know-how in preparing the ball. An early and unreliable incarnation of how to reverse-swing has already been mentioned. A more surefire way requires the ball to be smooth and slightly clammy on one side, with a reasonable shine. The other side is then allowed to become worn and pitted, but must remain scrupulously dry.

The teams most proficient at achieving this, such as Pakistan, who were the first to harness it to great effect, tend to rely on sweat not spit to prepare the smooth side. To roughen the ball on the other side, or at least to hasten the effects of natural wear and tear, fielders often throw it in short of the wicketkeeper. It usually takes about 30 to 40 overs for the ball to become ready for reverse-swing, legally, though international umpires have begun to clamp down on teams who persistently throw the ball in on the bounce.

Before the methods of achieving reverse-swing were widely known, some would attempt to accelerate the process by means that were mostly foul. Imran, Pakistan's World Cup-winning captain, has admitted to using a bottle-top he kept in his pocket to hasten the roughening process. Cricket-ball leather is tough, so quick fixes tend to be drastic, such as the occasion when Chris Pringle, a pace bowler for New Zealand, also used a bottle-top to lacerate one side of the ball during a Test against Pakistan in 1990. It worked, too: he took seven for 52.

Essex's reliance on JK, and therefore traditional swing, meant the team was well versed in looking after the ball well. One of the ways we'd do that was to use Lipice (a brand of lip balm) to help shine up the ball. In those days of three-day matches, teams only got one ball per 100 overs and needed to look after it, something Fletch drummed into every one of us, ten times over. Lipice had become the ball-preserver of choice after Bob Massie had swung England to defeat at Lord's in 1972, when the Australian took 16 wickets for 137. Accusations that he'd used the stuff arose on the back of that incredible performance, though they were never proven. Even so, swing bowlers everywhere took note and Essex were not alone in buying it in bulk.

Most of us would put some on our lips, while a few specially designated team members, including Fletch himself, would stripe up their upper sleeve with it. It would need a particularly violent strokeplayer like Viv Richards to play a long innings, or a very dry pitch and outfield, to ever stop an Essex ball retaining its shine throughout the innings. If the Laws were broken, the umpires, most of them ex-players, might occasionally tut-tut the practice, but generally they turned a blind eye. It was only when TV cameras and stump microphones were able to get in close and personal, and expose the chicanery for all to see, that umpires suddenly had to become policemen as well.

Essex often pushed up against the invisible line now delineated by that woolly concept known as the 'Spirit of Cricket'. For hardened pros, such fanciful concepts were for the birds, especially in an age when cricketers were paid a pittance. As such, it came low down in our order of priorities. For Fletch and the Essex team, the equation was simple – to earn more, we needed to win matches and, by extension, competitions, as that way lay prize money and bonuses. It was a perpetual struggle, and he would occasionally push the boundaries of acceptability in order to prevail.

One ruse, used on pitches beginning to break up, was for the batsmen to wear long spikes in order to facilitate the process. This was only done if Essex, who always had excellent spinners in the

1970s and 1980s, were in the ascendancy and batting third rather than last. It wasn't legal, and in a Championship match against Kent at Canterbury in 1981, John Lever, wearing his bowling boots for added effect, was warned by umpire Bill Alley after he'd dragged his feet straight down the middle of the pitch. A fine former cricketer himself, Alley was not fooled by Lever's excuse that he was using his feet to combat Kent's spinner, who was of course Derek Underwood.

'You can't do that, JK,' said Alley.

'Sorry, Bill,' answered JK, 'I already have.'

There was no censure available to Alley apart from ticking Lever off, and that was seen by players as unavoidable collateral in the dogged pursuit of victory. JK's blatant gamesmanship didn't prevent Alley giving left-arm spinner Ray East two lbws as Essex romped home by 140 runs. In the kind of result you don't often see these days, now that most pitches possess a high loam content which does not disintegrate, Essex's spin twins East and Acfield took all 20 of the Kent wickets – the split falling 11–9 in favour of off-spinner Acfield.

For all his brilliance and pragmatic solutions, Fletch was not immune to doubt or nerves. Although at his best when in the thick of it, he used to get the wobbles during Essex run-chases in one-day cricket, especially if he was already out and stuck watching helplessly from the sidelines. Actually, he couldn't watch, not if it was getting close. On those occasions, he would lock himself in the lavatory but demand up-to-date bulletins, which were then relayed to him by the 12th man through the locked door. If a wicket fell, he might pop out quickly to relay instructions to the ingoing batsman, but otherwise he couldn't bear to see what was going on – Essex's propensity to mess up run-chases being legend. It is why, in limited overs cricket, we generally liked to bat first, another departure from modern trends.

*   *   *

Essex had three overseas players in the Fletcher sides of the 1980s. They were Ken McEwan, a stylish batsman from South Africa who'd ventured to England in the 1970s; Norbert Phillip, an all-rounder from Dominica; and the Australian captain, Allan Border, one of the greatest batsmen to have graced the game.

McEwan, or Forty-foot Fred as he was sometimes known, for reasons I never discerned (it was a reference to snakes, apparently), was hugely popular, being both modest and quietly spoken, two characteristics against type for most South African sportsmen of the age. Those traits meant he had a strong affinity with Gooch, a similarly undemonstrative presence in one of the more colourful and crazed dressing rooms.

Neither was shy or less than forthcoming with bat in hand, however, and together their aggressive strokeplay provided the impetus around which Essex's game plan of quick scoring revolved. If they failed, which wasn't all that often, the less gifted were there to do the rebuilding. If everyone went quickly, you still knew it was game on, as there was obviously something in the pitch for the bowlers, and Essex's attack were good at getting much from little.

With bat in hand, McEwan was a marvel to watch. While Essex's bowlers would towel themselves down quickly in order to be ready to watch Gooch take on the opening bowlers, with its promise of fireworks, there was a languid ease to McEwan's batting that made even the oldest toms in the team purr with pleasure. Enjoying him was best done from a comfortable chair. Like David Gower, his grace with the bat sometimes made him seem too nonchalant, to the point where some dismissals looked the result of carelessness. But Kenny Mac cared deeply for this motley bunch he played his cricket with; he just didn't need to throw bats and dressing-room fits to show it.

One memorable innings was the 178 he made at Derby in 1983. The home side had been rolled for 92 on a spicy pitch which continued to favour the bowlers. Only four people got into double figures for Essex, one of them Goochie, who made 83. But McEwan was just another class that day, scattering Derbyshire's pace attack and its sole spinner, Dallas Moir, to all parts of the Racecourse Ground.

He was also particularly severe on Ole Mortensen, Derbyshire's Danish fast bowler, a big, expressive man known as Stan, after the England and Blackpool centre forward from the 1950s, Stan Mortensen. Stan was a bowler whose success, or lack of it, could be measured in outbursts of noise. From the 'oohs' and 'aahs' that issued forth from the great Dane, a blind person might have been forgiven for thinking that Mortensen had been getting the better of McEwan and beating him all ends up. Anyone with clear sight, though, would have seen a very different picture, the reality being that instead of beating the edge, the ball kept whistling to the boundary. When Mortensen finally got his man, caught at deep square leg going for another six, the triumphant bellow he emitted – a futile blast given Essex went on to win by an innings and 25 runs – could be heard in Matlock.

Ken's effortless ease when batting made him very popular with Essex supporters, which had its perks, at least for him. One couple, Maurice and Elaine Berkeley, a retired High Court judge and his wife, felt him so wonderful and his batting so aesthetically pleasing on the eye that they invited him out to dinner at every away match they attended, which was most. Although this might not have been everyone's idea of a rip-roaring night out, Ken never wavered in accepting their hospitality, which they also occasionally extended to Fletch, Goochie and Ackers. You see, although good manners in accepting their invitation would have come into it for Ken, it was also a way of saving on the meal allowance. Despite his popularity and easy-going nature, Ken was always getting stick for being tight. It must have been those Scottish forebears.

I was invited to dinner by Maurice and Elaine, once, but was obviously considered too boorish and not up to snuff enough to be asked back. But unlike Gooch, whose faux pas saw him end up with his nose in the soup, at least I'd managed to stay awake during the meal.

Ken, who retired at the end of the 1985 season to take over his parents' dairy farm in South Africa, did leave an unintended legacy in his naming of the 'Mole Hole' at Chelmsford. A small hut with equally small outside area, the Mole Hole was where the players' wives, girlfriends and children would congregate to gossip and drink Pinot Grigio, which they would have to bring themselves. Ken had played a season for Western Australia and for reasons he never explained, WAGs were known as 'moles' out there, though I suspect it was a bastardisation of 'moll', as in gangster's moll. The less-than-salubrious nature of their area at Chelmsford saw the Hole bit added, which is how it is still referred to, despite today's WAGs having moved to slightly smarter premises.

Norbert Phillip, who played alongside Ken in the days when counties were allowed two overseas players, was also quiet and unassuming, another in contrast to the Essex dressing room he entered in the late 1970s. A West Indian from Dominica, he played his cricket with the dynamism and flair associated with the Caribbean. Bowling had to be quick, with plenty of bouncers, while batting was all about giving it a lash, blocking essentially being for wimps.

Known to us as 'Nobby' or 'Nobbler', Phillip played nine Tests for the West Indies during the Packer years, but did not add to them once the cream of the team had returned by 1979. Although light on all-rounders, the West Indies had a fearsome team back then, with fast-bowling talent and hard-hitting batsmen queueing round the block. There were also rumours of a rift between him and Clive Lloyd, captain of West Indies, which acted as a further impediment to Test caps. This was never confirmed by Nobby, though there appeared to be something in the theory. Whenever we played Lancashire, he always bowled at the speed of light to Lloyd and peppered him with bouncers – a combination that hardly denoted affection.

A very private man, he had a wife and twin sons, though they rarely came to the cricket. The boys were called Frank and Frankie, which proved Nobby must have had a sense of humour. He took the day job very seriously, looking after himself to the extent that he joined neither the 'curry crew' nor the 'scum burger' clans within the team. Instead, he'd either dine with Fletch and Ackers or take himself off for 'soup and steak', a combination he favoured when-ever he ate out on away trips.

I don't know what he'd consumed before playing Surrey in 1983, but he and Neil Foster got the ball to swing so profusely that they bowled them out for 14. Yes, 14. Nobby finished with the heady figures of six for four; Fozzy four for 10. And there was nothing much in the pitch, as Essex, who'd won the toss after rain washed out the first day, had just finished batting and made 287 – Fletch having scored 110 of them.

JK and I were both injured and did not play, though we had come to the ground for treatment, so watched the 'impossible' unfold from start to finish, which didn't take long. Although not close enough to see what was happening in the middle, we were on the players' balcony, just a few yards from the Surrey dressing room, so could see and hear the mayhem going on there.

As mentioned, the ball swung, a lot, but the way the dismissed batsmen were telling it to those waiting to go in, you'd have thought they were up against fire-breathing dragons. Every time a wicket went, and they were falling almost at the rate of one an over, the eyes of the ingoing batsman would open wider and wider. Fear stalked them.

There was disbelief, too, in their predicament. Sylvester Clarke, Surrey's demon bowler, and down to bat at number 10, refused to get out of the bath when told he needed to get padded up. He thought it a wind-up and was only persuaded otherwise when three of his team-mates lifted him out of the tub and carried him naked onto the balcony to show him the scoreboard. His response, when he did get in, was to have an almighty slog at Fozzy, the resulting inside edge running away for the only boundary Surrey scored.

It was clearly one of those freak things which happen from time to time, and while no doubt chastened by their shocker, Surrey knuckled down to make 185 for two in their second innings to draw the match. More rain having also helped their cause.

With typical British humour to the fore, the Surrey players involved had ties and T-shirts made. The seven who had made ducks had theirs emblazoned with 'The Magnificent Seven'. Meanwhile the four who'd managed to get off the mark had the words 'The Fabulous Four' printed on theirs. Unsurprisingly, considering it had happened at the end of May and therefore early in the season, both sets of players were banned from wearing them by Surrey's coach, Mickey Stewart. His reasoning was that Surrey needed to put Chelmsford behind them, quickly, which might not happen if they wore constant reminders.

The match also caught out Henry Blofeld, who'd been there to report for the *Guardian*. Eager to get away early on the second evening for dinner in Norfolk, Blofeld filed early, his report based around Fletch's fine hundred, with a final sentence which read, 'At the close, Surrey were __ for __.' To this he attached the instruction 'Sub-editor, please fill in the relevant details.'

It was unprofessional, but with Surrey having about 50 minutes to bat before the end of play, time in which a story-changing narrative was unlikely, Blowers felt the risk was worth taking, especially when faced with a two-and-a-half-hour drive. Having dined well and drunk a splendid Gevrey-Chambertin or two, Blowers still had the wherewithal to check with the sub, which happened to be Matthew Engel, soon to become the paper's cricket correspondent.

'Hello, old thing, Blowers here, to see if you have any queries over my copy.'

'We do, Henry,' said Engel. 'You know those figures you asked us to fill in at the end of your piece. Well, the relevant numbers are 14 and 10.'

'I'm not with you, my dear,' said Blowers.

'Well, Henry, Surrey were bowled out for 14, and you appear to have neglected that rather salient fact in your report.'

These days Blowers would have been sacked on the spot by the sanctimonious clots that populate most national newspapers. But back then there was a feeling that it could have happened to anyone, most journalists being fairly venal. Anyway, the *Guardian* had enlightened editors who quite liked the story, and not only the one Blowers missed.

Towards the end of Nobby's time at the club (his final season was 1985, the same as Kenny Mac's), his appearances with the first team became less frequent. His increasing absence from the side led to the rise of a small but unsavoury faction among Essex supporters. When Nobby wasn't picked, a group of them by the River End sightscreen at Chelmsford would bear a placard that read 'Keith Fletcher's White, White Army.'

Racism was fairly overt back then and black players endured some shocking slights. Gloucestershire's David 'Syd' Lawrence had bananas thrown at him when fielding against Yorkshire at Scarborough, while others had to endure racist taunts on a weekly basis. Even Viv Richards, a man no sane person would want to mess with, had run-ins with such bigots.

The ugliest it got with Nobby at Chelmsford was during a tense, low-scoring John Player Special League match against Somerset in 1984. Nobby bowled a no-ball at a crucial moment during their run-chase and some bloke in the Members' Pavilion went crazy, calling him a 'useless black ----', and asking why he didn't '---- off back home'.

I was fielding on the boundary right in front of the abuser and decided I couldn't take an Essex supporter, especially a club member, spouting such racist bile.

'There's no need for that,' I said, in my haughtiest public-school voice. 'He's trying his best. Give him a break.'

Far from quelling the situation, my attempted ticking-off just inflamed the matter.

'Don't you tell me what to do, you jumped-up prat, I pay your bloody wages,' said the member.

'Well, I tell you what,' I said, summoning as much sarcasm as I could, 'I'll take sixpence cut and you ---- off back home,' a riposte that went down well with the crowd around him, who began to cheer.

Although chastened by the reaction of the other members, he wasn't quite done and seemed determined to have the last word.

'We'll see what Peter Edwards [Essex's general secretary] has to say about this. I'm a club member; you can't speak to me like that.'

'Be my guest,' I said, confident that when Edwards heard what had happened, the loathsome bigot would be drummed out of the club.

We won the game and subsequently the Sunday League that year, but that did not stop Edwards drawing me aside the following week to tick me off about a complaint he'd received from a member about me bad-mouthing him.

When I told him what had gone on, he reminded me that Essex was a members' club and that each one should be treated with respect at all times. As for the rights of players not to be abused in the workplace, not a thing was said.

The Fletcher years during the 1980s were not always harmonious. While most revered Fletch – who was seen by the players as part patriarch and part mystical guru from a mountain top – there was one member of the team with whom his relationship wasn't entirely friction-free: Raymond Eric East.

Easty loved an audience, as it justified his need to perform, and not just when playing cricket, though he was damn good at that. Japes were his thing and some were better than others. Most who experienced them enjoyed them too, such as the time at freezing Fenner's (the thermometer actually read 0 °C), when he borrowed a spectator's trenchcoat and then fielded in it at cover point, and not just for a few balls. These days they'd have you up before the beak for pulling a stunt like that, with charges of bringing the game into disrepute. Back then, though, the crowd just laughed, as did the umpires.

Easty was not above the odd sledge, though his could never be construed as anything more than banter. In a game already mentioned, in which JK cleaned up Sussex at Hove in 1983, John Robert Troutbeck Barclay, Sussex's captain, was bowled by him for 21 in the first innings. As he wandered off past Easty, who was fielding in the gully, Barclay muttered, 'It didn't strike me as a particularly tricky delivery as it came down.' In the second innings, as we pushed for victory, JK knocked back Barclay's off stump with one of those balls you wish TV cameras had been there to record. JK had swung it about all game, but this one shaped in on the sea breeze and then moved away off the seam after it pitched. It would have dismissed better batsmen than Barclay, who departed in silence.

He'd got about halfway back to the pavilion when Easty shouted out, at the top of his voice, 'Was that a tricky enough delivery for you, Johnny?'

Where East's tomfoolery sometimes jarred with Fletch was when a game was in the balance and demanded our full attention. Any distraction then – and Easty's japes often came at times of stress – could prove an irritant. One such occasion came when Essex were trying to chase down 240 in 48 overs against Northants at Wantage Road in 1980. Easty was already in a funk, having bowled most of the morning while awaiting the declaration. Being used as a declaration bowler was the lowest of the low and Easty was fuming. So he was not in a great state of mind when, later that afternoon, having messed up the chase, Essex needed him to go and block out the draw.

In those days, Easty used a Warsop Stebbing bat, from a batmaker in Essex, which was flat on both sides. He used to tell the opposition that one side was for slogging, the other for blocking, but that only he knew which was which. His schtick was to ask bowlers, especially spinners, if they knew which side was facing them that ball. 'Are you sure you've got the right field?' he'd ask. He'd then hold up the bat, before spinning it around to show the other side, which of course looked identical. It was like a magician rolling up his sleeves to show there was nothing hidden up them.

On this occasion, with Essex attempting to hold on, there was only one choice Easty needed to make and that was to block. This he did, though not without his usual tomfoolery, in this case getting into a forward-defensive position on one knee before the ball was bowled. His reasoning was that Richard Williams, Northants' off-spinner, was about 5 ft 3 in tall and he wanted to make sure he wasn't lbw to one that didn't bounce that much.

When Fletch saw this, he marched onto the players' balcony and made his displeasure known with a full teapot – a gesture of annoyance in which both hands are placed on the hips. Undeterred, Easty kept mucking about. When he was bowled by Jim Griffiths, a pace bowler, at the other end, a wicket that quickly brought another when Griffiths dismissed Neil Smith, Fletch blew his top.

Despite us clinging on to save the match, Fletch drew Easty aside afterwards and told him not to bother turning up to festival week at Colchester, Easty's home patch and where our game against Derbyshire began the following day. Easty did not respond well to being treated like a naughty schoolboy and had a stand-up row with Fletch – the only time I can recall a player doing so in my time at the club. By banning him from playing, instead of hitting him in the pocket, Fletch had denied Easty the audience he most adored. It was tough love, but it worked. He never took on Fletch again.

6

THE REAL IAN BOTHAM

MY SURPRISE SELECTION for England in 1982 meant I had to cope with the tag of being the 'new Botham', despite the old one being very much alive and kicking, and in the same England team.

It had never crossed my mind to be compared to Beefy; the notion came from Fleet Street's sports editors looking for convenient pegs upon which to hang their stories. But if I was slow to catch on there, I was quick to rationalise the way I needed to play in order to flourish in a professional game demanding quality and consistency – and it wasn't like him.

Happily for those who relish spontaneity over predictability, Beefy was less willing to curb his questing ways, an attitude for which everyone in cricket had cause to be thankful. Beefy began the 1980s as England captain, picked his mates, got sacked, then flayed the Aussies from what seemed to be the point of no return to become the most famous sportsman in Britain. People forget now, but in his 1980s heyday Botham was bigger than any footballer in Britain. When Nike advertised their new football boot on hoardings around the country, it was the bearded Botham, not a permed Kevin Keegan or a bouffant Glenn Hoddle, who featured.

For many, cricket is a complex, introverted game played as much inside the head as outside on the field, and one requiring skills honed by hours of practice. Not for Beefy. He treated it very much as an entertainment in which he demanded to be the centre of attention. He also personalised it, making encounters a me-versus-you situation from which opponents often shrank. It was a very different approach from that of today's players, for whom team talks revolve around 'controlling the controllables', which I'm told means focusing on their own game and not that of their opponents.

With Beefy, it was forever a battle of wills on a cricket field and one that he was used to winning. On the odd occasion that he came off second best, a truly remarkable thing would occur: instead of having to deal with the self-doubt that would arise in the rest of us when faced with a setback, he would dismiss any reversal as an aberration under the laws of nature, or at least as they were constructed in Universe Beefy.

In other words, he never blamed himself when things went wrong. Instead, he would reboot with a night's carousing, ready to take the next challenge head on. As such, any failure would be erased from history, at least from the one running in his head. Even against the West Indies, the one team he never dominated, he would regard failure as the impostor. As for the rest of us, we'd feel the ones out of our depth.

My first real contact with Beefy came just a few months before his Ashes heroics of 1981, when Somerset played Combined Universities in a Benson & Hedges group match at Fenner's. Although yet to leave a permanent imprint on the folklore of the land, he was still a figure of some awe following feats like his century and 13 wickets against India in 1980, during a one-off Test at the Wankhede stadium in Mumbai. Often overlooked amid the deeds that followed, it remains arguably the greatest all-round feat in Test cricket, more so given that he'd partied hard throughout the match.

Here was a man who knew he was physically gifted but who also had an immense appetite, not just for competition in the sport he played, but for the life of excess it was possible to lead around it. A life many of his contemporaries chose to avoid. It gave him the edge, in my eyes, over the other great all-rounders of the era – Imran Khan, Richard Hadlee and Kapil Dev. All were super-talented, and while there were endless arguments between me and my mates as to who really was king, I'd always try to settle it by saying that Beefy achieved what he did on a skinful and never going to bed before 2 a.m. Not for him bottles of Evian water and early nights. In that respect, he was not just up against his opponents but his own rebel self.

It came as a surprise, then, when some of the Cambridge contin-gent in the Combined Universities side met up with the Somerset team before the match and Beefy, then England captain, declined the invitation to come to a student party thrown by some friends of mine. Many did, Joel Garner jumping at the chance. In fact, Big Joel enjoyed it so much that he still brings up the occasion whenever we meet. Beefy, though, was not persuaded as to the charms of cheap wine and rough punch, so we left him in the bar of the Blue Boar, where Somerset were staying.

The B&H match was largely a non-event, with Somerset winning comfortably by seven wickets. Beefy's contribution was an unbeaten 29, though he didn't manage a wicket from his 11 overs as Combined Universities, batting first, made 111 for nine off their 55 overs.

The next time we met was towards the end of that 1981 season, when Essex played Somerset at Taunton. Beefy had been relieved of the England captaincy by then but the loss had freed him up to perform some of the most remarkable deeds with bat and ball ever seen on a cricket field. Even better, they'd been inflicted on Australia, the old enemy, to the extent that the Ashes, which looked at one stage like being relinquished without much of a fight, had in fact been retained.

The first of Beefy's blitzkriegs was the miracle of Headingley in mid-July, which I didn't see live on the telly as I was playing for

Essex against Lancashire at Southchurch Park in Southend-on-Sea. Matches at festival grounds were well attended back then, and at Southchurch sponsors' marquees lined the eastern boundary. When the flags fluttered on the sea breeze it had an Agincourt grandeur completely at odds with the scuzzy pavilion and its splintery floor and dribbling showers. Visiting teams hated playing there and couldn't get out fast enough, praying the fixture list never sent them that way again.

Yet, at that game, even Southend knew something special was afoot, albeit in the Test. And we knew it because all we could see were people's backs in the marquees. Instead of watching the live cricket taking place in front of them, they had turned instead to watch the drama unfolding up north on TV. Then came the roared cheers of approval from the tents, as Beefy warmed to his task. It sounded more like a football crowd than anything I'd previously experienced at the cricket. We couldn't even kid ourselves that the cheers were for us, so out of kilter were they with the rhythms of our game against Lancashire.

It was a moon-landing moment, a time when everyone, and not just cricket lovers, knew what they were doing that manic Monday when Beefy, and Graham Dilley lest we forget, defied all the odds to flay the Aussie bowlers around Headingley. It was pretty much the same the next day, too, when Bob Willis ran amok with the ball. Excuses are often the last refuge of the pretender, but it was more than a little off-putting knowing that such great deeds were going on 180 miles away. Try as he might, Fletch could not get us to concentrate wholly on the task in hand and we failed to finish Lancashire off, despite having made them follow on. At least we didn't lose, a fate that befell Australia after they'd made England do the same in Leeds.

Beefy's derring-do at Headingley, where he smashed 149 in what looked for the most part like a lost cause, captured the imagination of the entire country, not just the faithful. There is something in the English psyche, despite many around the world feeling we have a superiority complex, that reveres the underdog, especially when it prevails.

Botham, by his standards at least, had been subdued prior to that match. As captain, he'd overseen defeat in the first Test, and when a tame draw occurred in the second, at Lord's, in which he made a pair, the knives were out. When the pressure mounted to intolerable levels, something unique to Ashes series, he resigned the England captaincy. Later, Alec Bedser, chairman of selectors, confirmed that Beefy would have been sacked anyway had he not stepped down of his own accord.

Beefy captained England in 12 Tests, though none resulted in victory. Of course, it was possible to argue that with nine of them being against the West Indies, when they were kings of the roost, and the other three against Australia, he was up against world cricket's two toughest opponents. Captains are chosen for many qualities, not least for bringing out the best in others. Yet the one person his leadership could not seem to inspire was himself. As captain, Beefy averaged just 10.6 with the bat and 36.7 with the ball in Tests, as opposed to 34 and 28, respectively, when under the command of others.

Such a huge disparity would have seen other players dropped from the team altogether, a fate that might have befallen Beefy had Mike Brearley, his replacement as captain, not insisted on retaining him. I doubt Beefy even considered that he might not be selected, or if he did, whether he paused for more than a second to ponder it. Instead, the ignominy of him losing the captaincy was followed by the glory of him performing noble deeds the rest of us could only dream about – a turnaround that suggested self-belief, or self-delusion, on an epic scale.

Headingley was only the start for him. After that match came the extraordinary bowling at Edgbaston, where he took five wickets for one run in five overs to halt what looked like another certain Australian victory. Kim Hughes's Aussies were 114 for five chasing 151 for a 2–1 lead, with two Tests to play, when Beefy took his first wicket of the innings. Half an hour later they were 121 all out, which meant England took the 2–1 lead instead. With no demons in the pitch, they'd been 'Beefied', pure and simple – mere mortals submitting to a now roused force of nature.

The destination of the Ashes was decided when England won the fifth Test at Old Trafford in mid-August, where Beefy, again among the wickets, played arguably his finest innings of the series. Dismissed by Dennis Lillee for a duck in England's first innings, he made amends by making 118 in the second, a knock that contained the memorable image of him hooking Lillee off his nose for six – a stroke made all the more thrilling for Beefy being helmetless, one of a select few to remain so as safety concerns grew during the decade.

A draw in the final Test saw England win the six-match series 3–1, each of their victories having been secured or inspired by an extraordinary feat from Beefy. If the outcome provided sweet redemption for him and the reclamation of some wounded pride, the country too was ready, this time to worship a new deity, albeit one with a pagan core.

As one social commentator at the time put it, 'Botham provided a wonderful antidote to the "Nagocracy" of the embryonic Nanny State beginning to form in the 1980s under Margaret Thatcher's Conservative Party.'

The public certainly took to him. Here was no namby-pamby public-school cricketer, but a champion from a comprehensive – which broadened his appeal. He certainly made it cool to like cricket. Suddenly, rock stars like Mick Jagger and Eric Clapton wanted to be seen with him, something he was only too happy to indulge, despite not knowing much about them or their back catalogues.

All the attention would have turned most heads; it would have been unnatural if it hadn't. So, when Essex played Somerset that September in 1981, the change in him was obvious. Although still defiantly a team man during play, he was not especially democratic when it came to discussions in the bar, or on such matters as where we might go and have a beer or something to eat. When I suggested a pub I'd read about in the CAMRA *Good Beer Guide*, which along with the AA road atlas was a constant travelling companion for the Essex team, he scoffed and told me to keep any such suggestions to myself.

Now, everybody enjoys a wind-up from time to time, so when the pub he took me, JK and Easty to proved something of a dud, with rubbish beer, I couldn't help piping up that we'd have been better off going to the one in the guide. Beefy did not react well. He pulled up his car, somewhere in the Somerset countryside, and told me to get out. 'I'm not having any more of his smart-arse comments,' he said, directing his words to JK and Easty. 'He can walk back.' It was eight miles to Taunton, where we were staying at the County hotel.

It was JK who came to my rescue and apologised for my upstart behaviour. Fortunately, Beefy loved JK from the various England tours the pair had been on together. As such, he was swayed, begrudgingly, by his testimony that apart from me being young and foolish, I was not a bad fellow really. He let me stay in the car on the proviso that I 'zipped that ------- mouth' of mine.

Often powerful, first impressions are not always accurate. When I got picked for England the following year, I was more than a tad apprehensive at meeting up with Beefy again, given our last encounter had not ended well. And yet I could not have been more wrong about the outcome as he welcomed me into the fold with genuine warmth in an effort to relax me and calm my jitters.

Once he'd realised that I was a man who sought adventure as much as him, at least off the cricket pitch, we became good mates. Obviously, he came with a health warning from those who'd known him a while, but I was young, impressionable and giddy with excitement that England's foremost sportsman should want to tolerate my company away from the confines of the dressing room.

Staying the course was the difficult thing, and I don't just mean remaining in the team, tricky though that could be in those fickle times of chop and change. There was stamina to consider. Beefy was a man of big appetites, especially for drink, and the price of keeping his company after hours was to either acquire a constitution like Oliver Reed's or learn to suffer hangovers that would cripple an elephant.

Fiercely competitive in all things, Beefy would see honour at stake in just about every social situation, especially when alcohol was taken. Once, when Somerset played Surrey at Weston-super-Mare in 1984, he took out, as in neutralised, Sylvester Clarke, Surrey's West Indian fast bowler.

The pair went on an extended pub crawl, where beer, wine and spirits were consumed in vast quantities until Clarke, no mean imbiber himself, had to be carried to his bed. He then spent most of the next two days of the match groaning on the physio's couch trying to remember his name.

Clarke didn't bowl again in the match, which was obviously the point of the exercise, though neither did Beefy in Surrey's second dig, which suggests there was a degree of collateral damage as well. Like many of his plans, its consequences were not quite as envisaged and the game was drawn.

There were limits to socialising with him, and on the 1982–83 Ashes tour I tended to avoid his little drinking school and their predilection for necking, often down in one, huge jugs of whisky and ice cream. Apart from the 1,500-plus calories in the concoction, it also contained at least a third of a bottle of whisky, which is where it started to get silly, especially as one jug was never enough.

That little cabal comprised Beefy and Chris 'Crash' Lander, the legendary cricket correspondent of the *Mirror*, for whom Beefy had a column. It also included the photographer Graham 'Morro' Morris, a big buddy of Crash's whom he used to extricate from all kinds of scrapes on tour. Botham was box-office copy at the time, so Crash was instructed to keep him on a tight leash away from other journalists. As a result, he would spend much of his time socialising with Beefy, which on that particular tour meant downing all manner of alcoholic beverages, though with particular dedication to said whisky and ice cream. It was a pricey combination, too, but Beefy knew Crash could claim it on expenses, so didn't hold back.

It all came to an ugly head one evening in Adelaide's Sebel hotel in the build-up to the third Ashes Test. Having just downed one of the jugs with great theatricality while standing on a table in the main bar, Morro was then handed half a pint of crème de menthe by Botham, also to knock back in one. Sensing an imminent visit to A&E if he did so, Morro engineered a swoon worthy of a stunt veteran, so that he went one way off the table and the crème de menthe went the other. Miraculously, he escaped serious injury, but the glass and green liqueur went everywhere, inevitably attracting attention where it shouldn't.

These days the press would have been all over it, with the moral mob on social media demanding a hanging at the very least, especially as England went on to lose that Test. For the most part journalists then were still at the heart of many capers on tour, especially Crash Lander, paying for both the drinks and clean-up bills as well. Perhaps that added cost caused a tipping point. Towards the end of that trip some had stopped turning a blind eye.

There was a cost to Beefy's predilection for this calorific cocktail – his waistline and his pride – and it was highlighted later on that 1982–83 tour during a one-day international at the Gabba in Brisbane. In a jape that to my knowledge has never been repeated, at least not with the same amount of elaborate subterfuge, some medical students released a piglet onto the field during England's innings. On one side of the animal, painted in bold capital letters, was the name 'BOTHAM', while on the other, also in capitals, was the name 'EDDIE', as in Hemmings. In the event, what particularly irked Beefy was not that he should be considered a porker, as those jugs of whisky and ice cream had definitely taken a toll, but that he should be bracketed with the less-than-svelte Hemmings, someone he was not especially matey with.

The pig, which gave the stewards the runaround before being apprehended by a policeman, one no doubt used to dealing with errant livestock, became a national sensation in the Aussie newspapers. So, too, did the medics who'd smuggled the animal into the ground, especially after revealing how they'd done it. Their ruse was certainly well planned, with the piglet first being anaesthetised, before being packed into a coolbox. It was then surrounded by ice and tins of beer. In a flourish that persuaded the stewards on the gate that it really was lunch, the piglet had an apple placed in its mouth. Once settled by the boundary's edge, the medics revived their patient and sent it on the field to run around during England's innings. Genius.

Naturally, piggy jokes and quips soon did the rounds in the team, such as 'I'm sweating like a Hemmings', or as Foxy once shouted to him when he was dawdling along in one of the courtesy cars, 'For

Christ's sake, Eddie, put your trotter down.' Nobody dared give Beefy any stick, though, especially as he was getting more than his fair share from the Aussie press.

The following winter, in a bid to shed some timber, he went and trained with Scunthorpe United. But staying trim requires ongoing discipline and Beefy was having too much fun to court abstinence for any length of time. He was, after all, called Beefy for a reason.

Beefy's love of a party and his retinue of famous friends certainly raised the level of post-match piss-ups from the beer in spit-and-sawdust pubs I'd been used to at university and with Essex. Once, while we were both mooching in the slips at Lord's during a Test against the West Indies in 1984, he casually asked me what I was doing later.

'No firm plans, though I expect some of my mates will be up for a pint or two,' I said.

'Do you fancy a party?' he asked. 'A few of us will be going.'

'Whose, and where?' I asked.

'Elton's. Out at his place in Old Windsor. Should be a cracker.'

I didn't demur, and promptly caught Malcolm Marshall off Willis to celebrate this entrée into Beefy's glamorous world.

Elton John had got to know much of England's cricket team the previous winter when his 1984 tour of New Zealand coincided almost venue for venue with England's visit. It was a trip I had not been selected for, and one which subsequently became known as the 'Sex, Drugs & Rock 'n' Roll' tour, for all the obvious reasons. Certainly the impression from afar, and I was just over the Tasman sea playing in Sydney, was that the cricket appeared of secondary importance.

In Windsor, Elton proved a genial host, friendly and attentive. The gathering was 99 per cent men, though, all recounting their experiences from New Zealand, which meant his wife, Renate, took on a permanent look of studied boredom. Elton and Renate Blauel, a German sound engineer, had got married a few months earlier in Sydney, where, coincidentally, I'd been playing Grade cricket for the University of New South Wales. I remember the hoo-ha around the city, but also the general surprise that someone who'd appeared openly gay should be marrying a woman. Inevitably, conspiracy theories abounded, not least in the bars of Darlinghurst, Sydney's gay heartland.

The celebrity-heavy wedding reception aboard a boat in Sydney Harbour was reported to have been lavish, though the rock 'n' roll element was compromised when Michael Parkinson, a guest, missed the boat's departure. Feeling he ought to make an effort to attend, Parky persuaded a police launch to take him out to his host's boat, where the party was now in full swing. Not knowing it was Parky on the police boat, Elton and his guests simply saw the Law approaching, suspected a raid and promptly jettisoned all their exotic pharmaceuticals into the harbour. Parky's cheery wave and subsequent boarding was not acknowledged with joy.

The party at Windsor was not quite as glam, but the informality did not stop me feeling like a spare part. Because I'd not been on the New Zealand tour where Elton and the team had bonded, I was not privy to the banter. Instead, while they reminisced, I busied myself admiring his art collection, in which there was a Magritte and several Lowrys. He also had a fab record player on which Elton John records appeared to be on heavy rotation, at least on that particular evening.

Most of his band were there, as well as lyricist Bernie Taupin, whom Beefy chummily referred to as 'The Scribbler'. Though all seemed perfectly charming, one had to wonder who or what the party was for, given there was food for 80, but just Elton, his wife, six musos and seven cricketers present, plus The Scribbler.

Beefy was more at ease than most in the assembled company. He was also feeling good, having just taken eight for 103 in the West Indies' first innings. The ball had swung and there was nobody with a better nose for wickets when it hooped about than him. The West Indies batsmen were vulnerable whenever there was sideways movement, their eagerness to take the ball early increasing any risk of dismissal. Even the great Vivian Richards had succumbed to him, his old team- and flatmate, though the inswinger from which he was adjudged lbw wouldn't have hit another set of stumps – it being one of the worst decisions I'd seen in a Test.

As a rule, team captains and crackerjack cricketers like Viv Richards tended to be immune from really bad decisions. But umpire Barrie Meyer, perhaps caught up in the buzz of Saturday's full house at Lord's, which itself had responded to Beefy's howled appeal, shot his finger up before any doubts could creep in. When he saw the replay at lunchtime, Meyer, a good and highly respected umpire, went immediately to the West Indies' dressing room to apologise.

But if Beefy was buzzing from his bowling performance, Elton seemed even more animated, hopping from foot to foot for most of the party. After a while, Bob Willis came over to me and said, jokingly, 'I want some of whatever Elton's on, he's been bouncing about like a Duracell Bunny for hours.' Alas, unless it was the champagne or the Château Giscours which had revved him up, it was never offered.

Although the rest day of the Test acted as a buffer before we resumed hostilities with the West Indies on the Monday, I doubt many of the players who came to Elton's party that Saturday would have turned down the chance had it fallen in the middle of the match. Experiences like that don't come round often and must be taken, which is where the common ground between Beefy and me was most firm.

When the match continued, we put our 41-run lead on first innings to good use, or did until we accepted the umpire's offer of light at the end of the fourth day. Our lead was 328 and I was batting with Allan Lamb. Facing the West Indies' pace attack of that era was not much fun at the best of times, let alone in murky light. But even so, we were on top in the game and the West Indies bowlers were tired, so it made sense to bat on even if it was gloomy. At least that was the point I made to Lamby, who was on 109 after another brilliant innings against pace.

In those days umpires offered the light to the batsmen rather than taking an executive decision themselves, as they do now. As such, they turned to Lamby, the senior player in the middle, to make the call. Sensing, perhaps, the odd incredulous headline, as well as my dissenting voice, Lamb told them that David Gower, the captain, must make the decision. So we all looked up to the players' balcony, England's being on the left side of the Pavilion as seen from the pitch, for guidance. Gower, or Lubo as he was known even when captain, was nowhere to be seen. It was only when we returned to the dressing room, Lamby having eventually decided to accept the umpires' offer to go off, that we discovered he'd been busy watching Wimbledon on the telly, the light in SW19 clearly better than it was in NW8.

Instead of declaring overnight, the decision to come off meant we batted on at the start of the final day, eventually setting West Indies 342 in roughly 80 overs. It proved immaterial. In an extraordinary assault from Gordon Greenidge, who made an unbeaten 214, and supported by a more measured 92 from Larry Gomes, West Indies reached their target in 66.1 overs. It was utter carnage, their effort still standing as the highest successful run-chase in a fourth innings at Lord's.

ENGLAND V WEST INDIES
(2nd Test)

Played at Lord's Cricket Ground, London, 28 June – 3 July 1984

Umpires: DGL Evans & BJ Meyer
Toss: West Indies

ENGLAND

G Fowler	c Harper b Baptiste	106	lbw b Small		11
BC Broad	c Dujon b Marshall	55	c Harper b Garner		0
DI Gower*	lbw b Marshall	3	c Lloyd b Small		21
AJ Lamb	lbw b Marshall	23	c Dujon b Marshall		110
MW Gatting	lbw b Marshall	1	lbw b Marshall		29
IT Botham	c Richards b Baptiste	30	lbw b Garner		81
PR Downton†	not out	23	lbw b Small		4
G Miller	run out	0	b Harper		9
DR Pringle	lbw b Garner	2	lbw b Garner		8
NA Foster	c Harper b Marshall	6	not out		9
RGD Willis	b Marshall	2	did not bat		
Extras	(4 b, 14 lb, 15 nb, 2 w)	35	(4 b, 7 lb, 6 nb, 1 w)		18
Total	(105.5 overs)	**286**	(9 wkts, declared, 98.3 overs)		**300**

WEST INDIES

CG Greenidge	c Miller b Botham	1	not out	214
DL Haynes	lbw b Botham	12	run out	17
HA Gomes	c Gatting b Botham	10	not out	92
IVA Richards	lbw b Botham	72	did not bat	
CH Lloyd*	lbw b Botham	39	did not bat	
PJL Dujon†	c Fowler b Botham	8	did not bat	
MD Marshall	c Pringle b Willis	29	did not bat	
EAE Baptiste	c Downton b Willis	44	did not bat	
RA Harper	c Gatting b Botham	8	did not bat	
J Garner	c Downton b Botham	6	did not bat	
MA Small	not out	3	did not bat	
Extras	(5 lb, 7 nb, 1 w)	13	(4 b, 4 lb, 13 nb)	21
Total	(65.4 overs)	**245**	(66.1 overs)	**344**

WEST INDIES	O	M	R	W		O	M	R	W	Fall of wickets:				
												Eng	WI	Eng	WI
Garner	32	10	67	1		30.3	3	91	3	1st		101	1	5	57
Small	9	0	38	0	(3)	12	2	40	3	2nd		106	18	33	–
Marshall	36.5	10	85	6	(2)	22	6	85	2	3rd		183	35	36	–
Baptiste	20	6	36	2		26	8	48	0	4th		185	138	88	–
Harper	8	0	25	0		8	1	18	1	5th		243	147	216	–
										6th		248	173	230	–
ENGLAND	O	M	R	W		O	M	R	W	7th		251	213	273	–
Willis	19	5	48	2		15	5	48	0	8th		255	231	290	–
Botham	27.4	6	103	8		20.1	2	117	0	9th		264	241	300	–
Pringle	11	0	54	0		8	0	44	0	10th		286	245	–	–
Foster	6	2	13	0		12	0	69	0						
Miller	2	0	14	0		11	0	45	0						

Close of play:
Day 1: England (1) 167–2 (Fowler 70*, Lamb 13*)
Day 2: West Indies (1) 119–3 (Richards 60*, Lloyd 32*)
Day 3: England (2) 114–4 (Lamb 30*, Botham 17*)
Day 4: England (2) 287–7 (Lamb 109*, Pringle 6*)

Man of the match: IT Botham, CG Greenidge
Result: **West Indies won by 9 wickets**

Inevitably, scapegoats were sought, with some even suggesting that Gower was at fault for setting them a target in the first place, the draw being considered a good result against the West Indies back then. I don't subscribe to that. England had not beaten West Indies at home for 15 years, so we needed to at least try to win. As Gooch, still banned for his part in the 1982 rebel tour, put it when I got back to Essex, 'England hadn't been in that kind of position against them for years. Lubo had to go for it.'

If Gower was at fault, it was in keeping Botham on for so long on the final day. The ball wasn't swinging as it had done in the first innings, yet Beefy kept persuading him to give him just one more over, a message he'd transmit by holding up his right index finger in Gower's direction as he took his short-sleeve sweater from the umpire. The 'just one more' charade went on for at least five or six overs. If Beefy had been beating the bat, or looking dangerous as he'd done in the first innings, his insistence on keeping going would have been justified. But Greenidge and Gomes were seeing it well and Beefy was leaking runs at nearly six an over.

His extravagance was not the sole reason we lost. The ball did nothing for anyone, the pitch having relapsed into a deep slumber. Also, the West Indies back then were a team that needed no persuading as to their greatness, so playing out the draw was not an option they even remotely considered, just something we'd half assumed on their behalf. The combination of those factors and the sheer brutality of Greenidge's assault caught us on the hop. Yet, try as we might, we had nothing to counter with once the hardness had gone from the new ball. Indeed, it was one of only a handful of occasions, in any form of cricket, that I ever ran in to bowl more in hope than expectation.

Somehow, I survived the inevitable cull for the next Test at Headingley in mid-July, though Neil Foster, Geoff Miller and Mike Gatting did not. Over the years, the consensus has been that Headingley suited bowlers like me, accurate brisk-mediums who wobbled it about off the seam or through the air. Back at Essex, Fletch certainly felt it was a good opportunity for me to make a mark. 'Just make sure you get on before that Paul Allott does,' he said as I headed off to Leeds. Allott, who'd come into the side in place of Foster, ploughed the same furrow as me. What Fletch was forecasting, in his inimitable way, was that come the end of the match, there would only be room for one of us for the rest of that summer.

As ever, it was sage advice, though when Allott, or 'Walt' as he was more widely known, was given the new ball by Gower and promptly took six wickets, I sensed my fate was decided. I was not disabused of the notion, either, and after West Indies had notched up another victory, this time by eight wickets, I was cast back into county cricket.

Usually, I was phlegmatic about setbacks. But this time I could not fail to ponder the small margins and bits of luck that seemed to separate success from failure, or at least survival from demise. For instance, why did Allott get the new ball when Beefy would normally have taken it? It is a question to which I still don't know the answer. Under heavy cloud, the new conker had zipped around, something it didn't really do much of when it was older and the skies had cleared.

There were other moments, too, that niggled. During our second innings, I'd been given out lbw to Malcolm Marshall to one that had nipped back sharply but had struck me, a 6 ft 5 in tall man, a few inches above the knee roll on the front pad. There must have been significant doubt as to whether it would have passed above the stumps, doubt that the same umpire, David Evans, had found for several of the West Indies' batsmen against whom I'd appealed for far closer lbws (my judgement, not his) the previous day. Continuing the hard luck tale, I'd also had a catch dropped off my bowling.

What I'm trying to get at is that if I'd taken those three wickets and made 30 in the innings in which I was sawn off, then in all likelihood I would probably not have been dropped, despite our defeat. By such desperately thin margins are careers decided, especially in a side losing as often as we were that series.

When players got the chop back then, the captain was meant to inform you before the squad for the next Test was announced, which was usually at noon on the Sunday before the match, in time for the radio news bulletins. It wasn't always easy. There were no mobile phones and with all the travelling cricketers did back then, it could be difficult to gauge when a player might be at home.

I discovered I'd been left out of the side for the fourth Test when I drove through the gates of the St Lawrence Ground at Canterbury, for a Sunday League match against Kent on 22 July. What gave it away was when the home supporters, spying my sponsored car with name emblazoned on the side, started jeering and making vulgar hand signs at me. You see, I'd been replaced by one of their own, Richard Ellison, an old rival of mine since schooldays, and this was their way of celebrating his promotion and my humiliation.

On the drive to Canterbury I'd been listening to one of my home-taped cassettes, so had missed the squad's announcement on radio. When Gower did finally make contact to inform me of my fate, at least 24 hours later, he said that he'd wanted me in the side but Peter May had vetoed my selection, saying that 'I didn't get upset enough when things didn't go my way.'

While it was true that I had a reputation for being, or at least looking, laid-back, this came as one of the more surprising reasons to be dropped. Had he said, 'You didn't take any wickets, didn't make many runs and we felt it was time to give someone else a chance,' I would have struggled to disagree. But short of abusing David Evans, the umpire, for adjudging me lbw but not giving me any of the ones I'd asked for, I wasn't sure how I was meant to show displeasure at my setbacks, or indeed if I did, how that might keep me in the team.

Beefy, of course, had never needed to have these internal dialogues as he'd never been dropped. Unusually, he'd had a pretty quiet match at Headingley, too, though he excelled in all kinds of ways off the field, not least in his kindness to strangers.

For Headingley we stayed at the Craiglands hotel in Ilkley, 18 miles to the north-west of Leeds. The trip to the ground, which took an hour during morning rush hour, went through Otley, a small market town whose Junction Inn became a regular stopping-off point on the return journey.

Beefy had become more cautious about mixing with the public but he was happy to stop here for refreshments with Paul Allott and me, both of us real-ale enthusiasts. While Paul and I favoured the beers of Keighley's Timothy Taylor's brewery, Beefy went for Theakston's Old Peculier, a strong beer often referred to in Yorkshire as 'Lunatic's Broth'. To enliven proceedings further, he had a whisky with each pint.

I also had two old schoolmates in tow, Kev and Steve, who'd come to watch the Test. As was their wont, they had not booked anywhere to stay, their constitution being such that any random floor, sofa or car seat would probably suffice following a good night out, especially if it was with Beefy.

We stayed until closing time, at which point we must have had six or so pints each, Beefy never wavering from his combination of beer and chaser. I'm not sure how it arose but somehow talk swung to cars, with Beefy being wound up enough to insist on driving Steve's souped-up VW Scirocco GTi the six and a half miles to the team hotel. Knowing how Beefy was with a challenge, I went back with Walt.

The route was uphill with many bends, but Beefy roared up and around them, arriving at the hotel with both tyres and gearbox smoking. 'There you are, lads, how was that? Pass muster?' At which point he promptly relieved himself all over the bonnet.

He then announced, over a nightcap in the bar, that he had a spare bed in his room and if one of Kev or Steve wanted to kip in it, they would be very welcome. I can't remember them fighting over the offer or how it even got decided, but Steve got the Beefy option, while Kev shared my double bed. Kev and I had been in different boarding houses at school, so this was the cosiest any sleeping arrangements had ever got. Remarkably, we have remained the best of friends.

Now, I'd known Beefy a while, but even I was taken aback by this act of generosity. After all, he'd only just met Steve, a short, balding scrap-metal merchant with a ginger beard. But Beefy trusted his mates and by extension their mates, so was only too happy to help out once it became known they had nowhere to kip. It was extraordinary when you think about it. Here was the most famous sportsman in Britain allowing some bloke he didn't really know to share his hotel room in the middle of a Test match, having just had a skinful with him and then peed on his car. That last act aside, it defied the rules of modern celebrity.

A few years later, during another Headingley Test against the West Indies, this time in 1988, Allan Lamb let Kev and Steve stay in his room at a hotel called Chevin Lodge while he and his wife, Lindsay, returned home for the rest day. On that occasion, another mate from school, Chris, kipped on my floor, though there were raised eyebrows the next morning when four full English breakfasts were ordered by four big blokes on just two room numbers, especially when one of those rooms was meant to be occupied by a Mr and Mrs Lamb. Even Fred Titmus, then one of the selectors, saw fit to peer over his Sunday paper in a bid to work out the dynamics of who fitted where. He didn't appear overly bothered. Fred had begun his cricket career with Bill Edrich and Denis

Compton, so capers during a Test match would have been nothing new.

There were no selectors in evidence in 1984, when Kev, Steve and I repaired for breakfast at the Craiglands (Beefy never did formal brekkers). But while the prospect of eggs and bacon held their usual allure, we were even more eager to hear of Steve's experience of sharing a room with the great man.

'Well, he snores,' said Steve. 'But the best bit was the look on the chambermaid's face when she brought him his morning papers and breakfast, and some fat, balding bloke with a ginger beard and wearing Y-fronts answered the door. It was priceless.'

The revelation, though, was Beefy's breakfast order. Instead of a full English, or even the three Shredded Wheat which he advertised for years on the telly, his order comprised two newspapers, the *Daily Mirror* and the *Sporting Life*, and two pints of full-cream milk.

'He grunted good morning,' said Steve, 'and then just sat there in bed studying the form and swigging the milk.'

Unfortunately, a pint a day of the white stuff, or even two, could not keep the West Indies at bay and not for the first time against them we went down heavily. On the back of losing, the landlord of the Junction, where we had stopped off most nights on the way back to Ilkley, sold a story about our drinking there to the *News of the World*. They quoted him as saying something like 'I'm surprised they could walk, let alone play cricket,' but then in red-top world hyperbole rules.

After that defeat I was dropped for the remaining two Tests, but it didn't matter who England's selectors picked that summer, the West Indies swatted them aside. It was, as the many placards borne by West Indies' supporters at The Oval proclaimed, a 'blackwash' – the second such inflicted on England in the space of 18 months, Gower the unfortunate captain on both occasions.

The Ashes had history and gravitas, but in the 1980s the West Indies were the team to beat, and everyone knew it, especially them.

Yet nobody, not even Beefy, could find a way of countering their battery of fast bowlers and aggressive batsmen, at least not for long enough to win a match. Small victories did occur, at the individual level. But as a collective force nobody really challenged them, at least not during that decade.

Beefy's generosity was often lavish, especially towards his mates. Soon after the 1982–83 tour of Australia and New Zealand had concluded, he invited me, Geoff Cook, his father-in-law, Gerry Waller, and David English, a 1960s scenester and friend to the stars, to watch England's Five Nations match against Ireland in Dublin. He even threatened to fly us over himself, though thankfully that never happened, as he'd not kept up the required flying hours to pilot the plane.

First, though, we had to watch him play football for Scunthorpe United Reserves on the Friday. His usual position was centre half but he persuaded the coach to play him up front, whereupon he promptly scored a hat-trick. 'Don't you just hate him?' said Cooky as the third goal went in, and we both agreed that, with him possessing such a sickening level of talent, we probably did.

The next day we jumped on a twin-prop aircraft to Dublin and watched England lose 15–25 to an Ireland team expertly run by Ollie Campbell, one which shared the Championship that year, 1983, with France. Much Guinness was taken and a cracking night in Dublin ensued, before a bumpy and sobering flight took us back to Blighty on the Sunday.

That kind of action-packed few days with much drink and little sleep left me knackered, but it was fairly standard for Beefy, who seemed to live his life with even more gusto than he played his cricket. Unusual and exciting things just seemed to happen around him, which is why so many, myself included, found him beguiling.

It wasn't all grand gestures. Once, when Essex were playing Worcestershire, after Beefy had joined them following his acrimonious departure from Somerset at the end of 1986, he invited me back to his cottage in the Herefordshire woods he shared with his minder, Andy Withers, for a 'cheeky' bottle of wine. The bottle in question lacked impertinence of any kind, being the legendary Château Latour 1961, a wine sipped by royalty and Texan billionaires on account of its cachet and eye-watering cost. It turned out that when the County hotel in Taunton had closed down, to be redeveloped into a shopping centre, the manager had discovered a few bin-ends in the cellar, which he'd offered to Beefy at a decent price. Among them were three bottles of the '61 Latour, generally regarded as one of the greatest wines ever made. To buy a single bottle today would cost between £2,500 and £7,000, depending on its provenance.

We both enjoyed wine but I'm not sure we treated this bottle with the deference it deserved. For starters, we'd already had a skinful of ale down his local pub, the Crown at Martley, as well as the odd spliff. We certainly needed food, though, if we were to do the wine any justice at all. The Taste Police would say a fine vintage Bordeaux like that demanded a rich lamb dish to complement it, but we did not have the time, the ingredients or the culinary expertise to knock up one of those at midnight. Instead, Beefy got the long-suffering Andy to do us bacon, sausage and eggs. This then served as blotting paper for undoubtedly the finest wine that I have ever drunk – a collision of the sacred and profane that was so Beefy.

The Crown at Martley was also the scene for one of the most memorable evenings of my career, being the place where Eric Clapton serenaded Beefy and the Essex team one Saturday, after play in the Championship match at Worcester had been rained off.

It was 1987, and the combination of Botham and Worcester's timeless ground at New Road had brought the celebrities flocking. There is a photo taken on the players' balcony there of Beefy flanked by Elton John, George Harrison and Eric Clapton. You never got VIP tonnage like that at Chelmsford, even on a sunny day, though Jimmy White and Gary Lineker did once pay us a visit during a charity match.

For this game just Eric had come along and he stayed with Beefy at the latter's place out in the sticks. Once rain had set in after lunch, reducing the chances of further play, a card school was started in the home dressing room. A few of the Essex boys got involved, but it was Eric who cleaned up the £450 in the pot. That caused more than a little resentment among the Essex contingent, who returned to our dressing room bleating things like 'There's no justice' and 'As if he bloody needs the money.'

Being a sensitive, artistic type, Eric sensed their rancour and made an offer to appease them.

'Listen, guys,' said Eric, 'Beefy's got one of my Stratocaster guitars in the boot of his car, and if the music shop in town has a certain Fender amp, I'll jam for you tonight down the pub.'

Now, even the curmudgeons hit in the pocket were excited by that prospect, everybody crowding round as Eric rang the local music shop from the payphone just outside our dressing room.

'Hi, do you have the Fender Twinolux amp?' asked Eric. 'You do, great, but you only have one. What time do you shut? Six on the dot. Right. I'll be round to pick it up around five-thirty.'

The shop assistant, wary of time-wasters late on a wet Saturday afternoon, asked Eric what name he should reserve the amp under. When the answer was, understandably, 'Eric Clapton', the assistant quipped sarcastically, 'Yeah, 'course it is and I'm Mick Jagger,' and slammed down the phone. Forty minutes later he was slack-jawed in wonder as Eric, with cash splashed on the counter, arrived to take ownership of the amp.

That evening down the Crown was one of true wonder. As a non-participant in the card school, I'd not met Eric properly at the ground. Yet here we were drinking pints of bitter together, him with a whisky chaser.

'Del, call me El,' were the words I most remember him saying, along with him asking me if I had Prince's *Sign 'O' the Times* album. When I said no, he offered to send me a copy, insisting it was a work of genius.

Eric then plugged in and began performing his songs in a side room with a dartboard. What floored me, along with the brilliance of his playing, was the contentment he seemed to exude. Here was one of the best guitar players ever, happy just to be in the company of his mate Beefy and winning a whole host of other friends, starry-eyed now as the magic of his guitar began to unfurl.

There was the odd misstep, like forgetting some of the words to 'Layla', which he played at a slower, less frenetic pace than the original. Yet the breathy intimacy of the performance was spine-tingling.

To stop us turning into drooling acolytes, Eric would chat between songs, doing his best to keep it casual and low-key, as if we were mates down the boozer having a sing-song, which I suppose we were. He obviously felt very close to Beefy, as he kept gazing into his eyes when singing some of his slower numbers, which disconcerted one or two unused to male friendships based on more than bonhomie and banter.

There was a vulnerability to Eric that seemed the opposite of Beefy's dismissive, insouciant self-confidence. Yet Eric must have been tough in less obvious ways to have survived the UK music business of the 1960s with its Svengalis, hucksters, social upheaval and enthusiastic drug scene. Whatever the attraction between him and England's greatest cricketer, it was touching, a true bromance before the term was coined.

Inevitably, word got round on the bush telegraph and people began piling into the pub to see if the rumours were true. But Eric was not for grandstanding and once the crowd had swelled beyond our cosy cabal he downed guitar, to a hail of jeers and boos from the latecomers.

'I'm sorry,' he said. 'I came to play for my friends, not to put on a show. I hope you understand.' They didn't, so Eric unplugged and we drank up and left.

It was an abrupt end to a magical evening, but we'd had him to ourselves for over an hour and felt blessed as a result. I've seen Eric perform at the Albert Hall several times since, big productions in front of an adoring audience. Yet none have come close to that evening where I sat at his right hand, that famous 'Slow Hand', and watched true virtuosity up close.

The next day, with the rain gone, the Sunday League match at Worcester was on as scheduled, though by the time we arrived at the ground, Eric was already there and looking agitated. We could see why: there was a huge scrape down one side of his yellow Ferrari Testarossa. When we asked what happened, he told us that Beefy had insisted on driving to the ground to put the Ferrari through its paces. All had gone well until the final 50 yards of the journey, which required him to negotiate the notoriously narrow gates at New Road. Beefy's heavy touch on the throttle had seen the Ferrari lurch through the gap, but not before making contact with one of the posts.

'I wouldn't mind, man,' wailed Eric, 'but the paint job is four grand alone.'

Hoping the guilt would sink in and affect Beefy's performance, we batted first on a slow pitch but kept losing wickets at the wrong time. Having been 141 for six, our total of 202 from 40 overs was a decent effort, but it didn't prove remotely competitive once Beefy had let rip with an extraordinary unbeaten 125, after he'd opened the Worcestershire innings. Even our cunning, Baldrick-like plan of sledging him with taunts of 'Boy Racer' and 'Emerson Fittipaldi' could not distract him from plundering our bowling.

The savagery was breathtaking. One six off Hugh Page, our overseas player that year, was hit so hard over extra cover that it completely dismantled the tea bar stationed five yards beyond the boundary there. It left those about to put sugar in their cuppa both shaken and stirred. With an unstoppable force like that, Worcestershire won by nine wickets with 51 balls to spare, which was a shellacking. The fact that Beefy outscored Graeme Hick, no slouch with the bat, two runs to one simply reinforced what a bravura performance it had been.

Despite the damage to his car, Eric was positively purring about Beefy's pyrotechnics when he entered our dressing room to offer consolation.

'Never mind, guys,' he said, no doubt feeling our pain. 'When the man is the man, the man is the man. There is nothing you can do about it.'

It was sweet of him, but with Goochie about to deliver a dressing-down for our flat performance, Eric's timing rather than his hippy-dippy sentiment caused Fletch – no longer Essex captain but still a player in the match – to issue a polite but curt message to our new best friend.

'Excuse me, Ernie,' said Fletch, 'but can you give us a moment, please.'

'Oh, er, sure man, no problem,' replied Eric, sensing we were perhaps not as enamoured of Beefy's knock as he was.

With the door closed, there was a disbelieving silence before one of the younger players turned to Fletch and said, 'What did you just call him?'

To which Fletch, incredulous that anyone should have the temerity to think that he didn't know his Cream from his Kajagoogoo, replied, 'Don't you know who that is? That's Ernie Clapham. He's a world-class guitar player.'

At which point any rollocking from Gooch was rendered entirely futile as the dressing room dissolved into laughter. Good old Fletch and his approximate memory for names.

The cult of personality can become an unwelcome distraction in the delicately balanced ecosystem of a cricket team, which is what appeared to happen to Beefy at Somerset. Used to having the run of the dressing room, as well as Taunton, Beefy was like a feudal lord running his fiefdom from the Four Alls pub in Corporation Street, now long gone.

For many visiting cricketers, a lock-in at the Four Alls was standard fare if Beefy was in town – post-match drinking time essentially being doubled. On one such occasion, during a match against Kent, Beefy settled a heated exchange between him and the journalist Stephen Brenkley by simply picking Brenkley up by the lapels of his jacket and hanging him on a coat hook. Trouble was, the move neither shut Brenkley up nor prevented him from dining out on the episode in perpetuity – a rare failure for Beefy, who liked to have the last word.

Beefy's power in his home town also extended to influencing umpires, as he did during Essex's Championship match at Taunton in 1985. There had been heavy rain after the first day's play and Beefy, who'd already made a brilliant 152, just did not fancy hanging around all day on the off chance of a few hours' play at the fag end of the day.

It was the opposite attitude to that of Keith Fletcher, our captain, who was always keen to play cricket if possible. On this occasion, Fletch, whose mantra was 'you can't win points sitting in the dressing room', had already put his tuppenceworth in with the umpires. Essex, though, were batting, so wouldn't be affected if the outfield was slippery underfoot.

'Watch this,' said Fletch from our dressing-room balcony. 'Beefy will try to get them to call it off for the day. He's already told me that he's booked golf down the road.'

And sure enough, after an arm-waving performance worthy of the Signal Corps' semaphore champion, in which Beefy helpfully pointed out all the treacherous wet patches, the umpires were persuaded to call off play for the day. Mission accomplished, Beefy then swung by our dressing room to ask who was up for some golf. It wasn't yet 11.30 a.m.

By that stage of his career, county cricket held less allure for Beefy than it did at the start, when Brian Close was his mentor and captain. Although there was always the challenge of getting Somerset to their first County Championship title to consider, something they have still not achieved, he did not treat playing for county and country as equals, at least not to the extent Goochie did with Essex. Nevertheless, Beefy was on fire for Somerset in 1985, at least with the bat. In the 11 Championship matches he played, he scored 1,211 runs at an average of 100.91, notching five hundreds and six half-centuries. His bowling, with just 11 wickets from 130 overs, was less impressive and suggested he was preserving himself for the Tests – the county toil being left to others.

His agent that year was a colourful character called 'Lord' Tim Hudson, a Mancunian who'd headed to America's West Coast in the 1960s, where he'd become a successful disc jockey in the emerging music scene. While living in Los Angeles, he'd also become the manager of two bands – The Seeds and The Lollipop Shoppe – who embodied the new 'Flower Power', a term the ponytailed Hudson claims to have coined. The Seeds, with their fey lead singer, Sky Saxon, were definitely touchstones of the West Coast scene. They even had two minor hits in the UK, with the psychedelic pop songs 'Pushin' Too Hard' and 'Can't Seem to Make You Mine', both cult classics.

Hudson persuaded Beefy to grow his hair long and to dye it blond, telling anyone who would listen that he was going to make his man a Hollywood movie star. It sounded far-fetched, but Hudson was the first to see the possibilities of holding music concerts at cricket grounds, something that happens all the time now, albeit mostly independent of the cricket. Although not shy of telling anyone, he was a visionary of sorts.

'Imagine it, man,' he once said to me over martinis at Birtles Hall, the impressive neo-classical pile in Cheshire bought by his wife Maxi, an American heiress. 'You get New Order on stage after a day's play at Old Trafford or the London Symphony Orchestra after the cricket at Lord's. It would be far out. Cricket and music, what could be groovier?'

Ever the sceptic, I pointed out that spectators would be seated for anything up to 10 hours if they committed to the whole package. If they didn't fall asleep, they'd probably get piles and sue. 'Such negativity, and in one so young,' was his riposte.

Hudson did take Beefy to Hollywood, but the only publicity I can recall is when he had a friendly hit-about with the LA Dodgers baseball team. Nothing much seemed to come of that and there were certainly no movie roles proposed.

Not long afterwards, Beefy's relationship with his agent foundered after Hudson told the press his client smoked marijuana – something still very much a secret at that stage. A year later, in 1986, Beefy admitted to occasionally smoking the drug after police found a small amount at his home in Epworth, South Yorkshire. That admission – one that did not surprise team-mates or most within the Test and County Cricket Board – saw Beefy banned for three months during the 1986 season.

On one level, the TCCB had to act, but it smacked of hypocrisy, cricket's image as a wholesome, morally upright sport being essentially bogus. Although invented by shepherds on the downlands of southern England in the 17th century, cricket only became organised when wealthy landowners and squires formed teams to fuel private wagers. Its reputation as the 'gentleman's game', filled with notions of 'fair play', came during the Victorian and Edwardian eras, when 'Muscular Christianity' was all the rage. Subsequently, as its popularity has spread globally, it has struggled to live up to those high ideals.

Naturally, column inches were filled with both sides of that debate. One bit of the moral argument I could never get my head around was the fear that 'it sets a bad example to kids'. Well, when I was a teenager, I was moved more by rock stars than sportsmen, and they gloried in drug-taking. Despite that, it did not persuade me to get high on anything other than best bitter and wine, fattening though both those things could be.

Beefy's enforced absence in 1986 saw me picked again for England, an opportunity I'd like to think I didn't squander, at least not against the first team of the summer, India.

In the three-match series against them, which we lost 0–2, I was England's leading wicket-taker, with 13 wickets. I also managed to notch my highest ever Test score in the first match at Lord's. Batting at six, I made 63 after England had been in dire trouble at 98 for four on a first-day Lord's pitch offering some nip and zip under cloudy skies. Just as satisfying was the 147-run partnership I had with Goochie, who made 114.

I always enjoyed batting with Gooch, not least because you had a close-up view of how a master batsman went about his business. As colleagues at Essex, we were pretty used to each other, but that did not dampen the inspiration I always felt in his company at the crease. You see, Goochie did not discriminate, and whether for county or country, he always made his cause seem a noble one, which occasionally rubbed off on the rest of us.

Despite our stand, the team were dismissed for 294, which was inadequate, and India, who took a 47-run lead from their first innings, assumed control to win the match by five wickets. They then won the next Test, which decided the series.

The rest day of that second match, at Headingley, fell on Sunday, 22 June, the day England's footballers played their World Cup quarter-final match against Argentina in Mexico City. That was the infamous game in which Diego Maradona scored two goals – one via the 'Hand of God', the other beyond even the conception of deities. The game was being shown live in the Wheatley pub not far from our team hotel in Ilkley. With our game just about done (India needed another four wickets on the Monday to complete a decisive win), we arrived there just after opening time, determined to drown our sorrows and maybe toast an England win in the footie.

The bitter they served was Tetleys and it went down well enough for us to keep drinking it despite the result from Mexico. Even without Beefy to lead the line (he was still serving his ban), I just kept sinking pints, to the point I'd knocked back 17 of them. At least, that was the general consensus; I'd stopped counting myself. It must have been a large number, though, as JK Lever, who'd been picked to play in that Test, christened me 'Half Man Half Tetley'. Although partly in homage to the band Half Man Half Biscuit, whose song '------' 'ell it's Fred Titmus' had brought great mirth to the Essex dressing room that season, it was probably an accurate estimate.

The incredible thing was I felt absolutely fine the following morning, though it didn't do me or England much good, as we were quickly toppled, losing our last four wickets within the hour. The defeat, by a massive 279 runs, was hard to accept. Headingley, a venue usually so toxic to visiting teams, had instead proved lethal to us. The pitch had been two-paced with variable bounce. JK and I had taken six and seven wickets respectively, but their seam bowlers, Kapil Dev, Madan Lal and Roger Binny, had got even more out of it.

Locals will always tell you that the overhead conditions at Headingley are crucial to how the pitch plays, with cloud cover causing havoc and sunshine inducing calm. 'Look oop, not down, son,' was how Fred Trueman used to put it. It will sound a pathetic excuse, but it seemed that whenever we batted during that game it was cloudy, and whenever India batted it was sunny. Our two scores were 102 and 128, theirs 272 and 237. Science may dismiss it as bunkum, but in that Test the correlation between fact and folklore was strong.

The other phenomenon I witnessed during that Test was Mike Gatting's capacity for food, though obviously I'd heard the rumours. One of the pleasures of a Headingley Test is the good ale and a visit to either Bryan's or Brett's fish and chip restaurants. Gatt, who had just taken over from Gower as captain after the latter was sacked following our defeat at Lord's, favoured Bryan's. On successive nights, he ordered two portions of the baby haddock, chips and mushy peas, with brown bread and butter. That is stupendous troughing. For starters, the 'baby' haddock was a misnomer and it actually had more fish, consisting as it did of two crisp battered pieces, than the 'large' haddock on the menu, which had one. A mountain of chips accompanied it. One was an effort for most people, but Gatt demolished two of them each night with scarcely a pause for breath.

The third and final Test at Edgbaston, which was also Sunil Gavaskar's last in England, was drawn, after which the second series of that 1986 summer, against New Zealand, began. I'd knocked Gavaskar over in India's first innings at Birmingham, bowling him off stump after he offered no shot. I never usually sledged opponents but I couldn't help having a word on this occasion. The reason had been Gavaskar's interview with BBC presenter Peter West, during a prolonged period of bad light. In it, West had made much of Gavaskar's skill of knowing where his off stump was, to which Gavaskar had replied, 'Yes, Peter, I'd like to think I'm a good judge of line.' Of course, when play resumed, and he misjudged the line of the ball from me, the urge to say 'Judged that one well, Sunny' was just too strong.

I missed the first Test against the Kiwis at Lord's, which was drawn, with illness, but played in the second, at Trent Bridge, which we lost by eight wickets. I had a poor game at Trent Bridge, going wicketless and not making many runs. What might have happened had I done well and we'd drawn or even won the game, I'm not sure, but my misstep paved the way for Beefy's long-awaited return after his ban. And boy did he return in style. Coming on to bowl first change in the final Test at The Oval, he dismissed Bruce Edgar with his very first ball back. Gooch, who caught Edgar's tentative push at second slip, demanded to know, immediately, who wrote Beefy's scripts. You couldn't make something like that up. Some people just play by different rules. Beefy wasn't finished either, taking two more in the innings, the first of them breaking Dennis Lillee's world record of 355 Test wickets. He even made a rapid and unbeaten 59 before England declared, though rain thwarted any possibility of levelling the series.

During that New Zealand tour, Goochie and I had invited Martin Crowe out for dinner to sound him out about becoming Essex's overseas player for the 1987 season. Allan Border had been with Essex that summer and had proved a fine and popular addition but could not return until 1988. Crowe, we felt, would be a worthy replacement, and he took little persuading. 'At last,' he said, 'I'll be part of a team that actually wins things.'

Being virtuous and well-mannered, Crowe, who'd spent the 1984 season playing for Somerset while Viv Richards and Joel Garner toured England with the West Indies, said he needed to clear it with Somerset first. Basically, he'd promised them first option, out of politeness, but foresaw no objection from them over signing for Essex, as Richards and Garner were still in place as the club's overseas players.

What he wasn't aware of, until he informed Somerset of Essex's desire to sign him, was the ferment brewing behind the scenes at Taunton. Peter Roebuck, Somerset's cerebral but highly strung opening batsman, had grown up with Botham and Richards at the club. Now, as captain, and persuaded by an argument that he was serving the greater good, Roebuck saw an opportunity to gather round him a team of young acolytes, something he'd always been fervent about. A complicating factor was that new rules had been introduced for the 1987 season, allowing counties just one overseas pro. Those with two existing overseas players could still register both, but new signings would be limited to one player only. If Somerset wanted Crowe – and Roebuck did, believing a new broom was required – Richards and Garner, two fine servants of the club, would have to go.

Just after Beefy's record-breaking wicket at The Oval, the pair were called in by the club chairman, Brian Langford, and sacked. A man loyal to his friends first, Beefy immediately issued Somerset an ultimatum: 'Reinstate them or I go too.' As a ransom demand it didn't work and the club called his bluff. A special meeting of the club's members was convened, but with heavy heart, a majority decided to support the committee and captain. As a result, Crowe never did play for Essex, who instead signed the South African pace bowler Hugh Page.

While it might be said that Essex had precipitated what many saw as Roebuck's betrayal of his team-mates (Beefy hung a sign above his clothes hook in the dressing room which read 'JUDAS'), our role had probably not become clear by the time we played

Somerset in Taunton a few days after news of the sackings had broken. If it had, it didn't prevent Beefy marching into our dressing room to offer his and Viv's services to Essex – 'as a package'.

It was typical Beefy: heartfelt, impulsive but slightly crackers all at the same time. It certainly caught Fletch and Doug Insole, Essex's chairman, on the hop. With Fletch about to hand over the captaincy to Goochie at the end of the season, it was felt that Beefy and Viv might be a bit too much superstar for a new captain to handle.

The match, which proved to be Viv's last for the club, was a thriller which Essex won by nine runs. The greatest batsman I have ever bowled at, Viv almost signed off with a winning knock, making 94 as Somerset chased 273 to win. He also made 53 in the first innings. It was a great and timely victory for us, though, as we marched to our third Championship title in four years.

At the end of that season Beefy went to Worcestershire and Viv left county cricket to concentrate on captaining the West Indies. It wasn't a final farewell for him, though, and in 1990 he returned to join Glamorgan for three seasons.

Nobody really mentioned 'Big Bird' Joel Garner, arguably the innocent bystander in Roebuck's machinations, due to his general happy-go-lucky nature. What probably did for him was his knees, which had begun to play up, forcing him to cherry-pick where he got on and off the treadmill of county cricket. Although he soldiered on for another two years for Barbados and West Indies, Bird bowled only another 494 overs in all cricket (an amount he used to surpass most summers for Somerset). He eventually called time on an illustrious career in 1988.

Beefy was not quite done yet, of course, and his move to Worcestershire saw them twice win the Championship, an accolade he'd not achieved before. He still had a few match-turning performances left for England, too, the best coming against his favourite foes, the Aussies, in the 1986–87 Ashes, when Mike Gatting was his captain. Though it was another England tour for which I was over-looked, I did manage to get a close-up view after spending the winter playing Grade cricket in Sydney for Campbelltown.

England retained the Ashes two Tests to one, but like their other successes against Australia in the 1980s, the reasons could be traced to a couple of decisive interventions from Beefy – the first with bat, in the opening Test in Brisbane; the second with ball, in the Boxing Day Test at the MCG. Although not wishing to detract from other important contributions such as Chris Broad's three hundreds in successive Tests, Beefy's two high points were the big moments which turned those two matches.

Put in to bat by Allan Border in the opening Test at the Gabba, Beefy turned a good start into an exceptional score with an aggres-sive 138, not that he ever really did passive. Merv Hughes, Australia's walrus-moustached fast bowler, came in for some severe tap, seri-ous enough to get sledged by Dean Jones, one of his team-mates. After one of the sixes struck by Beefy, Jones chirped, 'Jeez, Merv, that one's gone so far it's qualified for frequent-flyer points.'

Faced with a big total of 456, Australia then wilted under the pressure of some fine swing bowling from Graham Dilley, who took five for 68 in what was arguably his most important contribution in England colours. Dilley, a tall, blond fast bowler who could swing the ball at pace, had twice taken more wickets in an innings for England. The difference this time, though, was that after making Australia follow on, England went on to win.

England held their one-match lead until the fourth Test at the MCG. Whether hangover-led following Christmas revelry, or because the pitch was tinged with green, Gatting put the Aussies in and was rewarded with their prompt dismissal for 141 in under two sessions. Beefy, who had missed the previous Test with a pulled intercostal muscle, took five for 41. Because of the injury, he'd come on second change to nurse it back to life and had bowled little more than gentle dobbers, which had nibbled off the seam. But with Gladstone Small knocking them over at the other end, the Aussies didn't know whether to attack Beefy or defend him. Like all efficient predators, he took advantage of the chaos.

England took a 208-run lead after Broad's third successive hundred and dismissed Australia cheaply a second time, though Beefy, his decisive play made, wasn't among the wickets in the second innings. The Ashes were retained, a fact celebrated by a lavish party in Sydney thrown by who else but Elton John, an event that saw Dennis Lillee, trying to leave the shindig at 2 a.m., get stuck in a lift until dawn.

England lost the final Test, but it was of little consequence. One of the perks of being an Ashes winner is that you are remembered long after time has scattered the other details of your career. Take Mike Gatting. He'll be remembered for two things: captaining England to that Ashes victory and for being the recipient of Shane Warne's ball of the century in the 1993 Ashes series. What people have long forgotten is that Gatt, who took 54 Test innings to score his first hundred, captained England 23 times in Test matches. Those two victories in Australia were his only wins.

After that series Beefy's powers were on the wane. A succession of injuries, including one to his back requiring the fusion of two vertebrae, began to mount up. He managed to keep on playing for another six years, though with less frequency for England. In fact, after the 1986–87 tour he played just 13 more Tests, passing 50 once and taking 17 more wickets. In one-day cricket, which he never took that seriously, there was a late flourish in the 1992 World Cup, in which England were runners-up to Pakistan. A year later, though, having moved to newly formed county Durham to see out his dotage, he called it a day at 37 – age being nature's way of avenging itself on those who try to defy its laws.

7

CHAOS THEORY – 1988

T HE SEOUL OLYMPICS, with its drugs cheats, were held in
1988, a leap year which saw the first internet virus mess with
the new technology in our lives. But if that had the capacity for
chaos, there was even greater mayhem on the cricket field for
England, whose summer schedule consisted of five Tests against the
West Indies followed by a one-off Test against Sri Lanka.

In what must still be a nadir for the England cricket team, an
unprecedented four captains were appointed that summer, five if
you count my two sessions at the helm in the final Test. It was a
head count that made Henry VIII look positively forgiving.

The mayhem began with the sacking of Mike Gatting after his
alleged dalliance with a barmaid during the first Test, something
Gatt has always vigorously denied. Thereafter, the despatching of
captains continued almost at the rate of one a Test until the final
match. Even then Gooch, the last of the quartet, required a stand-
in, me, after splitting his finger. England cricket had never seemed
so shambolic.

West Indies were still the number-one Test team in the world,
though some felt they might be vulnerable following the retire-
ments of Clive Lloyd, Michael Holding, Joel Garner and Larry
Gomes. What did they know? In their place came the tall and lethal
Curtly Ambrose, the effing rapid Patrick Patterson, whom Jeffrey
Dujon, the wicketkeeper, felt was the fastest bowler he'd ever kept
to, and Carl Hooper, a silky strokeplayer of talent and cool. Oh, and
they also had a supremely proud man, Vivian Richards, eager to
leave his own legacy as West Indies captain. Vulnerable? My arse.

If we'd had an off-field spinner as good as Alastair Campbell became for Tony Blair's Labour a decade or so later, you might have argued that England's 4–0 defeat was actually something of a minor triumph. After all, the previous two series against the West Indies had ended in 5–0 whitewashes. Yet nobody dared venture that thesis as the summer wore on and England got through 28 players, four captains and one chairman of selectors.

Ian Botham, so often English cricket's saviour earlier in the decade, was absent following surgery to his back. Wear and tear, something he had always dismissed as footling, had developed into something more serious and it took him about a year to get over it.

Even without him, it might have been different had the team been able to retain the confidence and quality of play produced during our own clean sweep, that of the Texaco series of ODIs which preceded the Tests. I was picked for that three-match series, in which England were led by Mike Gatting, and I bowled pretty well. Indeed, I won the man-of-the-match award in the second game, at Headingley, where, on a tricky pitch, I was England's top-scorer (39) as well as its top wicket-taker (three for 30).

It was the second award I'd won against the West Indies and I had a theory as to why that might be, since I'd never won one against any other country. Batting at six, seven or eight and bowling first or second change, as I did, normally limited one's scope for producing the kind of match-turning performance that won man-of-the-match awards in one-day cricket. Against a side like the West Indies, though, things were different. Their barrage of fast bowlers and aggressive batsmen meant players were less able to cope than against other teams. The West Indies basically reduced the competition from within your own side, which I suppose improved one's own odds, providing the match was won and you'd played a reasonable part in achieving that win. Which at Headingley I had.

In fact, I bowled a ball there, to Jeff Dujon, that I'm fairly confident would have defeated any batsman in cricket history. It swung away from Dujon, a right-hander, but as he shaped to cut it past cover, it hit a crack, nipped back sharply without getting more than eight inches high and bowled him middle and off stump. Patrick Eagar, the doyen of cricket photographers, captured the moment, and Dujon's despairing gesture really says it all.

Though we had bossed the one-day series, Test cricket was an entirely different beast. For a start, bouncers were not restricted in the way they were in the limited-overs arena, while pitches were built to last five days instead of one, so tended to do less for those relying on seam movement – which was pretty much every England bowler bar Graham Dilley, who had proper pace when he slipped himself.

People who have not faced bowlers like Patterson or Ambrose, who was a good yard quicker then than the bowler who later settled down to life probing line and length, will have no inkling as to the effect intimidation has on a batsman's mind. Helmets might have been standard by then, but gloves were still not fracture-proof. Also, chest guards were bulky and uncomfortable, so more likely to be discarded than worn.

Even with helmets, trying to cope with three or four 90 mph balls every over aimed at your chest or above wore batsmen down. In any case, full-on impact with your helmet at those speeds still did damage, with concussion very much an associated risk. Even those who played the hook shot, a stroke filled with risk, rarely had a lasting solution. Instead, you needed courage, mettle, a high pain threshold and a positive outlook, things that rarely came in fours even among top Test players.

Australia's Mitchell Johnson showed the immense value of a fast bowler with pace and aggression when he blew England's batting away in the 2013–14 Ashes. But there was only one of him and he was limited to two bouncers per over. Against West Indies in 1988, there were four quicks – Marshall, Ambrose, Walsh and Patterson, with Ian Bishop in reserve – all eager to let fly with as many bouncers as the umpire decided to let them get away with.

Brutal pace wasn't their only unique selling point, either. While Patterson might have been a blast-you-out kind of bowler, Marshall, Ambrose and Walsh were skilful manipulators of the ball as well. Marshall, in particular, had studied other bowlers. Like Dennis Lillee, he prided himself on adapting to both the conditions and the opponent facing him. If he bowled to Gooch, for example, he'd try to get him caught behind with the new ball. If that didn't pay off, he'd try to work the lbw by getting Gooch to play around his front pad by holding the ball outside off stump for a period, then trying to spring the plan with a crafty inswinger. He knew that Gooch was one of the finest batsmen against balls bouncing above the knee roll, so persistent short stuff, unless the pitch was really quick, was generally wasted on him.

What made Gooch such a worthy opponent was that he relished the challenge of playing fast bowling. His adage that 'Nobody likes fast bowling, it's just that some are better at playing it' was based on his experiences of facing the West Indies home and away. With his upright stance at the crease, bat raised, he backed himself and his reactions to cope with whatever came his way from the fast men. Only once did he admit that he felt helpless about not being able to react in time, and that was against Patrick Patterson at Sabina Park in February 1986. It was Patterson's debut in front of his fellow Jamaicans and he bowled fast and furious. 'Rapid' was the term Gooch used. Yet, it was the pitch, which had slight corrugations, that gave him most concern, not the 97 mph those present reckoned Patterson had been reaching.

'The rippled nature of the pitch, which was concrete-hard, meant one ball would shoot low from just short of a good length while another would fly past your chin,' said Gooch in his autobiography, *Gooch*. 'It was the one time I thought I might get hit in the face and not be able to do anything about it.'

Despite the danger, he still wore a helmet without a grille, top-scoring with 51, one of just four scores to reach double figures as England were dismissed for 159.

A home series would be different, we hoped. As we assembled for the first Test at Trent Bridge in June 1988, we were greeted by Nick Stewart, a debonair gent who, among other things, had once been an A&R man for Island Records. Stewart had brought with him several cases of decent claret, a thank you, he said, from some city traders who'd made a killing betting on us in the one-day series. Thank you, we said, and divvied it up, with David Gower and Paul Jarvis the luckiest recipients, given neither had played in the one-day series.

As was Peter May's policy, we stayed about 40 minutes from Trent Bridge at a hotel called Rothley Court, just north of Leicester. It was pleasant enough, with medieval suits of armour standing in the lobby. When I joked that we could perhaps do with borrowing them to face the West Indies, Allan Lamb tried to climb into one but found it too small even for a short-arse like him.

In the match we batted first and made 245. I came in at six, which I'd done in the one-day series. With no Botham, we looked a bit light on the batting, and while I'd been in decent nick with Essex, six was too high for me against a side like them. It meant we had a long tail, something Marshall, who'd been bowling with his ribs strapped, and Ambrose exposed. We'd been 220 for five at the end of a tricky first day, but were skittled for 245 before noon on the next.

I had been on 39 overnight but did not add to my score as Marshall bowled me off my pads. Some people I knew put my prompt dismissal on the second morning down to the previous night, which I'd spent with Gooch and Emburey at the Crown Inn at Old Dalby, a village halfway back to the team hotel. In truth, it had been a fairly standard night, involving a few pints of beer and a meal with wine. The only unusual thing was that we'd played a game or two of pétanque, the evening having been warm and pleasant enough to spend outside.

To my acquaintances, who just happened to be at the same pub, we'd obviously been giving it a thrash. As a result, they made the correlation, a false one as it happened, between that and my early dismissal the following day. In any case, I'd been a bit unlucky with Marshall's inswinger, which had been missing leg before it hit my pads and cannoned into the stumps.

Our total was still below par and West Indies easily overhauled it, to reach 448 for nine declared. By then, bad weather had consumed almost a day's play and with the help of a fine unbeaten 146 from Goochie, we comfortably played out the draw.

We hadn't lost, which was a major advance over the previous 10 Tests played against the West Indies. Two days later, though, it felt like we had, after two tabloids, the *Sun* and *Today*, accused Gatting and four other England players of engaging in naked sex frolics at Rothley Court during the match.

Part of the case against Gatting was the kiss-and-tell account of Louise Shipman, a 20-year-old barmaid at the Red Lion Inn in Rothley. Shipman had a boyfriend who was a freelance journalist, which made the whole thing reek of a set-up. Gatting has always denied he had sex with Shipman, saying that he just invited her back to his room for a drink. Looking back, I tend to believe him as most cricketers would brag about any conquests to the dressing room. There was none of that from Gatt, despite the papers quoting eyewitnesses dining at the hotel who said that they had seen sex romps on the hotel lawn and 'a chap's bottom in the air'.

One of my Essex team-mates, Brian Hardie, was also caught up in the scandal. Back then, the 12th man from the original squad would return to play for his county and be replaced by a player whose county did not have a game. Because somebody felt the pitch might turn for Emburey, Hardie, a brilliant short-leg fielder, had been summoned, despite his Scottish nationality.

For the first few days Hardie, or 'Lager' as he was generally known, stuck with me and Goochie after play, joining us on our nightly visits to the Crown Inn. But the rest day saw us mooch around Rothley, so there was no appetite, as we were not coming from Nottingham, to drive all the way to the Crown. Instead, we went to the Red Lion in Rothley, the local hostelry Gatt and the non-real ale drinkers had been frequenting during the match.

Gatt was already there having dinner with some of the selectors. Graham Dilley and I just slouched by the bar, taking in the scene, which seemed lively for a Sunday night, though maybe not if word had got round that England's cricketers had been using the place.

I can't be sure that Gatt was targeted, but I do know that Shipman was keen to come back to the hotel along with two other female friends of hers. Gatt did not come to the bar at Rothley Court, where Dill and I had one more drink before calling it a day. What went on thereafter has only ever been revealed in those two news-papers in the aftermath of that Test.

On Wednesday, 8 June, the *Sun* broke the story with the front-page headline 'TEST STARS IN SEX ORGY', but did not name anyone until the following day.

I saw the naming-and-shaming story in the *Sun* while travelling to Chelmsford by train. Essex had been playing Hampshire in the Benson & Hedges semi-final. The match had been rained over into a second day and I'd stayed with my old friend Kevin and his wife after going out with them for a curry. Because both of us had enjoyed a drink or two, we'd left our cars at the restaurant, hence the train journey. As I alighted at Chelmsford station, I passed Fiona Hardie, Lager's wife, on the steps as she went to catch the London train. Her cheery 'Morning, Derek' told me she had not yet seen the papers naming her husband in the scandal.

She did not remain in blissful ignorance for long. It took me 12 minutes to walk from the station to reach my peg in the dressing room, which was next to the players' payphone. Fiona rang just as I was about to hang up my jacket. Her voice, terser than before, asked if she could 'speak to Brian, please'. He wasn't there. The club's lawyers were already at work.

Mickey Stewart, England's coach at the time, was asked to investigate and questioned all the players who'd been involved in the Test. He also spoke to the manager of the Rothley Court hotel and the landlord of the Red Lion. Yet Stewart had been caught unawares by the story when it first broke. He was breakfasting near some cricket journalists in a Swansea hotel, and they couldn't understand his good mood – until they realised that he'd been reading the back pages of the papers, not the front.

'Turn the paper round, Mickey,' Martin Johnson of the *Independent* remembers telling him, recalling too the pained look on Stewart's face as he stomped off to make the first of many fraught phone calls.

Paul Downton, who'd kept wicket in the Test, recollects being summoned to Lord's to be quizzed by Fred Titmus and Phil Sharpe, two of the selection panel under May.

'I just remember feeling furious that I was being dragged into something that did not involve or concern me,' said Downton. 'Having been on the losing side to West Indies, constantly, I really felt that we had a chance of competing with them after our decent showing at Trent Bridge. Yet here we were essentially shooting ourselves in the foot with a witch hunt.'

Others, too, like Phil DeFreitas and Allan Lamb, were summoned to Lord's for the inquiry. DeFreitas, who had not been staying at

Rothley Court because he lived in Leicester, had only popped in for a quick drink on his way home.

'I had to drive all the way to Lord's, so I wasn't happy,' said DeFreitas. 'I had no helpful information to give them. I do remember, though, that as I drove out of the Grace Gates Lamby drove in. He was fuming and gave the assembled press and photographers a right roasting for what he saw as deliberate destabilising of the England team.'

Lamb had been the subject of newspaper scandals previously. This time, though, he'd not even been in the vicinity, having gone home to Northampton after Saturday's play to nurse a flu virus. When asked for a comment by the *Sun*, once the story of the 'orgy' had broken, he quipped, 'Looks like I missed all the fun.' He then added, 'Maybe Ian Botham was involved – he needs the exercise after his back surgery.'

I don't recall the findings of Stewart or anyone else's report ever being made public, but some barmy decisions were made over the incident. Peter May, who'd publicly stated that he believed Gatting's version of events, then went and showed his support by sacking him as captain. May's justification was that Gatting, who'd admitted to asking Shipman to his room for a drink, had placed himself in a position in which he'd imperilled the highest honour in the game – the England captaincy.

The warped logic didn't end there. Gatting, who some in authority felt had been pushing his luck with the TCCB ever since his spat with umpire Shakoor Rana on England's tour of Pakistan seven months earlier, had just written a book titled *Leading from the Front*. Contained within was a contentious chapter about the Rana incident which the TCCB did not want included. Unhappily for them, the publishers had already printed hardback copies and were not about to remove the offending pages.

Eventually, after a few months of wrangling, and this after Gatt had been sacked as captain, he was fined £5,000. And yet a day earlier, which shows how conflicted the hierarchy must have been about him, he'd been awarded the OBE for services to English cricket.

Emburey was appointed Gatt's successor as England captain for the second Test, at Lord's. May, though, made it plain that it was very much 'play as you go', and the leadership issue would be reassessed at the end of the match.

We bowled first, after the West Indies had won the toss, and had them in deep trouble at 54 for five. Dill had found a killer rhythm from the Nursery End, with some good swing, and had nipped out four in his opening spell, including Viv Richards for six. He should also have added Gus Logie soon after, but I spilled the chance at first slip. It wasn't what I'd call regulation, being low to my right, but it should probably have been snaffled seven times out of 10.

Quite a few catches in the slip cordon get put down at Lord's and I believe the slope plays its part by fooling the brain that the ball is on a slightly different trajectory than it really is. I felt Logie's catch was only a few inches above the turf, so snatched at it, whereas it was probably shin-high. I reckon the slope gave me that impression, though I've no idea if the science stacks up, optically.

To compound my woes, Logie went on to top-score, with 81. In league with Jeff Dujon, who made 53, he fashioned a crucial partnership of 130 for the sixth wicket. It left me and my compadres contemplating what might have been, not least how a total that should have been nearer 120 ended up as 209.

It is not easy or pleasant explaining how such culpability feels. The team rallies behind you and tells you, 'Never mind, catch the next one.' But you know that the depth of disappointment runs far deeper than the surface banalities. This was the West Indies, the best team in the world, and one which had humiliated us on a regular basis. We had them in deep trouble, a position from which they had now wriggled free. 'You absolute prat' scream a thousand silent voices, of which my own is the loudest.

Their total proved more than enough for the mighty West Indies attack to work with. With Malcolm Marshall on top of his game, and with the remaining three quicks keeping pressure on at the other end, we were shot out for 165, which gave them a lead of 44 precious runs.

They didn't squander their advantage, either, making 397 in their second innings. Gordon Greenidge scored a hundred, while Logie added to his first-innings heroics by remaining unbeaten on 95. Deserving though he was of such an accolade, it was not enough to get his name onto the Lord's honours board.

I took two wickets, including Viv Richards in front of a full house on the Saturday, but any joy was tempered by the fact that we were about to take a good hiding and go 1–0 down. That night, at my old mate Magoo's wedding reception back in Cambridge, I got thoroughly bladdered, knowing that I had the rest day at home to get over it.

We made 307 in our second innings, but that flattered us. While Allan Lamb scored a fine hundred, the rest of the top six made just 32, with me failing to trouble the scorers. Yes, I was still at six. The tail wagged but it was a futile gesture. We lost by 134 runs – normal service against the West Indies had been resumed.

As I expected, the selectors dropped me for the third Test, at Old Trafford. Emburey retained the captaincy, though not for long. The match in Manchester was, by general consensus and this from an admittedly generous sample of shockers, England's worst performance of the summer.

Batting first after winning the toss, England were dismissed for 135 off 60.2 overs, so a slow death. West Indies then got 384 before bowling England out again, this time for 93, Marshall taking seven for 22. In that second innings only two batsmen, Gower and Martyn Moxon, reached double figures. It doesn't get more dispiriting than that.

The frustration of that result saw the selectors visit their wrath upon the team, making seven changes for the next Test at Headingley. Out went Martyn Moxon, Gatt, Paul Downton, Emburey, David Capel, Phil DeFreitas and John Childs, and in came me, Tim Curtis, Bill Athey, Robin Smith, Jack Richards and Neil Foster, with Chris Cowdrey as the new captain. Only Gooch, Gower, Lamb and Dilley retained their places. Changes that swingeing put everyone on edge – those surviving the cut as well as those coming in. Essentially, every player in the team had been placed on notice.

Cowdrey seemed embarrassed by his promotion, and not just because Peter May was his godfather. Actually he made mirth of the fact, telling the press that the England captaincy was the best present a godparent could give. Cow had played five Tests for England under David Gower on the tour of India three and a half years earlier, but had not been part of an England team since. Those five matches may still have swung it his way, as apparently Mark Nicholas, the Hampshire captain, was also in contention for the job. In the end it was felt that making a Test debut against the West Indies as both batsman and captain was too great an ask, and Cowdrey got the nod.

Cow's first job in his new role was to inform those who'd been dropped of their fate, including Paul Downton, someone he'd known since the age of 12. Downton, with whom I'd roomed during the 1987 World Cup in India and Pakistan, recalled the moment Cowdrey told him of his fate.

'Cow phoned and said, "I've got some bad news, matey. They want changes and they've given me a choice between you and Gower, and I'm afraid I've gone for Gower." I never played for England again.'

Normally, you'd think that a fair enough trade-off, except that Gower and Downton were hardly vying for the same spot. Unless Cowdrey was being disingenuous, in order to break the bad news more softly to his old mate, it seemed the selectors had just rolled the dice.

Cow's speech at the pre-Test dinner was almost as brief. I felt for him. The series and selection had become an utter farce.

'What was I meant to say?' said Cowdrey, recalling the moment decades later. 'I'd been told that I'd be taking the side to India in the winter, but suddenly I'd been drafted in to captain the fourth Test against the West Indies.

'I'd never played a Test in England before, never played against the West Indies, or been to a pre-match dinner. The preparation was minimal. I'd just come out of a county match for Kent, and although we were top of the table, I hadn't got a run for weeks.'

Inevitably gallows humour came to the fore, until Goochie, fired by a few glasses of claret and fed up with the defeatist chatter, asked if he could say a few words.

'I'm tired of losing to this lot,' he said. 'Yes, they are a bloody good team, but they've never really been tested, at least not by us. We've got to believe we can compete with them. To do that we've got to get behind the new captain and give him all we've got.

'None of us should come off that field wondering if there was any more we could have done. The series has gone but we've got the opportunity to try to salvage some pride, so let's go and do that. Anyway, I'd like to wish Chris all the best.'

Goochie wore a hangdog expression at the best of times, but the serious look he maintained while delivering his oration stilled the room and cut dead the pessimistic chatter. Whether it stopped most players feeling they had but a single Test to prove themselves, I don't know, but it gave us something else to ponder as we went to bed that night. Knowing Gooch pretty well, I don't believe the speech was a deliberate bid for the captaincy, though he would have known that Cow was unlikely to have what it took, talent-wise, to stay in the side for long, at least against the West Indies.

Everyone involved with England appeared to lose their bearings that summer, which meant that everything seemed up for grabs all of the time. It was chaos. Tim Curtis, who came in to make his Test debut as Gooch's opening partner, remembers it all feeling very dislocated.

'There seemed to be an old boys' club, headed by Allan Lamb and David Gower, who seemed intent on being welcoming and keeping everything jolly,' said Curtis. 'But there was also this sense of disarray. Mind you, I didn't feel it was quite as bad as the Ashes in 1989, in which I also played. England used even more players that series.'

Curtis also recalls the bizarre start of the match, when England were put in by Viv Richards after he'd won the toss, though he kept our batsmen on tenterhooks by leaving his decision to inform them until the last possible moment (then 20 minutes before the start). Play began on time, though there had been a sharp shower just before. After two overs, and with the score still 0–0, Curtly Ambrose complained that he couldn't keep his footing after water had seeped out of the ground onto his run-up. Umpire Dickie Bird investigated and play was held up until after lunch while ground staff set about sorting the problem and mopping it up.

With the sun shining, usually cause enough for celebration in Leeds, it made for a farcical scene and one the crowd were loath to accept. They booed Bird, who tried to reason with them, saying that it wasn't his fault water had oozed up through the ground. Although it was never explained satisfactorily at the time, the culprit was thought to be Keith Boyce, the groundsman. In those days, the Headingley pitch used to crack alarmingly when it dried, which made the bounce inconsistent and very difficult for batsmen to counter as the match wore on. That challenge would have been intensified by the pace and height of the West Indies bowlers, so Boyce, presumably with patriotic intent, had tried to keep moisture in the pitch by blocking some of the drains. When it rained, the run-off could not discharge via its usual channels, so bubbled up right up under Curtly's feet.

Neither the delay nor the soggy run-ups deterred Ambrose, and he took four for 58 as we were dismissed for 201. If anything, it provided extra motivation for him, and he cut a fearsome sight with his blistering pace and steepling bounce.

We should have scored more and might have done but for a calf injury to Allan Lamb when he was on 64. He and Robin Smith, another making his Test debut that match, added 103 for the fifth wicket, though their efforts were squandered when none of the last five batsmen reached double figures. The score was 183 for four when Lamby hobbled off and 185 for eight a few overs later. You've heard the one about giving suckers an even break – well, don't even think about doing it with thoroughbreds like the West Indies pace attack.

I made nought, caught by Dujon off Marshall. It was a snorter which had sprung up off a good length and flicked my right glove. I can remember watching the TV highlights later that night and Richie Benaud musing over how one might play a ball like that and not get out. In the end he decided that you'd have to miss it, something I'd not managed to do.

Bowling was more pleasurable, as it usually was for me at Headingley. Coming on first change, after Dill and Fozzy had taken the first three wickets, I proceeded to take the next five, as West Indies were bowled out for 275. They remain the best bowling figures of my Test career, which offered some solace when our second innings capitulated for 138. It left our opponents needing 65 to win, a total they knocked off in 14.3 overs without a glitch.

ENGLAND V WEST INDIES
(4th Test)

Played at Headingley, Leeds, 21–26 July 1988

Umpires:	HD Bird & DR Shepherd	
Toss:	West Indies	

ENGLAND

GA Gooch	c Dujon b Marshall	9		c Hooper b Walsh		50
TS Curtis	lbw b Benjamin	12		b Ambrose		12
CWJ Athey	lbw b Ambrose	16		c Dujon b Walsh		11
DI Gower	c Dujon b Benjamin	13		c Dujon b Marshall		2
AJ Lamb	retired hurt	64	(8)	c Dujon b Ambrose		19
RA Smith	c Dujon b Ambrose	38	(5)	lbw b Marshall		11
CS Cowdrey*	lbw b Marshall	0	(6)	b Walsh		5
CJ Richards†	b Ambrose	2	(7)	b Ambrose		8
DR Pringle	c Dujon b Marshall	0		b Benjamin		3
NA Foster	not out	8		c Hooper b Benjamin		0
GR Dilley	c Hooper b Ambrose	8		not out		2
Extras	(1 b, 18 lb, 6 nb, 6 w)	31		(3 b, 8 lb, 4 nb)		15
Total	(69.1 overs)	**201**		(61.5 overs)		**138**

WEST INDIES

DL Haynes	lbw b Pringle	54		not out	25
PJL Dujon†	c Smith b Dilley	13		not out	40
CL Hooper	lbw b Foster	19			
IVA Richards*	c Curtis b Foster	18			
AL Logie	c Foster b Pringle	44			
KLT Arthurton	c Richards b Pringle	27			
RA Harper	c Gower b Foster	56			
MD Marshall	c Gooch b Pringle	3			
CEL Ambrose	lbw b Pringle	8			
WKM Benjamin	run out	9			
CA Walsh	not out	9			
Extras	(15 lb)	15		(2 lb)	2
Total	(81.2 overs)	**275**		(14.3 overs)	**67**

WEST INDIES	O	M	R	W		O	M	R	W	Fall of wickets:				
Marshall	23	8	55	3		17	4	47	2		Eng	WI	Eng	WI
Ambrose	25.1	8	58	4		19.5	4	40	3	1st	14	15	56	–
Benjamin	9	2	27	2	(4)	5	4	2	2	2nd	43	61	80	–
Walsh	12	4	42	0	(3)	20	9	38	3	3rd	58	97	85	–
										4th	80	137	85	–
ENGLAND	O	M	R	W		O	M	R	W	5th	183	156	105	–
Dilley	20	5	59	1		4	0	16	0	6th	183	194	105	–
Foster	32.2	6	98	3		7	1	36	0	7th	185	210	127	–
Pringle	27	7	95	5						8th	185	222	132	–
Cowdrey	2	0	8	0		3.3	0	13	0	9th	201	245	132	–
										10th	–	275	138	–

Close of play:	Day 1:	England (1) 137–4 (Lamb 45*, Smith 23*)
	Day 2:	West Indies (1) 156–5 (Arthurton 1*, Harper 0*)
	Day 3:	West Indies (1) 238–8 (Harper 31*, Benjamin 7*)
	Day 4:	West Indies (2) 27–0 (Haynes 10*, Dujon 17*)

Man of the match:	CEL Ambrose
Result:	**West Indies won by 10 wickets**

It was another drubbing. In the past, any internal scarring I'd suffered had soon repaired itself, but these defeats disorientated. It was as if all purpose had been lost. Although one began every Test with optimism of a kind, it wasn't long before you were wishing for it to end as quickly as possible. At times like that it was hard to know why you put yourself through the humiliation, except for the money. There was certainly no glory in getting annihilated like that.

There wasn't even that much joy at Essex that season, so it was not as if Goochie and I could go back and lose ourselves in another cause. We did, however, finish third in the Championship after winning four of our last five games, though it wasn't enough to overhaul Worcestershire, who won by a single point from Kent.

Before that denouement we had one more Test against the West Indies, at The Oval, and the team picked included the talented young players Rob Bailey and Matthew Maynard. Back, too, came Phil DeFreitas, David Capel and John Childs, Essex's left-arm spinner.

It wasn't all change. I survived, as did Neil Foster, Tim Curtis, Robin Smith and Jack Richards. But not Gower, Bill Athey, Graham Dilley or Lamby, though Lamby was still injured with a torn calf muscle. That injury made it even more curious that May should get rid of Gower, one of our most experienced batsmen. But selection by then was obviously being done on a roulette wheel.

Most interesting was their choice of England captain, which had fallen to Graham Gooch after Cowdrey had been diagnosed with a broken toe, courtesy of a yorker he'd received at Headingley. Ever doleful, Gooch believed he was chosen because he was the last man standing and there were no alternatives, at least not among those guaranteed selection. Through a summer exhibiting more chop and change than David Bowie's hairstyles, he was the only player to feature in every Test.

There was a different dynamic to the team as well. It felt like the West Indies had wiped out a generation of England players that summer. From so often feeling like the junior man in the side, I was suddenly the third eldest after Gooch and John 'Charlie' Childs. Third eldest did not mean third most mature, though, and I remember having a very late night in the bar with Matt Maynard, then 22, the night before he made his debut. I didn't lead him astray, as he'd already acquired a reputation for being thirsty, but I should have led by example by heading to bed before midnight. Yet by then, that series had turned most of us into hard-drinking fatalists and another late night wasn't going to alter a thing.

It was the first time four Essex players had ever represented England in the same Test, so Goochie, Fozzy, Charlie and me had a group photo taken in front of the gasometer before the start. We even brought a bit of Essex magic to bear with the ball, too, taking nine of the West Indies wickets to fall after we'd batted first and made 205 – Fozzy finishing with five, me three and Charlie one.

The other wicket to fall, as they were dismissed for 183, was a run-out, though I also had a hand in that, being the man who broke the stumps. In truth, Roger Harper, the batsman involved, should not have been given out. In collecting David Capel's wild throw from mid-on, I'd inadvertently broken the wicket. As the Laws stood then, I was supposed to place the ball and any standing stump together and pull it from the ground. Instead, I put the ball and the already uprooted stump together and appealed. Not knowing the Laws, Harper walked off and was not recalled by the umpires, though a piqued West Indies dressing room soon informed him of his ignorance.

It gave us a first-innings lead for the first time in the series, which we promptly squandered when we were bowled out for 202. Again the Essex contingent, or at least some of them, prospered. Goochie made 84, with Fozzy, who'd gone in as nightwatchman, the second highest scorer, with 34.

When people ask what facing that West Indies attack was like, with its quartet of fast bowlers, I tell them it was relentless – the fear of danger to body and wicket ever present. Keen competition for places kept them quick and mean, in both senses of that last word. Even if you could cope with the pace, and there weren't many throughout world cricket who could do so, they just wore you down – your patience, your resolve, everything.

During his knock of 84, Gooch had remained on 40 for 69 minutes on the third morning, and he was one of the best players of fast bowling there has ever been. They were quick, aggressive,and accurate – and bowled no rubbish. You might chance your arm and come off against them once in a series, but mostly you had to earn your runs through concentration and courage, and with a sturdy cut and pull shot. Without them, you were cannon fodder.

Quite frankly, most of the players picked that summer weren't up to it, the exceptions being Gooch, Lamb, Smith and Gower, though only the first two managed to average over 40 with the bat. England's batsmen notched two hundreds and seven fifties in that five-match series, all bar one of the fifties scored by that quartet.

The West Indies still needed 226 to win on a wearing Oval pitch, more than they'd made in their first innings. It was Gordon Greenidge's way to attack run-chases like that, something he'd done to us at Lord's in 1984. By the close he'd rushed to 53, with his partner Desmond Haynes on 15.

Not long before the end of play, Gooch split his finger dropping a difficult chance at second slip. Seams on new balls can be sharp and it cut him badly enough to need stitches and for the doctor to recommend that he did not take the field the following day. With no official vice-captain, and me the next senior in terms of caps, I was given the job of trying to fashion a rare victory when we resumed hostilities on the fourth morning, with West Indies needing another 154 runs to win. The situation was not without hope.

Our bowling attack of Fozzy, Daffy DeFreitas, me, Charlie Childs and David Capel had bowled well in the match so far. Also, the pitch had begun to dust up in places, which would make Charlie's spin a handful.

Just as I was about to take the side out onto the field, Goochie came over to issue some last-minute instructions.

'Good luck, mate,' he said. 'If we can get early wickets, you never know. Anyway, open up with Fozzy and Daffy, then you come on Daffy's end and follow Fozzy with Charlie; that end looks like it will spin more. Give him a long spell while you, Fozzy and Daffy alternate from the other end. Whatever you do, don't give Capel the ball. We haven't got enough runs to play with.'

Armed with my orders, I led out the England team, the first and only time I did such a thing. Did I feel inordinately proud of leading my country? Not really. I'd been too long part of a team oppressed by our West Indian opponents. In any case, taking charge in the way I did had nothing to do with merit and everything to do with our shambolic summer, so counted for diddly-squat. It's true that in the immediate aftermath of leaving Cambridge many had predicted that I would one day captain England. More fool them, as it was an ambition I never shared. They obviously didn't know me and my healthy scepticism towards power and leadership, or the Establishment's antipathy towards those who didn't play the greasy-pole game. Anyway, this was by default rather than design, so in no way justified their soothsaying.

Even so, it was a little bit scary. Instead of hiding behind the decisions of others on the field, I suddenly had to make a few myself that would affect the collective – not that anything I did was likely to bring us that elusive win. Early wickets would have brought hope, and we might have had one, too, had Jack Richards not dropped Haynes off me after I'd replaced Daffy at the Vauxhall End. The ball had gripped in the dusting surface and seamed away a tad, so our cause was not entirely hopeless, especially as Charlie had spun a couple quite sharply. But as the morning wore on our means of striking began to reduce, so when Charlie eventually had Greenidge caught behind for 77, they were more than halfway to their target.

Charlie posed the most threat and was our main hope, the old ball now doing little for the seamers. But he was new to this Test lark and had tensed up a bit, which is never ideal for a precision skill like spin bowling. Carl Hooper had spotted that as well, and while his 23 was but a brief cameo, he attacked Charlie in an attempt to knock his confidence completely out of kilter. One six, which he eased over long-off, was simply outrageous in its dismissal of convention.

Charlie knew Hooper was quick on his feet and a brilliant player of spin, so had come over the wicket to him. His aim, following Hooper's desire to always dominate spinners, was to bowl it into the footholes, now amalgamated into a small dustbowl after three days' play, the plan being to frustrate him into error. Hooper was having none of it. In a shimmy that was left so late as to defeat any adjustment of line or length on Charlie's part, he was down the pitch a yard outside leg stump to caress the ball, and there really is no other word for the shot with its clean, smooth aesthetics, for six into the Oval pavilion.

There are strokes which reveal a lot more than the runs they bring, and this one told me and Charlie that the game was up. We'd tried everything (except Capel), and here was Hooper simply toying with our most dangerous bowler. Hooper was out soon after, chopping on to Fozzy, but with Desmond Haynes set and Gus Logie continuing his good form, we'd lost by eight wickets just before tea, with four sessions of the game remaining.

The margin suggested no change in the expanding canon of humiliating defeats at the hands of the West Indies, and yet it felt like we had at least competed. The selectors must have thought so as well.

For only the second time that summer they retained the captain, Gooch being appointed for the one-off Test against Sri Lanka at Lord's.

They did not show the same faith with the rest of the team, though, making seven changes. In came Tim Robinson to partner Gooch at the top of the order, while in for their Test debuts came Jack Russell, Phil Newport, David Lawrence and Kim Barnett. Allan Lamb returned, as did John Emburey, the selectors clearly feeling that Charlie Childs should have done better at The Oval.

I too survived, but I did not play much of a role in the match against Sri Lanka, which we won comfortably by seven wickets before lunch on the fifth day. That early finish enabled Gooch to receive his winner's medal, shower, pack his bags and still get across London to The Oval in time to take the field for Essex for the last two sessions of play in the first day of a Championship match.

He asked Fozzy and me if we'd like to join him, but bowlers rarely volunteered for anything, not being infected with the same keenness or sense of duty as Gooch. Our priority, as we saw it, was to our ailing bodies, and playing a match we had always been scheduled to miss by dint of playing in the Test would mean placing unnecessary strain on them. As warranted by his selfless gesture, Gooch made a hundred for Essex, though rain thwarted the ambitions of both teams by washing out the third day's play, so the match was drawn.

It wasn't long before the TCCB introduced a regulation to prevent players from representing two teams on the same day. It was classic TCCB. The national game was in turmoil, but instead of making reforms that might actually address the mess created that summer, they directed their efforts at pursuing those who had found loopholes in their regulations. It was pettiness personified and reminded me of the time, at boarding school, when I was summoned by my housemaster.

Why, he wanted to know, given my role as a house prefect, had I not punished anybody that term?

'Because I've not caught anyone doing anything wrong, sir,' I replied, all punishments having to be registered in a book.

'I don't care. Just go and punish someone.'

So I did, just to get him off my case.

As that crazy summer mellowed into autumn, there was one final twist. Gooch was made captain of England's winter tour to India. It was a trip for which I was not selected, which hacked me off no end.

I understood all the arguments that I was an English-conditions bowler who would not be suited to the dry, bare pitches of India, but I was resourceful. Anyway, I'd been the best all-round player on an England Schools tour to India a decade earlier, as well as playing a part in a World Cup there, so knew what to expect.

In the past, I'd fully accepted most of the occasions I'd been dropped from the side. But not this time. I'd played in four of the five Tests against the West Indies, something only five other players, from the 23 used, had managed. What about all the Johnny-come-latelies who'd come in for the Sri Lanka match and then found themselves picked for the tour party, where had they been when the flak was flying against the West Indies? Back in the safe haven of their counties, that's where.

The sense of injustice was acute, and it only got worse when India's government called off the tour because Gooch, Kim Barnett, John Emburey, Graham Dilley and one or two others were on a United Nations blacklist for having had sporting contacts with South Africa. Full pay and they didn't have to tour either – that was doubly galling. So I took myself off that winter, away from cricket, and into the wilds of the Kalahari and Namibia. Like those who joined the Foreign Legion, I felt the need to forget, otherwise there was the very real danger that I would end up embittered, and that was not my nature.

Peter May resigned as chairman of selectors in November 1988, to be replaced by Ted Dexter, a former England captain known as Lord Ted because of his regal bearing. Dexter was also seen as a progressive, having been known to wear leathers and ride a motorbike, though these things can be deceptive.

By making Gooch captain, May had at least managed one good deed that summer. Before his appointment, initially for the final Test against the West Indies, Gooch was close to chucking it all in with England, to spend his time playing for Essex in the summer and Western Province, in South Africa, during the winter. He'd even gone as far as to sign up for WP, though he got them to release him from the contract once he'd been asked to lead England in India.

'When they appointed me captain it ignited something in me,' said Gooch. 'I'm glad it happened. The impetus of that then gave me four or five of the best years of my career.'

Before that transpired, Gooch had to suffer one further setback. Dexter, an admirer of the Corinthian spirit and a cavalier at heart, abhorred the idea of Gooch, tethered as he was to Oliver Cromwell's roundhead creed (puritanical, hard-working, graft over craft). Describing the prospect of being captained by Gooch as like being 'slapped in the face by a wet fish', Dexter, after the 'no tour' winter was over, once more appointed Gatting to the England captaincy.

But if Lord Ted had forgiven Gatt all his sins, Ossie Wheatley, a team-mate of Dexter's in the Cambridge teams of 1957 and 1958, and now chairman of the TCCB's cricket committee, was not so clement. In his position, Wheatley had the right of veto and he used it. It is thought that he was backed in his decision to block Gatt's return as captain by Raman Subba Row, the chairman of the TCCB and another former England player who'd been at Cambridge. Poor

Gatt. Reappointed as captain by one member of the Cambridge mafia, he suddenly found his path blocked by two others. It was such a mess that even the Establishment seemed divided.

The move, which many within the county system felt gave too much power to a position of middling rank (Wheatley's), caused changes to be made. Indeed, the power to veto today's choice of captain lies solely with the chairman of the England and Wales Cricket Board and not the head of the ECB's cricket committee.

Denied Gatting, Dexter then chose David Gower to captain the team in 1989, an Ashes year. Gooch would have to wait another season to be captain and for another debacle to unfold, this time against the Aussies, one that called upon even more players than in 1988.

Those two seasons were a nadir for England cricket, which resembled one of those Victorian freak shows. 'Roll up, roll up, my friends, and see the cricket team that cannot win.'

8

QUIRKS OF THE ERA

Benefits

For the professional cricketer, the 1980s was largely a decade of promises unfulfilled. The battles with clubs for better salaries had been fought on the back of Kerry Packer's circus in the late 1970s, but wages were not much improved. To make up for the parsimony, Benefit years were awarded for long service.

A Benefit was something most players relied upon even when playing for England, where the pay was better but still not that generous. Some counties – Essex included – even used the promise of a Benefit to depress wages. Their reasoning ran thus: 'Yes, we might not pay as well as Lancashire, but you'll get a better Benefit here.'

It was not guaranteed, of course, and could not be written into a player's contract. To be awarded one required longevity, usually a minimum of 10 years as a capped player for a single county. It was a reward for loyalty and long service. Getting one was just the start, though. As the fund-raising, or glorified begging as some called it, was the player's responsibility, Benefits consumed much of the time and energy previously dedicated to preparing one's game. As a result, they often caused form to diminish and waistlines to increase.

Players, and their Benefit committees, would dream up ways of getting cricket supporters to part with their hard-earned cash over and beyond what they spent supporting their team. During Ray East's Benefit, in 1978, pontoon jars in pubs were the rage. People would buy the scratchcards within and see if they'd won one of the cash prizes offered. They probably broke the strict protocols of charitable status, which did not allow Benefit items to be sold for a set price. Instead, all monies raised had to be via a donation, which could be as little as half of one new pence in those days.

The jars proved popular money-spinners, each raising about 100 quid profit, of which the pub would take a cut. When one landlord absconded with the proceeds, his chief barmaid in tow, Easty was offered the chance of revenge by John Collins, a diehard Essex supporter and a man who, legend claimed, had once worked for the Krays.

'Heard you've had a bit of bovver, Raymondo,' said Collins one day, in the kind of voice Ray Winston has since adopted whenever he does menacing, which is often. 'I can make the scumbag pay if you like.'

'What have you got in mind, JC?' asked Easty, unsure of where this was going.

'Well, for 30 nicker I can have him kneecapped. Or, for 50, I can get the full shooter job done on him,' said Collins, without a scrap of irony.

'What, shoot him dead?' said Easty, the two-octave rise in his voice betraying his incredulity.

'Yeah. Your choice, son.'

Easty knew Collins was not a man to be trifled with. Once, while umpiring a local league game at Ilford, the visiting bowler had let fly his frustration after JC had turned down yet another lbw shout. A bad mistake. A heated exchange took place which ended with Collins pinning the bowler down with a stump, pointed end at his throat.

There had also been the occasion when JC had been dining with Easty and Geoff Miller in Southend during an Essex v Derbyshire match there. For pudding, Miller had asked if there was cheesecake, only to be told that the restaurant had run out. Feeling his hospitality might be compromised, Collins summoned the manager and, fixing him with a cold stare, said in his iciest monotone, 'If the man wants cheesecake, get the man some cheesecake.' It appeared, too, brought with some haste from another restaurant.

With clout like that, Easty, a man scared stiff by nothing more than a fast bowler's glare, wasn't about to call JC's bluff when real violence was on the menu. Instead of embracing some natural Essex justice, he wrote off his loss, the only surprise being the lack of support among team-mates, who wanted to see just how far JC might go.

By 1984 the novelty for pontoon jars had worn off and beneficiaries needed more exotic enticements to get punters to part with their money. Ian Botham, whose Benefit it was during George Orwell's year of reckoning, decided to have a junket to Spain at the end of the season as one of his fund-raising activities. Filmed by ITV with a view to being shown as a Christmas special, the trip pitted half a dozen cricketers against a similar number of celebrities and sports-men from other disciplines. The idea was to play each other at golf, tennis and double-wicket cricket. All this would take place at the La Manga resort near Alicante, though we all met up at a hotel in Gatwick first to get acquainted.

The celebrities and other sportsmen were a motley lot. There was a Macdonald and a McDonald, footballer Malcolm and newscaster Trevor. Jim Watt and his wife Margaret were also involved, as was comedian Lennie Bennett and his wife, also called Margaret. Making up the group were actor Patrick Mower and a man who almost missed the flight, Peter Cook, his companion not Dudley Moore but a woman he called the 'Contessa', whom he'd met at a party just days earlier.

Apart from me, the cricketers joining Botham were Chris Cowdrey, Phil Edmonds, Eddie Hemmings, Ian 'Gunner' Gould,

Jan Brittin and Rachael Heyhoe Flint, Jan being the leading England Women's player at the time, chaperoned among this group of ne'er-do-wells by Heyhoe Flint.

Beefy also had dispensation to bring about 15 mates as cheerleaders, which included his agent, Reg Hayter, close mate David English and two of Somerset's more likely lads, Trevor Gard and Richard Ollis. Colin Milburn also came along for the craic, as did a mate of mine from university, Muttley, who also got on well with Beefy. Basically, these were people who enjoyed consuming copious amounts of alcohol.

I cannot recall exactly how long the trip was, which was sold as a one-off holiday to the public, but it must have lasted at least five days. I do remember that it was mayhem, a booze-fuelled bacchanal, with Peter Cook its nihilistic orchestrator.

Mind you, I'm not sure Cooky's trip panned out quite as he'd envisaged. The comely Contessa who had accompanied him seemed to have taken to other beds. His plaintive 'Has anyone seen Contessa?' as he stalked the La Manga clubhouse became one of the refrains of the trip, though none of us were sure how much of the self-pity was real and how much was being played for laughs.

Whichever it was, Cook still glugged down industrial amounts of booze. Nearly everyone did, though nobody, not even Beefy with his incredible constitution, could cope with quite as much cerveza, wine and brandy as Cook did on what seemed a non-stop 24-hour loop. Day and night were rendered as one through the meniscus of Cook's drinking cup. He didn't wash, shave or change his clothes for at least four days. By the fifth, his body odour now roaming free, he was out of control. Having done his duty on the golf course, he staggered off the 18th green, threw his clubs in a hedge and flopped into the swimming pool, fully clad, before paddling to the other end. If that didn't startle sunbathers enough, he then clambered out and disrobed, flinging all save his underpants over their sautéing bodies before padding off to his room, presumably to see if the elusive Contessa had returned.

Cook was perpetually drunk, yet still able to deliver his lacerating wit. When faced with his dinner bill one night, he told the waiter he would not pay unless he, the waiter, bit the Contessa's neck and drew blood. A Spanish waiter, with both the task and humour more than slightly lost in translation – the scene could have been pitched as the 13th episode of *Fawlty Towers*. It was a brilliant but cruel humour, which ended with the waiter biting the Contessa's neck, albeit lightly. Yet excruciating though it was, you could see why the man was hailed a comic genius.

If that jape ended with minimal humiliation, Cook overdid it at the 'meet and greet' sundowner, where the punters on the trip had paid a premium to mingle with the stars. With Botham his new chum and drinking buddy, Cook decided to protect him from the banalities of polite conversation – on this occasion a middle-aged woman recalling the times she'd seen Beefy play.

'I was there at Headingley, you know, against the Aussies in '81,' she purred, certain that Botham would be charmed by the memory. But instead of a gracious response from Beefy she got a dishevelled Cook, leaning in close, his breath a hot Komodo stink of fags and alcohol.

'If you don't ---- off, now, I'm going to kill you,' he hissed with utter conviction.

A lady of northern England, at least from her accent, she looked at Cook, then at her husband, who shrugged the shrug of a man thinking, well, it is Peter Cook. Relatively comforted by her husband's nonchalance, she continued her eulogy.

'And then of course, Ian, there was your eight wickets against the West Indies at Lord's in the summer when you got the ball swinging from the Nursery End.'

'---- off or I'll kill you,' interjected Cook for the second time, the extra menace tangible in both his eyes and voice.

She shot another look at her husband, who appeared more apprehensive than before. Although more hesitant now, she ploughed on nonetheless, determined to say her piece.

'Whenever I've watched you I always think you bat better when you've taken a few wickets first. In fact, I reckon—'

She did not get to finish her point because Cook, his voice fracturing with rage, screamed '---- OFF!' with a venom beyond mere performance. As she reeled back in genuine shock, he then flung the contents of his glass in her face, just in case there was any lingering ambiguity.

The stinging exchange did the trick, as she was quickly led away, wet, confused and sobbing, by her husband, who wisely did not seek to further inflame a situation none of us, perhaps not even Cook, had fully anticipated.

If the first interjection was amusing, the sudden violence of the coup de grâce shocked me. If anything, it revealed the high-tension tightrope Cook must have walked every day inside his head. People talk about functioning alcoholics, and judging from Cook's unerring aim with the wine, he fitted that particular bill. What his actions lacked, utterly, was any kind of judgement or humanity, though with at least three bottles of wine downed since midday, and an eagerness to show off to Beefy, that was hardly surprising.

Fate caught up with him a few days later, this time in the shape of Margaret Watt's fist. Drunk again, he tried to stick his hand down her cleavage, only to be handed a right hook husband Jim would have been proud of. For Cook, the subsequent black eye and the yarn he spun around it was all part of the grotesque theatre of his life. In that world, it was a sin to be boring, or too serious, two things he felt Lennie Bennett, his partner in the double-wicket competition, was certainly guilty of.

Bennett, whose mouth seemed rather larger than his talent, had not stopped talking since everyone convened at Gatwick. Indeed, with his wife Margaret in close harmony, he never tired of telling us what a fine cricketer and golfer he was, over and over and over. Like Cook, though, fate was on hand to deal him a cruel comeuppance.

Walking round the boundary while another match was in progress, Bennett tried to catch a six struck by Phil Edmonds. Steadying himself under the steepler, he chose the Australian way to take the catch, with hands inverted and above the face. Trouble was, while he lined the catch up well enough, he allowed the ball to pass through his fingers with scarcely a reduction in velocity. The result: a scream of pain, an impressive blood spurt and four teeth scattered upon the La Manga turf. As Cook said after Bennett had been led away in search of first aid and sympathy, 'The only result better than that would have been if the ball had rebounded and hit his missus in the gob as well.'

That evening, when it became clear that Bennett would have to stay for another night before a flight from Alicante became available, Cook got the supper-club singer to belt out a rendition of 'Feelings', while people were commiserating with Lennie in the bar. The joke being that it was how the Spanish pronounced 'fillings', of which Lennie had lost several. Dosed up on painkillers and brandy, and with a cold flannel to dab away excess blood and dribble, Lennie, understandably, did not see the funny side.

His parting shot, when he and his wife left the following day, was that he would sue the La Manga club and everyone involved with the event – a preposterous gesture considering he wasn't even playing in the game that caused his injury, and the ball was over the boundary line when he interjected. Still, he must have seen a good dentist, because he was back on TV a few months later flashing the old Lennie Bennett smile on a show called *Names and Games*. Yet he could never quite pull the smiles inside enough to invite Peter Cook, or anyone else on that La Manga trip, to be a guest.

The press

What began mostly as a symbiotic relationship in which both parties benefited ended as a parasitic one – at least, that is how many players viewed it as newspapers began to use sport as one of the battlegrounds in the circulation wars of the 1980s, after the main one – Princess Diana.

I was still at Cambridge when England toured India in 1981–82, an ill-tempered trip which saw the visitors, captained by Keith Fletcher, beaten 1–0. Although it was a dull series on the field, I marvelled at the reports in the *Guardian* by Frank Keating. As John Arlott had done before him, Keating had clearly hit it off with Ian Botham, and the pair's drinking sessions in the Suhag hotel in Indore, as well as the cricket, were writ large for us to enjoy over our cornflakes. The story Keating related was that while he nursed the mother of all hangovers, Beefy flayed Central Zone for 122 off 53 balls in England's three-day tour match against them, an incredible strike-rate even now in the age of T20.

The hardships of travelling in India in those days threw press and players together more readily than, say, a tour of Australia, there being at most two first-class carriages on the Jullundur Express. Yet in less than a year that relationship had soured to the point where Doug Insole, England's manager on the ensuing Ashes tour Down Under, had to invoke a curfew. The reason being that some elements of the press were beginning to report on players' post-match carousing – something unthinkable in India just 12 months earlier.

The relationship took a while to sour completely, though, and as with most things cricket in the Eighties, Botham was at its heart. Being the most famous sportsman in Britain by 1982, he was big news. Signing him to your paper, as the *Daily Mirror* did for an exclusive deal, was a coup. As a result, the *Mirror*'s closest rivals

– the *Sun*, the *Star* and the *News of the World* – would try to run stories discrediting Beefy whenever they could.

One of the most infamous was by Lindy Field, a former Miss Barbados. On England's 1985–86 tour of the West Indies, she claimed that Beefy had snorted cocaine and made torrid love to her, even breaking the bed. The *News of the World* ran the story. They ran another, two weeks later, in which Vivien Kinsella, the 'Zelda' already mentioned in Chapter 4 on the 1982–83 Ashes tour, claimed she'd given Beefy heroin on the 1983–84 tour to New Zealand. I wasn't on either of those trips, and while both stories sounded just too preposterous, they still had to be dealt with. It explained why Beefy, unlike the rest of us whose dealings with solicitors mostly began and ended with purchasing a house, had a full-time legal team ready to mobilise at a moment's notice.

That year, 1986, seemed to be something of a peak for revelatory stories about cricketers in newspapers. Not long after the *News of the World*'s claims, Beefy was busted for possession of marijuana and served a three-month ban from cricket. The *News of the Screws* was clearly out to get him.

With him out of the picture, the papers turned on other cricketers. During a one-day series against New Zealand in July 1986, the *Mirror* ran a story headlined 'HIC, HIC HOORAY', in which it described the England team as 'Champagne Charlies'. They'd been hoping for us to lose, after a member of the public had tipped them off that seven of us, me included, had been drinking in the Hale Wine Bar the evening before our match at Old Trafford. Unhappily for them, we won, easily, despite New Zealand posting 284 for five off their 55 overs.

For me, some of the quotes from eyewitnesses that 'champagne was going down their throats like water' betrayed just how much is made up in stories like these, or at least exaggerated for effect. For starters, I tend to drink champagne only when there is nothing else, and that night I was drinking beer along with most of the other players there. Only David Gower and Lamby might have been on the champagne. The report also claimed that I was being chatted up by three beautiful women at the bar, which was definitely fabricated, as I can only remember talking to Richard Ellison, another team member. With that level of porkies being told, it is easy to imagine how they might have spun it and revved it up further had we lost.

The reporter responsible, Paul Weaver, was a decent bloke. But tabloid editors were ruthless and he had been told he had to go to the team hotel where we were staying, Mottram Hall, and if necessary bribe the receptionist to reveal which players were not yet back in their rooms. When he demurred, he was threatened with the sack.

These days players say they don't read newspaper reports, and they may be telling the truth, following the myriad ways of finding out information now. Back in the 1980s, though, most players read about themselves on a daily basis, counties allowing them to order a paper on their hotel bill when playing away from home. At Essex, those orders tended to be split between the *Telegraph* and the *Sun*, a combination that gave you cricket reports alongside more visual stimulation. For variety, I would order either the *Guardian* or, after 1986, the *Independent*. To round it out, Clem, our scorer, got *The Times*.

Matthew Engel of the *Guardian* and Martin Johnson of the *Independent* were very different kinds of writers, but as cricket correspondents of those papers they provided entertaining reads, much as Keating had done before them. They didn't need to quote players very often, so any conversations with them in the bar would be strictly informative and not spread verbatim across the next day's back pages.

If a player did appear in a big story, they would nearly always claim to have been misquoted. I always maintained a healthy scepticism about this – until it happened to me, in 1990, and it cost me another fine. The journalist involved was Rob Steen and he was writing for the *Independent*. Rob was a good egg and wanted to know what I made of the excessive run-scoring that year, exemplified by the drawn match between Surrey and Lancashire at The Oval, where Surrey's 707 for nine and 80 for one played 863 all out from Lancashire.

To my mind, the extra volume of runs being scored at most counties was due mainly to two changes brought in that season by the TCCB – the first one reducing the size of the seam on the ball from 15 strands to 11, the second being a directive to groundsmen to produce straw-coloured pitches (i.e. without live grass on them). What I said to Steen was that as an experiment it was a bit of a cock-up, as the TCCB had changed two variables, so wouldn't know how much importance to apportion to which for all the runs being scored.

This was turned into a quote from me which read, 'It's a typical TCCB cock-up, says Pringle,' which is a heavily spun version of what I actually said. Unsurprisingly, the TCCB were not impressed and instructed Essex to fine me, otherwise they would, heavily. I was duly relieved of £500 of my hard-earned, which did not please me greatly. To soften the blow, I asked Steen if the *Independent* would stump up half the fine, but their sports editor refused, saying that he trusted their man to have quoted me accurately. When I asked for a tape recording or note to be produced to back this claim, none was forthcoming.

To his credit, Steen was sympathetic to my cause and offered to make it up to me by buying dinner in a London restaurant of my choice. When I said, 'Deal, book Le Gavroche now,' he reneged, eventually taking me for a burger on the Charing Cross Road. I never did ask if he claimed it on expenses.

*   *   *

The press conference is where players and press are thrown together in an awkward symbiosis. I never did many, but one that has stayed with me was after a one-day international against the West Indies at Headingley in 1988.

In a low-scoring game I'd been made man of the match for top-scoring with 39 and taking three for 30. After the captains had done their bit before the media I was put up as well. Two journalists asked questions. One I'd never seen before, but the other was Graham Otway of the *Today* newspaper, a recent addition to the news-stands founded by the entrepreneur Eddy Shah.

Otters, as Otway was known by his colleagues and players alike, clearly had a story in mind, one that involved my love–hate affair with Headingley's notorious Western Terrace. So he tried to lead me into supplying him with quotes to augment it.

'Derek, I loved the way that, after taking a wicket, you went over to the Western Terrace and pulled an imaginary knife out of your back. After all, they'd been stabbing you in it all day, hadn't they?'

'Um, I did nothing of the sort,' I said.

'Well, I clearly saw you take an imaginary knife from your back,' said Otway, desperately trying to get his quote.

'I didn't, I gave them a little bow,' I said. 'There was no knife.'

'No, no, I clearly saw you withdraw a knife from your back,' Otway insisted.

'If you did,' I countered, 'it was mere prestidigitation, as I intended a bow.'

'Hah, spell that, Otters,' shouted Martin Johnson, a jibe that seemed to silence my inquisitor.

Then came the final question from the journalist I didn't recognise, something about was I surprised I'd done so well. 'Not really,' I said.

And that was that, my big moment in front of the British press.

Groupies

Groupies were also a feature of the era, though not in the numbers which attended rock bands when they toured the land, their music and antics being infinitely more exciting and attractive than those of cricketers.

The groupie, or enthusiastic supporter as I liked to call them, doesn't really exist now in the age of Tinder, where one's inner urges can be satisfied at the swoosh, left or right, of a finger on a smartphone. Back then, though, it was a young cricketer's rite of passage, when they played at Trent Bridge, to be introduced to Amazing Grace, a long-standing supporter of both cricket and cricketers.

Grace's fame preceded her and I knew of her and her coterie of like-minded female friends long before I first played against Nottinghamshire. So it was with a mixture of apprehension and anticipation that I entered the Supporters' Bar there after play one day early in my career.

'Grace, have you met young Derek Pringle, our new all-rounder?' said Ray East, with a heavy glint of mischief in his eye.

'No,' she purred. 'But we have all evening to get acquainted, don't we, petal, so why don't you come and sit next to me?'

And so began a ritual of humiliation, at least for me, as Grace, perfumed and matriarchal, with double entendres and flashes of suspenders to the fore, set about a process that seemed part seduction, part mothering.

Some groupies were said to keep scorebooks, though not ones that kept tally of runs and dot balls. Yet I never sensed that Grace actually hankered to chalk me up. This was theatre, for the delectation of my team-mates and her friends, and she was good at it. If I'd had any luvvie bones in me, I could have hammed it up into a scene from *Are You Being Served?*, what with all the Mrs Slocombe-style innuendoes. But I was young, naive and awkward, which meant Grace had to make all the running – something of which she began to tire, especially as I'd not been gallant enough to even buy her a drink. Eventually, her attentions turned elsewhere and I was left to slope off to the pub and a comforting pint of ale.

As I grew older, I came to appreciate the company of Grace and her ilk, which was never less than cheery and conversational. I don't know whether my libido was abnormally low, but I was never inclined to take it further than a few drinks in the bar after play. Of course, that made me something of a challenge, and some never gave up trying to get me into their team.

Back then, every county seemed to have its group of dedicated female supporters, most of them given a nickname. So there was Dubry, Motorbiker, Scoreboard, Kermit, Karl Malden, Cold Norton, the Birmingham Bombers, the Ripon Runners, Peanut, the Netball Team and Monkey Wrench, to name but a few. Others, like Grace, were even known by their given names.

Some would follow a team for years, then disappear, never to be seen again. Marriage, a change of job or circumstance, or even a loss of interest in cricket, were all potential reasons for losing one's allegiance. The diehards, though, continued on through the generations, their support and dedication unstinting to all things bat and ball.

Fan letters

Most pro cricketers will receive at least one fan letter in their career. Most get many more, the majority mundane requests for autographs or to sign things like photographs, scorecards or first-day covers depicting cricket grounds and events.

Occasionally, there were variations on the above, such as the time Ray East got a letter which began:

Dear Ray East,

I have long been an admirer of your left-arm spin bowling. You are a real asset to Essex CCC. Please can you get me Graham Gooch's autograph.

With all good wishes etc.

PS – I enclose an SAE for your convenience.

Then there was the typed letter from India which Gooch received, seeking guidance from him, and not just on cricketing matters.

Dear Grahm Gooch [sic],

Your batting is a feast of spectators. One cover drive from you lights a path to the heavens. You are without doubt my No 1 favourite cricket player, which is why I now write to you for guidance.

Gooch dearest, I must disclose to you my most terrible problem – I have been enjoying myself by hand at night.

Love has lost away and my dearest has left me. But while this has made me sad, with a feeling of great shame for how I miss her, it has also affected my batting with my scores suffering as much as my heart. Have you any recipe for how I might end this torment, so I can get back my love and start scoring runs again?

Yours, most sincerely etc.

When Goochie had finished reading the letter, which was post-marked Dehra Dun in India, he just sat shaking his head in disbelief. He didn't write back, though I did take the liberty of photocopying the letter, which is right up there, in terms of unusual content, with the one Beefy got at The Oval in 1982, as discussed in Chapter 2.

Responding to letters could be a time-consuming business if you were someone like Gooch or Botham and received hundreds every month. But while Gooch dutifully replied to all reasonable requests, Nasser Hussain used to throw most of his fan mail straight into the bin unopened, not being one for unnecessary distractions.

Maybe Nasser feared hate mail from the trolls of the analogue age, though you tended only to get those when on England duty. Generally, county fans weren't moved to write to you when you were rubbish. Instead, they'd just shout their displeasure from the stands. It was a quicker way to get your message over than the GPO.

I received loads of letters slagging me off when I first played for England, class prejudice to the fore. I still have most of them, sharp reminders that not everybody is happy to share in one's good fortune, especially when you have been to public school and Oxbridge.

The most interesting letter I received, though, arrived just before I was fined £500 for flicking a V-sign at the Somerset members – an action that cost me £250 a finger. Plenty of cricketers had been upbraided for showing their displeasure this way, me included after that close Test we won at Melbourne in 1982, though I don't recall any being fined for it. My excuse was that I was provoked after receiving a torrent of abuse following a poor showing in the first Ashes Test at Headingley in 1989, which England lost.

Essex were down at Taunton playing a Benson & Hedges semi-final, a nail-biter we won by four runs. For whatever reason, the home fans got stuck into me about England's recent defeat. The amount and nature of the abuse that came my way reminded me of the stick I got at the MCG. I never minded a bit of flak or mickey-taking from opposition supporters, or even from the Essex faithful, but this was nasty, personal stuff. Goochie and Fozzy had both played in the same Test, but neither attracted a peep of disapproval. I felt picked upon, which made me indignant and determined to fight fire with fire.

I needed an opportunity to retort, which came when I finished our innings with a flourish that included striking the final ball off Neil Mallender for six. As I came off, I removed my right batting glove and, with a gesture worthy of the showiest impresario, gave the boo boys and girls the full Harvey Smith. The Somerset faithful did not take this affront sitting down and I was immediately pelted with lunchboxes, half-eaten drumsticks and any projectile-sized bit of food which came to hand. It was like a scene from the Middle Ages, the only thing missing being me chained to a set of stocks.

The furore was witnessed by Somerset's secretary, Tony Brown, a man never less than convinced of his own importance. Once captain of Gloucestershire, he'd also been England's manager for their tour to India in 1984–85, which had got off to a difficult start. Indira Gandhi had been assassinated just hours after England arrived and many of the England players felt it might be prudent to leave India until the ferment had settled. Brown saw this as a challenge to his authority. So, at a team meeting in Mumbai, he threw all the passports onto a table and in no uncertain terms told those who wanted to leave to take their passport and '---- off.'

I've never much cared for autocrats like him, and while I wasn't on that tour, he knew I wasn't a fan of his – which is probably why he made it his season's mission to get me punished for my insurrection against Somerset's members, using the full force of the TCCB's disciplinary committee. Naturally, this all made the press.

It had been a feisty game as well, so to calm matters between the clubs, Doug Insole, the Essex chairman, ordered me to write a letter of apology to Somerset. He then demanded to see it before it was sent. I was in no mood for contrition, having received scores of letters from Somerset fans condemning the behaviour of their fellow supporters, so I wrote:

Dear Somerset Members,

Regarding my behaviour at Taunton last week, I give you the words of Edith Piaf – 'Je ne regrette rien.'

Yours in cricket,

Derek Pringle

Insole was apoplectic and demanded I write something showing remorse, or Essex, too, would take action against me. So I did, hating myself for being so easily swayed.

As I later pointed out to the TCCB's disciplinary panel, it was a particularly unfeeling and unrealistic person who would expect me to take such abuse and not react to it. My point was given short shrift. But then the panel did look like a bunch of Low Church Protestants rather than followers of the Old Testament, with the eye-for-an-eye vengefulness that I'd sought in the heat of the moment.

Anyway, before I was hauled before the beaks at Lord's, a lady from Kent sent me a letter which read:

Dear Mr Pringle,

I hear you've been upsetting people, you really must learn to keep your cool. Here's a picture of me in Barbados keeping mine.

Enclosed was a full-length photo of the letter's author, at least I assumed she was the author, in the buff – which beat a request for an autograph hands down. It didn't ease the pain of the fine, though, the first of several I incurred as the old freedoms of self-expression came under renewed scrutiny.

Overseas players

I may be biased, but it seems to me that county cricket in the 1980s attracted the greatest concentration of overseas talent there has ever been.

Winning doesn't always mean grinning. Beefy Botham and Big Bob Willis show different emotions after our three-run win over Australia in the 1982 Boxing Day Test at the MCG.

Keep calm and have a cup of tea. Keith Fletcher, after we'd duffed over Warwickshire at Ilford in 1984, and Graham Gooch, after his match-winning hundred against India in the 1987 World Cup semi-final (though he settled for bottled water).

Above: David Gower, a batsman with an exquisite touch and carefree attitude – a combination that thrilled and frustrated in equal measure.

Right: The unstinting and brilliant John Lever in full flow – a perennial sight in Essex's glory years, of which 'JK' was a principal architect.

Teams can become blasé about their colleagues, but we all took our seats to watch when Goochie went out to bat. Here he hooks Joel Garner en route to 129* against West Indies in 1986.

Right: A fearsome quintet? Norman Cowans, Robin Jackman, Bob Willis, Ian Botham and me try to look intimidating at the start of the 1982–83 Ashes tour. I'm not sure it worked: we lost 2–1.

The only way is Essex, as Goochie, Neil Foster, John Childs and me prepare to play West Indies at The Oval in 1988: the only time four Essex players have represented England in the same Test.

Above: Creaming one through the covers against New Zealand at Headingley in 1990. Over the course of my career I did not do myself justice with the bat.

Left: Smell the cordite. Allan Lamb and Tim Rice, a big cricket fan, with a knock-off Kalashnikov in Pakistan's lawless Tribal Areas during the 1987 World Cup. Today's teams wouldn't be allowed to take such risks.

Truly unplayable balls are rare indeed, but this one, to West Indies' Jeffrey Dujon, during a 1988 Texaco Trophy match at Headingley, fitted the bill. It swung away, hit a crack, nipped back sharply and kept low.

The Essex team of 1989 won more Championship games than any other but still came second after the TCCB deducted 25 points for a substandard pitch – an injustice that still irks today.

Leaders' forum. President Mugabe of Zimbabwe meets the England A team in Harare in 1990. Our captain, Mark Nicholas, at Mugabe's right shoulder, was particularly thrilled.

Snake charmers in India on the 1987 World Cup tour. The king cobra has had its poison sacs removed, allowing its handlers the chance to make a living.

Essex celebrate yet another County Championship. The club had champagne perpetually on ice during the 1980s.

Royal tea. On the Oval balcony with the Queen during a match against Surrey. She'd come to open the Indoor School there and had stayed for a cuppa. Surrey's president, Bernie Coleman, is the other person present.

The flotsam and jetsam of a cricketing life. At home in my kitchen signing bats amid the laundry (we had to wash our own kit). The room has since been updated.

During that decade at least up until 1987, each county was allowed to field two overseas players, something most did. The sole exception was Yorkshire, who defiantly insisted that its players must be born within the three ridings which comprised the county before the Local Government Act of 1972 blurred the boundaries. It was no surprise, then, that they never won the Championship during the 1980s, their successes limited to the Benson & Hedges Cup in 1987 and the John Player Special League in 1983.

With fast bowling the holy grail, most counties went for a thoroughbred quick. So in 1982, batsmen playing most of the season could expect to face:

Malcolm Marshall at Hampshire
Wayne Daniel at Middlesex
Sylvester Clarke at Surrey
Winston Davis at Glamorgan
Colin Croft at Lancashire
Imran Khan at Sussex
Garth Le Roux at Sussex
Hartley Alleyne at Worcestershire
Andy Roberts at Leicestershire

All were top-notch and fast, with most able to walk into any Test team of any era. It meant every top order was sorely tested just about every match, helmets and ice packs at the ready. Fracture clinics also did good business, while squads were tested for their depth of batting, gloves not being quite as good at protecting players' digits as they are now.

A few mph below them but still a handful were:

Joel Garner at Somerset
Richard Hadlee at Nottinghamshire
Clive Rice at Nottinghamshire

Franklyn Stephenson at Gloucestershire
Sarfraz Nawaz at Northamptonshire
Norbert Phillip at Essex

And that before mentioning some of the overseas batsmen who kept English bowling talent honest, such as:

Viv Richards at Somerset
Peter Kirsten at Derbyshire
John Wright at Derbyshire
Ken McEwan at Essex
Javed Miandad at Glamorgan
Zaheer Abbas at Gloucestershire
Gordon Greenidge at Hampshire
Asif Iqbal at Kent
Clive Lloyd at Lancashire
Geoff Howarth at Surrey
Brian Davison at Leicestershire
Alvin Kallicharran at Warwickshire
Glenn Turner at Worcestershire

The only notable absentees were Australians, wicketkeepers and spin bowlers, otherwise this was as good as it got from around the world. In fact, it was talent of such eye-watering brilliance that I reckon you could form a side from it and beat just about any other in cricket's long history, providing the pitch wasn't a raging bunsen burner.

Being in the midst of such greatness could be both uplifting and disheartening for the county pro. Get Viv Richards out cheaply, and you would be cock of the walk for a week. Get deposited all round Taunton by him, and it could seem a very long journey home.

It was the fast bowlers, though, who drew most talk from among the other players. At Essex it became almost a ritual before we played Hampshire in Southampton to gather in the bar of the Polygon hotel, also known as the Dead Parrot, and dredge up all the horror stories about Malcolm Marshall and what he'd done to us in previous matches. There we'd sit, beers in hand, ratcheting up the anxiety levels for the next day when – our prophecies uncannily self-fulfilling – he'd charge in and rip through us once again. Goochie, of course, would have nothing to do with our defeatist nonsense, despite the hilarious way Easty and Keith Pont would ham it all up.

Marshall always seemed to try extra hard against Essex, a perception he later confirmed when he told me that it was all Brian Hardie's fault. You see, Hardie had smashed him around when he first came over to pro for Hampshire as a 21-year-old in 1979 – the Scotsman's unconventional and unbeaten 146 against them at Bournemouth propelling Essex to a massive innings win. In his Bajan patois, spoken almost as fast as he bowled, Macco, as he was known, explained his Hardie obsession:

'If Hardie open the innings, I bowl quick to get he out cheap. If Hardie bat five, I bowl extra quick to get through the top order to get to Hardie. He the man I after, though I like to get Gooch too.'

He also used to bowl extra quick to fellow West Indians, as well as to Vic Marks, Somerset's jovial off-spinner. When asked why he always gave Marks a working over, Macco said he didn't like his rustic gait as he walked out to bat. 'He taking the pee-pee, maan.' To Macco, you could only swagger to the wicket like that if you were a gun batsman, and useful though he was, Vic wasn't quite one of them.

With such a plethora of quicks, you'd have thought English pros would have become highly adept at playing them, though that never seemed to be the case. What did arise was a never-ending string of theories of how best to play fast bowling, with few if any finding the secret formula. I batted against all the fast bowlers listed above and was in the Essex and England dressing rooms while others prepared to play them. Everyone's method was different, the only common factor being the almost reverent hush that would prevail before the day's play if the opposition had someone rapid in their ranks.

Gooch, who was regarded as one of the best batsmen against true pace, would seek a bit of calm and a cup of tea before hostilities began. He would also brush his teeth just before leaving the dressing room – something about feeling fresh for the challenge. Thereafter, he seemed to relish the confrontation, facing up to it by standing tall, bat raised.

Not many enjoyed facing fast bowling. Let's face it, when something hard and round weighing five and a half ounces strikes the human body at 90–95 mph, especially an unprotected part, the impact is like being hit by a combination of a Mike Tyson right hook and a rubber bullet. It can kill, as a few unfortunate players have discovered.

While death was not in most players' minds, the prospect of pain most definitely was, which led to a range of coping strategies. For instance, Graeme Fowler, who opened for Lancashire and England, used to prepare for the onslaught by driving at 90 mph down the motorway on his way to the match, trying to focus on the road markings as they whizzed by. It got his eye in and he swore by it. That, and a good chest guard.

My own method, which had very limited success, was to go back and across and get into line, reduce the backlift of my bat and duck anything banged in short. I'd seen the perils of swaying to avoid bouncers after Andy Lloyd was struck by Marshall during the Edgbaston Test of 1984 – a blow that detached his retina and ended his Test career there and then.

The trouble was, against the best quicks, unless you hooked well or could uppercut over the slips, there was precious little for you to take advantage of, front-foot drives not really being on offer. So, even if you survived for any length of time, the score didn't really go anywhere.

I was never scared, though the anticipation that one might wear a bit of pain did create a distinct unease not experienced when facing spinners or medium-pacers. That is how fast bowlers used to intimidate. Yet it was only an initial feeling. If you could hang around long enough to almost get used to it, playing fast bowling was exhilarating, in a masochistic sort of way.

There was certainly a sense of immense satisfaction if you could ever get on top of it, though that was rare, especially against those teams who had more than one speedster, like the West Indies. Their power and prowess in that department meant they went unbeaten in Test series between 1980 and 1995, a period of dominance unmatched by any team.

The 1980s was also a golden age for West Indians in county cricket. Back then, international fixtures between countries never impinged on a northern summer, while teams like Zimbabwe and Bangladesh were not considered suitable for membership of the 'Test club', which left playing schedules busy but not overcrowded. That enabled the world's best cricketers, bar Australians who had jobs outside cricket to look after, to play county cricket, and they were glad of it.

Eventually a few Aussies came over to play too – Allan Border and Mark Waugh at Essex, Terry Alderman at Kent, Dennis Lillee at Northants, Steve Waugh at Somerset and Carl Rackemann at Surrey – but generally they were a stay-at-home lot in the 1980s.

Over-rates

There was a bane of the bowling classes and it had nothing to do with batsmen. Over-rates were one of those things, like prices, which kept shifting in the direction the game's administrators didn't want them to go. So while prices went up, over-rates went down.

To stop this inexorable creep, the TCCB insisted upon a minimum amount of overs being bowled per hour in Championship matches. Failure to do so – and a team's rate was measured twice a season – would result in swingeing fines for both the county and the players.

The rate expected in Championship matches when I first joined Essex was 19.5 overs an hour. Typically, a day's play, which comprised three sessions, would last six and a half hours. In that time you were meant to bowl a minimum of 108 overs. The maths makes that 16.6 overs an hour, but time would inevitably be taken out of the day to change ends, set fields and so on, which is how the TCCB calculated that teams would need to bowl at 19.5 overs an hour in order to give paying spectators their money's worth by close of play at 6.30 p.m. With a rate like that you couldn't tarry.

Time would be given to the fielding side for taking wickets, sightscreen changes and any other hold-ups, such as changing the ball, boots, sweaty shirts and the like. Today, drinks breaks and the 12th man bringing on water for batsmen tend to hold up play all the time, but not then. In the 15 years of county cricket I played, I can count the number of drinks breaks on one hand – Fletch only allowing them at Essex if temperatures crept above 90 °F, which wasn't very often.

It is not an especially proud boast, but Essex never paid an over-rate fine in the 1980s, though that was mostly due to Clem Driver, the team's brilliant scorer. A large and genial man with a fine intellect and wit, Clem would charm the umpires into being generous with the extra time they gave us when play was interrupted. To smooth any negotiations, Clem always carried a bottle of whisky with him. He was partial to a drop, but so, generally, were the umpires, and it was amazing how a dram or three shared at the end of the day would increase the time it took for the sawdust to arrive, for batting gloves to be changed or for bowlers' footholes to be chamfered down. He used to reckon on an extra two minutes a nip.

Thanks to Clem's negotiating skills, as well as his creative accounting, we were rarely in debt when it came to over-rates. Once though, in 1983, when even his talents were looking unlikely to save us, a boring draw against Middlesex proved our salvation. The game also revealed how frustrating the pitches could be at Chelmsford. On the first day, we'd managed to bowl Middlesex out for 83 in 27.5 overs on a green top, me taking a then career-best of seven for 32. We then batted and made 289. But two heavy rollers and two days of hot sun later, and the pitch was unrecognisable as the one which had seen 20 wickets fall in the first four sessions of play. Three batsmen got hundreds for Middlesex as they racked up a massive 634 for seven in 211 overs over the next day and two sessions.

The docility of the pitch and the parlous predicament Middlesex had extricated themselves from meant that a declaration by their captain, Mike Gatting, in order to make a game of things, was out of the question. So on and on and on they batted, repelling with ease our increasingly obtuse attempts to make inroads. So easy was the pitch that even John Emburey, one of the most awkward-looking batsmen around, began to resemble Wally Hammond. Fletch got so fed up with Middlesex's attitude of not wanting to play a game that he just lay down in the field at extra cover. To show solidarity, I grabbed a chair and sat on it down at long-off, the crowd cheering loudly when I was able to field a ball driven to me without getting up.

When even that failed to embarrass Gatting into declaring, Fletch brought on Goochie and Keith Pont to improve our over-rate. With the collusion of Emburey, a close friend of Goochie's since they had first played for London Schools together, the pair got the over-rate up to 48 overs an hour, with Gooch at one stage getting through an over in just 18 seconds. He'd bowl it slow enough so Emburey could pat it straight back to him, whereupon he'd scamper back to his mark, turn and then bowl the next ball, all in the same motion. Emburey, by now past his hundred, would then do the same thing again and again, until it just looked like two mates mucking about in the back yard.

It was taking the mick – especially as Goochie and Ponty bowled 82 overs between them – and probably flirted with bringing the game into disrepute. But with most umpires being former cricketers, there was little desire to see fellow pros out of pocket for something as petty as over-rates. So they let it pass and we escaped a fine without Clem having to deplete his whisky stocks or fudge the numbers.

Eventually, with the fine jar largely bare, the TCCB decided to introduce something completely different for the 1984 season – the never-ending day; or that's what it seemed like when you couldn't get through the overs as Goochie and Ponty had done against Middlesex. I don't know how it was calculated, but for that summer the TCCB decided that a day's play would comprise 117 overs – one of several barmy directives by which they hoped to make three-day cricket more palatable to the public. With no fines, you had to stay on until the overs were bowled, bad light permitting.

For Essex there was an early reckoning with this new workload in the game against Hampshire, away at Northlands Road. JK was Essex's most popular cricketer during my time at the club, but we rounded on him that match. Oh, how we swore and cursed him that early summer's day, damning the very existence of this consummate professional and dedicated team man.

We fulminated with good, if selfish, reason, our ire having ignited long after the usual close of play. Hampshire were without their regular overseas stars Malcolm Marshall and Gordon Greenidge, and we had just bowled them out cheaply and then enforced the follow-on. As we pushed to inflict further damage, it was natural for Graham Gooch, deputising as captain for Keith Fletcher, to turn to JK to deliver the telling blow.

The trouble was JK had a 35-yard run-up, and that did not include his expansive follow-through. Usually, thanks to Clem's creativity, we rarely noticed how long JK's overs took. But that season there were no fines and teams had to bowl the overs come what may – which turned chop-chop into tick-tock. With the pavilion clock pushing 7.30 p.m. and 15 overs still remaining, with little prospect of bad light hastening an early bath, a collective plea broke out from the Essex fielders: 'GO OFF YOUR SHORT RUN, JK!'

It was only after he ignored us that the air turned blue, our collective disquiet proving Bob Marley's dictum that hungry men are angry men. Indeed, we didn't get off for almost another hour, by which time the only eyes watching us belonged to the groundsman's dog. Still, we went on to win the match, one of 13 victories that brought us our second Championship in a row.

Unlike the Essex team that season, the experiment of 117 overs proved unpopular and short-lived, with the TCCB once more reverting to fines which only the naive ever seemed to pay.

Sponsored cars and travelling companions

Cricketers rarely get any sympathy from the public when claiming fatigue. Most people view spending long hours outside as a bit of a doss. But factor in all the knackering travel that county players do, especially since road usurped rail, and even the hard of heart might concede they have a point.

I reckon I used to travel 20–22,000 miles during a cricket season, which then ran from 1 April to 30 September – at least that was the period they paid you for. About two-thirds of that mileage would have been racked up driving to away games, something you tended to do with a travelling companion. Over a 15-year career, mine varied from a batsman called Mike McEvoy, to Keith Fletcher, to Ray East, to Clem Driver, our scorer, and Nick Knight.

With McEvoy, all the driving was initially done by him as I did not pass my test until 1981. As junior men, we got to take the kit van on away trips, a job that meant an eternity on the road. As a goods vehicle, the kit van was fitted with a governor, which meant it could not exceed 50 mph. While others in cars would get from Essex to Worcester, say, in time for a nutritious meal and a couple of pints, Mac and I would be lucky to arrive by midnight. The only food available then was a round of ham sandwiches from the night porter.

The other thing was that until 1986, the M25 was no more than a tease of a motorway, being only partially built, which meant taking on the inner suburbs of London more often than was good for one's sanity, the gateway to Essex being through that great city's north-east quadrant. The number of times I used to go past the Blind Beggar pub on the Whitechapel Road and hear the same story of how the Krays had murdered George Cornell there back in the 1960s.

With Mac at the wheel, I was given the task of navigating using a map that had obviously seen long service, judging by the missing pages and the unhelpful notes scrawled over crucial road numbers. Difficult enough to decipher in daylight, it was almost impossible to read on the move at night. But with a combination of Mac's memory, my sense of direction (I had read Geography at Cambridge, after all) and general guesswork, we didn't get lost too often.

When pairing players to travel together on away trips, Brian Hardie, the team's travel manager, used to pick those who lived relatively near to one another. When I first started at Essex, I still lived with Mum in Marks Tey. While there, a fast bowler called Steve 'Piggy' Malone was my closest 'neighbour'.

Piggy, who used to pick me up even when we were playing at home (mostly for the Seconds back then), owned a VW Beetle, which he'd drive pretty fast down the A12 to Chelmsford. About three minutes before the junction we'd want, he'd take out this fancy hairbrush and start to assemble his hair using the rearview mirror and both hands to get it just so – all the while steering with his knees.

Quite why he needed to give his hair this kind of attention was curious. To me, with his dark moustache and luxurious locks, he looked like a German porn star, or at least those in the mucky mags some of the lads used to keep in their cricket coffins. Surely, a tousled look would work best. Anyway, he was doing me a huge favour taking me to Chelmsford, so I couldn't complain, despite the recklessness of his morning ritual.

By the time I was a regular in the first team Piggy and Mac had moved on, Mac into teaching at Colchester Royal Grammar School and Piggy to Hampshire. Happily, I'd passed my driving test and been picked for England, two things that helped to secure me my first sponsored car – a white Porsche 924, no less. Lancaster Garage of Colchester were the sponsors. As I was single and sported a tan from the day job, they obviously saw me as some kind of eligible-bachelor type. Why else would they possibly want to entrust a sports car to someone whose only previous driving experience had been a Citroën 2CV and a Renault Roho 4? It just didn't make sense, except as a marketing ploy.

Also, the Porsche had my name plastered all over it, which was just inviting trouble. I mean, one-time-ear-stud-wearing-England-and-Essex-cricketer, recently of Cambridge University, drives flash sports car with name written on it. Forget about it being a red rag to all the chippy ne'er-do-wells. If I hadn't had a responsibility towards it, I'd have run a coin over it myself. Disaster beckoned, and although I didn't wrap it around a tree, I did slide it into one or two ditches when going to meet mates at the Messing Crown, a country pub in east Essex protected by a series of sharp bends.

Far from being a chick magnet, the Porsche only managed to attract the attentions of the police and I got stopped several times for nothing in particular. Once in Leicester I had about five of the team squashed in, including two in what we called the goldfish bowl at the back. Fortunately, I had not touched a drop of alcohol, and the boys in blue let us carry on with our search for the best curry house in a city boasting hundreds.

The deal lasted for two years, 1983 and 1984, before it was suddenly withdrawn by the garage. I was abroad at the time playing club cricket over the winter when word reached me that they were horrified by the condition in which I'd returned it, something I couldn't understand as I'd had the car valeted before handing it back. When I asked for some clarification they said the engine had been covered in an unknown white substance, which had also got into the air vents.

The penny dropped. One of our last away games had been at Lancashire. While parked at Old Trafford, one of the Lancashire players, Steve O'Shaughnessy, had thought it a good wheeze to douse the Porsche in whitewash. And boy did he douse it. My response was to take it to a car wash, which got rid of the visible layers. It never occurred to me to look under the bonnet before handing it back. Even so, the garage must have wanted to terminate the deal. I mean, it was whitewash, for goodness' sake, not sulphuric acid, and it wasn't exactly my fault that it was there in the first place.

While I still had the Porsche, Neil Foster and I were both picked in the 12-man England squad to play the first Test against the West Indies at Edgbaston in 1984. A young man brash with confidence, Fozzy asked me if I wanted to travel up with him. But before I could respond, he'd spotted a flaw in his offer. 'Ooh, better not,' he said. 'It would only complicate matters. You're bound to be made 12th man and have to go home.'

I'm not sure *Schadenfreude* was a term that had made it to Essex back then, but it should have done. When England's captain, David Gower, decided to go into the match with two spinners (a mistake, as it happened), it was Fozzy who was left out and who had to make the despondent drive back to Essex.

Not that Fozzy's presence would have prevented us getting beaten. It might, though, have pushed Gower into bowling first on a greenish pitch after he'd won the toss, which would have at least made it a contest. Because he'd opted for two spinners, he couldn't put West Indies in; the papers would have been reporting a crucifixion had it gone wrong. So he batted first and we were dismissed for 191, Joel Garner ripping through us after the ball seamed sideways.

Some of the journeys we used to make appeared to be designed for maximum inconvenience, especially when a Sunday League match was scheduled in the middle of a three-day match against a different county from the one you were playing. One such combination I remember saw us play Saturday, Monday and Tuesday at Derby, but with the Sunday match against Glamorgan at Neath.

Just packing up all the kit was hassle enough, let alone getting down to south Wales and then back again after play the following day. Still, some teams claimed worse journeys in such circumstances, such as one who had Canterbury for the Championship match and then Scarborough for the Sunday League.

Essex once had a seemingly random Sunday game at Scarborough, the fixture coming in the middle of a small break in the itinerary. Instead of driving up, Goochie and the club had the not so novel idea of hiring a coach from Chelmsford to take us up on the Saturday and bring us back after the match – ETA back in Essex, the wee hours of Monday morning.

By now I was living in Cambridge, as was Nick Knight, which meant driving an hour to Chelmsford to catch a coach that would travel right past the Cambridge junction on the M11. After much wrangling, Goochie agreed that the coach would pick us up at Junction 12 just outside Cambridge at a pre-agreed time to save us two hours of additional travel to and from Chelmsford. He even agreed to make sure our cricket coffins were placed on board, providing they were packed and ready to go.

The plan proved a calamity. Not only did the coach driver turn off at the wrong junction, a move which cost us a good 40 minutes while he sat at Junction 11 and we at 12, but when we unloaded the kit the following day, my cricket case was not there. I had what I called my soft gear – cricket shirts, trousers, socks, jockstrap, contact lenses – but none of my hard gear, such as bats, pads, helmet and, most crucially, boots. With nobody else in possession of size 13s (wide), it looked like I was going to have to sit this one out.

Goochie, though, was determined not to let me off the hook, especially as he blamed me for my kit not being loaded onto the coach. It being Sunday, no shops in Scarborough were open. But through some do-gooding Yorkshireman, he got the home number of the local sports-shop owner and arranged for him to bring in his biggest boots, which he claimed were a roomy size 12.

The club paid for them, but they were not spikes, so I couldn't bowl. Also, they were nowhere near roomy enough to make up for being a size too small. Indeed, the only way I could squeeze into them was to not wear socks. Even then they hobbled me, which meant my only role in the field was to provide a statuesque presence at mid-off. Two yards either side of me and the ball was through.

I did get to bat, though, at five. Borrowing Goochie's railway sleeper of a bat, I made 21 at a crucial time, though running singles and twos was painful. We won the match, which made the return journey a little more bearable, at least to begin with. With Sunday traffic and a supper stop at the Bluebell Inn at Wentbridge, it took eight hours to get back, by which time dawn was just about breaking on Monday morning.

It was the first and only time Essex used a coach during my career.

Of course, cars created their own problems: those long journeys tended to cause more damage to bowlers in terms of niggles than their workloads, hefty though those were. Nor were the leather-flingers the only players to suffer. Alan Knott, arguably the finest wicketkeeper ever, reckoned long journeys used to make his legs seize up and stiffen his Achilles tendons, especially his right one, which worked the accelerator.

Knotty had a reputation for being a hypochondriac, but I reckon he was just deeply in tune with his body. To combat those issues, he kept in the car a sleeping bag with the bottom cut out of it and a block of wood, which he'd place beneath the pedals. The first, which he'd step into, would keep his leg muscles warm when sitting at the wheel, while the second ensured he would not overstretch his Achilles while driving the many hours from venue to venue. There must have been something to it: his career as a brilliant wicket-keeper spanned 21 years.

Goochie was sponsored by a Toyota garage in Wickford not far from Southend, and he was fastidious in looking after both his car and the sponsors. Which was just as well, as he had a lot of bad luck with his motors, though none of it self-inflicted.

One scrape occurred when travelling from Northampton, where we were playing a Championship match, to Trent Bridge, for a Sunday League game against Notts. Nasser Hussain had just come into the Essex side as a precocious but naive 21-year-old and as such did not know the highways and byways. So he asked if he and his travelling partner, Nadeem Shahid, could follow Gooch and his companion, Alan Lilley.

As it was a nice summer's day, Goochie decided to take the back roads but had to stop at some roadworks just over a small bridge. Being young and feckless, Nasser came barrelling over the arched span but could not pull up in time to stop his car from ramming Goochie's. Aside from the damage to both cars, we had to field three players with whiplash. No wonder we lost.

On another occasion at Trent Bridge, this time during a Championship match, persistent rain had prevented any play before lunch. Needing to get some medication from a chemist, Don Topley, one of our seam bowlers, asked Goochie if he could borrow his car to go into Nottingham. Reluctantly, Goochie agreed but told him that he must be be back by 2 p.m., just in case the rain stopped and we got a start. The rain did not relent, but neither did Topley make the deadline. When he did eventually return, just after 3 p.m., it was in a taxi. The reason: he had lost Gooch's car.

Apparently, Topley had parked the car in a multi-storey car park but had not taken note of where it was, the rain apparently making everywhere look drab and grey. In his panic, he'd done a quick tour of several city-centre car parks to see if any rang a bell. Unfortunately, none did, hence his late return, eventually, by taxi. Goochie's face was a picture of disbelief. With no likelihood of the penny dropping for Topley as to the car's whereabouts, the police were informed and given the car's registration. With them looking, it was found within the hour, a lot quicker than it took Goochie to forgive.

Once I'd moved back to Cambridge, which I did from the 1985 season, my travelling companion was Clem Driver, the Essex scorer. Although he lived about 20 miles away in a pretty village called

Langley, right on the Essex/Hertfordshire border, he was my closest neighbour for the purposes of travel to away matches.

Wise beyond even his 70-odd years, Clem was in many ways the perfect companion for a road trip and its aftermath. A superb navigator and conversationalist, he'd lived a varied life and taken down the details. He even tolerated the music I played, an experience he called 'listening to Pringle's handwritten tapes'.

It was a description that caught on. My obsession with vinyl discs meant I largely eschewed CDs. Armed with a decent deck (I'd now progressed from the JVC one I'd got from my Ashes sponsors in 1982–83 to a Roksan Xerxes) and a Sony Walkman Pro (the Pro bit is important for quality), I'd tape my favourite tracks onto cassettes to play in the car, the place I tended to do most of my listening back then, because of the long hours spent in it.

Personally, I never considered my tastes in music that challenging, but with team-mates getting a constant dose of Van Morrison if they travelled with Gooch, or the Electric Light Orchestra if they drove with Fletch, a typical selection of mine – the Smiths, Lee 'Scratch' Perry, Miles Davis, Nick Drake, John Martyn, Husker Du, Love, the American Music Club and the Meat Puppets – might have seemed a little out there.

Clem, however, never complained, though I did hear him saying to someone once that it helped to be deaf, at least in the ear that faced the speaker in the door. Anyway, whenever music of an uncommercial hue was being played, the reference was always that it could be from one of 'Pringle's handwritten tapes'.

A man of exceptional intelligence and knowledge, Clem would complete both the *Times* and *Guardian* crosswords every day, generally by the time we'd reached the ground. As an additional challenge, Clem would often accomplish this sporting a hangover, especially if he'd had what he called 'a drinking day' the night before.

When Essex weren't at home, Clem would separate the time away into drinking and non-drinking days, though nothing alcoholic would pass his lips until after play. When I asked what each entailed he told me, 'Well, a drinking day involves at least three-quarters of a bottle of whisky, preferably Famous Grouse. A non-drinking day, on the other hand, is two bottles of white wine.' To him, only spirits represented a 'proper drink'.

There was another bonus to travelling with Clem and that was his wife, Betty, a charming lady who rarely left Langley on account of her agoraphobia. That affliction aside, Betty was a superb cook who'd always have a feast prepared whenever I dropped Clem home. She, too, loved Essex cricket and saw feeding us up as doing her bit for the cause.

As a bachelor, my weight when travelling with others hovered between 15 and 16 stone. Once I began to travel with Clem, it shot up to 17 stone, most of the gain and blame laid squarely on Betty's roast joints with all the trimmings, and that before the pud and cheese and biscuits sent me sated back to Cambridge. Once Nick Knight became part of our travelling band, after he'd moved to Cambridge, the dining table would groan under the weight of the food. Despite that, Betty was as thin as a stick.

9

THE OFF-SEASON AND OVERSEAS TOURS

England 'B' – Sri Lanka 1985–86

Once the selectors had decided I was an English-conditions bowler, I rarely toured in the winter after that Ashes tour of 1982–83. Apart from the odd England 'A' and 'B' tour, and one-day trips to World Cups and other tournaments like the Nehru Cup and Sharjah, I was left largely to my own devices between October and April.

In the beginning, the desire to improve my game fashioned my winters. In 1983–84, 1984–85 and 1986–87, I played club cricket in Australia, South Africa and then Australia again, with only the last trip, at a club called Campbelltown in the Sydney Grade, proving worthwhile and enjoyable from a playing point of view.

Thereafter, having decided the experiences were not really progressing me as a player, I decided to travel, first to Peru, Ecuador, Bolivia and Venezuela in 1987, and the following year to Botswana and Namibia. Both were memorable trips to parts of the world beyond my comfort zone, and they expanded my world view far more than playing club cricket.

An official tour would occasionally intervene, however, such as the England 'B' tour to Sri Lanka early in 1986. Although it began life as two and a half months of 'missionary' work, taking in Bangladesh, Sri Lanka and Zimbabwe, politics intervened because some of the squad appeared on a blacklist featuring people thought to have sporting ties with South Africa. I'd played club cricket in

Pretoria the previous season, yet my name was not on it, presumably my efforts there for Oostelikes Cricket Club had sneaked beneath the radar.

As ever with preening politicians, there was a lot of brinkmanship at play, and we got as far as the airport before being told that legs one and three, to Bangladesh and Zimbabwe, had been cancelled. Happily, a solution was at hand courtesy of Sri Lanka. Eager to move their cricket to its next phase after being awarded Test status four years earlier, they offered to extend our visit there to take up the slack.

This was done so promptly that a flight was organised within a week, which meant most of us left our luggage in a room at one of Heathrow's airport hotels. One who didn't was Jonathan Agnew, who'd brought a gross of Mars bars to ease his passage through the original tour. I think he felt they might go walkies if he left them in the team room, so he took them home, before returning with a somewhat reduced pack a few days later.

The tour began with a match against Sri Lanka Colts in Colombo on 12 January. Although January is meant to be one of the coolest months in that part of the world, it was all relative for somewhere situated just seven degrees north of the equator. With the high humidity it felt as hot as Hades to us, especially when wearing our tour uniform of grey slacks, white shirt, tie and blazer. Imagine our surprise, then, when we attended an official sundowner one day, at which we sweated cobs in our tour regalia, to find that the opposition were wearing cardigans beneath their jackets. When I asked one of them what was going on, he said, 'Well, it is a bit chilly at the moment.'

Unsurprisingly, that was a tour where temper and temperature were inextricably linked. The hotter it got, the more we lost our rag, though the provocations were plenty, including the worst umpiring

I've ever seen – and that includes Steve Bucknor at the 1992 World Cup final.

It was frustrating, especially for the bowlers. Once the Sri Lankans noticed that we'd picked a lopsided squad, with only one frontline spinner, Nick 'The Beast' Cook, they prepared slow turners which essentially dusted up whatever the format. In fact, so rough did they make the pitch for the four-day 'Test' at Kandy, that Mark Nicholas, our captain, decided to play our assistant manager, Norman Gifford, then 45 but still playing first-class cricket for Warwickshire. Giff bowled left-arm spin and Marky had to get special permission from the TCCB to play him, which was granted. It bore fruit, too, Giff taking seven wickets to the five snaffled by The Beast.

What was also lopsided was the amount of time we spent in stifling Colombo, the capital. While the Oberoi hotel we stayed at was perfectly good, residing there for all but 15 of our 50 nights in Sri Lanka meant that it began to pall for many, though creatures of habit like Bill Athey loved it. Ath, never one for sampling local culture, used to dine in the same hotel restaurant (and more than one choice was available), at the same time, and eat the same meal, night after night. He'd then repair to his room in time to catch Clint Eastwood in *For a Few Dollars More*, a film they screened at the same time every night. By the time we left for a rare excursion to Kandy, Bill knew every line – not that there were many.

To amuse myself, I grew a beard, which I then shaved from one half of my face. My team mates knew about my ruse, but the game was to see how long it would take for the manager, Peter Lush, to notice. At team meetings I'd sit with my bearded side towards him, then change seats and show him my clean-shaven side. In the end, after several meetings, I had to stand in front of him face-on to make him notice. With powers of observation that poor, he would never have made a spy.

One briefly redeeming feature of the hotel was the bar on the top floor called the Supper Club, though with familiarity breeding contempt, it wasn't long before we'd rechristened it the 'Suffer Club'. With the hotel being the stopover place of choice for the world's major airlines, air hostesses of all stripes would congregate there most nights after a few sharpeners in the crew room. There was a fair selection too, with British Airways, Air Finland, Gulf Air and Lufthansa all represented. Swimming-pool lounger and a spot of shopping by day, Supper Club by night, perhaps followed by a bit of rough and tumble, seemed to be their routine until the return flight home.

There used to be a close association between England touring teams and BA back then, not necessarily in terms of us flying with them, but certainly in the understanding of them allowing us to use their crew room. Essentially, we were two teams stuck in far-off places with an urge to let our hair down. Allowing us access to some decent wine and whisky pinched off the plane, as well as some British banter, was really just an extension of flying the flag. You can forge great friendships in a short space of time in conditions like that. No surprise, then, that several England cricketers of the era ended up marrying or going out with air hosties.

In comparison with the socialising, the cricket proved tough. Apart from the physical trial of coping with the heat and humidity, Sri Lanka's cricketers were pretty good, at least on their own patch. They were determined, too, along with their umpires, to give no quarter, which made for some feisty matches.

Generally, stalemate prevailed, with only the 45-over one-day matches being decided, Sri Lanka 'B' winning three to our two. Of the seven three- and four-day matches played, every single one ended in a draw.

If most of the cricket and routine of being in the same hotel was dull, Sri Lanka was not. The climate allowed exotic flora and fauna to flourish, while its colonial past meant there were some grand old buildings, most of them in decay. The civil war with Tamil Eelam meant money was not being spent on propping up fading colonial facades.

Although we were well away from that conflict's main theatre in the north and east, there were still reminders of it, such as the bomb that went off in the middle of Colombo while we were at practice. It was an explosion we both heard and felt, that distinctive percussive *whap* heard as the pressure wave compacts human flesh even a few miles away. While one or two of the players felt jittery about the incident, the consensus was that we were not targets and therefore not in much danger unless we went wandering around the middle of town.

Unsurprisingly, not that many had been going walkabout. Although far fewer beggars tugged at your sleeve than in India, you would still get hassled if you wandered beyond the confines of the hotel. Most of the nuisance came from touts enquiring as to whether you wanted 'Hash, boys or pushy?' And pushy they were.

It wasn't the only misunderstanding between us and the locals. Our baggage man, Siripally, a slip of a man who could nevertheless haul ten times his bodyweight in cricket gear, was one of those people destined for sainthood, so sweet was his nature. He also had an unintended comic timing, or at least I think it was unintended, as he kept the straightest of faces when delivering his one-liners. The first of them came out one day in Colombo after he'd taken Chris 'Kippy' Smith's sweaty shirt off him and handed him a cold bottle of water after nets.

'Cheers, china,' said Kippy, his way of thanking anybody, and not just Siri, whenever they did something for him. You see, although 'china plate' was Cockney rhyming slang for 'mate', it was also part of the vernacular for white men brought up in Durban, South Africa, as Kippy had been. Siri didn't know this, and after the third or fourth time Smith thanked him with a 'Cheers, china,' he'd had enough.

'Sir,' said Siri, with more than a hint of indignation, 'I am Singhalese not Chinaman. Please remember this.'

Later, at the same net session, a brass band suddenly struck up just outside the ground, a big raucous sound with a sleazy New Orleans swagger.

'What's that music all about, Siri, a wedding or something?' asked the Beast.

With a grave face, Siri leaned in close and said, with as much gravitas as he could muster, 'No, sir, Christian died.'

His best performance, though, was in the dressing room at Colombo Cricket Club, or CCC as it was known locally. It was mid-February, so a few degrees hotter than when we'd arrived, and the penultimate four-day 'Test' of the tour was under way.

England had spent a fairly fruitless morning in the field trying to make inroads. When they came off for lunch, Siri, as ever, was ready to minister to their needs. He was shrewd enough to know there was a hierarchy and that he must pamper Jon Agnew, the leader of our attack. So he handed Aggers a large bottle of cold water, before taking his sopping shirt off to the dryer. He then pulled off Aggers's bowling boots for him, before plodding off to get him some lunch, returning soon after with a large plate of curry and rice. But instead of the 'Thanks, Siri' he was expecting, there was an explosion of expletives as Aggers hurled the plate to the floor and went into meltdown.

'I hate this ------- place,' Aggers screamed. 'You go out on the field to play and it's ------- red hot. You come off the field into a changing room with one bloody fan and guess what, it's ------- red hot. And then, you go for lunch and what do you get? ------- red-hot curry. Aaargh. I've had it with ------- Sri Lanka.'

Throughout this tirade, Siri, who was just inches from Aggers, had not moved. As the hysteria finally blew itself out, he looked at Aggers and said, calm as you like, 'No like, Aggy?'

Although never one to undersell himself as a drama queen, Aggers was broadly right about the cuisine, it was ------- hot. If you ate local fare, as I tended to do on tour, you needed to be able to cope with some serious capsaicin heat, the active ingredient in chillies. Sri Lankans like them with everything, and I mean everything, devilled cuttlefish being the ultimate mouth-burner. I had that once and it was like a splinter grenade going off in my throat.

The heat, without and within, was impossible to escape in Sri Lanka. At most of the grounds you'd get vendors selling drinks but also big, juicy pieces of freshly cut pineapple. Nuzzi, they called them. Healthy, cool and refreshing, any visitors making a purchase would take them straight, no chaser. Not the locals. Unless the chunks were doused in a mixture of salt and powdered chilli, they weren't interested.

Being a fast bowler was particularly trying in Sri Lanka, as David 'Syd' Lawrence discovered. In one match against Sri Lanka 'B' at CCC, he steamed in and bowled fast. Unfortunately the pitch was comatose and he was a bit too wayward and got belted everywhere, especially by their captain, a pudgy left-hander called Arjuna Ranatunga. We eventually dismissed them for 428, but as we walked off, Syd, with spumes of sweat leaking from him like mini water sprinklers, was almost inconsolable.

'It's a shit game,' he said. 'When people read *Wisden* in a few years' time they will see I bowled 28 overs and got nought for 114. But it won't say how hard I tried. It's a shit game.'

Syd was right. He kept charging in even when the ball kept disappearing to the boundary even quicker than he bowled, which was quick. He also had a temper on him, like most fast bowlers, and a stubborn streak which revealed itself when we were given new room-mates.

I don't know what Syd's beef with Nick Cook was, but he told manager Peter Lush he did not wish to share with him. Lush, in the paternalistic mould of the era, told him to get on with it and do as he was told. Syd refused and booked a room for himself, which he paid for with his own money, a financial sacrifice few players would have made back then. After two nights, Lush relented and gave him a different room-mate, but the incident showed Syd was not someone to be easily swayed from his principles.

At the end of the tour, most players flew home, though Wilf Slack, one of our openers and a man who died tragically four years later while playing cricket in Gambia, was called up by England for their tour of the West Indies. Good luck, we thought, he's gone from cricket in the slow lane to cricket played on the speedway.

Given our proximity to the Maldives, Kippy Smith and I decided to head there for a week, the opportunity unlikely to present itself again. I'm glad I went. Although not the luxury destination it is now (our island of Furana was so basic we showered in cold sea water), there was a pristine nature to it all that I found captivating. Having got my PADI scuba-diving certificate in three days, I spent most of my time below the waves, marvelling at the myriad fish species which inhabited the many coral reefs there.

By contrast, Kippy spent most of his time in a hammock reading one of those self-help books on how to become a millionaire – time well spent for him, as it happens. The reason for his sloth was understandable. On an early snorkel not long after we'd arrived, a shark had come within 20 yards of us. In Durban, where Kippy was from, sharks killed people on a regular basis. This one was a black-tipped reef shark, and while not renowned for its man-eating, Kippy wasn't taking any risks and returned to dry land post-haste.

And that is where he stayed until it was time to return to Colombo and one more night in the Suffer Club before our flight home. The place hadn't changed much, the only difference being that it now had one of the world's most eligible bachelors prowling its banquets – Imran Khan, Pakistan's captain, his team now being on tour in Sri Lanka. Kippy and I had a chat with Imran, who in the absence of any cute hosties was quite voluble, especially in his disgust at Sri Lankan umpires.

'Everyone complains about Pakistani umpires, but this lot are far worse,' he said. 'In Kandy, they gave four of our top five out lbw, including Javed Miandad. He was so upset he later ran out to the middle with a *Wisden* opened at the page for the lbw Law. He'll get punished for doing it, but it was the umpires who were bringing the game into disrepute.'

Imran, who went into politics after retiring from cricket, has since become Prime Minister of Pakistan, surely the first cricketer to hold such a lofty office. Back then, his experiences with the umpires of Sri Lanka, and elsewhere, persuaded him to lobby the International Cricket Council to provide neutral umpires for all international matches and bilateral series. Some 30 years later, that is exactly what we have, at least in Test matches. Poor decisions may still occur, but at least there are none of the accusations of bias, or worse, that poisoned so many overseas tours in the 1980s.

England – 1987 World Cup to India and Pakistan

Being an ICC event, neutral umpires were already in place for the 1987 World Cup, held jointly in India and Pakistan, during October and November, and the first where games comprised 50 overs a side. It was a good thing, too, given that Javed Miandad's lbw dismissal in our match against Pakistan at Rawalpindi was said to be the first time he'd been given out that way during an international match on home soil. Phil DeFreitas was the pioneering bowler, India's Ram Gupta the brave umpire.

Armed with about seven vaccinations, including a trio of painful intramuscular jabs to combat hepatitis B, we flew to Lahore aboard a British Airways flight which Allan Lamb tried his best to drink dry before we touched down on the forbidding plains of alcoholic abstinence. He had a good go, too, draining most of the decent champagne he managed to blag from the hosties working in First Class (we were in Club).

His thirst had consequences, though, the first being to upset Ludovic Kennedy, whose foot Lamby squashed while drunkenly trying to regain his balance. Kennedy was en route to Hong Kong to see his daughter. Like many on board he'd taken off his shoes and popped on some flight socks. He'd risen to stretch and was having a chat with me and Paul 'Nobby' Downton in the galley when along staggered Lamby, with painful consequences.

It didn't get any better for Lamby, who kept on drinking until the alcohol anaesthetised him. Unable to rouse him as we circled to land in Lahore, Nobby and I had to fill in his visa form. We managed the basics like passport number, date and place of birth, but couldn't get any answers out of him to questions like father's name, and the last three countries visited, questions that immigration officials in Asia always seemed to demand. So we made them up, hopeful that as we were all dressed up in our blazers we'd be waved through en masse. We weren't, but on the other hand nothing was queried, including Goochie's cricket case, which had 10 bottles of wine stashed beneath the pads and gloves.

I'd never toured Pakistan before and had brought along V.S. Naipaul's *Among the Believers*, a book of non-fiction he wrote while travelling through Asia's Islamic countries, Pakistan included, in the late 1970s and early 1980s. As is often the case with Naipaul, the book has divided opinion over the years, though I found it a provocative read. The Pakistan I experienced on a daily basis that trip was in thrall to cricket, the colonial game. The one Naipaul saw when he travelled there was obsessed with creating a modern Islamic State, albeit one hampered by the contradiction that Islam itself seemed unreconciled to modernity. It was fascinating to see how the two co-existed.

The TCCB saw it differently again. For the first time I can recall on an England tour, we travelled with a doctor. Not just a GP, but a leading medical man from London's Hospital of Tropical Medicine, Dr Tony Hall. Whether it was an extra nod to professionalism or simply because World Cup squads had 14 players rather than the 16 of Test squads, and were therefore more vulnerable to illness, the Doc was hired to keep us well.

As part of the same brief, someone decided that we needed some home comforts to keep us sane but also regular in our morning ablutions. With that in mind, crates of corned beef, baked beans, English tea bags and packets of crisps were flown out to appease those suspicious of the local cuisine. With only one or two players indulging themselves, they travelled all round Pakistan with us, though not India, stacked high in the team room at each hotel.

To help us stay healthy, Dr Hall also handed out a sheet of 'Dos and Don'ts'. In the first column were things like washing our hands at every opportunity, something he enforced by pointing us to the basins every time we left the field or net practice. He also insisted that all food in the dressing room be freshly cooked on site, while every hotel we stayed at was not given the green light for dining until its kitchen had been inspected by him, clipboard in hand.

In the Don'ts column were things to avoid, such as ice cream, salads, tap water, the local sweets and stray dogs. By way of an experiment, Dr Hall, ever keen for data from the field, tried every item on his forbidden list, except for the dogs. He'd then note any effects. Except that there weren't any. By the time the tour had reached the halfway point, he'd not even experienced a wobble, let alone full-blown dysentery. So he tore up his Don'ts sheet and suggested we do the same.

Not all of us were hale and hearty throughout. I took ill in the first week and was poleaxed for two days as I paid hourly homage to the porcelain gods of Armitage and Shanks. Fortunately, I was rooming with caring Nobby Downton, who sorted out bottled water and Dioralyte for me, so at least I was hydrated.

Those like our coach Mickey Stewart, a man whose idea of exotic food was some chopped chives on scrambled eggs, felt it was my comeuppance for eating the local curries and kebabs. In Asia, Mickey, untrusting of local cuisines, ate eggs three times a day every day. But I reckon, and the Doc concurred, judging from the time it had taken for my guts to start flip-flopping, that the culprit was the steak and kidney pie I'd eaten at the club in the British High Commission.

That club, based in a compound in Islamabad, was a godsend for those desperate for alcohol and reminders of home, like week-old copies of the *Daily Telegraph*. With colonial club protocol to the fore, you could buy books of tickets to pay for drinks and food, of which for us at least, wine and beer were the most popular.

Some of the High Commission staff seemed a bit put out at being invaded by us, though there was a group of women, plainly bored with their life in that bubble, who seemed up for some fun. In a closed environment like that any hanky-panky would have gone round the rumour mill in a shot, so was out of the question. There was, though, a hilarious game of impromptu strip darts played, in which most of the contestants, me included, got down to our knickers. It was about as X-rated as things ever got in Pakistan. Naturally, there were accusations that the exhibitionists were throwing badly on purpose. Yet, with all visitors having to be off compound by midnight, not even the worst throwers had time for full exposure.

*　　*　　*

On the field, we were still casting about for our best combination. I started off in the side against the West Indies, Pakistan and Sri Lanka, but was dropped in order that we might play a second spinner, which given the state of the pitches – slow, baked and bare – seemed fair enough. Chris Broad also started off in the team, but like me he too was left out, in his case for Bill Athey, who was a better player of spin.

The Windies match – the second of the Group B matches – was held at the Municipal stadium in Gujranwala, a nondescript town 60 miles north of Lahore. We travelled there on the day of the match for a 9.30 a.m. start, due to dusk falling at about 5.30 p.m. That meant setting off at 4.30 a.m., when it was still pitch-black.

The day before our match some of us had met Muhammad Ali. As an ambassador of Islam, he'd been on his own short tour of Pakistan. Now here he was in the lobby of the Lahore Hilton, clearly damaged but still exuding an aura gifted to the very few. He hammed it up a bit with Phil 'Daffy' DeFreitas, doing a quick shimmy and a half-thrown combination, to which Daffy was unsure how to respond. Although Ali moved very slowly and deliberately, there was still the occasional gleam in his eye.

He also wished us luck, not that any of it rubbed off on me against the Windies. Although we won the match, I had to wait until last to come on to bowl. When I did get a go, I got belted all round Gujranwala. As captain, Gatt believed in players taking responsibility. So, specialist bowlers did the bowling and specialist batsmen did the batting. As a result, I was given my full allocation of 10 overs, including three at the death, despite getting hammered by Richie Richardson, Jeffrey Dujon and Roger Harper.

I conceded 83 runs from my 10 overs, then the most ever by an England bowler in one-day cricket. In some ways it was nice to know that Gatt had enough faith to persist with me. But it was also curious that he didn't bowl Goochie, or even himself for a couple of overs, just to spread the load.

To add insult, it was also the most conceded in a World Cup match, though Ashantha de Mel, Sri Lanka's opening bowler, took that accolade off me four days later when he also got collared by the West Indies. His 10 overs cost 97 after Viv Richards had cut loose with an incredible 181 in Karachi.

In truth, I didn't feel I'd bowled badly. There'd been quite a few edges for four and I'd had Richardson, their top-scorer, dropped before he'd reached 20. When I told Goochie this afterwards he thought I was having a laugh, but I meant it.

It was also the most uncomfortable, physically, I'd ever felt on a cricket pitch. Whether the pre-dawn start had anything to do with that, I'm not sure. But the concrete bowl of a stadium certainly did. With some summer heat still lingering in northern Punjab, it had turned into a tandoori oven by 11 a.m.

It was so hot and humid that Daffy was sick on the outfield after pulling up during one of his overs. The press were told he'd swallowed a fly but the bright orange liquid that spewed out seemed a bit extreme for that. By mid-afternoon the place was like a furnace. Happily, the West Indies were bowling by then, trying to defend 243.

They might have done it, too, had their captain, Viv Richards, not left Courtney Walsh with six overs to bowl at the death. Walsh would have experienced heat and humidity before, but not like this. There was a sapping quality to it in Gujranwala that sucked the life from you. As he tried to get through his overs, it wasn't long before Walsh, a man with a loose-limbed action anyway, began to resemble a deboned chicken. In one of his finest World Cup knocks, Lamby was on hand to take advantage. Like a patient predator, he pounced on the ailing Walsh, his unbeaten 67 off 68 balls seeing us through to victory with three balls to spare.

With no Beefy or Gower that tournament (Beefy was having a fusion of two vertebrae and Gower a shoulder operation), I was coming in at six. Although confident in my abilities as a one-day batsman, number six, even though it fed into Gatt's ethos that the top five must take responsibility to do most of the batting, was a place too high.

The subsequent move to two spinners, with Eddie Hemmings replacing me, was the right one from a bowling perspective, though it weakened the batting. Despite that, we kept beating everyone in our group except Pakistan, gaining enough impetus for a semi-final meeting with India in Mumbai on 5 November. The other semi pitted Australia against Pakistan in Lahore.

Prior to that encounter we'd played a group match against Sri Lanka in Peshawar, a regional town close to Pakistan's notorious and lawless Tribal Areas, as well as its border with Afghanistan. We won the game easily (Sri Lanka were not the one-day force they are now), yet the four days spent there were among the most incident-packed of my cricket career.

For starters, Peshawar, at least then, was something of a base for mujahideen fighters on R&R. Indeed, Osama bin Laden, then backed by the CIA and fighting the Soviets who'd invaded Afghanistan seven years earlier, was said to have funded 'rest' houses there for that purpose. As a result, when a bomb went off near the main market, the first theory was that it had been KGB trying to kill resting mujahideen.

England teams did not travel with their own security detail then, though a few armed police were provided for us whenever we travelled to the ground or airports. The bomb caused a bit of anxiety among the team, but there was no thought that we should head home or even elsewhere in Pakistan. Instead our manager, Peter Lush, told us to be sensible and stay around the team hotel, the

Pearl Continental, now thought to be the most bombed hotel in Pakistan, since the Taliban's rise in that area.

The PC, as it was known, didn't have much to offer apart from a Green Room and a few shops, the Carpet Palace the most interesting of them. Discreetly tucked away, the Green Room was where foreigners like us, on presentation of a permit declaring ourselves to be alcoholics, and Christian, could buy locally brewed Murree beer, an apricot liqueur from Hunza or some dodgy Scotch whisky, distilled, it seemed, anywhere but Scotland. The permits could be obtained at a kiosk near reception and cost 150 rupees. Still, they were worth it. The beer was drinkable and the place was a magnet for intrepid travellers needing to unwind for a night, so you got a few interesting stories as well.

Some of us had even been to Murree, a hill station about 35 miles north-east of Islamabad, where the beer was brewed. Murree was where British memsahibs used to escape the summer heat in colonial times, and the spa-town atmosphere persisted. We went there by road along the twisting Karakoram Highway, our driver happy to overtake gaudily decorated and heavily laden lorries on blind bends. When someone shouted at him to be less reckless he'd just smile and say, 'Inshallah,' then continue to make progress his way.

The Carpet Palace in the PC, owned by Waqar Samad, was every bit as intriguing as the Green Room. Ever since Dad had returned home from Mombasa one day with two 'Persian' rugs he'd bought off a dhow captain, I'd been in thrall to their beauty and the craftsmanship involved. Here, though, was a cornucopia of them, with a master salesman to entice the unwary into purchase. Dazzled by both, I was putty in Waqar's hands, as was Goochie.

'I guarantee you this rug is antique Tekke Turkoman, brought across the mountains by Afghan refugees,' he would say, while his assistant would unfurl it in such a way as to reveal its intricate patterns and hues. 'At least 1,200 knots per square inch and made with vegetable dye, not mineral,' he would add, stressing the 'not mineral'. In rug world, mineral dyes were modern and inferior.

Waqar was charming and sharp as a tack. He was also a master strategist. After I'd set aside three rugs for purchase, he insisted that I accept a fourth, this time as a gift. It was a fine rug and, although flattered by his generosity, I told him it would be an insult for me to accept such a lovely piece for nothing.

'Pringle,' he said, without hesitation or a hint of irony, 'it would be an honour to be insulted by you. Let's say 350 dollars to avoid any such feelings, and it's yours.'

It was in the same league as the logic of those who guarantee your safety in Pakistan by offering 'presidential-level security'.

'But you've had three presidents assassinated,' I remember saying once when this came up, pointing out what I felt was an inherent flaw.

'Yes, but you are not president,' came the answer. 'Presidential-level security good if you are not president.'

Helpless in the face of Waqar's verbal dexterity, I cashed some more traveller's cheques and paid up, the victim of a beautiful mugging.

I had no way of proving the rugs' authenticity, but Waqar's tales had the ring of truth about them, despite the excessive patter. After all, rugs and carpets were the only means of barter and wealth available to the many thousands of Afghans housed in the refugee camps near Peshawar. That and their portability, which enabled them to be brought across borders without too much hassle, made them almost as good as hard currency.

One thing Waqar did stiff us on was his claim that the rugs would attract neither duty nor VAT when they arrived back in the UK. 'Shipping costs only,' he assured us. 'British Government classes them as "arts and crafts". Which makes them free from such tariffs. I guarantee you this,' he said, with impressive authority.

Caressed by Waqar's charm and plied with endless cups of tea and chapli kebabs, Goochie and I ended up with half a dozen rugs between us, which were promptly despatched, by sea, to await our return. When Goochie picked them up at Tilbury dock just before Christmas, he rang to tell me I owed him £400. 'Arts and crafts, my arse,' he said. 'Customs charged both duty and VAT.'

Lamby had ogled the rugs, too, but felt them expensive. 'Let's go to the market in town,' he said to me the day before our game against Sri Lanka, 'they'll be cheaper there.' When I pointed out that the manager had essentially banned us from going there after the bomb, he said he had to do something away from the hotel or he'd go stir-crazy.

So I asked our local liaison officer, Namen, where we might go, now that the town was off limits. 'We can visit a good friend of mine in Tribal Area,' he said. 'Very interesting person, very safe.'

Namen arranged a car and together with Tim Rice, of *Evita* fame, who happened to be travelling around watching the cricket, and photographer Graham Morris, Lamby and I headed off into Pakistan's lawless lands to meet Gulshad Khan.

The first thing you noticed once beyond police jurisdiction is that everyone carried a firearm, mostly knock-off Kalashnikovs. Even the stray dogs seemed to have ammo belts. En route, we stopped to visit a gun factory in Dara, where we could have bought anything from a gun disguised as a fountain pen (a firing pin on the end of a tube which could shoot a single bullet), to a rocket launcher.

The area was a paradise for contraband, so it was no surprise when we arrived at Gulshad Khan's fortified property to discover that our host smuggled hashish for a living. He was also a cricket nut, so treated us like VIPs. He even showed us, and allowed us to photograph, his smuggling operation, which was fascinating.

From what I could see and determine, great bunches of cannabis leaves were placed in a hole about 15 inches deep and 20 inches in circumference and then given a good bashing with a heavy metal ball on the end of a wooden jib. There were at least six of these contraptions pounding away. It was all done manually, the end product being a compacted dark, browny-green resin with bits of foliage in it which looked uncannily like a cowpat at the firmer end of the spectrum. This was then placed in moulds, where it stiffened into rectangular blocks.

For some reason, and this may have been for our benefit, it was stamped 'Deluxe Leather', and then wrapped in goatskins for onward shipment to places unknown, at least to us. There was a store room full to brimming with the stuff, its street value significant. 'HASHISH, ya', shouted Gulshad Khan when he saw the look of incredulity on our faces.

The smell was heady. 'Where's Beefy when you need him?' joked Lamby. Mind you, Gulshad Khan didn't offer us any 'product' to sample. I'm not sure where Islam stands on narcotics like hashish, but he told us that neither he nor any of his workers smoked the stuff created in those dark holes. But as for producing it for purposes of commerce? Well, that was just business – good business.

We took tea and watched the West Indies lose to Pakistan on the TV, an exciting game that the Windies could have won, had Courtney Walsh run out the non-striker for backing up too far off the last ball of the match. Instead, Walsh only warned him and the home side got the single they needed to win. In an outpouring of gratitude from the Pakistan public, Walsh was given rugs galore for his good sportsmanship. As I later pointed out to Lamby, that was the way to get a cheap one.

Before we departed, Gulshad Khan allowed Lamby and me to fire his Kalashnikov, which he assured us was 'genuine, not copy'. With his permission to 'shoot anything but the chickens', I blazed away into the dusk sky, amazed at the powerful kick it gave to my shoulder. It was the first and only time I have fired a gun that could kill a human.

We kept quiet about our adventure, though Lamby must have said something to Tony Lewis, as it appeared in the *Sunday Telegraph*. As a result, Peter Lush gave us a rocket about reckless behaviour, though we were not fined.

It was while we were in Peshawar that news of Britain's great storm of 1987 filtered through. With international phone calls from hotel rooms extremely expensive, most made brief calls home to check that loved ones were fine and that the house had not blown down. A few days later, after we'd got to Karachi, Lamby was on the blower a lot more often, this time to his stockbroker – Black Monday had happened and global financial markets were in meltdown.

Most players I knew didn't make enough to speculate on shares, but Lamby had negotiated himself a deal with Northants that saw him get not only his Test fee, which was paid per match back then, but also the money the county received whenever England picked him.

Each time I was selected for a Test, the TCCB would pay me £1,500 and Essex £1,500, a sort of compensation payment to the county for taking me from them. When I heard that Lamby and one or two other players had negotiated all or part of that second fee to be paid to them, I asked Essex if they would pay their fee into the players' pool. After all, it was the team that would miss Goochie, me or Fozzy more than the club. Their response was brief, and in the negative.

Like India, Pakistan was sensory overload, save in one respect – there were hardly any beggars. My theory was that the regime, under General Zia-ul-Haq, had stuck them all in the army or the police, a move which produced an equally intimidating presence on the streets.

There were no coppers around, though, when I ventured to Clifton Beach in Karachi, a desirable suburb popular with all manner of living things, of which people, camels and dogs were the most numerous. I'd heard you could watch mongoose fights with cobras there and was not disappointed, though you needed a strong stomach to watch as the snakes were shredded by those razor-sharp teeth.

My guide for this brief excursion was Maju, our liaison man for this part of Pakistan. Maju was a Parsee, a group which had originated in Persia, so was not a Muslim. Even so, he considered himself less an outsider in Karachi, which was the capital of Sind province, than in the Punjab a few hundred miles to the north. Pakistan is very parochial and tribal in its approach to most things, regional differences being just one of them.

Parsees were also quite numerous in India, though not so much in Delhi, where we spent a few nights before travelling to Jaipur for our penultimate group match against the West Indies, which we won.

A group of us – Goochie, Lamby, John Emburey, Nobby Downton, Tim Rice, a journalist called David Norrie and I – all dined at the Bukhara restaurant in the Delhi Sheraton. For lovers of food cooked in the tandoor this was the ultimate, with something called sikandari raan, a charbroiled leg of lamb, especially fine.

Pudding, though, was something else altogether, with Embers challenging us all to a crème caramel-swallowing contest. With speed being the essence, this was not done with spoons but by sucking the whole wobbling confection clean off the plate in one big slurp. The technique advised was to exhale all breath from your lungs, lean forward with mouth poised just above the quivering pud and then inhale suddenly and deeply through your mouth, sucking hard as you did so.

If you got the technique right, and Embers was the undisputed king, the entire thing would disappear down the hatch at about the speed of sound. When he did it, it was like a magic trick. One second the crème caramel was there, the next it was gone, with not a single particle remaining as evidence of its existence.

I had a go and my epiglottis did not close quickly enough to stop bits of crème caramel from hurtling into my lungs. At the time I felt as if I might choke to death, and I was still coughing up bits of gunge days later.

The organisers, sponsors and broadcasters, not to mention the cricket-mad public, wanted nothing more than an India–Pakistan final in Calcutta. First, though, the two home sides had to get past Australia and England in the semis, with us playing India in Mumbai and the Aussies playing Pakistan in Lahore.

That India failed to fulfil the fantasy of their billion-strong fanbase was down to one of the greatest one-day innings, in terms of context, planning and execution, that I have ever seen – and I saw Viv Richards's unbeaten 189 at Old Trafford in 1984 from the sharp end after he'd belted me clean out of the ground.

Goochie has always been one of the best batsmen I have played with or against, yet he excelled himself in that semi-final. It all began a day or so before the match. We'd monitored the grounds-man's pitch preparation closely, so knew that it would be left bare and dry to benefit India's spinners Maninder Singh and Ravi Shastri. Goochie's plan, after it became plain that timing the ball with conventional strokes would be difficult, was to sweep, sweep and sweep again. It was a shot he played well, but he honed it to perfection in the build-up by getting young Indian spinners to bowl at him on the outfield. With the bounce and turn unpredict-able, he proceeded to sweep every ball, irrespective of line or length.

One of the young spinners hired for the occasion was so confused that he felt that he had not provided proper practice. 'Mr Gooch, I now realise that you treat me with total disdain as a bowler, because you sweep every delivery to leg,' he said.

Come the match, it worked like a dream. Put in to bat by India after they'd won the toss, England made 254 off their 50 overs, with Gooch scoring 115 of them. This was not a knock that wowed with its majesty of stroke. Instead, it was that rare thing – an innings that had been pre-conceived to perfection.

Slow to respond to Goochie's strategy of sweeping just about every ball Shastri and Maninder bowled, India were poor with the bat as well. Only Mohammad Azharuddin threatened to get India close, though when he went, sixth man out for 64, the game was up.

With Australia beating Pakistan in Lahore, the first World Cup outside England had the finalists it didn't want. It was also a match in which I was unlikely to play a part. After all, I'd been surplus to requirements since Peshawar three weeks earlier.

When we arrived in Kolkata, the place was ablaze with burning effigies of Indian players, mostly Sunil Gavaskar and Ravi Shastri. A message to Shastri, who as a Maharashtran was anathema to Kolkata's Bengalis anyway, stated, 'They sacked me as vice-captain. This is my revenge.'

When not undertaking their pyromania, thousands of people would congregate outside our hotel, the Oberoi Grand, just to catch a glimpse of us. We were barred from leaving the hotel on foot without an armed escort of 10 soldiers for fear of being mobbed, so we didn't bother. We were there to get a job done, so didn't mind being confined to quarters for three nights.

The final was on 8 November, a Sunday. Such is the power of cricket in Kolkata that St John's Church, built by British jute barons in the eighteenth century, shifted its Remembrance Day service to the Saturday so as not to clash.

It wasn't only the religious timetable that was affected by the big occasion. Chris Broad, with whom I was now sharing, had been out of the side for as long as I had. Yet, as we lay on our respective beds killing time before our final team meeting, he suddenly had an outbreak of optimism that he would play in place of Tim Robinson, his opening partner at Notts.

When I asked why he felt that way, he pointed to his excellent record against Australia the previous winter when, under Gatt, he'd scored three hundreds in England's 2–1 Ashes victory. I wasn't so sure and told him that it made no sense. Test cricket in Australia 12 months earlier and one-day cricket in India now was like comparing concrete with dust, or at least the difference between the pitches was.

'They'll go with Ath and Robbo,' I said. 'We've got to the final playing them and two spinners, so they won't change now. You and I are carrying the drinks, mate.' But he wouldn't have it.

Sadly for Broady, my logic prevailed, which didn't surprise me, as it had seemed obvious. What did surprise were the tears he shed. He must have persuaded himself that he would play, a belief he probably felt was justified later on after we'd lost the final and Robbo had failed to score.

In hindsight, I certainly should have played. The pitch at Eden Gardens dusted up on a medium-pacer's length, which allowed Simon O'Donnell, Australia's all-rounder, to be the most effective bowler in the match. Grand claims after the event are always futile, but I have always maintained that if I couldn't outbowl Simon O'Donnell on any given day, then I might as well have not been there.

Still, we came within seven runs of winning and probably would have prevailed but for some uncustomarily loose bowling with the new ball by Gladstone Small and Phil DeFreitas – and that infamous reverse-sweep by Gatt.

Chasing 254 to win, we were 135 for two and seemingly cruising when Allan Border, Australia's captain, brought himself on in a last-ditch effort to change the pattern of the match. Gatt was a fine player of spin and Border a competent but part-time slow left-armer. Instead of waiting to see if the first ball was a loosener, Gatt tried to be cute and reverse-sweep him to third man for four. In those days, few played the shot, which carried unnecessary risk. And with good reason. Gatt was through his shot early and gloved a simple catch to wicketkeeper Greg Dyer.

A team should be more robust than to believe the game is up after losing their third wicket, but under Gatt, the top five had to shoulder most of the batting burden. The tail could not be left with too much to do, something that looked likely when Athey was needlessly run out for 58 with 84 runs still wanted.

Lamby played well for his 45 to get us back in the hunt, but when he was seventh man out, bowled by Steve Waugh, we still needed 34 runs off three overs and only the tail to get them. A flurry of hitting from DeFreitas, who made a quickfire 17, got us close but not close enough, as Australia clinched the match and their first World Cup by seven runs.

Although favourites before the start of the final, we had not played to our potential. Whether Australia or the occasion had caused that was not clear. What is clear, however, is that the win by Border, with a young side, heralded a renaissance for Australia which continued for the next 20 years, well into the next century.

Naturally, there was the inevitable despondency which comes from losing a big match where you have not done yourselves justice. But we'd just come straight out of a long, tiring season in England, so fatigue must have played a part, if only with some of the woolly decision-making.

With that in mind, I felt for those team-mates who now had to head back to Pakistan for a Test series and some more one-dayers.

For them, umpire Shakoor Rana and more naan bread awaited. Not that Lamby, Nobby, the Doc or I would be among them. We had not been selected for that tour and were set to leave the next day.

At that stage, the idea of a Club Class seat on a British Airways flight home would have been many players' idea of heaven, but Lamby always sought that little bit extra. Espying Colin Moynihan, the Minister for Sport in Thatcher's government, at the post-final dinner, he went straight up to him and asked if he could swing an upgrade to First Class for those of us flying back to Heathrow.

Moynihan's contacts apparently extended to the top at BA, as First Class is where we spent the flight home, Lamby essentially finishing off where he'd started six weeks earlier – with champagne all the way.

England – 1989 Nehru Cup in India

Two years after that World Cup we were back in India, in October 1989, for the Nehru Cup, a tournament held to celebrate the centenary of Jawaharlal Nehru's birth. Only six teams were invited: India, Pakistan, Sri Lanka, England, Australia and the West Indies. For some reason, New Zealand were excluded, presumably because seven sides would have made the schedule more complicated.

There were some new faces in the England side, now picked by a selection panel chaired by Ted Dexter. Goochie was captain but Alec Stewart, Nasser Hussain, Jack Russell, Angus Fraser and David Capel had all come into the side within the previous 12 months. Then there was Wayne 'Ned' Larkins, a man who'd played for England a decade earlier, but had fallen out of favour until his considerable gifts as a batsman had found support from the new regime.

I roomed with Ned while we were in Delhi and he was an intriguing companion. Keen on a fag and a beer, he felt it his duty to drain the minibar on a nightly basis. He'd also phone his girlfriend every night, locking me out of the room. Whenever I knocked, he'd shout, 'Just a few more minutes, mate', though it never was. I spent a lot of time that tournament hanging around hotel corridors waiting to be let in by Ned. With international calls prohibitively costly back then, Ned, who would would spend 30–40 minutes phoning home every night, did most of his tour fee within weeks. It was one of the hidden perils of touring.

Despite his naivety with collect calls, Ned was an incredible batsman to watch when he came off, as he did in the match against Australia in Hyderabad. They'd set us 243 on a slow pitch on which all but Allan Border had struggled to score quickly. Adopting a baseball hitter's pose, something today's batsmen do all the time in T20, Border had struck 84 off 44 balls with five sixes.

One of them, off Angus Fraser, had gone clean out of the ground, a strike that prompted Gooch to go up to his bowler to ask if he bowled a slower ball. Gus, a curmudgeon from birth, said, 'No. Do you think I ought to start?'

I don't know if Border's knock spurred Ned on, but he went out and spanked the Aussie attack led by Terry Alderman, England's nemesis during the disastrous Ashes series a few months earlier. Although he was out before victory had been completed, Ned's 124 off 126 balls had broken them. As team-mates fussed round to pat him on the back for his brilliant knock, he looked up with a cheeky grin on his face and said, 'Terry who?'

By way of celebration he got stuck into the beer, not that he usually needed an excuse for that. 'Right, who have we got next?' he asked mid-session.

'India, in Kanpur', said somebody, though this was not true, as Pakistan in Cuttack was before them.

'Who've they got to bowl?' asked Ned, clearly considering this as good a time as any to get mentally prepared for the next match.

'Kapil Dev, Madan Lal, Maninder Singh, Chetan Sharma,' came the reply.

'Kapil Dev,' interjected Ned, who'd played with him at Northants. 'He's just bloody lovely to face.'

Ned had a 'tell' when alcoholic capacity had been reached – his right eye would start winking at you. That night, it had been flickering for a while when he told us where and how far he would hit Kapil.

When we did play India, after beating Pakistan in Cuttack, Ned made a circumspect 42 on a pitch custom-made for India's bowlers. Later, as we tried to defend 255, he was pelted with pieces of concrete while fielding on the boundary. Such perils were not unusual in India. Nor was the fact that a man with a hammer was breaking up the stand and selling the bits, for a few paisa, to those throwing them at any England fielder within range. The umpires were powerless to prevent it, as were the fielders, though the moderate size of the missiles suggested that distraction rather than injury was the main object of the exercise.

With Goochie's appointment as captain for both the Nehru Cup and the tour of the West Indies later that winter, the latter part of which I had not been selected for, the first vestiges of professionalism with a capital P began to be inflicted upon England cricket teams.

The initial thrust into this brave new world came in Delhi, after our warm-up match against an Air India XI in which two 16-year-olds had made fifties against us. Their names were Sachin Tendulkar and Vinod Kambli, two Mumbai schoolboys who'd been creating a stir in that mighty metropolis.

Afterwards, one of India's selectors asked Gooch whether he felt Tendulkar might be ready to play against Pakistan, whose trio of fast bowlers – Imran Khan, Wasim Akram and Waqar Younis – had made them an attack to be feared.

'I wouldn't if I was you,' he said, his argument being that young talent like that could be set back if traumatised by fast bowlers. They didn't listen. Tendulkar played, got hit on the head by Waqar in his first Test, and went on to become one of the greatest batsmen in history.

In the kind of curio that only happens in India, we also met a man at the match who held the Guinness Book of Records title for the world's longest fingernails. With it being impractical to have both hands growing nails over 20 inches long (how otherwise would you eat or wipe your bum?), only one hand's worth was cultivated, each nail meticulously taped to protect it from breaking. It seemed a grotesque sacrifice to make. The arm bearing the long nails was so devoid of muscle condition from not being used that it either hung limply by his side or was supported by the other. There was freak value, for sure, and clearly good money to be made, judging from the number of acolytes who pandered to his every need.

Increased muscle and fitness had always been high on Goochie's agenda, though until that trip he'd never imposed it on an England team. That was about to change, as he marched us off to the national hockey stadium in Delhi, where instead of the nets most of us assumed we would be doing, there were a punishing series of shuttle runs around a 400 metre track. Lawrie Brown, the physio, kept our times.

It was stiflingly hot inside that enclosed stadium and one or two of the old school, such as Ned, Nick Cook and I, were not best pleased with this new regimen, though Ned at least had the benefit of going on to the West Indies. For those not on that trip, it felt like chasing a horse which had already bolted. Coming as it did, on the back of a long, hard season, it was intended to send a message – that Goochie and coach Mickey Stewart meant business. It was like football's pre-season training, which is why I took to calling Stewart 'Mick McManager'.

What it also meant, when we did eventually get a day or an afternoon off, was that most players were even more reluctant than usual to take in a bit of culture. Even when I suggested a trip to the Taj Mahal, most opted to lie by the pool instead. Only Robin Smith, and then after a lot of arm-twisting, came with me on the 6 a.m. train to Agra. He still remembers the day we spent at Fatehpur Sikri, Agra Fort and the Taj Mahal, Shah Jahan's memorial to his favourite wife Mumtaz, something he wouldn't have done if he'd spent it sipping lime sodas on a sun lounger by the hotel lido.

Nasser Hussain, then 21, had also been picked for both tours that winter. A young man whose passion for cricket and success could quickly spill over into anger, he also possessed a mind like a sieve. Perhaps flustered by the amount of relatives he never knew he had descending upon him with requests for complimentary tickets, he proceeded to leave bits of gear and items of clothing at nearly every venue we visited, including his England blazer.

In Cuttack, the team bus had to be stopped and turned around after net practice because he'd forgotten his batting gloves, of which he'd brought only two pairs. When we returned, an ox of undiscerning palate was busy chewing them. Naturally, his sponsors, Gray-Nicolls, were contacted to send replacements, except something like that was never straightforward in India, despite the place's love affair with cricket. When Nasser's new gloves did arrive, manager Peter Lush had to spend most of the day clearing them through Customs, his refusal to indulge the time-honoured system of baksheesh, or bribery, costing him time instead. Speedy conclusions in India have always borne a price.

Another trait of Indians I found trying was the inability for those mostly in service roles to say no. Whether it was because they were in awe of us as cricketers (and Lord knows they shouldn't have been), or just the fact that we were visitors to their country, their fear of disappointing us by admitting something was not possible created a whole new category of frustration.

One example I can give was the day I ordered breakfast in the Usha Kiran Palace hotel at Gwalior, a small city off the main tourist track, but not remote enough to be devoid of all luxuries, such as toilet paper and air conditioning.

'Good morning, sir, what would you like for breakfast?' asked the waiter on my first morning there, beaming from ear to ear.

'Can you do poached eggs?'

'Yessir.'

'Good. I'd like two poached eggs on toast and a pot of black leaf tea, thank you.'

'Two posh eggs [sic] and black leaf tea,' he said, repeating the order.

'Yes, thanks,' I said.

The tea arrived reasonably promptly, but after about 30 minutes there was still no sign of the eggs. In a now empty dining room, I summoned the waiter.

'Are the poached eggs coming?' I asked.

'I will check, sir.'

He returned a few minutes later to tell me, 'It is coming, sir.'

After a further 15 minutes had elapsed I asked again, an inquiry which set in motion the same routine and answer: 'It is coming, sir.'

When nothing had appeared some 20 minutes after that, I called him over and vented my exasperation with an accusation: 'You can't do poached eggs, can you?'

'No, sir,' he said, with a grin not quite as wide as before.

'Why didn't you tell me that an hour ago? I've been sitting here wasting my time.'

There was no explanation, just that ambiguous shake-cum-nod of the head they do in India, and another 'Sorry, sir.'

Yet India delights in unexpected ways, too, and it was in Gwalior that I saw the most wonderful health warning on a bottle of beer. Back then, almost every Indian city with over three million people would have its own beer brands, rather than the ubiquitous Cobra and Kingfisher that you find everywhere there today. This particular beer was called Black Partridge, and written on the label in the kind of flowery English beloved of India's bureaucrats were these cautionary words: 'Drinking alcoholic beverages can be injurious to your health.' They were probably not wrong. Just below that was the amount of alcohol by absolute volume – a head-banging 8.5 per cent.

Most of those beers were topped with glycerine, which acted as a preservative. You could see it floating on top of the beer in the bottle. The old hands reckoned that the glycerine was a prime suspect in causing the trots. Acting on this belief, they used to pour it off prior to filling their glass. To the uninitiated, everything went down the hatch, none the wiser if that little bit looser the following morning.

There were other products which amused, such as 'Crazy Brand' toilet paper, probably only noticed due to the additional time one spent on the loo. On this was printed 'Manufactured by Jay Pee Traders. Local taxes extra.' That was the thing about India, it taxed you at every turn.

Somehow, and this despite losing two of our four matches, we had a semi-final meeting with Pakistan on 30 October in Nagpur, a place whose sole and brief entry in my guidebook had it as the orange-growing capital of India.

We needed something much stronger than fruit juice when we arrived there from Mumbai. Our plane had made three aborted attempts to land but pulled out each time, without explanation. When we did finally manage to touch down, on our fourth attempt, there was spontaneous applause from the passengers.

It wasn't the first time an internal flight that trip had caused sheer terror. In Delhi, as we taxied into position for take-off, another jet swooped in to land just in front of us. It probably missed us by 60 yards, though some of the tabloids presented it as an 'England team cheats death' story to titillate their readers.

Our apprehension was made worse by Lamby telling us that the airline flying us around India had the worst safety record in the world, matched only by some unpronounceable carrier from one of the Soviet satellites. Not that Lamby was phlegmatic about flying or indeed a picture of calm – he was straight onto the beer the moment we left terra firma.

To our horror, there really was nothing strong to drink in Nagpur. Although it was not a 'dry' city like Ahmedabad, we'd arrived just in time for Diwali, a public holiday, which meant alcohol could not be served. To make matters worse, any jangling nerves we had from our journey were not calmed by the booms and bangs of fireworks that were exploded until dawn.

This went on the following night, too, and while it was the same for both teams, we were certainly not at our best when it came to playing the semi-final, a rain-reduced match of 30 overs a side which we lost by six wickets.

We set Pakistan 195 and they got them without too much bother, after Rameez Raja anchored the innings and Saleem Malik played the shots. Saleem's 66 off 41 balls was like something Jos Buttler might produce today, though he did not attempt anything so outrageous as a ramp shot. He did, however, take a liking to Gus Fraser, carving him to all parts of the off-side fence. Gus's six overs cost 58, something I still bring up whenever he starts to get uppity.

England XI – Netherlands 1989

There was another short 'overseas' tour in 1989, even briefer than the Nehru Cup – a three-day stint in the Netherlands during mid-August. Billed as an England XI, the team comprised players who had either played for England or who were on the fringes of selection.

The other criterion for selection for two one-day games on Dutch matting was that players could not be involved in either of the NatWest Trophy semi-finals on 16 August, which ruled out those from Hampshire, Middlesex, Warwickshire and Worcestershire. Also discounted were the England players recently signed up for a second rebel tour to South Africa, though the final composition of that breakaway squad had not yet been finalised.

Neither did the team to Holland involve the cream like Goochie or Lamby, or indeed any who'd played a regular role in that summer's Ashes series, which although not yet completed had already been decided in Australia's favour. It was a somewhat mixed crew, then, which flew to The Hague very early one morning in order to catch a coach from there to Amsterdam to play that afternoon.

Captained by the bespectacled and eccentric Peter Roebuck, we were greeted by rain, which made the matting pitch treacherous, especially as we were not allowed to wear spikes. Previous England teams would have erred on the side of caution and not played in such conditions, but Roebuck was a zealot when it came to cricket. He told us we were missionaries and had to spread the word and put on a show, which we did, playing a 40-over match once the rain had relented to a fine drizzle. He even won the toss and fielded when conditions were at their most difficult underfoot, a real evangelist.

Roebuck's team talk was a peach, too: 'Gregory and Simon [fast bowlers Greg Thomas and Simon Base], I'm going to give you the new ball. Simon, I want you to bowl fast, fast, fast. The matting pitch will bounce for you if you do that. Greg, I want you to swing it away just short of a good length on middle and off and we'll get them caught at slip.'

'I've been dreaming of bowling a ball like that my whole life, boyo, and you're making it sound routine,' said Gregory, looking confused.

As so often happens when you try to do the right thing, Roebuck's good intentions misfired, leaving us a laughing stock as we lost to the Dutch by three runs.

It is true that the matting pitch took some getting used to, and it was hard for bowlers to stand up on it and bowl properly in trainers. We still should have won, though some dawdling by Nasser Hussain and David Capel in the final 10 overs, as we chased 177, cost us dear.

Of course, as somebody pointed out, no Dutch-born player reached 20, the majority of their runs, 77 of them, having been scored by Nolan Clarke, a Bajan good enough to play eight years for Barbados in the Shell Shield. Even so, we bowled badly at him – banging in short to a West Indian being one of the dumber things to do on a small ground with short boundaries.

The press who'd made the trip had a field day. Not only did the result and match provide them with good copy, adding further mayhem to the overall chaos England cricket found itself in at the time, but the press conference given by Roebuck was a collector's item.

I wasn't present, but afterwards Matthew Engel from the *Guardian* asked me if there was any animosity going on behind the scenes. When I asked why he wanted to know, he said that after Roebuck had given his take on the defeat, the coach, Mickey Stewart, had rushed up to the journalists and asked, somewhat hysterically, 'What's he been saying, what's he been saying?'

Not much, was the answer, though Mickey had become suspicious after he'd discovered that the press's agenda, following another disastrous Ashes, was for Roebuck to be the next England captain following Gower's presumed resignation at the end of the series. Mickey's paranoia was as misplaced as the media's assumptions about Roebuck. For one thing, he wasn't even first choice to lead our ragtag team to Amsterdam. That honour had fallen, initially, to his Somerset team-mate Vic Marks. But Vic was about to join the *Observer* newspaper as cricket correspondent, so turned down the honour.

As far as I've been able to make out, there had never been any intention of making Roebuck England captain after Gower, so goodness knows where the press had got that idea from. As ever, confusion reigned until Ted Dexter, the chairman of selectors, no doubt choking down some humble fish pie in the process, appointed Gooch.

Unlike Mickey, the players on the tour had not given a thought to the lines of succession of who would or wouldn't be England's next captain. After a night of fine Dutch hospitality, which included a trip round Amsterdam bars in the wee hours with Greg Thomas and Steve Watkin, we revisited the pretty Amstelveen cricket ground for our second match, this time over 55 overs. With the weather dry, we won easily after batting first and setting the Dutch 262. John Stephenson, a team-mate at Essex, scored a hundred. It was proba-bly what swung his selection for the final Test against the Aussies at The Oval, the following week.

Greg Thomas didn't play the second match. He'd been offered, along with several others, the opportunity to play in the rebel tour of South Africa. I got on well with Gregory and he'd always claimed he'd rather play for England. But he wanted guarantees from Mickey Stewart that he would be selected, something Mickey couldn't give him. As a result, Greg, 29 at the time, told him that he'd be heading to South Africa, so Mickey pulled him from the second match. No point in playing someone about to take the krugerrand.

I played in both games despite having broken the little finger on my left hand. I'd done it taking a diving catch against Lancashire in the Sunday League match a few days before our Dutch jaunt. When

I saw the physiotherapist at Old Trafford, a stand-in for Lancashire's usual physio, Lawrie Brown, who also doubled as England physio, she sent me on my way with a 'Nothing wrong with that.'

That wasn't the opinion of the Dutch doctor I saw before the first game in Amstelveen, who informed me that not only had I broken my finger, but I'd torn the tendon off the bone as well. 'It's a classic hammer fracture that should have been picked up,' he told me. 'It will mean six weeks in a splint, otherwise the tendon will not take and the finger will have a permanent drop.'

As it wasn't my bowling hand and I could get it into a batting glove, with splint, without too much discomfort, I continued playing. Indeed, like John Stephenson, I was even picked to play in the final Ashes Test, though not before seeking guarantees from Mickey Stewart that he'd back me if I dropped a catch. Fielding was the only thing the splint compromised.

Fortunately he did and I played in one of only two Tests against Australia that summer (out of six) that England didn't lose.

England 'A' – Kenya and Zimbabwe 1989–90

In early 1990 there was a tour to Kenya and Zimbabwe, this time with a team called England 'A'. With sports psychologists having begun to apply their nostrums to cricketers, someone in a position of power obviously thought it would be too demeaning to call the side England 'B', as we had been a few years earlier against Sri Lanka. One thing that didn't change was the captain: Mark Nicholas.

The serious cricket action at the time was actually taking place 7,500 miles to the north-west of Harare in the Caribbean, where Goochie's England team had won the first Test against the West Indies in Jamaica. Compared to that, what we were up to seemed very small beer indeed.

At 31, I wasn't sure what I was doing on the trip, though I did get to see some future England regulars like Mike Atherton and Graham Thorpe. With their uncompromising approach, sure touch and firm but understated confidence in their own abilities, both looked destined for the big time. I also got to see some of those who became stalwarts for Zimbabwe, like Andy and Grant Flower, and some who might have been just as revered had they got international recognition sooner, like Dave Houghton.

Harare-born Graeme Hick also turned up to visit his parents, who still farmed in Zimbabwe. Unable to play for the country of his birth because he was in the process of becoming England-qualified, Hick cut a curious, somewhat embarrassed-looking figure while he sat around waiting for his time with England to start. Most of the white population there wished him well in his quest for stardom, as he was a seriously gifted batsman, but the indigenous Africans had more pressing matters to worry about than Zimbabwe cricket losing a talented cricketer.

The most exciting it got in Zimbabwe, for me at least, was an argument with two white Zimbabwean blokes at a Harare nightclub. Syd Lawrence had already had a run-in with their ilk in Mutare, where a drunken white farmer had punched the African security man on dressing-room duty. Seeing a 'brother' in bother, Syd had got the drunk in a headlock and dragged him out of the room before flinging him into a hedge.

I was not as bold or proficient at dealing with violent people, so when one said that I'd got 'the most punchable face in Africa' (I had been winding them up a tad), I prepared to duck.

Fortunately, the Bicknell brothers, Darren and Martin, were on hand to intervene. Although not exactly the Krays, they were big and menacing enough, far more than I was in my National Health glasses. Their presence ensured that the most punchable face in Africa remained unpunched.

Soon after that we got to meet Robert Mugabe at Harare Sports Club, independent Zimbabwe's first president arriving there in a blare of sirens and a cavalcade of armed guards, even though his residence, State House, was about 100 yards away. His handshake was so limp I assumed he had a gammy arm, but was told that was not the case. Which made me think, as he went down the line floppily shaking away, that it must have been weakened from taking all those bungs.

Not all harboured such cynical thoughts. Upon meeting him, Mark Nicholas, our captain, and never one to shy away from hyperbole, announced, 'Meeting you, Mr President, has made this the greatest day of my life.'

The trouble was that MCJ, as we mostly called the skipper (the initials of his three christian names), had already had two 'greatest days of his life' that trip – the first when we'd chanced upon a mother cheetah with five cubs and freshly killed Thomson's gazelle in Nairobi Game Park; the second when we'd stood in the spray gazing at Victoria Falls. I could see his point on those two, but Mugabe was just another despot. As someone brought up in Africa, I knew they were ten a penny.

10

OTHER MAVERICKS

Phil Edmonds

Botham was not the only player to cut a singular path in what outsiders assume to be a team game. Phil Edmonds was a tall, spinning all-rounder with a regal bearing and an insufferable attitude – at least to authority. Like me, he'd also been born in Africa, in Lusaka, Zambia, which made him something of a kindred spirit.

He was also a fellow Cambridge man, one who was even a member of my college, Fitzwilliam. Whether because of those connections, or maybe in spite of them, I always found Philippe-Henri (the name his Belgian mother gave him, but Henry to others) to be a fun team-mate for England. Others, though, found him exasperating.

He certainly wound up his various captains something rotten with his arrogant insouciance, and both Mike Brearley and Bob Willis, captains of Middlesex and England respectively in the early 1980s, could scarcely tolerate him.

He was a damn fine cricketer, though, something he was not shy of telling people, though I also heard it from an independent and expert source, my captain at Essex, Keith Fletcher. He ventured his opinion while we were driving back from Scarborough, a six-hour drive to Essex back then, so plenty of time to field inane questions from me such as: 'Who is the better spinner, Fletch, "Deadly" Derek Underwood or Phil Edmonds?'

'Well,' said Fletch, pausing a moment for some mental calculation, 'Deadly was unplayable on a sticky dog, but you don't really get them any more, now that pitches are covered. But that Phil Edmonds, he's got such a strong action, he can turn it on a pane of glass.'

He didn't actually commit to saying who was better, but in my book there could be no higher accolade than being able to turn a ball on glass, so Edmonds got the nod.

He also got the nod from Peter May and his selectors to play against India in 1982 after Deadly, along with 14 other England players, had suddenly found themselves banned for going on the first rebel tour to South Africa.

That first Test at Lord's was my England debut, as well as being Willis's first international match as captain. We'd somehow made 433 batting first and Beefy had struck quickly in their first innings, trapping opener Ghulam Parkar lbw. The next batsman in was Dilip Vengsarkar, arguably India's best after Sunil Gavaskar, who was at the other end. Vengsarkar preferred to play off the front foot if possible, so Willis, who was bowling from the Pavilion End, had posted a short leg. Henry was that man.

Although helmets, shin guards and arm guards had all started to be worn by those brave, foolhardy souls who fielded at Boot Hill, Henry just used to crouch there in a Bill and Ben sunhat with a neckerchief for protection. I don't even recall him wearing a box, though he must have done. On this occasion, and no doubt because he felt Vengsarkar was susceptible to a bit of chirp, he started sledging him. I'm not certain what he said, but it was salty enough for Vengsarkar to pull out of his stance just as Willis was about to release the ball.

'Umpire, umpire,' Vengsarkar implored as he pointed accusingly at Henry, 'he is abusing me.'

David Evans was not one of those umpires who saw mirth in much, so when Henry said in that flippant southern African drawl of his, 'Honestly, Dave, I was just wishing him good luck,' he went into officious mode and summoned Willis for a powwow.

With Big Bob not best pleased at having to pull up after completing most of his 40-yard charge to the crease, Edmonds was given a dressing-down. Evans even warned him as to his future conduct, which seemed a bit harsh considering nobody, except Vengsarkar, had heard what had been said. It did the trick, though, and Vengsarkar missed one soon after and was lbw, Evans upholding Big Bob's snarled appeal.

The saga was not yet over and in India's second innings, after they'd followed on, an early wicket saw the same protagonists in the same positions as a day earlier. Except that, instead of being the umpire at Big Bob's end, Dai Evans was now at square leg. This time, as Big Bob hurtled in to bowl at Vengsarkar, Henry, with neckerchief now tied round his mouth like a gag, turned to Evans and waved, just to show him that he couldn't sledge even if he'd wanted to.

Evans did not see the funny side and Willis was again summoned to deliver another rollocking to his rogue left-arm spinner. But that is where the pattern ended. Instead of being distracted and then dismissed, Vengsarkar went on to score 157, albeit in a losing cause.

In that same match I met the Queen, along with the other members of each team. Before we shook her gloved hand we were given a crash course in protocol, in this instance by Jack Bailey, MCC Secretary. Bailey had a sense of humour and a fondness for a preprandial snifter, but he seemed unusually serious that day when he addressed us prior to our royal engagement before the start of play.

'You do not speak to Her Majesty unless she speaks to you, and you shake her hand with a firm but light grasp. When she is introduced to you by your captain, you address her with the words "Pleased to meet you, Your Majesty," or "Pleased to meet you, Ma'am." By the way, that last word is pronounced "mam" as in "ham" and not "marm" as in "smarm".'

He might well have added 'you horrible lot' but didn't. Although most of us were as compliant as boy scouts, Bailey hadn't reckoned on Henry, a true maverick and no respecter of courtly ritual. As the Queen, wearing a scarlet shawl, moved along the team, all seemed well, until Henry delivered his faux pas.

'Pleased to meet you, Your Majesty,' he said on cue, before adding, unbidden, 'Can I just say that red is also my favourite colour.'

There was a hush, then a pause, as the impertinence sank in. But while Bailey's glare was set to stun, the Queen, who fixed her own cool gaze on Henry, replied in that withering tone monarchs muster when dealing with minor irritants, 'How nice for you,' and moved on.

Needless to say, Bailey let rip with an almighty bollocking once we were back inside the dressing room. Henry could not give a toss and, far from proving a deterrent, it actively encouraged him to break convention once more when he met the Queen four years later, during another Test against India at Lord's.

Like naughty schoolboys, we egged Edmonds on for a repeat performance. Of course, he protested that his previous interjection had been strictly off the cuff, and that he could not perform to order. But he was a showman, and we knew he wouldn't be able to help himself.

As a variation, this time he posed a question, an affront tantamount to treason in less enlightened times – ones you suspect Bailey, again on hand to chaperone the Queen, wished would return, so that Edmonds could be carted off to the Tower.

'Pleased to meet you, Ma'am,' said Henry. 'By the way, have you had a say in choosing Sarah's wedding dress?' – a cheeky reference to the impending wedding of Prince Andrew and Sarah Ferguson.

Given the thousands of people she meets every year, it is doubtful that the Queen recalled Henry's previous insolence. But she looked at him, nonetheless, with a curtness that could cut more than ribbons. 'No,' she snapped. 'She chose it herself.'

I didn't play that often with Henry, him being considered a valuable asset on overseas tours, something I wasn't. Mind you, he needed a sympathetic captain to get the best from him, something Willis wasn't.

Henry did test Big Bob's patience, though, such as the time in 1982 when he found himself on a hat-trick against India in the final Test at The Oval. The batsman coming in to face the hat-trick ball was left-hander Surendra Nayak, a player Henry had not seen before but who had played in the tour match against Essex the previous week.

'Anyone seen this bloke play?' said Edmonds to no one in particular.

'Sure,' I said, 'he played against us at Chelmsford last tour game.'

I was fielding at mid-off, so Henry marched over to quiz me as to the best way to dismiss him.

'Not sure,' I said, 'we didn't get him out. But as I remember, he did like to get on the front foot.'

Henry then repeated everything, presumably to ramp up the tension on the batsman. The only person who seemed irate, though, was Willis, who wore the exasperated look of a parent dealing with a petulant child.

'Can we get on with it, Goat,' said Willis, using Henry's nickname.

But Henry didn't do orders and marched over to me again just to check that he had the info right, though the smirk on his face suggested he was deliberately pratting about.

By now, Willis was steaming and had ordered him to 'bowl the bloody ball'. Which he did, sending down a bouncer to Nayak which our wicketkeeper, Bob Taylor, standing up, parried for three byes. They were the only extras he conceded that innings.

'Well, you did say he liked to get on the front foot,' said Henry at the end of the over, pleased with the farce he had created and not at all concerned about missing out on a Test hat-trick.

His flippant approach – he treated cricket as a diversion – led many to believe he just didn't care about the game or the rest of his team. But he had a tough competitive streak when it mattered, something he took into the City when he finally quit the game in 1992.

His thirst for a business venture was apparent long before he retired and I remember him asking me how I was going to spend the rest day of our Test against India at Headingley in 1986.

'Game of golf in the morning, maybe, then watch England play Argentina in the World Cup,' I said.

'Are you sure?' he said. 'I'm off to Middlesbrough to see an old supermarket I'm thinking of buying. I've got to start the Edmonds empire somewhere. Come with me. Surely you retain an interest in all that after your degree?'

'Not really,' I replied. 'Anyway, we're watching England in the World Cup.'

I don't know whether Henry bought the supermarket, but 20 years later he was well established enough in business to have a reputation in the City. And, surprise, surprise, it wasn't for observing protocol.

David Gower

Another player who didn't always obey the rules of engagement, especially in cricket, was David Gower, aesthete and fun-lover, with or without bat in hand.

There was a time when I sensed that David, an intelligent and sensitive man, felt we might become good friends. But while he was a fixture in the England side, I was in and out of it, so the closeness needed to build a strong friendship never materialised. Which is a pity, as we both had Africa in our hearts and, as often as not, red wine coursing through our veins.

As a batsman, David, or Lubo as most of us called him, after a steak restaurant in Adelaide he used to frequent on his first Ashes tour, could play shots others merely fantasised about. Left-handedness makes most batsmen of that persuasion appear more stylish than their right-handed counterparts, but Lubo was blessed with a silken touch even among lefties. Cricket, though, can be cruel in its juxtapositions, and just as we would marvel one minute as he flashed one away past point with scarcely an inch of tolerance in either the ball's length or line, we'd harrumph the next when the same shot would bring a nick and with it his departure.

The posh end of cricket, the champagne and stripy blazer set, claimed him as one of their own, though their lionisation of him was based on the misperception that he was a bit more cavalier than he actually was. Although he'd attended The King's School, Canterbury, and London University (briefly), he'd learnt the business end of cricket under Ray Illingworth at Leicestershire CCC, and there were none with fewer airs and graces than Raymond.

It meant that Lubo had a good cricket brain when he chose to engage it, though one that did constant battle with his regular one, bored as it was by the longueurs, routine and analysis that dogged the game. Instead, he was into improvisation and embracing the moment on the field, as well as the cultural opportunities it afforded him when off it. Stuff I would also like to have embraced had the need to plot a steady path for my limited skills not been so pressing.

Like a lot of public schoolboys of that era, he thought it uncool to care too much about anything, especially something so footling as a game of cricket. Though neither realised it at the start of their time together in England teams, it's why he and Gooch clashed so terribly later on, their ideologies as distinct from one another as the shiny and rough sides of a used cricket ball.

It all came to head on the 1990–91 tour of Australia, a year into Goochie's tenure as England captain and another trip I was not picked for. A man used to doing what he wanted when he wanted, preparation-wise, Lubo did not care much for Goochie's regime, based as it was on hard practice and even harder training.

It probably didn't help either that there were few allies to Lubo's way of thinking left in the side. Beefy had not yet returned to England duty following injury, while Allan Lamb, as Goochie's vice-captain, had to side more with authority. Meanwhile, Mickey Stewart, the coach, was fully supportive of Goochie's tough work ethic as a means of improving England's lot.

Essentially, Lubo felt the regime lacked levity, though his attempts to jolly things up on that tour backfired because of poor timing. England were 2–0 down in the Ashes by the time they played against a Queensland XI at Carrara, late in the tour. In what had been a frustrating trip, one where Goochie had needed an operation on an infected hand, the Carrara match was a rare event where almost everything had gone to plan.

England registered their first win of the tour in a first-class match, thanks in part to a Robin Smith hundred. But just as Smith reached the milestone, the ground was buzzed by a Tiger Moth aircraft bearing Lubo and another player, Johnny Morris.

The Gooch I know was not immune to humour and the stunt might have gone down well had Lubo bought into his leadership style more. But the players aboard the Tiger Moth, both of them playing in the game, had not sought permission to leave the ground, an unwritten rule for touring teams. In his position as captain, Goochie could not overlook the infringement.

What compounded matters was that the press had been informed of the stunt, with Lubo and Morris having posed for photographs at the airfield. The set-up nature of it fanned the flames of indignation that this was a big two fingers to authority. As a result, the disciplinary committee fined Lubo and Morris £1,000 each, an amount Lubo felt excessive.

If that was an irritation for Goochie, it was nothing to the emotions stirred in him by Lubo's dismissal in the next Test at Adelaide. On the final ball before lunch, with England 160 for three and battling to get on terms with Australia's first-innings score of 386, he nonchalantly flicked a leg-side ball from Craig McDermott straight to Merv Hughes at fine leg.

It was a deliberate trap that a six year old would have spotted, but Lubo, 113 Tests under his belt by then, had fallen for it. It was probably also the moment when Goochie felt that Lubo was a luxury item on tour his team could not afford. After that trip, Lubo never played abroad for England again.

Many, and not just Gower fans in the media, painted it as Roundheads v Cavaliers, or as one of the last professionals v amateurs spats that had pervaded cricket for most of the 20th century. Yet, Goochie's take on it has always seemed perfectly reasonable to me.

'When David was captain and I was in the team, I was happy to do what he asked of me with regards to preparation and playing in the matches,' explained Gooch to me one day. 'But now that I'm captain, David is not so keen to do as I ask.'

For Lubo fans, and I counted myself among them, Goochie's stance could be seen as a hard taskmaster at variance with a player whose motivations he'd never completely understood. What swayed me that Lubo was at fault was the testimony of Clem Driver, the Essex scorer, who'd been co-opted to score for England. Clem was never less than fair in his judgements of others, and he told me Lubo had been out of order for most of the tour. Although not entirely neutral, I trusted Clem to give a spin-free version, even if it did condemn one of England's finest and most stylish batsmen.

I don't know whether the loss of England's captaincy had affected Lubo, but I suspect it had, as it had not ended well. Twice whitewashed by the West Indies while he was in charge, he captained England 32 times, winning five Tests, losing 18 and drawing the remainder. It was not a distinguished record, but like Gatt, he did win an Ashes series.

Apart from his captaincy debut in 1982 against Pakistan, where he stood in for an injured Bob Willis, his time at the helm was done in two phases: 1984–86 and then again in 1989. That second stint, a home series against Allan Border's Aussies, changed him, or at least brought out a stroppy side which had not surfaced much previously.

That 1989 Ashes series was a debacle as we went down 4–0. I played in the opening Test and the sixth and final one, as England used even more players than they had done the previous year, when the four captains had lost to the West Indies 4–0.

That hammering against the Windies plus the cancelled tour to India that followed led Ted Dexter, the new chairman of selectors, to return the captaincy to Mike Gatting. When that was subsequently vetoed by the TCCB's cricket chairman, Ossie Wheatley, Dexter went for Gower over Gooch, the man in possession before the winter tour had been cancelled. As a result, Lubo probably felt he was third choice as captain before a ball had been bowled.

It did little for his sanity when the Aussies won four of the first five Tests. He also had a stalker, a woman, who would send huge bouquets of flowers to every venue on the opening day of each Test. By the time of the sixth and final Test, at The Oval, Lubo was nearing his wits' end. He'd lost the toss and we were preparing to field. But just as he was about to give a team talk in which he probably had nothing constructive to say, the dressing-room attendant handed him the flowers.

It is never pretty seeing a great talent at a low ebb. Instead of giving his talk, Lubo just yowled and, in true John Cleese fashion, used the flowers to give his cricket case a damn good thrashing.

Until that moment I'd never quite understood the principles of primal-scream therapy, but Lubo's howl as he destroyed the bouquet suddenly gave it meaning. He was very quiet afterwards, as the dressing-room attendant put his dustpan and brush to work, though so was everyone else. Perhaps not the ideal state to confront an Aussie team cock-a-hoop at having won the Ashes.

Not that it affected us that much, as the match was drawn, one of only two not lost during the series. One reason for that might have been the type of ball used. By 1989, most counties had twigged that the Reader ball, with 15 strands of twine in the seam, was the one most bowlers preferred. It felt small in the hand, stayed shiny, kept its shape and on pitches that offered purchase it would seam and spin more than the other brands. It also swung for the technicians among us.

Naturally, Australia objected to its use in the Ashes. Their bowlers were used to Kookaburra balls back home, which did little, while their batsmen were vulnerable to the moving ball, liking to hit through the line with firm hands and minimal foot movement. Obviously Kookaburras were off the menu, so they pushed instead to use the Duke ball, which, by general consensus, didn't move about as much as the Reader.

Incredibly, the brains trust at the TCCB upheld their request and allowed them to toss for which ball to use. All six Tests were done at once, at Headingley, and although he flipped the coin, Lubo won the right to use the Reader ball just once, in that final Test. What a useless tosser.

Can you credit it? As the home side, we couldn't even get the ball we wanted to bowl with. Paranoia stalked England teams back then, what with the almost random nature of selection and groundsmen producing pitches to last five days rather than ones that might actually assist our bowling, so this was just another boot in the delusionals.

At the end of the six-match series, lost 4–0, Lubo resigned and Gooch was appointed. What followed – better preparation, better fitness, fewer crazy capers – really signalled the end of the maverick era.

Before the England captaincy soured him, Lubo possessed a keen sense of humour, with an appreciation of the absurd. Good friends with JK Lever, from their time together on England tours in the 1970s and early 1980s, he used to take a fearful ribbing from him whenever Essex played Leicestershire at Grace Road.

A county forever cash-strapped, Leicestershire was run by the parsimonious Mike Turner. As such, drinks after play for the visiting side was a crate of light ale, something that had not changed from before the War. It was insipid stuff and there weren't many takers. At Essex, after-play drinks were bespoke, with the players and scorers of both sides placing their orders with the 12th man at teatime.

Essex also had sponsors' marquees, where a few more drinks could be taken once you'd showered and changed – something that got the evening's consumption off to a good and free start, especially for the visitors who didn't have to drive home. Fed up with taking stick and even faintly embarrassed by Leicestershire's stingy hospitality, Lubo bought a two-man tent and erected it just beyond the boundary's edge at Grace Road for Essex's next visit.

We had no idea what he was planning, though we found out at the end of play. As we trudged off, he'd placed a sign outside it which read 'SPONSOR'S TENT'. He then popped his head out of what was really a very small tent and said, 'Come on then, in here, drinks.'

It went down well with the Essex sense of humour, though our mirth quickly subsided when all there was to drink was that standard-issue case of light ale. That evening, in protest, we opened every bottle but did not drink them, an act that angered Turner, who complained to Essex's committee about our ungrateful attitude.

Although it didn't happen in that tent, I have to acknowledge a debt to Lubo for being largely responsible for my interest in wine. On an earlier trip to Grace Road, when I was still at university and before I really knew him, Lubo invited JK and Easty round to his house for a snifter or two after the pub. With them my unofficial guardians, I tagged along.

When Lubo asked if I wanted a glass of wine, I declined, my sole experience of the stuff to that point having been from student parties, where the wine could masquerade as paint-stripper.

'Well, I haven't got anything else,' he said. 'It's wine or tap water.'

So I gave it a go and, lo and behold, it was rather good. I made a mental note to learn a bit more about this wine malarkey, something I have done to the point where I have gone on to bore many a dinner companion since. Yet Lubo's flat, in some nondescript suburb of Leicester, is where it all began.

Lubo's love of good wine made its way to England team dinners. Although the TCCB were happy to pay for food and wines of their choice, they drew the line at the fine white and red burgundies Lubo ordered at Mottram Hall before we played a one-day match against the West Indies in 1984. When Peter May saw the cost of the wines Lubo had chosen he told the hotel that the person responsible would have to pay for them. That was when it got messy. Trying to recoup this unexpected bill, Lubo spent the next few days going round working out who had drunk how many glasses of what so he could bill them for their share.

There is one other thing about Lubo, a cricketing one. He played, after Javed Miandad, the most memorable first-class innings against

Essex I have ever seen. It was in 1988, a month after he'd been dropped from the final Test against the West Indies, so he was probably still seething.

Javed's knock was for Glamorgan in the fourth innings on a wearing pitch at Colchester in 1981. I wasn't playing for Essex but I did field the whole of that final day as 12th man. It was incredible watching him toy with Easty and David Acfield, our spinners, as if they were novices.

Glamorgan needed 325 to win and reached 311 all out, with Javed unbeaten on 200. His innings was another level. After him, the next highest score for Glamorgan was 36, with only two other batsmen reaching double figures. His 43-run partnership with Robin Hobbs for the eighth wicket was ended when Hobbs was out for nought first ball. Yes, that's right, first ball, so expertly had Javed pinched the strike.

Lubo's knock came in different conditions, though the circumstances were not dissimilar, with Essex on top. Unlike Javed, who batted at four, Lubo opened the innings for Leicestershire after we had made a monolithic 592 for eight declared, so it was a fairly docile pitch. Being one of the early four-day matches, there was plenty of time to build a big score. Even so, Lubo did not tarry, smashing it from the start, albeit with his customary elan.

There was certainly nothing so uncouth as a slog. There must have been dot balls when he didn't score, though I don't recall them as he lay about me and the other Essex bowlers with a savage beauty. We, literally, could not bowl to him.

John Childs eventually trapped him lbw for 172, a score which contributed a mammoth 64.1 per cent of Leicestershire's total of 268. They followed on, as did he with his blitzkrieg, though this time he nicked one before much damage could be done, and we won by an innings and 83 runs. Typical Lubo, the exquisite and the hum-drum constant bedfellows.

Derek Randall

One of the craziest mavericks of the era and one whose barminess came without a scrap of affectation was Derek Randall, a brilliant batsman and fine athletic fielder.

He was bonkers, with an almost childlike view of the world. There were those sceptical about whether he could really be as artless as he came over, but he ate, lived and slept wackiness whenever I played with or against him.

Except he didn't seem to sleep that well, at least not on tour. On the 1982–83 Ashes trip I roomed with Randall, or Arkle as he was better known, quite a lot. The first time I was paired with him was at Sydney's Sebel Townhouse. On our first night together he woke me with a gentle shake of the shoulder at about 3 a.m.

'Wake up, youth, wake up,' he said.

'What's up?' I asked.

'I can't sleep, youth,' he said.

'What? You woke me up to tell me you can't sleep?'

'Yes, youth. Do you want a cuppa tea?'

And that was his default solution to every crisis or moment of apprehension – tea. On that tour he must have made hundreds of pots of the stuff, though I got the impression the making was more important than the drinking, as he rarely finished a cup.

His other comfort was books. Not that he actually read them. When waiting to bat on that Ashes tour, I noticed he always sat quietly with Roald Dahl's *Charlie and the Chocolate Factory*. By the fifth Test he'd been rumbled when Foxy Fowler suddenly said to him, 'You were on that page two matches ago.'

'Oh, I don't read it,' said Arkle.

'What do you do, then, look at the pictures?' sniggered Foxy.

'No, I just look at the words,' admitted Arkle. 'They keep me calm before I bat.'

With the story irrelevant, it explained why he rarely turned the page. A constant fidget on and off the field, he needed to be distracted before batting, especially when taking on the quicks. In that series, a combination of Geoff Lawson, Dennis Lillee, Jeff Thomson, Rodney Hogg and Carl Rackemann, all of them 85 mph plus, clamoured to bruise Pommie flesh. He knew it was going to be scary, and the banality of an open book, one he'd probably read to his kids, was his way of staying calm before the inevitable storm.

Once plunged into it, he relished the fray, though he did take personally the attempts by fast bowlers to try to maim him. Once, at the Sydney Cricket Ground on that 1982–83 tour, Beefy tried to gather a group of us to go and have a drink with the Aussies in their dressing room after play – as was the custom for the team which had not been in the field.

When Arkle was asked if he'd like to come, he refused point-blank. 'What? Come and have a drink wi' that bloody gorilla, Thommo? You must be joking. He's just spent t' last hour trying to take me head off me shoulders. Am I hell going to have a beer wi' him.'

His eccentricity was such that it invited a deep fondness, for only a churl could fail to be amused by his antics. He could be annoying, though, especially to those who'd tolerated his quirks on previous tours. Beefy, for instance, refused to share a room with him on account of his constant fidgeting, tea-making and snoring. I, though, found him fascinating and enjoyed being billeted with him – the two Dereks.

I first met him, properly, when we played together for MCC against India at Lord's in 1982, a game which preceded the Test series against them. During that match, we'd stayed in a place called the Clarendon Court, a hotel of faded charm on the Edgware Road about 400 yards from the Grace Gates.

During the first Test at Lord's, three weeks later, the England team stayed in the Westmoreland hotel, a new establishment 200 yards away from the Grace Gates, but in the opposite direction to Clarendon Court. After one of the days' play, Randall left Lord's in his whites and, not thinking, turned right out of the Grace Gates, which took him to the Clarendon Court, where he'd stayed just weeks earlier. He asked for, and was given, a key corresponding to his room number at the Westmoreland. It was only when he'd disrobed and flung his whites onto a bed with someone asleep in it that he realised he was in the wrong hotel.

If that was done in error, his hilarious turn as a prostitute in Adelaide was deliberate. Dared by Beefy that he couldn't pick up a 'punter' outside our hotel, the Sebel, which was flush in the middle of the red-light area on Hindley Street, Arkle took up the challenge with gusto.

First, he persuaded an off-duty nurse to swap clothes with him, his slim build fitting her dress well and she his slacks and polo shirt. He then got her to apply a bit of her make-up and lippy on him and he was off, swinging her handbag as if made for the role.

We all crowded round the windows of the ground-floor bar to watch, certain that nothing would happen. After all, even in a dress he wasn't the most alluring sight on the strip, especially standing there in his man's shoes (his feet had been too big for a swap with the nurse).

We were wrong: within a few minutes a car had pulled up and after a short conversation, in he got. Apart from Beefy losing his bet, it had been a hilarious evening all round, especially watching Arkle persuade a complete stranger to swap clothes with him and then watching him ham it up as a woman. Expecting him to be gone about five minutes, our mirth soon turned to concern when, after half an hour, he'd still not returned.

'Perhaps he's enjoying himself,' suggested Beefy. 'He is a loon, after all.'

Yet just as we started to think about informing the team management, or how we might explain it all to the police should they need to become involved, in he walked, a little dishevelled but still in one piece.

'What happened?' we chorused.

'Well, this bloke stopped, I got in his car and we drove off to a quiet place, where we parked up,' said Arkle. 'He then put his hand on me knee and grabbed me chest.'

'What did you do?' we asked.

'I hit him wi' bloody handbag, of course, wha' do you think? Of course, he kicked me out of his car, so I've been all this bloody time trying to get a taxi back.'

I was used to some wacky japes with the Essex side but this was the most bizarre caper I'd ever seen. The strange thing about it was that Arkle had not demurred even for a second once Beefy had laid down his challenge. That spoke volumes for his crazed, impulsive nature when in company and why, in the main, he tended to opt for the quiet life of making cups of tea in his room.

Not that his odd behaviour was limited to tours. Once, when Beefy called on him at his home outside Nottingham, he found Arkle and his wife doing the washing-up together, both of them wearing a set of cricket pads. Intrigued, Beefy asked why they needed leg protection for such a routine domestic chore.

'Well,' said Arkle, 'it's start of t' new season and t' missus is helping me break in me new pads around the house.'

Although crackers, boy could Arkle bat, especially when the ball was away from his body and he could free his arms through the shot. He'd announced himself during the Centenary Test against Australia in 1977, when he'd made a brilliant 174 against Lillee and co. at the MCG.

I'd seen his brilliance up close against Lillee a few years later in two matches at the WACA on the 1982–83 Ashes tour. In four innings there – the first two in a tour match against Western Australia, the second two in a Test match a week later – he made 14, 92, 78 and 115. On a pitch where England's batsmen have routinely been humiliated over the years, that was some going.

For reasons never explained, the selectors felt him susceptible when playing the West Indies. His one and only Test against them, which also happened to be the last of his England career, was in 1984. Joel Garner dismissed him for 0 and 1.

The following year, the pair of us found ourselves in an intriguing shoot-out at Lord's in the 1985 NatWest Trophy final: me bowling the final over for Essex; him facing it and needing 18 runs for a Nottinghamshire win. An equation, then, that was overwhelmingly in my favour.

Lord's finals were packed to the rafters in those days, often with spectators fitted onto the grass. That was not the reason the off-side boundary, to which I bowled the last six balls of the match from the Nursery End, was only 60 yards long – the pitch was over that side of the square. Randall may have played the idiot much of the time, but with bat in hand he was rarely less than compos mentis, and he targeted that short side with ruthless precision.

Along with John Lever I'd been Essex's 'death' bowler for a while by then, so this wasn't some unexpected role foisted upon me. Accuracy and yorkers were the qualities required to do the job back then, slower balls having not yet entered the zeitgest.

I knew Arkle would move around the crease to give himself room to target that off side. But even knowing that, and bowling the ball full and well outside leg stump to try to prevent it, I could not stop him striking three boundaries there from the first five balls – the other two deliveries having gone for two runs apiece.

Having begun the over with a cushion of 18 runs, I stood at the end of my run with one ball to go, Notts now needing two runs to win and me contemplating sporting suicide. Blood was pounding in my head. I could hear it along with the Essex supporters, with whom I was not overly popular at that stage of my career, as they began to get on my case.

Fletch, who'd never won a 60-over cup final during his 20-odd years at the club, was doing his best to stay calm, but I could sense displeasure in his body language.

Of the five balls that over, I felt I'd bowled just one bad one, the fourth, which had not been full enough. Arkle had pounced on it and smashed it away to wide long-off for four. But otherwise I thought I'd cramped him for room most times, though he'd countered that brilliantly by staying calm, picking his spot and timing the ball down the slope to the Mound Stand rather than slogging it. But should I stick with my original plan for the final ball or try something different?

There was a short delay while Fletch and I tinkered with the field and Arkle told his young batting partner, Duncan Martindale, to run two come what may.

Although there was a lot riding on that ball, I felt the humiliation had already happened with me conceding 16 runs off the first five balls. I just thought, 'If he does move outside leg stump again, I'm going to try and hit the outside of his front foot with a yorker.' I had to stop him getting a decent bat on the ball or it was all over, and that seemed the best option.

Arkle did go the same way (why change a plan that has worked?) and I did shove it well outside leg stump. It was a deliberate reaction to his action, which is why I can never get over those people, and BBC commentator Jim Laker was one of them, who said, 'If only Randall had stayed still it would have been a wide.' Yes, that's true, but I wouldn't have bowled it there if he'd stood still.

He still got more bat on it than I would have liked, and but for him hitting it straight to Paul Prichard at midwicket, he would probably have got the two required for victory. Happily for me and the team, Prich clung on and we won by a single, solitary run.

ESSEX V NOTTINGHAMSHIRE
(NatWest Trophy Final)

Played at Lord's Cricket Ground, London, 7 September 1985

Umpires: DJ Constant & BJ Meyer
Toss: Nottinghamshire

ESSEX

		Runs	Balls	Mins	4	6	S-rate
GA Gooch	b Pick	91	142	169	8	1	64.08
BR Hardie	run out (Hemmings)	110	149	176	15	–	73.83
KS McEwan	not out	46	39	47	4	1	117.95
DR Pringle	not out	29	30	40	2	–	96.67
PJ Prichard							
KWR Fletcher*							
AW Lilley							
DE East†							
S Turner							
IL Pont							
JK Lever							
Extras	(1 b, 3 lb)	4					
Total	(2 wickets, 60 overs)	**280**					

NOTTINGHAMSHIRE

		Runs	Balls	Mins	4	6	S-rate
RT Robinson	c Hardie b Turner	80	142	149	4	1	56.34
BC Broad	run out (Pont/East)	64	107	137	6	–	59.81
CEB Rice*	c Hardie b Turner	12	19	26	1	–	63.16
DW Randall	c Prichard b Pringle	66	54	72	6	–	122.22
RJ Hadlee	b Pont	22	17	20	2	1	129.41
DJR Martindale	not out	20	22	33	–	–	90.91
BN French†							
EE Hemmings							
RA Pick							
K Saxelby							
KE Cooper							
Extras	(14 lb, 1 nb)	15					
Total	(5 wickets, 60 overs)	**279**					

NOTTS	O	M	R	W		Fall of wickets:	
						Ess	Not
Hadlee	12	4	48	0			
Cooper	9	3	27	0	1st	202	143
Saxelby	12	0	73	0	2nd	203	153
Rice	7	0	38	0	3rd	–	173
Pick	8	0	36	1	4th	–	214
Hemmings	12	1	54	0	5th	–	279
					6th	–	–
ESSEX	O	M	R	W	7th	–	–
Lever	12	2	53	0	8th	–	–
Pont	12	0	54	1	9th	–	–
Turner	12	1	43	2	10th	–	–
Gooch	12	0	47	0			
Pringle	12	1	68	1			

Man of the match: BR Hardie
Result: **Essex won by 1 run**

We celebrated in London that night, but not too hard, as we had to drive up to Trent Bridge the following morning to play, guess who, Notts, this time in the John Player Special League. We won that game, too, which set us up to take the title a week later when we beat Yorkshire at Chelmsford.

In that penultimate match, Goochie smashed 171 as we set Notts 253 to win. They didn't come close. In a neat twist, I dismissed both Arkle and Martindale, two men who, 24 hours earlier, had come within a whisker of turning me into Essex's No 1 villain. That is how fine the line between success and failure in sport can be, and also in the response of those who follow it. Chump or champ? At that moment I was the latter.

Arkle and Notts got their revenge in the 1989 Benson & Hedges Cup final, also held at Lord's. In that match John Lever bowled the final over, which saw Notts needing four runs off the last ball to win. Eddie Hemmings did it for them, too, his sliced drive finding the cover boundary just behind square, obviously a favourite area for Notts players in one-day finals.

Although I felt devastated for JK, Essex's greatest ever servant along with Goochie and Fletch, I felt pleased for Arkle who, true to form, celebrated with a cup of tea.

11

MIGHTY ESSEX –
THE GOOCH YEARS

AFTER A DOZEN years of answering to Keith Fletcher as our esteemed leader at Essex, Goochie's ascent to the captaincy took place in 1986, or at least the first phase did.

It proved a curious experience. Goochie had one of his worst years in terms of runs for the club (778 at an average of 37) and was one of four players who captained the team over its 24 Championship matches that season. We still won the title, though, as well as coming runners-up in the John Player Special League.

With Goochie floundering runs-wise, and JK Lever not our leading wicket-taker for once, the Championship was secured by alternative means. Allan Border, in his first year as our overseas pro after the departure of Ken McEwan and Norbert Phillip, made 1,287 runs in 29 innings, while Paul Prichard, no doubt inspired by having the feisty Border as a room-mate, scored 1,165 runs.

Bowlers, though, tend to win you three-day matches and the fact that Neil Foster (fast) and John Childs (spin) excelled as well, with 100 and 85 wickets respectively, meant that we still had a team to tackle opponents whatever the conditions. JK also played his part, with 58 wickets, while I took 41, though the fact that both of us were involved in England's series with India that summer, along with Goochie, meant that none of us played all the games.

Perhaps most remarkable was the fact that the Championship-winning side had to respond to four different leaders. Goochie, the club's official captain, was in charge 13 times and achieved five wins, four draws and four defeats. Fletch, who stood in for Goochie when he was on England duty, captained eight games, winning five and drawing three. Then, after Fletch broke a finger, there was Brian 'Lager' Hardie, who captained two games, and JK, who took over for one fateful match against Lancashire.

The Essex handbook that year acknowledged Fletch's vital contribution to the cause, its cover depicting both him and Goochie with their mitts on the trophy. As mentioned, a shrewd journalist had already christened the amalgam 'Flooch', though that was very different from fluke – something this triumph, by 28 points, most certainly was not.

A handful of games revealed the team's character at this time of flux, as well as its strengths and weaknesses. Interestingly, two of those matches were actually defeats: one against Hampshire at Ilford week during June, and the other against Lancashire at Old Trafford in early July. The third, a victory, came against Kent at Folkestone in late August.

In the first, we were not quite at full strength, missing both Lager Hardie and Fletch. We were then further disadvantaged by losing the toss on a dry pitch which was always going to break up with unknown consequences. I did my bit with the ball, taking seven wickets across Hampshire's two innings, but the nub of the match came down to us chasing 198 on a pitch where the ball was bursting the top – against an attack containing Malcolm Marshall, then the best fast bowler in world cricket.

We were four down in no time, which is when I joined Allan Border at the crease. Wearing only an Essex cap, AB had already exhibited great courage, taking several body blows from Marshall as the ball reared off the surface, leaving a pockmark and a puff of dust in its wake.

I did my best to stay with AB, but the irresistible thing about facing someone as fast and lethal as Marshall, on such a tricky surface, is that the other bowlers appear as light relief, even if they merit due care and attention themselves. Try as you might not to get lured into imprudence, it is nigh-on impossible to treat them with the same reverence.

So, although AB and I added 41 together for the fifth wicket, and I ended up as third-highest scorer in our innings with 22 (worth four times that much on a flat deck), I was the only one to succumb to Nigel Cowley, Hampshire's off-spinner, someone who couldn't frighten my old gran.

Whenever people ask which was AB's best innings for Essex, I cite this one. Obviously he made hundreds for us which helped to secure victory in other matches, but this was one of those occasions when the batsman was never in control of his destiny. The dreaded unknown, in terms of what the ball might do from either end, was a constant, gnawing threat. To survive required both bravery and skill. To thrive as AB did, though, demanded an intimate knowledge of risk assessment. Strict discipline was crucial when it came to deciding which ball to play and which to leave alone, all of it processed through a hail of body blows. Just watching it was utterly absorbing and exhausting.

It helped that AB was one of those masochists who like extreme challenges because they make them feel alive. Batting in those conditions without a helmet was foolish in the extreme, but it got his juices flowing, as did the many bruising blows he took, most of them with barely a flinch.

That we got within 13 runs of winning was mostly down to him negating Marshall with bat, body and bravado. Inevitably, when two great forces like that clash something had to give and Marshall eventually produced the snorter with AB's name on it – ironically, just as the main prize hove into view.

Marshall's figures in the second innings read 21–7–26–4, while AB made 54, to go with his fine 71 in the first innings, two of only four scores to exceed 50 in the entire match. Although we lost, AB's innings was inspirational and it lifted us all to know that we had such a skilled, committed and gutsy player on our side.

And he was gutsy. During his second stint with us in 1988, he was struck a fearsome blow by Tony Merrick, Warwickshire's strapping and very quick Antiguan fast bowler, on a spiteful pitch at Edgbaston. He was wearing only his Essex cap, and the ball cut his ear so badly that it needed 10 stitches. It also bled profusely, leaving a memento mori at the crease for incoming batsmen. Paul Prichard was batting at the other end and recalled the moments after AB had been hit.

'He was down on his knees holding his head and there was blood everywhere,' said Prichard. 'Asif Din, who'd been fielding at short leg, started to take AB's pads off. I don't know what motivated Din to do that, but AB just looked at him and shouted, "Why don't you just ---- off!"'

'Maybe it was AB's way of coping with the pain, but as he was led off with a towel round his head he started sledging other Warwickshire players, including Merrick, who'd not shown the slightest concern for his welfare.'

Against his wishes, Border was persuaded to wear a helmet in the second innings, though he struggled to get it on, with all the crêpe bandage wrapped round his head.

'He looked like Vincent Van Gogh, though we didn't tell him that,' said Prich, who was rooming with him. 'I'd been hit in the ribs by Merrick, so had heavy strapping round them. What with AB's head bandaged as well, our room looked more like a field hospital.'

The measure of Border was revealed in the second innings of that match. As Merrick smelt blood and went for the kill, only four players made it to double figures and only one of those made it to three:

AB. It was the only hundred of the match. A magnificent, valiant, brave knock that counted for little in the context of the game, after we lost by five wickets. As an example of getting stuck in after a sickening blow, though, none could have been stronger.

Back to 1986, and the second defeat mentioned earlier, one of five to befall the team that Championship campaign, was to Lancashire at Old Trafford in July. The losing margin was an innings and 22 runs, somewhat shameful after the home side had made a paltry 240 in their only innings of the game.

With Goochie and me away playing for England, and Fletch hors de combat with a broken finger, JK captained the side. It was a horror show. From the moment he lost the toss on a quick grassy pitch, abject humiliation ensued as Patrick Patterson, arguably the fastest bowler in world cricket at that stage, destroyed us.

Across two innings, Patterson, with that high-kicking front leg of his promising bone-breaking speed, took 10 wickets as Essex were blown away for 71 and 147. Only two scores exceeded 20, one of them by AB, who made 51 in Essex's second innings. It was a shellacking completed inside two days and it showed our vulnerability to express pace when Goochie wasn't playing and AB didn't fire in the first innings.

A lot of teams would have taken a while to get over such a mauling, but one of Essex's great qualities was the ability to put humiliation behind them, quickly, and move on. For us, defeat, however swingeing, was no more than a minor bump in the road, though this one also served to give us a collective kick up the jacksie.

Even though most teams knew it was futile to dwell on setbacks, recovering confidence quickly wasn't possible for all. Indeed, I recall Hampshire a few years later, in 1992, going to pieces after losing to us in Bournemouth, where they'd made us follow on.

Given we were again without Goochie on England duty, it was one of our best wins during my time at the club. Before that match, which took place between 19 and 22 June, Hampshire were top of the Championship. After their humbling defeat they won just one of their remaining 13 matches, to finish 15th out of 18. Not everyone could shake off a setback as well as us.

The 1986 season proved a bit of a stinker for me with the bat, though I did score 97 against Kent at Folkestone at the end of August. It was an innings I consider one of my best for Essex, setting up a winning position for us in tough conditions at a crucial moment in the season.

The pitch at the Cheriton Road sports ground always posed a challenge when we played there, which admittedly was not often. Mostly, it suited the brisk left-arm spin and cut of 'Deadly' Derek Underwood, for whom I suspect it was specially prepared. This game we had Goochie back as captain, but AB had returned home to Australia, so we were missing our leading run-scorer. Despite that, we batted first, after winning the toss, and were three down quite quickly, with Underwood the bowler on a roll.

Goochie clung on for 74, knowing that the pitch – and this was why we'd batted first – would not stay knitted together for long. It was like Headingley in the Eighties. You knew the pitch there would be hard work if you batted first, especially if it was cloudy. But if you could survive long enough to post a competitive score, it was always going to get more difficult to bat on as the game went on.

I batted at six that game and together with Fletch, who made 47, helped to put on 62 for the fifth wicket. Our plan was to sit on Deadly Derek and make him bowl a lot of overs if necessary, which he did, notching up 40 during our first innings, to finish with four for 96.

At the end of the day, I was unbeaten on 75 along with David Acfield, our number 11, who had not yet scored. The following morning, knowing that Goochie was keen to get Kent in (three-day cricket was like that), I got on with it but fell three short of my hundred, caught at long-off trying to reach the milestone with a six off Graham Dilley. Like most who played for Essex, I'd completely bought into the team ethic, so did not dwell on not having reached three figures.

Our total of 280 proved more than competitive when we bowled Kent out for 224 in 105.2 overs. With less than a day left in the game, we bashed a quick 127 in 28.2 overs and got them back in to chase 184 on a pitch turning square. They never fancied it and lost wickets at regular intervals as John 'Charlie' Childs spun them out for a second time, with seven for 58 to go with his three for 65 in the first innings – an immaculately conceived victory.

Charlie had joined us the previous season from Gloucestershire, where he'd been surplus to requirements, the mighty Glos having opted for the left-arm spin of David Graveney instead. Idiots. Grav was a decent enough left-arm tweaker, but Charlie had real gifts. If only he'd known that and been more confident in his exceptional abilities, he might have enjoyed a 40-cap Test career instead of the two he did manage.

His arrival and subsequent thriving at Essex was typical of the club. Not in the habit of approaching superstars to join them (even AB joining us was more his doing than ours), Essex liked to grow their own talent or pick up wastrels and strays from other counties and then turn them into Crufts champions. We were damned good at it, too, and after Charlie came Peter Such, another spinner unable to hold a place at other clubs but who went on to play for England after passing through Essex's cricketing crucible.

Charlie had another great quality prized by team-mates during those times of shared rooms on away trips – he didn't snore. John 'Stan' Stephenson mostly roomed with him and reckons he was so quiet and still in the next-door bed that he had to hold a mirror beneath his nose to see if it would mist up and so prove he was still breathing.

Charlie's 10 wickets in the win at Folkestone meant we needed just three bowling points against Nottinghamshire in our penultimate game to win the 1986 Championship, which was just as well, as we didn't earn any batting points, being dismissed for 139 in what ended as a draw. Being away from home at Trent Bridge, there was a sense of anticlimax. There was certainly no whooping from us after Goochie had taken their seventh wicket. We simply shook hands, satisfied at a job well done.

We might have won the John Player Special League that year as well, but we faltered against Surrey at home in our third-from-last match. We lost by one wicket without both Goochie, who was playing in the final Test against New Zealand, and Allan Border, who'd returned home.

Having no equivalent in Australia, AB hadn't been sure how to approach the 40-over stuff when he first came across it. At the start of the season he simply tried to tee off against opposition bowlers, with only limited success. A purist, at his best scrapping out long Test innings, he saw the Sunday League as a frenetic slog to have some fun with. Except that it wasn't much fun when he kept getting out cheaply. It took a few stern chats from Fletch before he realised there was more to it than hit and giggle. Even so, he never did quite get the hang of it that first season with us, passing fifty just twice in the 13 matches he played.

There were a few other 'cultural' differences for both him and the rest of the team to get their heads round. One was that he hated deference, so when, during his moderate trot in the Sunday League, he chopped on one day for not very many, a dismissal that brought a dressing-room chorus of 'Bad luck, AB' from the junior players, he went ape.

'Stop saying "bad luck"!' he shouted as he smashed his bat against his cricket coffin. 'I'm playing like a busted arse.'

Another habit of his was that he liked to earn a drink. So while the rest of us pretty much hit the beer rain, hail or shine, AB only went for it when he felt he deserved it, which was usually after he'd made a big hundred.

One game, against Glamorgan at Swansea in June 1986, he decided to celebrate after he'd made 150. That's when the boys saw him attack the Oranjeboom lager with a vengeance. Later, in the wee hours of the following morning, the hotel fire alarm went off, something that happened from time to time in the grotty hotels Essex stayed in. The drill usually demanded that guests assemble in the hotel car park, but Paul Prichard, Border's room-mate, could not get him to stir as a result of the Oranjeboom consumed.

'I'd rather ------- die,' said Border, who refused to leave his bed even when the hotel manager went to rouse him. Fortunately, like most alarms, it was a false one and Essex's bit of prime Aussie didn't end up on a Welsh barbie.

AB couldn't return as our overseas player in 1987, so we engaged the services of Hugh Page, a pace bowler from South Africa. Quite how a tall leather-flinger was considered an equivalent replacement for a short, nuggety batsman still confuses me, but that's what happened, with dire consequences.

It wasn't Pagey's fault that he couldn't fill Border's shoes. Most of us underperformed that year, including Goochie for a second successive season, as the team collectively had a stinker. As a result, we came 12th in the County Championship, our lowest position during my 15 seasons at the club and one of only four occasions in that time that we finished outside the top five. The best-laid plans and all that.

Ironically, Goochie began the 1987 season with 171 against Gloucestershire, but then bagged a series of ducks. That led to him not being picked for England, except for a single Texaco one-day international against Pakistan. As a consequence, he became increasingly fretful about his form, even dropping himself down the order for Essex towards the end of the season.

On top of his batting woes, he was captaining the most successful county of the past 10 years. Not the best time to have, by his stellar standards, another modest season. To compound the not-inconsiderable matter of our best batsman being below par, John Lever, our stalwart with the ball, endured a series of injuries and took just 26 wickets.

Although we had been over-reliant on JK and Goochie generally, others had managed to step up and fill the void the previous year. That season, though, nothing seemed to click. Even the addition of Geoff 'Dusty' Miller, who joined us from Derbyshire, did not seem to improve the performance of the team, despite fitting in well.

Brought in to replace off-spinner David Acfield, who appeared to have fallen from favour under Goochie, Dusty quickly showed his credentials for joining our wacky dressing room by embarking on his infamous curry marathon of having one 17 nights in succession. But if his spicy diet kept him on his toes, it led to constipation on the pitch, in terms of runs and wickets, and by 1990 he'd returned to Derbyshire without any of the trophies he'd hoped to win by moving south.

Another reason for our stagnation that season was Neil Foster's absence on England duty. He missed half the games, which meant that, with JK ailing, Essex were relying on me and Charlie Childs to supply the firepower. I finished the season with 54 wickets from 21 matches and Charlie took 33, but it was not enough for us to compete as in previous years. We ended the season with a paltry two wins and an unforgivable 17 draws, a number that would have pained Fletch, who would rather lose trying to win than end up in stalemate.

It wasn't that Goochie, who led us for 20 of the 24 Championship matches that season, was a negative captain. But he liked to lead from the front and nothing much was going his way. Bad weather, which struck us more that year than normal, also played a part. Yet, for some reason, the team didn't really gel as in previous years.

Pagey, who began the season well, faded fast after a chronic knee injury was made worse by the demanding treadmill of county cricket. Although determined to soldier on, he managed to play only half the games, few of them with distinction. One of the nicest men you could wish to meet, Pagey still apologises to me every time I see him for letting Essex down that season. But it wasn't solely his fault. He was just one piece of a jigsaw that never fitted together.

Fletch remained a member of the side, but due to Goochie not being selected for England, he only captained four matches. Yet even his magic wand didn't work that year and all four were drawn. It was a confusing time and one that did not gain in clarity when Goochie decided, at the end of the season, to jack in the captaincy. His beef with the job was that he was expected to be captain, manager and opening batsman all at once. Suddenly, time and effort spent previously on preparing himself to bat had to be spent on dealing with the often-trifling problems and quibbles of others. When his form with the bat suffered, he withdrew to the thing he knew best, his own game.

'I never seemed to have enough time to prepare myself or plan the way I was going to bat,' he said in *Gooch*, his autobiography. 'Often, it seemed I hardly had time to put my pads on before I was out there to face the first ball.'

More introverted than many in the dressing room, Goochie was forced to undergo much self-analysis in which he seemed to lose faith in himself. Paul Prichard remembers him returning to the dressing room after another low score and saying to him, 'I just can't bat any more.'

'I was floored,' said Prichard. 'I said to him, "How do you think that makes the rest of us feel?"'

During the World Cup in India and Pakistan which followed that 1987 season, and for which both he and I were perhaps fortunate to be selected, he got all maudlin one night in Lahore as we shared a bottle of his smuggled wine before our first match. Totally unbidden, he suddenly blurted out that he felt he had little time in the game left, believing his eyes to have gone. I told him that was rubbish and he just needed a couple of big scores to rekindle the joys of batting again. Fortunately, he made several, including a brilliant 115 against India in the semi-final in Mumbai, one of the greatest of all World Cup knocks. Happily, for all concerned save his opponents, faith in himself was soon restored and the next six years proved the best of his career.

Goochie's introspection during his low point might have seemed selfish to outsiders, but it is one of the risks teams take when they make the best player captain. So, for 1988, at the age of 34, and with Allan Border back as our overseas player, he gave up the role and Fletch returned to take control once more.

Although nowhere near as dire, performance-wise, as the previous season, there was still an element of musical chairs to the captaincy in 1988. Now mindful of the need to plan for the future, and with some talented youngsters like Nasser Hussain and John Stephenson pushing for regular inclusion, Fletch decided there was a need to blend youth and experience.

There was also the issue of who would follow Fletch as captain, as he couldn't go on for ever. Goochie had tried to do the job but found it difficult to incorporate into his ambitions to be a consistently world-class batsman. But other than me or Neil Foster, nobody else seemed a contender.

The men who ran the club, chairman Doug Insole and cricket chairman Graham Saville, were not enamoured of those alternatives, so they let Fletch start off in charge. Then, once Goochie had regained his mojo, they persuaded him to have another go, with the promise that Fletch would help to ease the burden of the job by being the team's part-time manager. I'm not sure when that was all agreed, but that season Fletch captained 12 matches, Goochie eight and Allan Border two, as we came third in the Championship, eight points behind the winners, Worcestershire.

For me, those eight points could be found lying on the outfield at Colchester's Castle Park, after we drew there with Glamorgan, our scores level – a result that earned us half of the 16 points teams then got for a win. With just a few weeks of the season to go, it was a pivotal match, as well as one I felt we'd actually won off the last ball.

At the crease with our last man and needing two off the final ball for victory on a turning pitch, I swept Rodney Ontong, their off-spinner, fine on the leg side, the connection good enough for it perhaps to have gone for four had one of the senior players been lurking at deep backward square leg. Shrewdly, their captain, Hugh Morris, had placed a young Matthew Maynard down there and he was quick to the ball and with his subsequent throw to the keeper. It was a fine piece of fielding. Even so, with my long reach I felt certain I'd made my ground for the second run, which would have got us home. Unhappily for us, umpire Barry Dudleston felt otherwise, and we ended up with a rosette that year instead of a trophy.

Mark Waugh joined us for a few games at the end of that 1988 season after Border had once again returned home early. Like

Ken McEwan, our overseas pro in the Seventies and early Eighties, Waugh was easy on the eye as a batsman. He could also catch flies, being the best slip fielder I have ever seen, including His Beefiness.

His return for a full season in 1989, alongside young homegrown players like Nasser Hussain and Stan Stephenson, contributed to the changing composition of the side. It helped that all three had good seasons with the bat, scoring 10 hundreds between them as we dominated the Championship once more.

Gooch was back as captain, while I was made his vice-captain, that latter decision, I sensed, made against the better judgement of those running the club. Fletch, when he wasn't involved with the Essex Seconds as mentor and coach, would help to manage the first team, as well as Goochie's workload. It was the first time since I'd joined the club 11 years earlier that we had someone not part of the playing XI become part of the daily decision-making process. In all but name, Essex had got its first coach.

We also had the Reader cricket ball for all our home games, having only dabbled with it in previous seasons. Possessed of a strong, large and proud seam, and retaining its shine for long periods, the Reader was a pace bowler's joy. I certainly relished it and swung my way to my best ever season for Essex. Mind you, I owed the swinging bit to a net session before the first Ashes Test at Headingley. It was there that Worcestershire's Phil Newport showed me his particular grip, which transformed the amount and frequency of swing I achieved thereafter.

Newps, as we called him, was a fine bowler who used to hoop it all round New Road at Worcester. On this occasion, we were both bowling in the nets with Readers. But while I was getting it to offer a bit, he was swinging it round corners. Casually, I asked him to show me his grip. Whereas I'd place my index finger one side of the seam and my middle finger the other, he had his middle finger placed directly on the seam and his index finger just resting on the ball, not playing much of a part at all. Essentially, he got the seam backwards-rotating as he bowled just through the action of his middle finger, like spinning a yo-yo.

It made sense. If the ball was to swing, and we are talking conventional swing here not reverse, you have to turn it into a gyroscope, which means a stable backwards rotation about the ball's own axis while it is in forward motion towards the batsman.

If you had two fingers gripping the ball either side of the seam, as I did, you would need both to release it in perfect synchrony for the ball not to wobble a bit. Although fine for achieving movement off the seam, wobble is no good for swing, which is why Newps's method, using just one finger to ensure its stability in flight, was genius.

Swing can be mercurial for those relying on it, but with this new grip and a Reader ball I found it virtually foolproof. Ironically, it didn't work for either of us during that first Test against Australia, which we lost by 210 runs. Apart from us both bowling badly, the ball did not swing, mainly because it was a Duke not a Reader, Allan Border having won the right to use them instead of Readers for the first five of six Tests that series.

That shocker at Headingley aside, I never looked back. My only regret was that, at the age of 30, I'd not discovered it and those Reader balls sooner. Still, my 94 first-class wickets that season was the most taken in the country, a total I shared with Glamorgan's Steve Watkin. I never did join the 100 Club, which boasted John Lever and Neil Foster among its recent members. But I reckon I would have got there that season but for the two Essex matches I missed when I was picked for the sixth and final Test against Australia, at The Oval.

The Ashes had already been lost, with Australia leading the six-match series 4–0, so this Test was largely irrelevant, except that it was against the Aussies. Following my execrable bowling at Headingley in the first Test of that series, after which I was rightfully dropped, I felt I was about 20th choice to get a recall. But a spate of injuries meant I was picked, despite nursing a hammer fracture to the little finger of my left hand.

I took four wickets in the Test, which was drawn, but missed out on a lot more, potentially, by not playing for Essex. Whether I'd have taken the 11 wickets I needed in those two matches to get to my century will never be known, but pace bowlers dominated the games I missed, so there was every chance. Because of that, it remains the only occasion I wasn't completely overjoyed to be picked for England.

A far greater injustice, though, lay in us not becoming County Champions that year. Worcestershire pipped us by six points, but only after we'd been docked 25 for a substandard pitch at Southend, which considering Yorkshire had won the toss and batted first, was laughable.

We won both our Championship matches at Southend's Southchurch Park that week in July, and while the pitches were a bit dry, both our opponents had first choice of what to do on them. Our groundsman, Andy Atkinson, had wanted to prepare the strips, but the council, which owned the ground, wanted their man to do the work. He was used to producing strips for afternoon games once a week, not two three-day matches and another in the Sunday League.

In the first, against Kent, we rolled them for 112, made 347 in 107 overs on the back of a fine Hussain 127, and then dismissed them again for 229, to win by an innings and six runs. I took 10 wickets in the match and promptly drove off to Kent, of all places, to attend the wedding of an old school friend. I arrived well before the speeches.

The dry nature of the pitch meant that one or two balls had burst the surface but nothing drastic, not like Folkestone whenever we played there. There had been murmurings for a while among the blazers at Lord's that Essex were playing fast and loose with pitch preparation, and that this, in conjunction with the big-seamed Reader ball that year, was making life hell for the poor batsmen. To protect them, they had brought in a penalty of 25 points for substandard pitches, though this was wholly arbitrary, as it relied on the entirely subjective judgement of umpires, who needed to report such pitches in the first place. As we were to discover.

The pitch against Yorkshire a couple of days later was more testing than the one used against Kent, though the match took a similar pattern. They won the toss and batted, and we knocked them over for 115. Our batsmen, this time led by a battling 85 from Stan Stephenson, made 248. They then got stuck in second time around, to make 239 and set us 107 to win, which we got with three wickets to spare.

It was hardly a minefield, with Stephenson saying it was a lot easier to bat on than the pitches he played on at Grace Road and Trent Bridge that season. What did for us was Yorkshire's low score in their first innings when the pitch was at its best; that's what piqued the interest of those sitting in their ivory towers in St John's Wood.

Reading of another low score against Essex, as well as the umpire's misgivings over it, Donald Carr, the secretary of the Test and County Cricket Board and a decent bloke, headed down to Southend for the second day's play. With him came Harry Brind, Surrey's head groundsman and the recently appointed TCCB Inspector of Pitches. The pair arrived just after lunch, right in time to see Richard Blakey's first ball from Neil Foster clang straight into his helmet off a fast bowler's good length. It was unfortunate. There was a patch about the size of a dinner plate where the pitch had crumbled at one end. If you hit it, which not many did that match, it would go through the top and take off. Carr's timing was immaculate for all those who felt we needed a comeuppance, and he was quick to invoke the new penalty. Suddenly, our 36-point lead at the top of the table had been pegged back enough to spur on the chasing pack.

We lost only two matches that season, both of them when Goochie was away playing for England. One of them was against Nottinghamshire at Trent Bridge, a week after the Yorkshire match which had seen us penalised. I was captain that match and was still smarting at our punishment. As such, I got the opportunity to make a point when we lost to Notts on a pitch I felt to be far worse for batting than the one at Southend. So I called a press conference afterwards to air my gripes.

It was not sour grapes, as we'd been outplayed comprehensively. The point I wanted to make, having made it plain that Essex were happy to play on any surface presented to them, was the flaw at the heart of the TCCB's protocols of what constituted a poor pitch. This one had not only been up and down with its vertical bounce, but had also jagged lavishly off the seam, in late July. What I wanted to know was why the umpires at Southend had seen fit to report our pitch there, while the umpires here had not considered the Trent Bridge pitch worthy of even the slightest mention.

The hoo-ha didn't end there. The umpires that match, Roy Palmer and Bob 'Knocker' White, had got wind of my complaints. To compound matters, Palmer had given me out lbw in our second innings to Kevin Cooper, a ball which had nipped back sharply and hit me several inches above the knee roll on my front pad. I'm 6 ft 5 in tall and in my opinion it would have gone over the stumps, so I showed a sliver of disappointment by holding my pose, looking back at Palmer and then gauging where the ball might have gone. It was mild dissent, but Palmer didn't see it that way as he barged into our dressing room 10 minutes after my impromptu press conference.

'What you giving it?' he demanded. 'Standing there looking at me like that when I give you out.'

'Well, I didn't think it was good decision, Roy,' I countered. 'Going over the top.'

'What? It hit you halfway up your pad, bang in front of middle and off,' said Palmer, by now shaking with rage. 'Where's that young Hussain? He was batting at the other end: let's ask him.'

Nasser was having a shower, but that did not stop Palmer from marching straight into the cubicle and demanding he tell me where the ball had struck me.

'I don't really want to get involved,' said Nasser, who'd had his own run-ins with authority that season.

'Tell him!' shouted Palmer.

'OK, if you insist – about three inches above the knee roll,' said Hussain. At which point Palmer went into such a tizz that I had to tell him to calm down.

'It really doesn't matter, Roy, it was a heat-of-the-moment thing,' I said. 'My real concern is that there seems to be ambiguity among umpires as to what a bad pitch looks like. That's why I called a press conference.'

But with Palmer as angry as a cut snake, that last point just seemed to make him more agitated as he stormed off to the sanctuary of the umpires' room.

It was highly unusual to have such a heated encounter between player and umpire, but there was history between us. Once, when I'd captained Combined Universities against Gloucestershire at the Parks in 1982 in a Benson & Hedges match, Roy and his brother Ken, with whom I always got on well, were both umpiring the match.

Like all counties, Gloucestershire basically saw the Universities side as a guaranteed two points, and were keen to despatch us as quickly as possible, whatever the weather. On this occasion they'd batted and we were chasing an unlikely 300. By the time our 55 overs was up, we'd reached 216 for eight, most of it in a steady rain that not only dampened the pitch but would normally have driven county sides from the field. If Gloucestershire had been playing another county, the game would have been suspended until the rain stopped, in this case causing the game to spill over to one of two reserve days set aside to complete the match, weather permitting.

I could understand Gloucestershire not wanting to hang around for another day and incur the extra cost of hotels, but for me it was a point of principle. So, in my captain's report, which would have been read by Donald Carr at the TCCB, I wrote that if Combined Universities were to continue in the B&H competition, then we ought to be given the same courtesies as the counties. I then went on to explain why I thought this had not been the case against Gloucestershire.

For some reason, Carr didn't stick it straight into the shredder and took it up with whoever ran the umpires back then. Whatever the chatter about it at the TCCB, I heard a rumour that somebody who worked there had told Roy Palmer that my report was part of the reason he had not followed brother Ken into umpiring Test matches, at least until the 1990s, when he did get to officiate two Tests. If true, it was perhaps not surprising that he blamed me.

Carr and the mandarins at Lord's obviously saw coverage of my press conference at Notts in 1989, and promptly conveyed their thoughts to Doug Insole, Essex's chairman. In those days the umpires' word was final and Insole, a stickler for such things, quizzed me as to my motives. For once, I think he sided with me, though he never let me know that.

It didn't quite end there. Three weeks later, in their first home game at Trent Bridge since they'd played us, Notts joined Essex on the naughty step by having 25 points deducted for a poor pitch against local rivals Derbyshire. So bad was it that the umpires, this time Barrie Meyer and Peter Wight, stopped the match and demanded the groundsman cut a fresh strip. Notts won, but ended up with minus four points from the match to Derbyshire's plus five.

We might still have won the 1989 Championship but for losing to Northamptonshire after setting them 264 in 75 overs at Wantage Road at the end of August. Neither Goochie, Stan Stephenson nor I were playing, as we'd all been picked for the final Ashes Test, so Lager Hardie was captain. From afar, it did look a generous declaration, but when you are chasing the title, and with no points for a draw, you had to entice teams with targets you might not have offered in the early part of the season.

As a team, it was the most frustrated we ever felt. With a fair wind, we should have won two trophies that year, but ended with nothing. The disappointment hit everyone, though it did for JK, who, at the age of 40, called it a day. In terms of putting your body through the wringer for a single cause, day after day, few gave as much as he did. Just as well that he loved bowling and loved playing for Essex.

JK's retirement meant that only Goochie and Lager Hardie survived from the team which had won Essex's first ever Championship a decade earlier. After that, of the regulars, I was next most senior, then David East and Neil Foster.

I'd enjoyed captaining the side in Goochie's absence, but that was to end after the 1990 season, another where we ended up as bridesmaids in the Championship, this time second behind Middlesex.

It was a trying year, not only for me after I picked up a few injuries, but for bowlers everywhere. The popularity of the Reader ball saw the brains trust at the TCCB decide to reduce the number of strands in the twine used to make the seam. For the 1989 Readers, 15 strands were used, but this was reduced in 1990 to 11. The seams on other balls were also reduced. Coupled with that, following the punishments meted out to us and Nottinghamshire for substandard pitches in 1989, the TCCB also issued a new directive to the counties' groundsmen. It stated that pitches must start dry, with any grass present being straw-coloured, not green.

The combination almost made the bowling fraternity head for alternative employment, as batsmen generally ran riot with runs galore. At Essex alone, there were 27 first-class centuries scored from 22 Championship matches, up 10 from the previous year. Compared to 1986, when Essex last won the Championship, there were 18 more hundreds made from two fewer matches. It was carnage.

Huge respect then to Neil Foster, who took 94 wickets that season. As one who'd opted to take the krugerrand the previous summer by going on the second rebel tour to South Africa, playing for England was no longer a distraction for him. Instead, Essex had his complete focus, with Fozzy playing all 22 Championship matches, something he'd never accomplished previously. His haul was 19 wickets better than the next man, Warwickshire's Tim Munton, while only John Emburey and Phil Tufnell bowled more overs than the 819 he sent down.

I'd known Fozzy since he was a teenager and he was always destined to be a successful cricketer, as long as his spare frame could cope with the demands of the professional game, which are many as a fast bowler. Because he was lean, there were always those telling him that he needed to bulk up, especially early on in his career. One such was Reg Hilliard, an Essex committee man, who suggested Fozzy eat a big steak and drink two pints of Guinness every other night just to put on some beef. Fozzy was playing for Essex Seconds at the time and I remember him telling Reg that even if such nutritional theories held water, he could not afford to indulge such a grand diet. So Hilliard offered to pay. After that, on every Second team away trip, while the rest of us nursed our chicken and chips, Fozzy lived it up on a steak-and-stout diet – the benefits eventually becoming evident that year of the small-seamed ball.

Like most meat-eaters Fozzy could be feisty, a good trait for a fast bowler, providing it is trained on the opposition and not your own team, which occasionally it was. I had a thick skin, but Fozzy's behaviour during a match against Warwickshire that 1990 season, one where I was captain in Goochie's absence, really annoyed me.

We'd batted first and, despite losing most of the first day to rain, declared our innings on 331 for five at the end of day two. I then suggested that Warwickshire chase our score on the final day after a double declaration of their first innings and our second, standard practice in three-day cricket when inclement weather struck.

Their acting captain, Dermot Reeve, didn't fancy that. Warwickshire wanted a shorter chase and a smaller target, 291 from a minimum 85 overs, which gave them less chance of losing. Most captains would have walked away, but I'd been imbued with Essex's philosophy to try to win in all circumstances, so I agreed.

First, though, we had to 'give' them 41 runs in 14 overs, so I put on Mark Waugh and John Stephenson. So as not to waste a new ball, Warwickshire handed us a used one, which just happened to be from the previous season, 1989, the year of the big seam. I didn't know that until later, so sat there at slip as my stand-in bowlers beat the bat with encouraging regularity, thinking, 'We'll absolutely walk this.'

Come the denouement proper, with us now using a 1990 ball and Warwickshire having applied another heavy roller to the pitch, it was a very different story. The ball did not get off the straight. Fozzy huffed and puffed, as did I, as well as the other bowlers who followed, but by tea the only success we'd had was a couple of run-outs.

In a last-ditch attempt to rouse the lads during the tea interval, I attempted a Churchillian speech coloured with some coarse language. When I'd finished, Fozzy stood up and said, 'I will not be spoken to like a child,' but then proceeded to behave like a spoilt one for the rest of the match, which we lost by five wickets.

By his high standards Fozzy had bowled poorly and went wicketless, so I put his petulance down to that and thought little more of it. But others in the team, unbidden by me, went and informed Goochie and Fletch of Fozzy's sulky insurrection. Ever the pragmatist, Fletch, still a major powerbroker at the club, clearly smelt trouble brewing. He knew it unwise to upset our gun bowler. So, that winter, once England had returned from a frustrating Ashes tour, I was summoned to Goochie's house for a meeting.

After a bit of dancing around the subject over a glass or two of wine, I cut to the chase. I told him that while I thoroughly enjoyed the challenges of captaining Essex in his absence, if he wanted somebody to captain in his image, then the club should appoint someone else. So they did: Fozzy.

I'd begun to have a few run-ins with Goochie during the 1990 season. Although we got on well most of the time, I sensed he felt that I was a bit of a dilettante, using cricket as a springboard to something else. If I was, I'd not yet planned what on earth that something else might be.

I remember having one argument with him, though not its exact subject, which ended with him saying, 'The trouble with you is that you have an answer for everything, and it usually involves either an easy solution or a short cut.'

'Well, Graham,' I said, 'finding a short cut is the price of a good education. Who wants to go the long way round when you don't have to?' Of course, my answer just reinforced what he felt.

Goochie was very close to Doug Insole, the original Mr Essex before Fletch, JK, and then Goochie joined the club. At about the same time as that conversation with Goochie, I was having some treatment from Jim Davis, Essex's physio, for a hamstring niggle that was proving hard to shake. Doug's assessment, and he was from the old school, was that I should be fitter; not that we might be playing too much cricket and that, at nearly 32, it might be taking its toll on me.

'Why don't you want to be as fit as a First Division footballer?' he asked, in the days before the Premiership was the elite league.

'I tell you what, Doug,' I said, 'you pay me as well as a First Division footballer and I'll be as fit as one.' It was another quip that did not go down well and one which probably led to not having the right people on my side when the vice-captaincy came up for scrutiny following Fozzy's hysterics.

I was not that upset to lose it. Captaincy excites some, but I did not play professional cricket to be fulfilled by leadership challenges, the demands of taking wickets, scoring runs and winning games being enough for me. I was disappointed, though, by how easily the club's powerbrokers had cast me aside for someone who'd behaved in such an un-Essex fashion. That's what hurt.

Their instincts were proved right, though. We returned to our winning ways in the County Championship, securing the pennant in both 1991 and 1992, their judgement of whose ego to soothe and whose to bruise, with the least fallout to the team, being spot on. For that, you had to admire them.

Having preferred someone who was single-minded as vice-captain (Fozzy), as opposed to someone who occasionally thought out of the box (me), it always amused me that Essex took so long to promote Nasser Hussain to a leadership role at the club. When both Fozzy and I retired at the end of the 1993 season, I suggested to the club's bigwigs that Essex make Hussain captain after Gooch. You could have heard the unanimous chorus of 'You must be ------- joking' in Ilford.

Hussain and Fozzy never got on when they played together, but they were very similar in their pursuit of excellence. They let nothing get in their way. Giving both some responsibility beyond themselves was a gamble, but in Hussain's case it paid off as he became one of England's better captains of the next 20 years.

12

ENDGAME

JUST AS MRS Thatcher fell at the start of the Nineties, so too did the maverick cricketer, at least in the professional game. The irony was that Thatcher's downfall came, at least in part, from her own authoritarianism – something that would do for cricket's flannelled individualists as well. It didn't come from any tinpot tyranny of their own, more from the rising power of coaches. From having artistic freedom in terms of preparation and play, on and off the field, they suddenly had to operate to a more rigorous code. As a result, organisation, dedication and discipline replaced improvisation, imagination and self-expression.

Remarkably, it seemed to suit the way England played, as Gooch, the new captain, was tasked with wringing the best from a young team. Mind you, it would have been interesting to see if the 'industry over enterprise' approach he and coach Mickey Stewart advocated would have worked a decade earlier, when players like Botham and Gower were in their pomp.

Had it been imposed then, it is possible we might never have seen some of those magical moments that are still talked about today, such as the miracle of Headingley and the marvel of Edgbaston in that '81 Ashes series. On the other hand, maybe instead of such incredible highs and their correspondingly stumbling lows, there might have been a more consistent course plotted through the decade. We shall never know.

I've always been conflicted about the switch of philosophy. My heart hankered for the nobility and romance of the dashing individual deed that changed matches. I badly wanted to be that player, but rarely was. Yet my head revered and respected the sanctity of the team, which usually responded best to discipline.

When I first got picked for England, people used to tell me what an honour it was for me to represent my country. They would then add that had the opportunity fallen to them they would have done it for nothing. Maybe, but I was less starry-eyed in my patriotism. My priorities, I used to tell them, were to my team-mates first, then me, and then to that amorphous entity England or Essex, or whichever mothership I happened to be representing at the time.

The dichotomy created an interesting tension. At every level of cricket I played I was brought up to be a team man. And yet my ambition was to be a buccaneering game-changer, even if that role rarely occurred once I'd left school. The one time it did, though, was in a Sunday League match against Warwickshire at Edgbaston in 1983.

Batting at seven, I scored 47 in 17 balls, caught on the boundary trying to reach my fifty with a six. It was a bravura knock where everything came out of the middle of the bat and everything I tried, including several reverse-sweeps, came off. There was a smallish boundary on one side, but no shorter than the boundaries which exist now in white-ball cricket matches. I mention this only because Jos Buttler recently set an England record for the fastest fifty in T20 internationals on the same ground.

It took Buttler 22 balls to reach his fifty, five more than it would have taken me if I'd managed an extra five yards more ooomph in the hoik that brought about my dismissal. And although he was up against international bowlers off their full run-ups, I did face Bob Willis and Norman Gifford that match, two England bowlers amid journeymen like Willy Hogg and Chris Lethbridge. Of course, they were limited to a 15-yard run-up but even so, with everyone these days thinking big hitting was invented with T20, there were plenty who could tonk it even then.

The force was with me that day, and we won, just. But generally when I tried to play like that I'd make a quick 20 and get out, which was no good to anybody. To be more useful, I became a more boring cricketer, so the move to a team-based gambit actually suited me better than the freewheeling self-expression encouraged for much of the Eighties.

Under the new ways you had a role which, if you stuck to it closely, enabled you to do a job for the team. It was prescriptive, but some players like being told what to do. In terms of creativity, it was reductive but effective, especially in the 1991 Test series against the West Indies at home. Instead of trying to fight fire with fire, as in recent encounters with them, their flamboyance was countered by discipline and a dogged persistence, with both ball and bat.

As we'd done in 1988, we'd whitewashed the West Indies in the three Texaco Trophy one-day internationals. A few days after that, and probably another week before the Test squad was announced, I was interviewed by Peter Hayter of the *Mail on Sunday*. I knew Peter from schools cricket, where he'd been a doughty opening bat for Aldenham, so the interview was fairly relaxed.

When he asked what I felt my chances were of being picked for the Test squad, I said, 'Well, they selected me before when we'd won the Texacos, but it's never worked out that well and I was quickly dropped. So I wouldn't pick me if I was them.'

The selectors obviously never saw the piece or, if they did, they ignored my self-deprecating twaddle, as there my name was, selected for the opening Test at Headingley on 6 June 1991, the first Test match to be played without a rest day.

It had probably helped my cause that Ian Botham had twanged a hamstring in the opening Texaco match and was unfit for selection. We had played in the same England side previously, but it had begun to dawn on the selectors, now headed by Ted Dexter, that we were probably mutually exclusive.

Although many twinned me with Headingley, believing that we went together as harmoniously as the Two Ronnies, it had been the scene of my worst ever bowling performance for England, nought for 123 against Australia in 1989, as well as my best, five for 95 against the West Indies in 1988. A schizophrenic ground for me. This time, though, it was definitely benevolent to England as we beat the West Indies for the first time in a home Test since 1969, a hiatus of 22 years.

The principal way it helped us was with the weather. A bitter wind blew for most of the game, making it one of the coldest Test matches anyone could remember. The West Indies attack of Malcolm Marshall, Curtly Ambrose, Courtney Walsh and Patrick Patterson, probably the highest aggregate mph ever assembled in a Test match, just could not get warm in the chilly conditions. On a tricky pitch, that was a boon.

We were also helped by Goochie playing what many consider to be the greatest ever Test innings in history, after he made an unbeaten 154 in our second dig.

Hyperbole swirls around sporting deeds like midges round a sweaty head, buzzing with opportunistic intent to proclaim the biggest, hardest, furthest, fastest and best. But that knock has been hailed as cricket's magnum opus after all the obvious factors such as opponents, conditions and match situation are taken into consideration. Seasoned observers such as John Woodcock and Robin Marlar, writing for *The Times* and the *Sunday Times* respectively, certainly recognised its significance at the time, though that wasn't the case with everyone. Woodcock said it was 'probably the finest

Test innings played by an England captain', while Marlar said its worth was 'beyond rubies'.

Gooch certainly acknowledges it as his best. 'In the context of the game and the opposition, it was my greatest innings', he said recently. He also recalled it was the only time he'd been offered the light against a West Indies attack and turned it down. 'It was a rare event to get on top of that pace attack and I wasn't going to let them have a breather while we were ahead.' He was true to his word, keeping them at bay for 452 minutes.

For those of us in the England dressing room, the action was perhaps too close to place into context during the match. On a challenging pitch against the greatest pace attack in world cricket, possibly of all time, Goochie had applied himself to bat for as long as possible, as only he knew how. We had taken a first-innings lead of 25 and our captain was not about to squander such a rare advantage, slim though it was.

The innings was not a feast that stirred the senses, more a massive concrete slab of concentration. Out went the speculative shots and swishing hooks, and in their place came a mental resolve to play only that which was necessary – never an easy task against an attack comprising those four bowlers of the apocalypse.

For starters, Marshall and Ambrose, even then, were considered among the best fast bowlers there have ever been, while Walsh went on to notch 519 Test wickets. Patterson wasn't quite in the others' class, but was the fastest of the quartet when roused. Thankfully, his ardour was quelled by the cold. Countering that, though, was the fact that all four had played county cricket, so they knew how to use the conditions.

It was Goochie's combination of craft and watchful defence, more than any eye-catching strokeplay, which probably prevented his team-mates from recognising the immediate worth of his innings.

Although his top score in Tests at Headingley to that point was 68 (he averaged a measly 25.2 before that Test), Goochie had enjoyed a fine record against successive phalanxes of West Indian fast bowlers. In that regard, we probably took his brilliance for granted. What we did realise, though, was that his knock had given us a good chance to win, a rare occurrence against the West Indies teams of that era – and win we duly did.

With a next highest score in the innings of 27, Goochie's 154 stands out like an Everest among molehills. Never before had someone carrying their bat for England contributed such a high percentage – 61 per cent – of the team's total. I was one of two who managed that second highest score (the other was Mark Ramprakash, on Test debut). To most, 27 will seem an extremely modest score, but while we were at the crease together Goochie and I added 98 for the seventh wicket.

While I clung on, playing and missing and working the odd single, Gooch, by then at least, seemed on top of the task. His innings was a masterclass in attrition, taking seven hours and 32 minutes, with fewer than half the runs coming from boundaries (18 fours). Very different from the innings profiles of today's batsmen.

The pitch was not quick, but with cloud cover present more or less throughout the Test, the ball moved both laterally and, as the match wore on, vertically too, as the bounce became less reliable. But while others found mere survival difficult, none of this fazed Gooch, who tended to thrive on such challenges. He trained hard for those days when batting became both mentally and physically sapping.

As one who'd spent much of his career being hammered by the West Indies, the slightest sniff of a chance to beat them excited his competitive instincts. Being England's captain helped too, Goochie being inspired by the job's noble calling.

He might have been out early on, had mid-off not been so deep and dozing, while West Indies were convinced that he had later got a touch to one down the leg side. Some refused to applaud his century as a result, but when asked about that incident, Gooch said he did not believe he had made contact with the ball. Crucially, nor did the umpire.

Later, when time had allowed some perspective, Goochie said he doubted he'd timed eight shots perfectly in seven and a half hours of batting. Which shows how well he must have battled despondency as well as the bowling. There were, he later admitted, not many red blotches near the sweet spot of his bat.

When the last man, Devon Malcolm, was out, Gooch had no time to dwell on his achievement. The West Indies needed 278 to win and he had to marshal his bowlers. The secret to bowling at Headingley is to maintain a good-to-fullish length tight to off stump. If you bang it in there, it tends to sit up and it can be a fast-scoring ground if the bowling is loose.

In the West Indies' first innings, Phil DeFreitas and Steve Watkin had been superb in maintaining those principles. They'd been backed by some spectacular fielding, especially from Ramprakash. His brilliant catch at cover to get rid of Phil Simmons in that first innings was a gem, while his run-out of Carl Hooper, soon after, caused jitters to course through their batting. Being a bang-in bowler, Devon Malcolm was not best suited to the pitch, something borne out by his figures of one for 95 in the match, but Dev kept charging in nonetheless.

In the first innings, I didn't get much of a bowl except towards the end of the second day, Daffy and Watty having bowled so well. When I did get on, I immediately found some extra bounce to take the edge of Viv Richards's bat. To my disappointment, Lamby spilled the catch at first slip, leaving us to spend the night ruing what might have been. Fortunately, in my opening over the next morning, I virtually replicated the ball, and this time Lamby clung on, with no real damage done.

That extra bounce I'd got from the Football Stand End was left for others to find in the second innings. The wind, which had switched to the south-west, had grown strong, and yours truly was given the job of bowling into it from the Kirkstall Lane End. The pitch had also slowed, so I just concentrated on giving nothing away and building pressure that way. In Goochie parlance, 'Don't give 'em any easy score balls.'

DeFreitas and Watkin were again magnificent while I plugged away. We took nine wickets between us, the last falling to Dev as Courtney Walsh slogged a skyer, which Mike Atherton ran round from gully to take. It was an easier catch for mid-off but Athers called early, fixed his eyes on the swirling ball and clung on for dear life to seal a rare win.

Afterwards, as the spectators crowded around the old pavilion at Headingley for the various presentations, they broke into a spontaneous version of the national anthem, singing: 'God Save Our Pring' as the refrain. As one who'd enjoyed something of a Marmite relationship with the Headingley crowd, it was a moment to savour.

To celebrate our rare win, the TCCB, in an uncharacteristic gesture of largesse, allowed us to stay an extra night in the team hotel, a remote place stuck on a moor above Otley called Chevin Lodge. Only four of us stayed – me, Michael Atherton, Steve Watkin and Robin Smith – though Athers and I had Benson & Hedges semi-finals to play on the Wednesday. The evening didn't fizz. Leeds on a Monday night in 1991 was beyond resuscitation. Anyway, it didn't feel right to be celebrating our win with two-thirds of the team having gone home. We did, however, toast Goochie's stupendous innings.

ENGLAND V WEST INDIES
(1st Test)

Played at Headingley, Leeds, 6–10 June 1991

Umpires: HD Bird & DR Shepherd
Toss: West Indies

ENGLAND

GA Gooch*	c Dujon b Marshall	34	not out		154
MA Atherton	b Patterson	2	c Dujon b Ambrose		6
GA Hick	c Dujon b Walsh	6	b Ambrose		6
AJ Lamb	c Hooper b Marshall	11	c Hooper b Ambrose		0
MR Ramprakash	c Hooper b Marshall	27	c Dujon b Ambrose		27
RA Smith	run out	54	lbw b Ambrose		0
RC Russell†	lbw b Patterson	5	c Dujon b Ambrose		4
DR Pringle	c Logie b Patterson	16	c Dujon b Marshall		27
PAJ DeFreitas	c Simmons b Ambrose	15	lbw b Walsh		3
SL Watkin	b Ambrose	2	c Hooper b Marshall		0
DE Malcolm	not out	5	b Marshall		4
Extras	(5 lb, 14 nb, 2 w)	21	(4 b, 9 lb, 7 nb, 1 w)		21
Total	(79.2 overs)	**198**	(106 overs)		**252**

WEST INDIES

PV Simmons	c Ramprakash b DeFreitas	38	b DeFreitas		0
DL Haynes	c Russell b Watkin	7	c Smith b Pringle		19
RB Richardson	run out	29	c Lamb b DeFreitas		68
CL Hooper	run out	0	c Lamb b Watkin		5
IVA Richards*	c Lamb b Pringle	73	c Gooch b Watkin		3
AL Logie	c Lamb b DeFreitas	6	c Gooch b Watkin		3
PJL Dujon†	c Ramprakash b Watkin	6	lbw b DeFreitas		33
MD Marshall	c Hick b Pringle	0	lbw b Pringle		1
CEL Ambrose	c Hick b DeFreitas	0	c Pringle b DeFreitas		14
CA Walsh	c Gooch b DeFreitas	3	c Atherton b Malcolm		9
BP Patterson	not out	5	not out		0
Extras	(1 lb, 5 nb)	6	(1 lb, 6 nb)		7
Total	(54.1 overs)	**173**	(56.4 overs)		**162**

WEST INDIES	O	M	R	W		O	M	R	W		Fall of wickets:			
												Eng	WI	Eng	WI
Ambrose	26	8	49	2		28	6	52	6					
Patterson	26.2	8	67	3		15	1	52	0		1st	13	36	22	0
Walsh	14	7	31	1	(4)	30	5	61	1		2nd	45	54	38	61
Marshall	13	4	46	3	(3)	25	4	58	3		3rd	45	58	38	77
Hooper						4	1	11	0		4th	64	102	116	85
Richards						4	1	5	0		5th	129	139	116	88
											6th	149	156	124	136
ENGLAND	O	M	R	W		O	M	R	W		7th	154	160	222	137
Malcolm	14	0	69	0	(2)	6.4	0	26	1		8th	177	165	236	139
DeFreitas	17.1	5	34	4	(1)	21	4	59	4		9th	181	167	238	162
Watkin	14	2	55	2	(4)	7	0	38	3		10th	198	173	252	162
Pringle	9	3	14	2	(3)	22	6	38	2						

Close of play:	Day 1:	England (1) 174–7 (Pringle 6*, DeFreitas 13*)
	Day 2:	West Indies (1) 166–8 (Richards 73*, Walsh 1*)
	Day 3:	England (2) 143–6 (Gooch 82*, Pringle 10*)
	Day 4:	West Indies (2) 11–1 (Haynes 3*, Richardson 8*)

Man of the match: GA Gooch
Result: **England won by 115 runs**

We kept our lead in the series into July, after the next Test, at Lord's, was drawn, the entire fourth day having been washed out by rain. That was also the day the Queen was due to meet both teams at Lord's. As it was tipping down, she didn't bother. Instead, once play had been called off for the day, both sides were invited to Buckingham Palace for tea.

It proved an enlightening experience, with the Queen showing a supremely human touch when she met Alf Gooch, Goochie's dad. Alf had come to Lord's to pick up his son and drive him home, but he got swept up into the tea invitation. When he explained to Her Majesty that his wife would not believe him when he told her where he'd been, she went and cut a slice of cake, wrapped it in a serviette bearing the Palace's coat of arms, and said to Alf, 'Take her this. She will have to believe you then.'

The Duke of Edinburgh was more forthright in his chat. Meeting both teams, he began to quiz Devon Malcolm as to why he wasn't playing for the West Indies, Dev's Jamaican accent being still quite strong back then. It wasn't just a passing enquiry either, the Duke interested to know at what age Dev had come to England and where he'd been to school. I told Dev afterwards that he should have said Gordonstoun, though he'd have needed to clip that last syllable to pass muster.

During that match, West Indies batted first and made 419, though I managed to take five wickets, swinging the ball from the Nursery End, to win a place on the Lord's honours boards. In reply, we'd been in a bit of bother at 180 for six, but Robin Smith batted magnificently, making an unbeaten 148 to ensure we avoided the follow-on.

I kept him company, our partnership of 89 for the seventh wicket helping him to see off a surge from Ambrose, Walsh and Marshall. But then I got ahead of myself, something you should never do in sport, not at that level.

It all began the previous evening when an old mate of mine, Nigel Taylor, had promised to clear my mortgage for me if I scored a hundred against the West Indies. Considering that I'd never even reached fifty against them before, both of us felt his offer was safe. Yet, as Marshall took his sweater for a well-earned blow and Ian Allen, playing in place of Patterson, came on, I suddenly thought the opportunity might be there, especially when I proceeded to drive Allen's first two balls for four.

Focus on the present, the head doctors in sport say, even if we didn't really have any back then. I was on 35, striking the ball well, and the big guns were unlikely to bowl for another hour. Suddenly, being mortgage-free seemed a distinct possibility, or it did until Allen banged his next ball in short and, eager for another boundary, I went for the hook.

I didn't catch the shot flush and it looped towards wide mid-on. Still, I felt it was probably safe. But then I hadn't reckoned on big Phil Simmons turning on a sixpence at midwicket and making a fine running catch. I was distraught, not just because the mortgage offer had died a sudden death but because, having done the hard work, I'd squandered the chance of a big score against the best bowling side in world cricket.

The draw meant we were still one up as we moved to Trent Bridge for the third Test, though our lead didn't last long as we lost there by nine wickets. We didn't have a great game with bat or ball, our 211 in the second innings being particularly tame. Mind you, we were worse in the next Test, at Edgbaston, where we capitulated to 188 all out on the first day, Marshall and Ambrose dominant on a pitch that nibbled around off the seam.

Apart from a couple of late reverse-swingers from Wasim Akram at The Oval in 1992, the ball that Ambrose knocked me over with at Edgbaston was one of the best I'd ever received in Test cricket.

Basically, it pitched about middle and off and held its line to hit off stump. Fred Trueman was on commentary for BBC's *Test Match Special* at the time, and he harangued me for missing what he saw as a straight half-volley. The TV replay showed just what an unplayable nut it had been, especially when bowled at the pace Ambrose had been generating.

When we bowled, the ball swung for me but I didn't take many wickets. I had the satisfaction of getting Viv Richards out, but the West Indies had decided, instead of trying to attack me, to sit on me instead. My 23 overs cost just 48 runs, but to get wickets I needed them to underestimate me, not treat me with undue caution – and they weren't playing ball.

Chris Lewis had come into the side for David Lawrence, who'd played in the previous Test at Trent Bridge in place of Devon Malcolm. Lewis had pulled out of the first Test of the series at the eleventh hour with a migraine. A superb cricketer and athlete, Chris was always more nervy than he let on. Yet if he got an early confidence-booster, he could be world-class, and so it was in that match, when he took six for 111.

His excellence could not prevent West Indies from taking a valuable 104-run lead, one that looked decisive when we'd slumped to 96 for six by tea on day three. That's when I came to the crease, a place I made home for the next five hours and four minutes, until last man out the following day for 45. Talk about rearguards, this was like blunting the bowling with an elephant's backside. There was a reason for my intransigence, and it came in the shape of a threat from Geoffrey Boycott, working at the match for the BBC.

At close on day three, I'd reached 26 and Chris Lewis seven, the team score having limped to 156 for eight. I had two mates at the game, Simon 'Leadbelly' Lewis and Alex 'Sneaky' Snyder, who'd come all the way from Hong Kong to see me. Even though I was still batting, I felt it would be remiss if I didn't socialise with them that evening. So we went on the razzle, ending up in a nightclub until the wee hours.

The next day, although only slightly hung-over, I was looking at the pitch when Boycott sidled up to me. 'My little spies tell me you were out clubbing to all hours,' he said. 'You better not get out or I'll tell everyone on the radio how you prepared for your knock.'

So I didn't get out, or at least not for another three hours. While I stonewalled, Chris provided the rococo flourishes with a fine 65. Only once he was out and I was left with number 11 Richard Illingworth did I venture beyond a cautious nudge.

Some journalists hailed my obduracy as heroic, and it might have been had we won or even come close to doing so. But after a flurry of wickets gave us the flicker of a smash-and-grab victory, in marched Viv, the Master Blaster, to settle matters with a quickfire 73. Suddenly, from our promising start in the series, we were 2–1 down with one match to go.

I didn't play in the last Test, at The Oval, which began on 8 August. Beefy had been brought back into the squad after some strong performances for Worcestershire, so I might have been dropped anyway. Instead, I made it easy for the selectors by falling ill sometime between the team dinner and the morning of the match 10 hours later, when I awoke with a fever and a temperature of 102 °F.

Whether I would have been first choice, I don't know. I never asked Goochie and he never let on. Hick, Lamb and Jack Russell had all been dropped, so the batting needed bolstering. Alec Stewart was brought in to do that and keep wicket, so Beefy would also have been needed to offer some ballast in the middle order. David 'Syd' Lawrence had also returned, while Phil Tufnell came into the side in place of Richard Illingworth.

On balance, I looked likely to be the one to make way, though with 12 wickets in the series, I was England's second highest wicket-taker after DeFreitas. I'd done a good, steady job, but this was a must-win Test and good-and-steady was probably ready to be sacrificed for a bit of mercurial magic. Not that Beefy provided it, at least not to turn the game.

His presence in the match did put Jonathan Agnew on the map as a broadcaster, though, after he trod on his wicket while facing Ambrose. In summarising England's dismissals with Brian 'Johnners' Johnston, the doyen of the BBC's *Test Match Special* team, Agnew said that Beefy 'didn't quite get his leg over'. This set Johnners off into a giggling fit that has been replayed far more often than the dismissal itself, unusual though it was.

England won the Oval match to draw the series, though not without controversy after suspicions of ball-tampering. Phil Tufnell bowled brilliantly in the West Indies' first innings, his six for 25 consigning them to follow on after England had made 419 batting first, Robin Smith superb with a feisty 109. Tufnell's threat had dried up in the West Indies' second innings, though Syd made amends with five for 106, as the ball reverse-swung at pace. It was during that spell that umpire John Holder warned Gooch that he felt the ball had been tampered with. Despite that, it wasn't changed. As was their wont, the West Indies just got on with matters, complaining not really being in their DNA back then.

I watched the match unfold on TV from my hotel room, though I'd recovered sufficiently by the weekend to play a Sunday League match for Essex at Northampton. We were thrashed, but that did not stop me returning to London for the denouement of the Test and our celebrations.

Viv Richards, a warrior of an opponent, was very gracious over the result. According to Goochie, he singled me out for praise, saying that I'd given them more trouble that series than any other bowler. It was a generous compliment and coming from someone like Viv, a player whom I admired and respected greatly, it meant the world.

So, too, did drawing a series against the best Test team in world cricket. In terms of their bowling, this team was arguably stronger than the ones which had destroyed us in 1984 and 1988. Yet it did not have the same batting power as those West Indies sides that contained Gordon Greenidge, and that made them vulnerable. Also, Viv was not long for retirement, something he did quietly soon after that Oval Test, calling time on one of the more glorious Test careers – West Indies having won 63 and lost just 19 of the 121 Tests in which he played.

There was one more Test to follow that summer, a one-off venture against Sri Lanka at Lord's, though I was not picked for it. Instead, I went back to county cricket with Essex and the run-in to another County Championship title, something we'd been threatening after coming third, second and second over the preceding three years.

As a result of our win, someone had the wizard idea that we, as County Champions, should play Victoria, the Sheffield Shield winners, in a challenge match at Chelmsford. A four-day game as well as a 50-over thrash were hastily organised. A modest pot of prize money was put up, and it might have been fun, except I broke the index finger on my left hand, badly enough to be rushed to Broomfield hospital for an operation the same night.

Neil Foster was bowling with the new ball when Wayne Phillips, Victoria's opening batsman, edged a catch between me and Goochie, at first and second slip respectively. It was one of those where I felt it was his catch and he felt it was mine. When I saw he wasn't going for it, I made a late snatch with both hands, which is how the ball came to mangle my left index finger before being held safely in my right hand. All this happened in a fraction of a second, which may have been why the surgeon was surprised not only at the extent of the damage to my finger but that I'd actually managed to cling on to the catch.

With a winter tour of New Zealand looming, as well as a World Cup, hosted by Australia and New Zealand, the last thing I wanted was a bad break to a finger in an unscheduled game tacked on to the end of the season. There was further concern, too, when it became known that the leading finger surgeon at the hospital had been away at a conference, which meant the operation to put a pin in my finger was done by a houseman. It remains misshapen to this day.

Despite the setback, I was picked for both tours on the proviso that my finger was not a hindrance, which was only likely to be the case for batting, not bowling. To make sure it wasn't, I spent the next two months attending rehab clinics at Addenbrooke's hospital in Cambridge three times a week until the finger could bend enough to fit into a batting glove.

In late November, the squads for New Zealand and the World Cup, essentially the same group of players, assembled at the National Sports Centre at Lilleshall in Shropshire. We were there to bond over a few days and to see if the fitness programmes we'd been given had been adhered to.

It was while sitting there in reception, soon after arrival, that I met Colin Tomlin, a builder keen on fitness who'd written to Mickey Stewart, England's coach, to say that he was a patriot and fed up with the poor showing of the national team. He wanted to help, he said, by getting us all fitter. This appealed to Stewart and Goochie greatly, though you'd surely have to question the sagacity of employing someone who'd approached you out of the blue like that. For the elite squad of a national sport, it just seemed a bit random.

'Colin Tomlin,' he said, hand outstretched.

'Hi, Derek Pringle,' I replied.

'Oh, you're Pringle, are you? I've heard that I'll be having a bit of trouble with you. In fact, I've heard that whatever I say, you will take the opposite point of view.'

'Really, you mustn't believe all that propaganda Mickey Stewart puts out,' I said. 'He's winding you up.'

Thommo, as he quickly became known, put us through our paces with shuttle runs, orienteering exercises and various callisthenics from the National Service book of health. One thing I did notice about Thommo was that training was a banter-free zone. Mirth was not his thing and he always seemed to be wound very tight. The following season Goochie got him to come and train Essex, where larks and banter were par for the course. It was not a good fit. A few years after I'd retired I discovered Thommo had killed himself by jumping under a train following money troubles – a sad conclusion even for a man as troubled as him.

There were some primitive indoor nets at Lilleshall, too, and bleep tests, along with other means of measuring our strength and flexibility. These were overseen by a chap called John Brewer, now Professor of Applied Sports Science at St Mary's University in London. Brewer was checking the results against a baseline that we'd provided two months earlier. Incredibly, my bleep test was worse than it had been at the end of a long, tiring season, and that in spite of me being pretty dutiful towards the bespoke training programme that Brewer had given to me and everyone else. Maybe those old players like Alec Bedser, who advocated bowling and walking home as the only fitness required by professional cricketers, were onto something.

I did have the greatest quadriceps strength among the squad, and was one of the most flexible when it came to hamstring stretches. Yet my upper-body strength was pitiful (Brewer's description) for someone my size, which showed I'd not really developed muscle-wise since that early criticism during my first year as a Test player. I suppose I used my wrists and long levers for batting power, while a big chest and big biceps have got nothing to do with generating speed on a cricket ball while bowling. In fact, big pecs can add unnecessary load on the back, so should be avoided by bowlers unless, like Surrey's Nick Taylor, who was once asked by his bowling coach why he pushed weights, you are doing it to look good on the beach.

Christmas was spent at home but we were in New Zealand in time to celebrate New Year, playing our first tour game on 2 January 1992 against Auckland. It was a 50-over game which we won by five wickets with a ball to spare. The only other notable thing about the match was that three people bearing the surname Pringle played in it. Two of them, Chris and Martin, turned out for Auckland, while I played for England, a tri-Pringle match being a first for me.

The itinerary was higgledy-piggledy. A one-day international was followed by a tour match, then a Test, then another tour match, before the final two Tests. After them, two further one-day internationals would conclude the trip before we flew to Australia for the 1992 World Cup.

That first one-day international, also at Auckland's odd-shaped ground (the oval of a cricket ground squeezed into the rectangle of a rugby stadium), was instructive in how closely the England team, in terms of personnel rather than tactics, resembled the one which took the field in the World Cup final just over two months later. The only two missing from that team were Ian Botham, who skipped the first half of the New Zealand trip because of his panto commitments alongside Max Boyce in *Jack and the Beanstalk*, and Richard Illingworth, whose spinner's role was fulfilled in that match by Phil Tufnell.

We won, but neither our strategy nor that adopted by New Zealand bore much resemblance to the ones we adopted in the World Cup. I only mention this as a contrast to the guff spouted by modern teams, who feel they must know who will be doing what 12 months in advance or a plague will befall their houses. Our plans only began to firm up in the ODIs after the Test series, which was concluded 2–0 in our favour.

The other notable events in that Test series were that Ian Botham played his 100th Test, in Wellington, the third and final match, and Syd Lawrence played his last Test, after suffering a horrendous knee injury. I'd pulled out of the match at the 11th hour with a shoulder problem, but was sound enough to help stretcher Syd off after he suffered a split kneecap, incurred while trying to bowl. It was horrible to see this big fast bowler, who always gave it everything when he charged in, screaming in agony as one half of his patella lodged midway up his thigh, the other bit partway down his shin.

It was a sudden and terrible way for such a whole-hearted cricketer to finish his England career, and while Syd attempted to make a comeback for his county, Gloucestershire, a return some five years in the making, he managed fewer than 100 overs before the problems returned. After that, he opened a succession of bars and nightclubs in Bristol before turning his urge to pump iron into becoming a professional bodybuilder.

Our one-day tactics only really coalesced once Beefy arrived bearing gifts in the shape of a carton of sunglasses from his sponsors Oakley, and a Yuletide paunch. Although he huffed and puffed his way through training and the last two one-dayers, something curious happened between those matches. From batting at five in the first one, a position that saw him make 28 off 43 balls, he somehow persuaded Goochie to let him open the innings in the final one, a role he had not performed for five years.

Modern teams are rarely so open to experimentation, but as we'd already won the series Goochie, who'd opened with Graeme Hick in the previous two matches, dropped down the order. You have to hand it to Beefy. If people were sceptical about him rekindling his glory days pinch-hitting in the 1986–87 tri-series in Australia, they were quickly won over as he belted 79, at better than a run a ball, against an attack containing Lance Cairns, Gavin Larsen and Chris Harris.

With fielding restrictions in place for the first 15 overs, Gooch was obviously swayed by Botham's argument that he was the man to take advantage, and he went on to open throughout the World Cup. The gambit could scarcely be hailed a success, though, the 192 runs he scored in that tournament came at an average of 21.3, with a top score of 53, made against Australia in Sydney.

If that was a late decision, so too was the one to give me the new ball. At the outset, my ambition was to be a regular team member who would bowl either first or second change, take one end during the death overs and bat at seven or eight. That all changed when Phil DeFreitas was injured for the second one-dayer in Dunedin and I was asked to open the bowling.

I don't know whether there was anything unusual about the Kookaburra balls of that vintage, or whether it was the cool breeze blowing through Carisbrook's 'House of Pain', but the ball swung, a lot. You needed to get your hands on those Kookaburras while they were new to get that kind of movement, though having a ball at each end helped in that regard, as neither would ever be more than 25 overs old.

If you look at the scorecard for that Dunedin match, my figures of one for 31 off 10 overs with two maidens do not look overly impressive. But Gooch was close enough to see how uncomforta- ble the batsmen were facing my lavish swing. He gave me the new ball again in the next game, at Christchurch, and this time I took two for 11, sealing my role as England's opening bowler for the World Cup.

While taking a long-view plan of events has its place, flexibility and the ability to think and make adjustments on the hoof is even more important. If anyone had suggested two weeks before that World Cup that Beefy, fresh from panto, would have opened the batting and me the bowling, they would have been frogmarched off to the nearest asylum. But Goochie and his think tank saw the potential and went with it.

If making such bold changes so close to a big tournament was unusual, even then, New Zealand's alterations were even greater as they made their final preparations for the World Cup. Martin Crowe, their captain, was always a cricketer who thought out of the box, though what he proposed now must have caused many to conclude that he'd placed one over his head.

With all New Zealand's round-robin matches in the World Cup being at home, Crowe wanted to open the bowling with an off-spinner, Dipak Patel, who'd not even been picked for the one-day series against us. He got his wishes, too, and it worked a treat, especially on the slow, bare pitches made especially for Patel and the other dibbly-dobbler bowlers in their team, like Larsen and Harris.

Largely thanks to this strategy, New Zealand reached the semi-final against Pakistan and were only prevented from going all the way by a dazzling innings from a young and lean Inzamam-ul-Haq. That, and the fact that Crowe was, after sustaining an injury while batting, unable to captain his team during the Pakistan innings.

If the policies of me opening the bowling and Beefy opening the batting were settled by the time we reached Perth for our first World Cup match on 22 February 1992, they were about the only things that were. A hamstring injury to Allan Lamb meant we were without our first-choice batting line-up, while Goochie was still undecided over which spinner to play between Phil Tufnell and Richard Illingworth. In the end, Tufnell played in four of the first five games before giving way to Illingworth for the remainder.

Lamb's problem kept him out until our seventh match of the campaign, against New Zealand on 15 March, which meant that when Gooch was injured in the field against Sri Lanka in Ballarat in our fifth match, we were missing our two most experienced batsmen for the next group stage match against South Africa in Melbourne. Fortunately, by then the team were playing slick one-day cricket and South Africa were despatched despite the barmy new rain rule (which took away the overs in which the fewest runs were conceded from the bowling side) doing its best to foil us.

The inevitable hiccup in form arrived when we faced New Zealand, who'd learnt well from the defeats we'd inflicted on them before the tournament. In a change of strategy, they prepared a sluggish, grippy pitch on which 30 of their 50 overs were bowled by a spinner, Dipak, and their slow-medium cutter bowlers, Larsen and Harris. By the time we played them they were second in the table, having been beaten just once. But with Gooch still out injured and Lamb ring-rusty, we were never in the hunt after making 200 at Wellington's Basin Reserve. Had we won, though, we'd have set a new world record for consecutive victories in 50-over internationals.

If that defeat did not overly bother us (we'd already qualified for the semi-finals), losing to Zimbabwe three days later in Albury in New South Wales was embarrassing. Although missing Chris Lewis, Dermot Reeve and me though injury, we were only chasing 135. I'd damaged a rib muscle and was unable even to train, so I spent the match doing commentary with Mike Gatting, who'd been hired by the BBC. It made for grim viewing.

In a bid to get fit for our semi-final against South Africa on 22 March, Lawrie Brown, England's physio, had taken me to various experts, who'd jabbed the affected area with cortisone. Apart from making me feel like a pin cushion, it didn't seem to help and I was unable to play in a game which remains contentious to this day after the infamous rain rule left South Africa needing 22 runs off one ball.

What South Africa's apologists fail to mention when they claim Kepler Wessels's team were robbed is that they had only bowled 45 of their allotted overs. It was a deliberate go-slow on their part, for they risked facing a total of around 300, instead of the 253 they eventually needed, had they completed their 50 overs. To my mind, their cynical tactics got their just deserts.

Melbourne was our base during the World Cup, so returning to the Stamford hotel for the final was like coming home. I shared a corner suite with Robin Smith which gave us 180-degree views over the city, including one of the MCG, where we would contest the final against a Pakistan team who would not have been there had our group match against them in Adelaide not been rained off.

We'd bowled them out for 74 in that match on a pitch made helpful by the first decent rain Adelaide had seen for six months. I finished with figures of three for eight from 8.2 overs. It then rained for a few hours before stopping long enough for the full horror of the rain rule, designed by Richie Benaud, to make itself felt.

Instead of chasing 75 off 50 overs if the sun had shone, we needed to score 64 in 16 overs, a figure arrived at by some strange Aussie alchemy. Because we'd dismissed Pakistan in 40.2 overs, those unbowled overs, plus the 14 maidens we'd sent down in the match, went against us. With time left for 16 overs, the rain rule took the 34 overs in which Pakistan had scored the fewest runs, including those they'd not faced, and removed them from the equation. With it being a low-scoring match, only 10 runs came off the total, despite us losing 34 overs. We were still massive favourites, having reached 24 for one after eight overs, but the rain returned and the match was declared a no-result, which gave Pakistan a much-needed point and us a feeling of being robbed.

During the match Javed Miandad had edged one off me to the keeper but stood his ground, as he was entitled to do. Umpire Peter McConnell gave him not out, but while many batsmen might have maintained the deception, Javed came up to me in the lunch break to admit he'd edged it.

'Just a little touch,' he said grinning mischievously, 'but you get me later anyway' – and I had, with a dismissal that went beyond the need for third-party adjudication, having flattened his middle stump.

That was our only game in Adelaide, but some strange things happened in and around it. I was rooming with Chris Lewis and, apart from wandering around naked most of the time, he had the curious habit of ordering 10 dishes on room service, tasting a fork-ful of each, and then leaving the food lying untouched for hours to stink out the room. Also his hair dryer, which I asked to borrow, gave me an electric shock that put me on my arse. I'm not even sure why he had one, his hair was tightly cropped at the time.

That was the match where our suspicions were confirmed that Graeme Hick was miming the words to God Save the Queen, the national anthems of each country being sung by the players before each match. As someone pointed out, 'Hicky's lips are moving but there's no sound coming out.'

The issue of nationality and patriotism came up again on the eve of the final, at a dinner given by the ICC in Melbourne for both sides. The great and good of world cricket, as well as Australia's Prime Minister, Paul Keating, were all there and the entertainment was provided by someone impersonating the Queen. Once it became clear that the impersonator's schtick and agenda was anti-monarchy and pro-republican, Goochie and Beefy walked out. Bemused by this, and clearly not taking the same kind of offence as our captain and senior player, the rest of us stayed put, happy to drink the decent wine on offer.

Sensing our lack of patriotism as compared to that of the departed duo, Imran Khan, the Pakistan captain, got his team's attention and said, 'Look, boys, only the bloody colonials are left.'

It was a quick-witted and keenly observed quip, for going round our table there was:

Graeme Hick – born Harare, Zimbabwe
Allan Lamb – born Langebaanweg, South Africa
Robin Smith – born Durban, South Africa
Phil DeFreitas – born Dominica, West Indies
Chris Lewis – born Guyana, West Indies
Dermot Reeve – born Hong Kong
Gladstone Small – born Barbados, West Indies
Me – born Nairobi, Kenya.

That only left Goochie, Beefy, Alec Stewart, Neil Fairbrother, Phil Tufnell and Richard Illingworth as born-and-bred Englishmen. No wonder the Aussie players called us the United Nations.

To me it was all part of having a Commonwealth, that needed to be serviced, as a part of the country's recent history. Both my parents were born and raised in England; it was just that my father went to Kenya for his work in horticulture and I was born there.

Nearly everyone had their own criteria for players born abroad wanting to play for England. Goochie was happy for them to represent the national team provided they wanted to make England their home. Most in that era have done so, though Robin Smith, his brother Chris, as well as Graeme Hick, have all now emigrated to Australia, thus failing Goochie's 'test' of qualifying to play for England.

The journalist Martin Johnson had a very different view. Would players who came from abroad to play for England laugh at *Dad's Army*? If they didn't, they could never be English and should therefore not be playing for the national cricket team.

Different again was David Steele's assessment of nationality. Steele, who played for Northants, Derbyshire and England, once told Allan Lamb that he'd never be English as long as he had a hole in his backside. Lamby holds citizenship for both the UK and Grenada (don't ask), but for Steele, his rule still holds fast.

As a proud Englishman, Lamby was now fit again, so that meant Robin Smith, my roomy, would miss out on playing in the final against Pakistan on 25 March 1992. It also looked likely that I would sit on the sidelines, too, my side injury having not responded to any of the many cortisone jabs I'd been given.

At nets on the day before the match, I decided to have a bowl and if it hurt, which it did, to just keep going. If I did myself real damage I still had about a month before the county season began. Anyway, this was a World Cup final, not a Sunday League match at Chelmsford. So I kept bowling, and incredibly the pain and movement began to get easier. I was also swinging the ball a lot, so I felt it all a bit too good to be true. I was a sceptic when it came to believing in miracles, but here I was bowling as I had been a few weeks earlier.

I told Goochie that although I was not 100 per cent, the problem had not stopped me bowling properly and that the ball had swung. Being the consummate pro, he never got too hopeful about such things and told me to get down early the following day for a late fitness test. If there was a reaction to me pushing it in the nets, another fitness test would help rule me in or out.

The final was scheduled for a 2.30 p.m. start, so I was down by noon, having a bowl. My side was sore and stiff, from the previous day's exertions, but it felt fine, at least for a 50-over match. I told Goochie that as long as he bowled me in two or three spells, and not more, that I was confident of getting through the match without alarm.

Many would not have taken the risk, but Goochie had known me for over 14 years at Essex by this stage, so trusted me not to jeopardise the whole project just because it was a final.

'You're in,' he said. 'Good luck.'

The slight chance of rain meant Pakistan batted first after they won the toss, or at least that's what Imran Khan told a TV reporter.

I took the new ball from the Southern End and immediately got it to swing. Mostly during the tournament I'd tried to build pressure through dot balls, so I didn't bowl a really aggressive line and length, which would have meant very full and at the stumps.

The atmosphere was strange. Because most of the 90,000 crowd were Australians, they were conflicted over who to get behind – the old enemy or Pakistan, a team they had about as much disregard for as England. As such, the noise made when I took the first wicket, Aamer Sohail caught behind, failed entirely to reflect the enormous size of the crowd.

Pakistan's other opener, Rameez Raja, followed soon after, lbw, when he whipped across an outswinger from me. It was probably out by the standards of today's Decision Review System, especially as I had 'umpire's call' in my favour, but it was not stone dead, at least not as dead as the two lbw shouts I had against Javed Miandad in my next over, both of them given not out.

What made Steve Bucknor, an umpire from the West Indies, so intransigent over those two lbws has never been explained. When I did finally ask him, some 20 months later at a cocktail party in Kingston, Jamaica, I was met with an even stonier silence than on the day.

The balls certainly weren't missing the stumps, something Javed himself acknowledged afterwards when I spoke with him. Wearing that impish smile of his, he tapped his left leg and said, 'Bad luck. Allah smile on me today.'

He made the most of Bucknor's poor judgement, adding 139 runs with Imran for the third wicket before he was dismissed by Beefy for 58. Imran played superbly for his 72 before handing over to Inzamam and Wasim Akram to have a thrash in the final 10 overs, which got Pakistan's score up to 249, many more than we felt they'd get after being 70 for two at the halfway stage.

I finished with three for 22 off 10 overs, excellent figures by any standards. They could and should have been better. Eight of the runs conceded came from three wides, which I accepted as they were down the leg side. Then there were five no-balls, which were contentious, plus whatever runs were scored off the extra eight balls I would have had to bowl because of them and the wides. Being a final, everything was scrutinised closely and Mickey Stewart told me afterwards that each of the no-balls was replayed and not a single one had been illegal.

I'd had a problem with no-balls throughout my career, especially with Essex. What annoyed me was that Bucknor had seen fit to call these ones, in error, during a big event like the final, essentially guessing that my heel had not cut the back line when it had, but not to give the lbws which were stone dead. Incredibly, the ICC named him umpire of the tournament.

Our pursuit of their total got off to the worst possible start when Beefy was caught behind off Wasim Akram for nought. He swore blind he never touched it and fumed for the rest of the innings. We kept losing wickets at regular intervals, so could not put a strong stand together. When Goochie was out, caught at deep square leg playing his favourite sweep shot off Mushtaq Ahmed, we were 69 for four and in a spot of bother.

Some hope was restored by a 72-run stand by Neil Fairbrother and Allan Lamb. Fairbrother had been our best batsman in the tournament, so while he stayed there was always a chance of chasing down any total. But just as they might have put us into contention, Fairbrother lost Lamb to a stonking ball from Wasim which, delivered from round the wicket, was fast and then snaked away in the air at the last moment to uproot his off stump. Wasim was a master of reverse-swing, though quite how he got a ball no more than 18 overs old into a condition that enabled it will no doubt remain one of life's mysteries.

He struck with his next ball, too, sending Chris Lewis back for a golden duck after he chopped an equally late inswinger onto his stumps. When Fairbrother went for a fine 62 soon after and Dermot Reeve followed him a few runs later, we were 183 for eight and looking dead for all money.

That team, though, could boast a first-class century for all eleven of its players, which meant that, the pressure of a huge occasion like that notwithstanding, we could all bat. So, through me and Daffy DeFreitas, the score was eased past 200.

Their total still looked a distant prospect, though that did not prevent Moin Khan, Pakistan's wicketkeeper, sledging me from behind the stumps in an attempt to distract. As I faced Mushtaq Ahmed, Pakistan's wrist-spinner, he kept up a constant barrage of swearing from his perch behind the stumps.

'You ------- ----. You ------- ----. ----, ----, ----,' he'd rap, even when Mushtaq bounced in to bowl.

Sledging has never bothered me, so when I swung Mushtaq

high towards the midwicket fence, a boundary of at least 90 yards, it was not Moin who'd driven me to play the shot but the match situation. I'd absolutely nailed the stroke, too, and felt it must be six. So I turned to Moin and said, prematurely as it happened, 'That's six, ----.'

Trouble was, it hit the very top of the advertising boards, which under the Laws back then meant it was only four and not the maximum I'd hoped for. Anyway, sharp as you like, Moin came back, 'Only four, ----, only four.'

When Daffy was run out – on a ground as vast as the MCG we needed to take ever riskier runs – we still required 42 runs, with last man Richard Illingworth at the crease. It looked forlorn, and was, though we managed to add 19 of those runs before Illy was caught off Imran with four balls of the final over remaining.

The Pakistan team went into ecstasy, prostrating themselves to Allah and kissing the MCG turf. At the presentation, Imran said that the win would provide the necessary impetus for him to build a cancer hospital in his mother's honour, which he duly delivered upon. Once he'd finished parading the cup in the stadium, the younger players grabbed it and took it on a victory parade around Melbourne.

Back in our dressing room, many were inconsolable. For Goochie, Beefy, Lamby and me, this would be our last World Cup. As such, the defeat tasted very bitter indeed. We'd been lauded as the best team at the tournament but had fallen short when it mattered most. Life felt very cruel indeed.

Of course, speculation as to 'what might have been' for me had Javed been given out – a World Cup winner's medal; man of the match; CBE; marriage to Liz Hurley etc., etc. – has been a game mates of mine have played ever since, or at least every time Sky TV replay those two lbw shouts. Despite the reminders, I have tried not to dwell on it.

ENGLAND V PAKISTAN
(World Cup Final)

Played at Melbourne Cricket Ground, 25 March 1992

Umpires: BL Aldridge & SA Bucknor
Referee: PJP Burge
Toss: Pakistan

PAKISTAN

		Runs	Balls	Mins	4	6	S-rate
Aamer Sohail	c Stewart b Pringle	4	19	20	–	–	21.05
Rameez Raja	lbw b Pringle	8	26	36	1	–	30.77
Imran Khan*	c Illingworth b Botham	72	110	159	5	1	65.45
Javed Miandad	c Botham b Illingworth	58	98	125	4	–	59.18
Inzamam-ul-Haq	b Pringle	42	35	46	4	–	120.00
Wasim Akram	run out	33	19	21	4	–	173.68
Saleem Malik	not out	0	1	2	–	–	0.00
Ijaz Ahmed							
Moin Khan†							
Mushtaq Ahmed							
Aaqib Javed							
Extras	(19 lb, 7 nb, 6 w)	32					
Total	(6 wickets, 50 overs)	**249**					

ENGLAND

		Runs	Balls	Mins	4	6	S-rate
GA Gooch*	c Aaqib Javed b Mushtaq Ahmed	29	66	93	1	–	43.94
IT Botham	c Moin Khan b Wasim Akram	0	6	12	–	–	0.00
AJ Stewart†	c Moin Khan b Aaqib Javed	7	16	22	1	–	43.75
GA Hick	lbw b Mushtaq Ahmed	17	36	49	1	–	47.22
NH Fairbrother	c Moin Khan b Aaqib Javed	62	70	97	3	–	88.57
AJ Lamb	b Wasim Akram	31	41	54	2	–	75.61
CC Lewis	b Wasim Akram	0	6	1	–	–	0.00
DA Reeve	c Rameez Raja b Mushtaq Ahmed	15	32	38	–	–	46.88
DR Pringle	not out	18	16	29	1	–	112.50
PAJ DeFreitas	run out	10	8	13	–	–	125.00
RK Illingworth	c Rameez Raja b Imran Khan	14	11	9	2	–	127.27
Extras	(5 lb, 6 nb, 13 w)	24					
Total	(all out, 49.2 overs)	**227**					

ENGLAND	O	M	R	W		Fall of wickets:	
Pringle	10	2	22	3		Pak	Eng
Lewis	10	2	52	0	1st	20	6
Botham	7	0	42	1	2nd	24	21
DeFreitas	10	1	42	0	3rd	163	59
Illingworth	10	0	50	1	4th	197	69
Reeve	3	0	22	0	5th	249	141
					6th	249	141
PAKISTAN	O	M	R	W	7th	–	180
Wasim Akram	10	0	49	3	8th	–	183
Aaqib Javed	10	2	27	2	9th	–	208
Mushtaq Ahmed	10	1	41	3	10th	–	227
Ijaz Ahmed	3	0	13	0			
Imran Khan	6.2	0	43	1			
Aamer Sohail	10	0	49	0			

Man of the match: Wasim Akram
Result: **Pakistan won by 22 runs**

*   *   *

There were a couple of amusing postscripts to the final, the first being the post-match press conference, which was attended by both captains.

The first question to Imran was: 'Imran, was Javed Miandad a great help to you out in the field during England's innings?'

'Javed was not on the field,' said Imran, his vice-captain having been replaced by a substitute fielder after he'd pulled a muscle during his innings.

The second question, to Goochie, ran thus: 'Graham, what did Beefy say about his dismissal when he got back to the dressing room? Did he think it was out?'

'I don't know,' said Goochie, 'I was in the middle at the time.'

Then, the killer question, from a veteran Australian journalist with a fondness for the odd sharpening scotch in the press bar: 'Can someone please tell me who bloody batted first?'

The other postscript to the final came when I unpacked back in Cambridge and spotted two complimentary tickets for the final lurking at the bottom of my contact-lens bag.

There'd been two mates of mine, Nigel and Richard, travelling round who I'd furnished with tickets at every game, though they'd lacked ultimate faith in our capabilities and cleared off before the knock-out phase. Their place had been taken for the semi-final and final by two friends of Geoff Miller's, one of whom, Mike Evans, had made a fortune from frozen chickens. I'd got them comps for the South Africa match in Sydney and had promised the same for the final in Melbourne, a promise I'd clearly reneged upon, judging from the unclipped tickets in my bag. I phoned Mike to apologise, but he was fine about it.

'Don't worry, chuck,' he said. 'I paid a tout over the odds but that's not a problem, we got in. Damn shame we lost, though. Your round next time we meet.'

After the 1992 World Cup, the third time England had been

runners-up in four tournaments, several high-profile careers moved towards their conclusion. Indeed, by the end of the 1993 season, both Botham and Gower had retired, along with Derek Randall and Chris Tavaré.

As for me, I also retired in 1993, migrating to the press box, where I spent the next 20 years covering cricket instead of playing it – a job that was almost as much fun. Almost.

BIBLIOGRAPHY

CricketArchive (www.cricketarchive.com)
Cricinfo (www.espncricinfo.com)

Patrick Ferriday and Dave Wilson (eds.), *Masterly Batting* (Von Krumm 2013)

Graeme Fowler, *Fox on the Run* (Viking 1988)

Graham Gooch, *Gooch: My Autobiography* (Collins Willow 1995)

Martin Johnson, *Can't Bat, Can't Bowl, Can't Field* (Collins Willow 1997)

Simon Hughes, *A Lot of Hard Yakka* (Headline 1997)

Andy McSmith, *No Such Thing as Society: A History of Britain in the 1980s* (Constable 2010)

V.S. Naipaul, *Among the Believers: An Islamic Journey* (André Deutsch 1981)

David Tossell, *Sex & Drugs & Rebel Tours: The England Cricket Team in the 1980s* (Pitch Publishing 2015)

Alwyn W. Turner, *Rejoice! Rejoice!: Britain in the 1980s* (Aurum Press 2010)

Simon Wilde, *Ian Botham: The Power and the Glory* (Simon & Schuster 2011)

Wisden Cricketers' *Almanack, various editions* (John Wisden and Co Ltd)

STATISTICS

Cambridge University in first-class matches – overall

Span	Matches	Inns	NO	Runs	HS	Ave	50	100	Balls	Mdns	Runs	Wkts	BB	Ave	Ct
1979–1982	33	50	12	1929	127*	50.76	12	5	4890	221	2051	79	6–33	25.96	20

Cambridge University in first-class matches – year by year

Year	Matches	Inns	NO	Runs	HS	Ave	50	100	Balls	Mdns	Runs	Wkts	BB	Ave	Ct
1979	10	13	3	404	103*	40.40	2	1	1485	74	559	22	4–43	25.40	8
1980	9	14	3	604	123	54.90	3	2	1447	57	652	24	6–90	27.16	10
1981	8	13	3	400	127*	40.00	3	1	1254	53	552	20	4–39	27.60	1
1982	6	10	3	521	127	74.42	4	1	704	37	288	13	6–33	22.15	1

Essex in the County Championship – overall

Span	Matches	Inns	NO	Runs	HS	Avge	50	100	Balls	Mdns	Runs	Wkts	BB	Avge	Ct
1978–93	193	248	46	5336	128	26.41	26	4	28714	1165	13055	520	7–18	25.10	99

Essex in the County Championship – year by year

Psn	Year	Matches	Inns	NO	Runs	HS	Avge	50	100	Balls	Mdns	Runs	Wkts	BB	Avge	Ct
2nd	1978	2	3	0	10	5	3.33	0	0	42	2	19	0	–	–	0
1st	1979	–	–	–	–	–	–	–	–	–	–	–	–	–	–	–
8th	1980	8	10	1	109	40*	12.11	0	0	667	25	324	10	3–34	32.40	4
5th	1981	8	11	3	116	24*	14.50	0	0	864	29	489	8	2–20	61.12	1
7th	1982	6	9	1	152	54	19.00	2	0	971	40	388	17	4–53	22.82	0
1st	1983	16	20	4	503	102*	31.43	1	1	1606	47	872	40	7–32	21.80	12

		Matches	Inns	NO	Runs	HS	Avge	50	100	Balls	Mdns	Runs	Wkts	BB	Avge	Ct
1st	1984	15	23	4	388	63	20.42	2	0	2524	100	1253	55	7-53	22.78	10
4th	1985	21	27	4	573	121*	24.91	1	1	3109	125	1374	45	6-42	30.53	15
1st	1986	15	22	2	370	97	18.50	1	0	2017	85	946	41	7-46	23.07	7
12th	1987	21	31	8	655	84*	28.47	4	0	3376	149	1365	54	5-70	25.27	14
3rd	1988	13	17	0	446	128	26.23	3	1	2115	71	1031	41	6-39	25.14	5
2nd	1989	17	20	4	388	81*	24.25	1	0	3492	152	1447	89	7-18	16.25	6
2nd	1990	15	13	2	318	84	28.90	1	0	1953	82	927	29	5-66	31.96	7
1st	1991	12	11	6	328	78*	65.59	2	0	2158	96	887	30	5-70	29.56	4
1st	1992	12	12	3	405	112*	45.00	2	1	1949	83	870	39	5-63	22.30	4
11th	1993	12	19	4	575	76	38.33	6	0	1871	79	863	22	4-33	39.22	10

Honours won by Essex 1978–1993

County Championship: 1979, 1983, 1984, 1986, 1991, 1992
NatWest Trophy: 1985
Sunday League: 1981, 1984, 1985
Refuge Assurance Cup: 1989
Benson & Hedges Cup: 1979

Tests – overall

Span	Matches	Inns	NO	Runs	HS	Avge	50	100	Balls	Mdns	Runs	Wkts	BB	Avge	Ct
1982–92	30	50	4	695	63	15.10	1	0	5287	192	2518	70	5-95	35.97	10

Tests – year by year

Year	Matches	Inns	NO	Runs	HS	Avge	50	100	Balls	Mdns	Runs	Wkts	BB	Avge	Ct
1982	7	11	2	166	47*	18.44	0	0	1091	43	495	11	2-16	45.00	0
1983	–	–	–	–	–	–	–	–	–	–	–	–	–	–	–
1984	3	6	1	81	46*	16.20	0	0	429	10	257	5	5-108	51.40	3
1985	–	–	–	–	–	–	–	–	–	–	–	–	–	–	–
1986	4	8	0	166	63	20.75	1	0	891	32	376	13	4-73	28.92	4
1987	–	–	–	–	–	–	–	–	–	–	–	–	–	–	–
1988	5	8	0	66	39	8.25	0	0	821	36	373	14	5-95	26.64	0
1989	2	3	0	33	27	11.00	0	0	518	12	306	5	4-70	61.20	0
1990	–	–	–	–	–	–	–	–	–	–	–	–	–	–	–
1991	4	7	0	128	45	18.28	0	0	769	33	322	12	5-100	26.83	1
1992	5	7	1	55	41	9.16	0	0	768	26	389	10	3-66	38.90	2

ODIs – overall

Year	Matches	Inns	NO	Runs	HS	Avge	50	100	Balls	Mdns	Runs	Wkts	BB	Avge	Ct
1982–93	44	30	12	425	49*	23.61	0	0	2379	53	1677	44	4–42	38.11	11

ODIs – year by year

Year	Matches	Inns	NO	Runs	HS	Avge	50	100	Balls	Mdns	Runs	Wkts	BB	Avge	Ct
1982	2	1	1	34	34*	–	0	0	132	1	93	4	2–43	23.25	0
1983	2	1	0	11	11	11.00	0	0	84	0	104	0	–	–	0
1984	3	3	1	16	8	8.00	0	0	174	3	123	4	3–21	30.75	3
1985	2	2	0	17	13	8.50	0	0	102	1	81	4	2–32	20.25	2
1986	4	4	2	105	49*	52.50	0	0	230	6	174	1	1–63	174.00	1
1987	3	2	0	20	12	10.00	0	0	144	0	148	1	1–11	148.00	0
1988	4	3	2	81	39	81.00	0	0	264	9	129	6	3–30	21.50	1
1989	5	4	2	55	25*	27.50	0	0	267	6	182	3	1–19	60.66	0
1990	1	1	1	30	30*	–	0	0	42	0	45	0	–	–	0
1991	3	1	0	1	1	1.00	0	0	162	2	130	2	2–52	65.00	1
1992	13	7	3	49	18*	12.25	0	0	652	22	369	18	4–42	20.50	3
1993	2	1	0	6	6	6.00	0	0	126	3	99	1	1–63	99.00	0

Tests – match by match

	Opposition	Ground	Batting	Bowling	Catches
10 Jun 1982	India	Lord's	7	2–16 & 2–58	0
24 Jun 1982	India	Manchester	23	1–33	0
8 Jul 1982	India	The Oval	9	0–8 & 2–32	0
12 Aug 1982	Pakistan	Lord's	5 & 14	0–62	0
12 Nov 1982	Australia	Perth	0 & 47*	0–37 & 0–3	0
10 Dec 1982	Australia	Adelaide	1* & 9	2–97 & 0–11	0
26 Dec 1982	Australia	Melbourne	9 & 42	1–40 & 1–26	0
14 Jun 1984	West Indies	Birmingham	4 & 46*	5–108	1
28 Jun 1984	West Indies	Lord's	2 & 8	0–54 & 0–44	1
12 Jul 1984	West Indies	Leeds	19 & 2	0–26 & 0–25	1
5 Jun 1986	India	Lord's	63 & 6	3–58 & 1–30	1
19 Jun 1986	India	Leeds	8 & 8	3–47 & 4–73	1
3 Jul 1986	India	Birmingham	44 & 7	2–61 & 0–33	2
7 Aug 1986	New Zealand	Nottingham	21 & 9	0–58 & 0–16	0
2 Jun 1988	West Indies	Nottingham	39	1–82	0
16 Jun 1988	West Indies	Lord's	1 & 0	0–20 & 2–60	0
21 Jul 1988	West Indies	Leeds	0 & 3	5–95	0
4 Aug 1988	West Indies	The Oval	1 & 8	3–45 & 0–24	0
25 Aug 1988	Sri Lanka	Lord's	14	2–17 & 1–30	0
8 Jun 1989	Australia	Leeds	6 & 0	0–123 & 1–60	0
24 Aug 1989	Australia	The Oval	27	4–70 & 0–53	0
6 Jun 1991	West Indies	Leeds	16 & 27	2–14 & 2–38	1
20 Jun 1991	West Indies	Lord's	35	5–100	0
4 Jul 1991	West Indies	Nottingham	0 & 3	2–71 & 0–20	0
25 Jul 1991	West Indies	Birmingham	2 & 45	1–48 & 0–31	0
18 Jan 1992	New Zealand	Christchurch	10	1–54 & 1–64	2
30 Jan 1992	New Zealand	Auckland	41 & 2	2–21 & 1–23	0
4 Jun 1992	Pakistan	Birmingham	0*	0–92	0
23 Jul 1992	Pakistan	Leeds	0	2–41 & 3–66	0
6 Aug 1992	Pakistan	The Oval	1 & 1	0–28	0

ODIs – match by match

	Opposition	Ground	Batting	Bowling	Catches
17 Jul 1982	Pakistan	Nottingham	DNB	2–50	0
19 Jul 1982	Pakistan	Manchester	34*	2–43	0
23 Jan 1983	Australia	Melbourne	DNB	0–47	0
23 Feb 1983	New Zealand	Wellington	11	0–57	0
31 May 1984	West Indies	Manchester	6	0–64	1
2 Jun 1984	West Indies	Nottingham	2*	3–21	2
4 Jun 1984	West Indies	Lord's	8	1–38	0
24 Mar 1985	Australia	Sharjah	4	2–49	1
26 Mar 1985	Pakistan	Sharjah	13	2–32	1
24 May 1986	India	The Oval	28	0–20	0
26 May 1986	India	Manchester	49*	0–49	0
16 Jul 1986	New Zealand	Leeds	28	0–42	0
18 Jul 1986	New Zealand	Manchester	0*	1–63	1
9 Oct 1987	West Indies	Gujranwala	12	0–83	0
12 Oct 1987	Pakistan	Rawalpindi	8	0–54	0
17 Oct 1987	Sri Lanka	Peshawar	DNB	1–11	0
19 May 1988	West Indies	Birmingham	23*	1–26	0

21 May 1988	West Indies	Leeds	39	3–30	0
23 May 1988	West Indies	Lord's	DNB	1–27	0
4 Sep 1988	Sri Lanka	The Oval	19*	1–46	1
25 May 1989	Australia	Manchester	9	1–19	0
27 May 1989	Australia	Nottingham	25*	1–38	0
29 May 1989	Australia	Lord's	0	1–50	0
19 Oct 1989	Australia	Hyderabad (Deccan)	DNB	0–42	0
30 Oct 1989	Pakistan	Nagpur	21*	0–33	0
23 May 1990	New Zealand	Leeds	30*	0–45	0
23 May 1991	West Indies	Birmingham	1	0–22	0
25 May 1991	West Indies	Manchester	DNB	2–52	1
27 May 1991	West Indies	Lord's	DNB	0–56	0
11 Jan 1992	New Zealand	Auckland	DNB	2–32	0
12 Feb 1992	New Zealand	Dunedin	14*	1–31	0
15 Feb 1992	New Zealand	Christchurch	5	2–11	0
22 Feb 1992	India	Perth	1	0–53	0
27 Feb 1992	West Indies	Melbourne	DNB	0–16	1
1 Mar 1992	Pakistan	Adelaide	DNB	3–8	1
5 Mar 1992	Australia	Sydney	DNB	1–24	0
9 Mar 1992	Sri Lanka	Ballarat	0*	0–27	0
12 Mar 1992	South Africa	Melbourne	1	0–34	0
15 Mar 1992	New Zealand	Wellington	10	0–34	0
25 Mar 1992	Pakistan	Melbourne	18*	3–22	0
20 May 1992	Pakistan	Lord's	DNB	4–42	1
22 May 1992	Pakistan	The Oval	DNB	2–35	0
19 May 1993	Australia	Manchester	6	0–36	0
21 May 1993	Australia	Birmingham	DNB	1–63	0

INDEX